The Art of the Impossible:
A Blog History of the Election of Donald J. Trump as President

Steven Kates

Connor Court Publishing

Published in 2017 by Connor Court Publishing

Copyright © Steven Kates

All rights reserved. No part of this book may be reproduced or transmitted in any form or by any means, electronic or mechanical, including photocopying, recording or by any information storage and retrieval system, without prior permission in writing from the publisher.

Connor Court Publishing Pty Ltd.
PO Box 7257
Redland Bay QLD 4165
sales@connorcourt.com
www.connorcourt.com

Phone 0497 900 685

ISBN: 978-1-925501-39-1

Cover design, Maria Giordano

Printed in Australia

Dedicated to

Matilda, Eve and Louis

Primary Poll Tracking of Donald Trump. Source: RealClearPolitics.

Introduction

The book is a complete compilation of my blogs on the 2016 American presidential election beginning in July 2015 as the election cycle began and ending with the tallying of the votes which was completed on November 9, 2016.

It is a blog history, and may be the very first of its kind. The entire book is comprised of blog posts on my website: www.lawofmarkets.com some of which were also then published on www.catalaxyfiles.com. And while most of these posts were written from inside Australia, as it happened I was there on the day Donald Trump emerged from just one of the pack to become the front-runner for the Republican nomination, which began with his presentation to Freedomfest in Las Vegas. This moment was discussed by Mark Skousen, the organiser of this annual event, in which all of the groups on the right side of politics get together once a year:

> "And to think the successful campaign gained the national spotlight on July 11, 2015, when Donald Trump made his surprise appearance at FreedomFest. It was his lucky day (7-11 in Vegas!). The media covered his speech and aired excerpts of it all day long. MSNBC played his entire speech. NBC led its nightly news with it. Even Playboy magazine showed up. It was a media frenzy. And, as you can see from this polling chart, it worked. Trump never looked back."

And the fact is, one does not have to be in the United States to follow an American election. With the world connected up as it now is, one needs only the internet and everything you might wish to know is there before you.

The posts were not written to be published. They were written, as all such posts are, to reflect the moment. It is only in looking back on the entire period that I can see how they capture the mood and the detail. I don't think there is a single moment of significance through to the election on November 8 that is ignored. Everything is there, but all of it is looked at from the perspective of someone who wished to see the Republicans win, and from someone who, very early on, recognised Donald Trump as the uniquely best candidate to become president.

I will just say something about the format, which is a different kind of history from those that are more traditional. This is history written parallel with the events described. What makes this particular account useful is that its author sided with Donald Trump almost from the very start and was certainly sympathetic to his message early on. It is therefore an account of how Donald Trump became president by someone who wished to see him become president. You are therefore able to feel the dynamic and experience almost firsthand what it was like to go through the election.

Blogs are now, possibly even more than the media, the first draft of history. The media have so completely sold out to the left that it is impossible to get anything like an objective sense from journalist accounts of what took place. I, of course, am also a partisan, but have no pretensions that I can and could affect the result, so I just react to events without attempting to shape them. That is all the more the case since I had been watching the election from Australia so was remote from even the most limited ability to affect the outcome. The media's aim is to get you to vote a certain way, and with only a few exceptions, the way they want to you vote is for the candidate of the left. This is therefore an account of the events by someone who wished to see Donald Trump become President of the United States who could only describe and reflect on what he saw.

Let me also note that the posts, as published online, often contain videos, pictures and cartoons which have for the most part been left out. If you would like to see the actual posts as they were originally displayed you can google "law of markets" and then add in the name of the post found in the text. That, of course, only works in the present as this is being written. The future of the internet and these postings is anyone's guess, as is so much else. There are already many video links that have gone dead although, so far, all of the links to print media sites remain alive.

I am, as ever, grateful to my wife Zuzanna, who allows me to blog away until I have finished saying what I wish to say. But the book is dedicated with the greatest love to our grandchildren, Matilda, Eve and Louis, since it is they who will inherit this world that we are in the process of shaping as best we can.

Politics is what you can get away with

July 2, 2015

Went to the Andy Warhol exhibit at the MOMA yesterday which is the kind of thing you come to New York for. But what caught my eye was Warhol's most famous quote, "art is what you can get away with". Watching politics in the US, what may be true about art – there being a sucker born every minute – in Obama's America it is true everlasting about politics. The media here, like everywhere, is to the left. But to mix the media with a presidential system emphasises all of the worst features of both. Obama routinely breaks the law in deciding what he will enforce that he, as the head of the executive branch, is sworn by law to do, while there are other things that he is forbidden to do but does anyway since there is apparently no ability to fight it, never mind the lack of will.

The American political system is corrupt from end to end. The combination of a lawless president and a media that will never criticise means nothing will be done since nothing can be done since the ability to create the storm before the resolution of a problem is entirely absent. This is a country evolving into masters and servants, with the tax gathering power and the ability to reward friends unprecedented in a democratic community. Once the richest country in the world, using average real incomes per head of population as the measure, the US is well down the list today and heading down even further. The elites will do well, and the rest will have enough to eat, mostly. But there is no freedom where it counts, which is the freedom to disagree with the majority view on anything.

But it is a Warhol presidency. Explain this[1] in any conventional way, which is the story of the day to be replaced by another just like it that will distract from this, just as the day after will distract from tomorrow's:

> *US blocks attempts by Arab allies to fly heavy weapons directly to Kurds to fight Islamic State*
>
> *Middle East allies accuse Barack Obama and David Cameron of failing to show strategic leadership in fight against Islamic State*

That's tonight on Drudge. I wonder whether it will even crack the

---

[1] *The Telegraph*, 2 July 2015.

first five pages of the NY *Times* in the morning. If it's not in the news, it effectively didn't happen.

~

Bern vs the Donald 2016
July 7, 2015

An underestimate but still closer to reality: Bernie Sanders Says 'Real' Unemployment Rate Is Actually 10.5 Percent, DOUBLE The Official Rate]'.[2]

Meanwhile, over on the other side, Trump: 'Infectious disease is pouring across the border'.[3]

Still waiting to hear what they think of the nuclear deal with Iran, but both have been able to overcome the media blockade and have brought genuine issues into the national conversation.

And perhaps funniest of all, the NYT thinks that being opposed by the Castros is political poison in the US. As the article points out, it can only do him good[4] except for those who vote for Hillary or Bern or work at the New York Times and Washington Post.

~

Marco Rubio as it happened
July 11, 2015

At Freedomfest – Marco Rubio: 'America's Dream: Restoring Economic Opportunity for Everyone'. This was written down as he spoke this evening.

There he is, right there, on stage. He's just like his pictures, young and apple cheeked. He is telling his life story. The American dream is about happiness and fulfilment as you define it. And why is it possible? Because

---
[2] *The Daily Caller*, 7 June 2015.
[3] thehill.com, 7 June 2015.
[4] *Commentary*, 6 July, 2015.

the US is founded on spiritual principles, where the rights come from the creator. The only power we give to the government is the power to protect those rights.

I love the system of free enterprise, he says. It is the only governing principle that allows success. I can become better off without someone else becoming worse off. His dad used to say that he had a job because someone else took the risk to open the business to employ him.

Two major changes. First, economy is becoming global. Now even America cannot get away with higher taxes and increased regs. Must work at being competitive whereas in the past no one was in their zone.

Second is improved technology. Ten years ago if I told you I was going "to google" you you would have been offended. Tech changes coming at a rapid rate.

We must become more competitive. Must fix the tax code. Tax reform is critical to become more globally competitive. We must also reduce regulations. Regs are used by established firms to prevent new firms from taking their place. He got rid of the taxi opposition in Florida to Uber! Regulatory reform is critical if we are going to be competitive.

Big on privatisation.

Need more skills. Four year degrees is the way to education at the moment. Higher ed is controlled by a cartel. Only unis can give degrees and the universities have created this monopoly for themselves. And loans are so expensive. We don't teach welding and plumbing. We don't teach people to do that any more.

We have single mothers working for $11 an hour who cannot educate their way up. MOOC should be coming. We need to open higher ed to competition. If you know something, you should get credit for it and then education will fill the gaps. What matters is what you know and not where you learned it.

There are things about other countries we might admire but America is the greatest. The 21st century is made for America. Big government is a disastrous idea for the 21st century. It is free enterprise that is the future. The world is going in our direction, so why would we go in theirs.

America owes me nothing. I owe America everything. My dad had to work for a living. He made sure that the life he could not have would be available to his son. That is the American dream. Whether we remain a special country will depend on whether the journey from poverty to wealth can be opened to more.

We can leave our children as the richest country that has ever been but the work is in front of us.

God Bless America!

~

Donald Trump live blog
July 12, 2015

The media man of the moment here in the US is Donald Trump,[5] no doubt because to them he is an oddball who belongs to the Republican side of politics. They think they have invented someone utterly without mass appeal, an obnoxious billionaire entrepreneur with a negative attitude to racial minorities. He is, nevertheless, the hottest ticket in town. Here is Mark Steyn discussing Trump's appeal:[6]

> *What he said may or may not be offensive, but it happens to be true: America has more Mexicans than anybody needs, and then some. It certainly has more unskilled Mexicans than any country needs, including countries whose names begin with "Mex-" and end in "-ico". And it has far more criminal Mexicans than anybody needs, which is why they make up 71 per cent of the foreign inmates in federal jails. Just to underline that last point, a young American woman was murdered for kicks in a supposed "sanctuary city" on the eve of the holiday weekend by an illegal immigrant from Mexico. He had flouted US immigration law for years – or, to be more precise about it, local, state and federal officials had colluded with him in the flouting of US immigration law, to the point where San Francisco's sheriff actively demanded the return of this criminal to his "sanctuary city", thereby facilitating the homicide of an actual citizen, taxpayer and net contributor to American society.*

Be all that as it may, Trump has invited himself to Freedomfest and here

---

[5] *New York Post*, 10 July 2015.
[6] steynonline.com, 10 July 2015.

he is, right there on the stage, the man himself.

Begins... Donald Trump says he was asked to come and was very happy to. It is an honour to be here at a meeting of conservative and libertarian groups. I happen to like Ron Paul. Played a round of golf. A very nice guy. So many of us believe in the same thing.

Went to see a meeting of parents who had lost their children to illegal immigrants. An amazing thing; hardened reporters were sitting there with tears in their eyes. Others are saying that this is becoming a movement. People don't know what is happening.

Yesterday in Phoenix. Thousands of people are calling and could not hold in the original venue. An amazing thing that's happening.

Many said I wouldn't run. He wouldn't want to show his financials and etc, they said. I am actually much richer than people think. I am richer than they say. The reason I bring it up is because my way of thinking is the kind of thinking that we need in this country. Growth with low debt. We need this kind of thinking in this country. We have incompetent leadership. And I might mention that the Tea Party loves me – they are wrongly trivialised.

Our vets are treated like third class citizens. Must take care of our vets. We can provide a better and cheaper healthcare system than Obamacare. Knows a doctor with more accountants working for him than nurses.

Need to make America great again. But you cannot be a country great or otherwise without borders. We have exported our jobs to China. They send a car and we send corn. We think we are not dealing from strength. We aren't but we can. We cannot get our products into China. They have a surtax on our manufactured exports.

I love China. I love Mexico. I love the Mexican people. But their negotiators are tougher than our negotiators. They send their worst people to the US.

Introduces a black man whose son was killed by an illegal immigrant. Son was walking home from the mall and as he was coming home within two minutes of his house, just shot dead in the street. The man already had three counts against him. You must, according to the Mexican mafia, commit a crime in a black neighbourhood to stay on the wrong side of the law. With Donald Trump we can see hope is coming. The thing is that Mr

Trump loves America. "I trust Donald Trump." He's the kind of man you want to be your dad. I have a lot of black friends who are willing to vote for Donald Trump.

Trump back. The entire thing is so sad. Once it was found out that an illegal immigrant had killed his son, the story was dropped. It was true in every case. "There is something really bad out there. There is something sick out there." People can come here. We can have immigrants.

The Mexicans send them to the US. Let the US take care of our problem citizens is the attitude in Mexico.

I talk about trade. Let me talk about NBC. We want to talk about "inclusion". NBC has a lot of bad people. The Apprentice has been running for 14 years. [He sounds so New York!] NBC didn't want him to run since they didn't want to cancel his show which cannot run if he's running for president.

I'll make great trade deals. I want to be great on the military. All politicians do is talk. Talk about Benghazi and then nothing. Hillary's emails, same. Hillary gets rid of her servers and the subpoenas. 48 hours of indignation and then you don't hear about it any more. If I get the nomination, you will hear about it.

It is hard for conservative libertarian to get decent press. Nobody takes a full quote. "The American dream is dead – but I am going to make it bigger and better." The media only quotes the first half.

Mexico sends us their problems. The political press is dishonest!!!! We have to deal with them. But I have a megaphone. Still 20% of the people who were there you wouldn't have thought were there at all from what they said.

If I get the nomination, I will win the Hispanic vote since we will bring back those jobs from overseas. I will create jobs, which includes stopping illegals from coming in to take those jobs.

Went to Wharton. Graduated and made a fortune. Wrote the *Art of the Deal*. Look at the Iran deal. Persians are great negotiators. We have four prisoners over there. If I were there, I'd say fellows, you have these people. We want them back, and if they said no I'd say goodbye and end the negotiations.

I have a "tapping" – delay while thinking. I know how to negotiate.

Q&A

What I do not encourage is people to come into the country illegal.

Q: Federal debt.

A: We owe 18 trillion money. We do all of this business and we owe them money. We are going to be Greece on steroids. A believer in free trade, but you must have good negotiators. I know most of them. I know the good ones. We would have the greatest smartest deals you ever saw.

Q: Bigger problem – persecution of Christians in the middle east?

A: If you are from Syria and a Christian you are not permitted into this country. If Islamic you can easily do it. We must do something about it. I'm a Presbyterian. Persecuted people can come in. We should let them sort it out in the middle east and then pick up the leftovers. Trump was supposedly against going in. If you attack Iraq, I said, you will destabilise the balance in the middle east. Spent billions and have nothing. Iraq is meeting with Iran. We are led by stupid people.

Hillary would be the worst president. Hillary was the worst sec of state. Who would you rather have negotiating with China, me or Hillary.

Q: Foreign policy with the focus on Russia?

A: Everybody hates us and they make money from us. With me, the US will make the money and the rest of the world will like us. I would get along very well with Putin. We can make our country great again. I think of myself as a nice person, I am a nice person. But it doesn't matter if I'm nice. But people are tired of incompetence. Hillary is not going to bring back jobs. Every single person who gave Hillary or Jeb money are lining up to get something back. Me, however, I don't need money. I don't want anybody's money.

Wraps up. Thanks everybody. Just angry that the conference was not in the Trump Hotel. And as I always end my speeches: "Make America great again!"

Trump not surreal at all
July 12, 2015

There's this news report, 'Donald Trump just gave an amazingly surreal speech in Las Vegas'[7] from which I will quote a bit to see how surreal the attitude of the headline writer is. The story is pretty accurate, and is worth reading through. The Drudge headline for the link is "Trump Rocks the House in Vegas". It begins:

> *Donald Trump just gave one of the most bizarrely captivating speeches of his several-weeks-old campaign.*
>
> *Standing in front of an animated screen in Las Vegas on Saturday, Trump spoke passionately for almost a half an hour, hitting some of his main talking points: President Barack Obama's weakness, a 'porous' southern border, his business successes, and even Benghazi.*
>
> *It was one of two similarly themed speeches in the day. Later, he spoke before a crowd of what his campaign said was more than 15,000 in Phoenix.*
>
> *Trump made illegal immigration the primary focus of both speeches, railing against the Mexican government for supposedly sending undocumented immigrants to the US.*

Although others like to compare him with Ronald Reagan, the closer comparison for me is with Dwight D. Eisenhower for whom his first elected office was also that of President. I thought it was a very effective speech, and while there are still lots of questions that must hang in the air for a while, there was nothing flaky about how he behaved or what he said. What made him different was that he was willing to take issues head on and not pussyfoot around. Hillary won't take questions from reporters, all of whom are her friends and supporters. Trump took questions from the floor and answered every single question that the audience was willing to put up, both friendly and hostile. And while there were some vacant areas that he will have to think through more carefully, he made no mistake on the night. You would not want to write him off, at least not yet. For me he was much more impressive than Marco Rubio had been the day before.

UPDATE: Trump's speech has had wide circulation here in the US. I am

---

[7] *Business Insider Australia*, 12 July 2015.

now at Stanford for the next couple of days and saw an AP story in the local press, garbled of course, and negative, but still mentioned. This, however, is the take from Breitbart: 'TRUMP IN VEGAS: SLAMS OBAMA, HILLARY, JEB… CROWD GOES WILD'.[8] Some of the flavour:

> *LAS VEGAS, Nevada – Republican candidate Donald Trump addressed the FreedomFest conference in Las Vegas, telling delegates of his underestimated wealth, his passion for securing America's border, the slanted portrayal of him in the mainstream media, and how he believes that China and Mexico have "smarter leaders" than the United States.*
>
> *Some libertarians, who the conference is aimed at, believed that Trump would receive a hostile reception at FreedomFest. But the crowd was generally supportive, or at least open-minded, to Trump's run. One delegate told Breitbart London, "He doesn't pretend to be anything. People were surprisingly supportive of him."*

The report captures the essence of the surprise in finding Trump make sense about the issues he dwelt on. But his trying to locate his support within the Tea Party movement, as discussed in the report, may be the largest surprise of all.

~

"60%, 70% of the political media is really, really dishonest"

July 23, 2015

Trump doing what no politician has done before, making the media the issue:[9]

> DONALD TRUMP, GOP PRESIDENTIAL CANDIDATE: Let me tell you. The people don't trust you and the people don't trust the media. And I understand why.
>
> COOPER: Right. And politicians.
>
> TRUMP: You know, I have always been covered, fairly, accurately because it

---

[8] Breitbart.com, 11 July, 2015
[9] *Real Clear Politics,* 22 July, 2015.

was usually a financial press. And you know numbers are numbers and my numbers happen to be great. So, I was always sort of treated fair.

With the media it's, not all cases, some, some of the political media is great. And really honest. Even if they've don't want to want to be, they're really honest. But I find that 60%, 70% of the political media is really, really dishonest.

The single most important political change needed today is to reduce – you will never remove – media bias. Obama could not be dog catcher without the media. As it is, he remains almost as strong as they day he first ran for office in spite of the disasters he has not just coincided with in office, but has personally caused by the political choices he has made. I hope this catches on with others, but it has taken someone like Trump to actually start a process that needs to continue as long and as hard as it can.

~

That is, of course, the point
July 27, 2015

Here's the link: 'New California: Mass Immigration Turning Virginia Blue',[10] blue meaning Democrat. This is how the story starts:

A remarkable transformation is underway in the Commonwealth of Virginia.

The birthplace and final resting place of George Washington, James Madison, Thomas Jefferson—and once one of the most reliably-red of red states—is being rapidly turned into a progressive stronghold.

These changes are not the result of an inside agency, or a natural evolution in political thinking, but rather the result of one of the most impactful yet least-discussed policies of the federal government.

Each year the federal government prints millions of visas and distributes these admission tickets to the poorest and least-developed nations in the world.

A middle-aged person living in parts of Virginia today will have witnessed more demographic change in the span of her life than many societies have experienced in millennia.

---
[10] Breitbart.com, 26 July, 2015.

This is the left's new road to perpetual power, and you can see the same thing being tried here in Australia. Why should Labor stop the boats when they are filled with people who will vote only for the parties of the left? And why won't they vote for the Coalition? Because only the ALP sees advantage in taking money from you and giving it to them.

~

How is the Iranian deal in America's interests?
August 2, 2015

I can understand how the Iranian deal is in Iran's national interests. I can also understand how it is not in the national interests of many of the countries of the Middle East, Israel and Saudi Arabia in particular. But tell me, how is the deal in the interests of the United States (aka the Great Satan)? In what possible way are any of America's foreign policy aims advanced by this agreement?

If you are an ally of the US, you are now looking elsewhere for protection and safety. No one can or will trust the US as they once did. It will not matter who is elected next or the time after that. The treacherous nature of the US, which can change with every election cycle, and which is often determined by domestic side issues of no real consequence to its strategic concerns, will leave each of its allies looking for alternatives. The possibility of a far-to-the-left ideologue as president would have once been seen as impossible. With Obama and the constituency he has built, it seems to have become almost mandatory.

And while it seems invisible to those who govern the US at the present time, the combination of its economic and open-borders policies will make the US a weaker country well into the foreseeable future. Built on top of that the fetish for green energy. It may still be the strongest military presence, but it will be able to enforce its will to only a limited extent should it even wish to do so.

Thirty years from now we will be living in a world so changed I can only barely begin to sketch it. The only thing I am near enough sure about is that the *Pax Americana* we have depended on since the fall of the *Pax Britannica* will have been vastly diminished.

In the meantime, 'Kerry is off to do the near impossible while leaving out trying to do the absolutely impossible':[11]

> *The Iran nuclear deal tops Secretary of State John Kerry's agenda as he meets with foreign ministers from Egypt and Qatar this weekend. Kerry will skip a visit with Israel, the main U.S. ally in the Middle East and a vociferous opponent of the deal. . . .*
>
> *"People in my region now are relying on God's will, and consolidating their local capabilities and analysis with everybody else except our oldest and most powerful ally," Saudi Prince Bandar bin Sultan wrote in a July 16 op-ed for Lebanon's Daily Star.*

With that, you do not even need to read between the lines. Diplomatic though Saudi Prince Bandar was, he could not have been more clear or more critical.

UPDATE: At least there isn't complete idiocy across the US, only among Democrats and their leaders:[12]

> *American voters oppose 57 – 28 percent, with only lukewarm support from Democrats and overwhelming opposition for Republicans and independent voters, the nuclear pact negotiated with Iran, according to a Quinnipiac University national poll released today.*
>
> *Voters say 58 – 30 percent the nuclear pact will make the world less safe, the independent Quinnipiac (KWIN-uh-pe-ack) University Poll finds.*
>
> *Opposing the Iran deal are Republicans 86 – 3 percent and independent voters 55 – 29 percent, while Democrats support it 52 – 32 percent. There is little gender gap as men oppose the deal 59 – 30 percent and women oppose it 56 – 27 percent.*

I should just add that 52-32 percent support is not "lukewarm".

---

[11] *Washington Examiner*, 1 July 2015.
[12] *Hot Air*, 3 July 2015.

Insane may be just the word for them
August 5, 2015

It is the left generally and the media in particular. They are soul sick, disgusting and deranged. This is from 'Why Trump Resonates & Why the left doesn't get it in one image'.[13] This is the headline Trump's interview was based on: "Trump: Compared to Chopping off Heads, 'Waterbording Doesn't Sound Very Severe".

> Here is the exchange that the headlines refer to:
>
> *KARL: Would President Trump authorize waterboarding and other enhanced interrogation techniques, even torture?*
>
> *TRUMP: I would be inclined to be very strong. When people are chopping off other people's heads and then we're worried about waterboarding and we can't, because I have no doubt that that works. I have absolutely no doubt.*
>
> *KARL: You'd bring back waterboarding?*
>
> *TRUMP: …you mention waterboarding, which was such a big subject. I haven't heard that term in a year now, because when you see the other side chopping off heads, waterboarding doesn't sound very severe.*
>
> *Now if you are not familiar with how things work. What both the right and the left will often do is grab something from an interview and note how radical it is, how unacceptable it is, how it shows a temperament that does not reflect well on the person in question.*
>
> *So take a look at that sub headline from Crooks & Liars and let this fact sink in.*
>
> *To the people at Crooks and Liars Donald Trump's statement that: "when you see the other side chopping off heads, waterboarding doesn't sound very severe." is a statement so outrageous that they believe they can make political hay out if it.*
>
> *However to any sane human being not only is that statement objectively true but I suspect to the American voter hearing about women being sold into sexual slavery by our ISIS foes*
>
> *But the Islamic State's "revival" of the institution of chattel slavery—sex*

---

[13] datechguyblog.com, 3 August 2015.

> slavery of Christian and Yizidi women and girls no less—has faded from public attention.
>
> Over the past decade, thousands of Iraqi and Syrian Christians—including, in 2013, an entire convent of Syrian Orthodox nuns—have been taken captive for ransom. Last August, shortly after ISIS established its caliphate, it began something new. After capturing non-Sunni women and girls, ISIS began awarding and selling them as sex slaves. The vast majority were Yizidis but some, according to UN reports, were Christians.
>
> Boasting about it and justifying it under islam:
>
> "One should remember that enslaving the families of the kuffar — the infidels — and taking their women as concubines is a firmly established aspect of the Shariah, or Islamic law," the group says in an online magazine published Sunday.
>
> ...said voters might conclude that waterboarding is much too good for them.
>
> But apparently not to those on the left, at least not to those who read crooks and liars.

And if you would like to understand Trump's appeal this, I think, comes close to it:

> After watching the pro-Obama mainstream media coordinate to effectively put Sen. John McCain (R-AZ) 43% and Mitt Romney on defense throughout almost all of their respective presidential campaigns, Republican voters understand that if we are going to beat the Clinton Machine and the media in 2016, whoever we pick as our nominee will have to know how to dodge the media's sucker-punches and fearlessly stay on offense.
>
> In the face of more than a month of withering scorn and hate from the media, Trump has been everywhere hitting back, taking on all comers, ducking nobody, and turning Gawker into Wile E. Coyote.
>
> The bottom line is that Trump is displaying something sorely lacking in the current Republican field: competence when it comes to handling a hostile, left-wing media.
>
> Competence always translates into votes. The media knows this, which is why in 2012 and 2008 they created a dynamic that said, "Obama can do no wrong, and his Republican opponent can do nothing right."

Without breaking the back of that media strategy, Hillary Clinton will be our next president, and right now only Trump is showing that he can break the media's back.

~

The moral depravity of the left
August 7, 2015

How many different issues there are. The Democrats overload the system with more outrage than could ever have been imagined and then let the media ignore every bit of it. Let's just go to three.

First is ISIS. Anyone not sickened by the Islamic State is morally dead themselves. From Mark Steyn:[14]

> *The self-absorbed hedonism of modern western life necessarily requires desensitization. Bloomberg reports an ISIS "sex slave" price list acquired in Iraq by UN official Zainab Bangura: A woman over 40 will set you back a mere 41 bucks, but if you prefer a girl aged nine or under – and who doesn't? – the price rises to $165. As Laura Rosen Cohen points out, this is the real "war on women". But nobody cares – because to care, seriously, either about an infanticide-industrial complex or nine-year-old sex-slaves in an American protectorate, would ask something of us. And to ask something – anything – more than a supportive hashtag is too much.*

You can read more here, but this time in the English tabloid press: 'ISIS executes 19 girls for refusing to have sex with fighters as UN envoy reveals how sex slaves are 'peddled like barrels of petrol'.'[15] The price list for women is presented as well. What is it about ISIS you don't know that would want you not to see something done?

Second, the revelations about the American abortion industry. The actual issue Steyn was discussing in his post above was the Planned Parenthood sale of baby parts that has been captured on video. Perhaps our civilisation does not deserve to survive:

> *The fifth in an apparent series of twelve Planned Parenthood undercover*

---

[14] steynonline.com, 5 August 2015
[15] *Daily Mail Australia,* 6 August 2015.

videos shows Melissa Farrell, director of research for Planned Parenthood Gulf Coast, discussing how to manipulate the abortion procedure in order to ensure the "fetus" is delivered "intact" and thus able to be cannibalized for body parts. As Ms Farrell puts it, if a client "has a specific need for a certain portion of the products of conception and we bake that into our contract, and our protocol, that we follow this. So we deviate from our standard in order to do that."

No newspaper or media outlet you know has covered this in anything other than a perfunctory way, assuming they have covered it at all. How morally sick do you have to be not to find this depraved to the fullest extent of its meaning.

Third, there is the manoeuvering by Obama and Kerry to remove every possible sanction on Iran developing nuclear weapons. This is not a deal. This is the action of someone who is, for all intents and purposes, an Iranian operative elected President of the United States. The only crafting involved was to structure the process so that it could be approved by first the Iranians, then by the UN and finally by the American Senate. This is not calculation on behalf of the United States. This is calculation on how the sell out can be sold. Even the Iranians don't quite appreciate the traitorous nature of the American President, as witness this:[16]

Obama's remarks about the deal are meant for domestic consumption and aimed at soothing fears among Republican and Jewish critics, [Iranian Brigadier General Mohammad Ali] Asudi claimed.

The common denominator is the American media who do as best it can not to discuss any of it. Unless you watch Fox or read right-side blogs – easily avoided if your aim is not to know, or even find out what there is to know that you prefer not to – you are virtually unaware of any of it. Even if you had seen any of it, nowhere will you have come across the slightest outrage in the media. It is a moral sickness that infects the entire left side of the political spectrum. If you still can vote for these people – if you still see Obama in a positive way – it is a moral sickness you share with far too many others who prefer to see themselves as moral giants when they are instead the worst of the worst.

---

[16] *The Washington Free Beacon,* 7 August 2015.

Trump would be a terrible president
August 9, 2015

I've been paying close attention to Donald Trump since we happened to see his speech in Las Vegas that took him to the top of the polls. But politics is not about having a set of opinions. It is about working with other people to achieve collective ends. The business with Megyn Kelly[17] is the finish of him so far as I am concerned, and I am unlikely to be alone on this.

It's not just the disgust he creates. It's his lack of proportion. It's his attitude to the views of those who disagree with him that is so disturbing. He has never run for or held political office. He has only run businesses, which is precisely the wrong kind of experience for anyone in politics. A business is an organisation that does work by command and control. There are decision makers and those who put those decisions into effect. That is not the way a free society works.

Obama has much in common with Trump and has turned out to be the worst president in American history. My way or the highway, with the result that everything of any significance he has become involved with has turned out a disaster. Trump would be no worse, but he would be no better.

A presidential system is the worst form of democracy you can have. The last few years have shown how flawed a system it can be. We can only hope for a better outcome after 2017.

~

"Beck quipped"
August 10, 2015

You really do have to wonder about political reporting. This is a brief story on Glenn Beck's reaction to Donald Trump:[18]

> Conservative radio host Glenn Beck called Donald Trump a "son of a bitch," and panned his performance in Thursday night's GOP presidential debate.
>
> On his Friday broadcast, Beck argued that the GOP front-runner was a "big

---

[17] *The Daily Beast*, 7 August 2015.
[18] townhall.com, 9 August 2015.

loser" in the first showdown between Republican candidates.

He is the most arrogant candidate next to the candidate called Barack Obama," he said. "I mean, there's nobody I've seen more arrogant than him.

"This guy will be Barack Obama times 10 with enemy lists," Beck added of Trump's unpopularity with other Republicans. "[He is] really dangerous."

Beck admitted that Trump's inclusion produced entertaining political theater, calling it the "best presidential debate" he has ever seen.

"I could watch this as sports [if] my country wasn't dying," Beck quipped.

Trump instantly drew boos on Thursday evening by refusing to rule out a 2016 Oval Office bid as an independent.

My guess is that Glenn wasn't being lighthearted.

~

The American leader of the opposition
August 12, 2015

Whatever you may think of the crash in the Chinese economy, who are suffering from the after-effects of their Keynesian stimulus – ghost cities anyone? – what I really find interesting about these headlines from Drudge is the comment from Donald Trump. The American system lacks a leader of the opposition; now it has one, of sorts. If Trump comments, it's news. It has nothing to do with Obama and American politics, but that's because it is hard really to see Trump as opposed to what Obama is doing anywhere outside of immigration, and even then it's not all that certain.

CHINA MOVES SPOOK STOCKS…
Roils Markets Second Day as Yuan Cut by 1.6%…
EXPORTERS REELING…
RISKS CLASH WITH USA…
DOW 'DEATH CROSS'…
TRUMP: Currency devaluation will devastate…

No one else is news. How do any of the established Republican candidates get a look in? He is leading the opposition, but just who or what he is opposed to is still to be determined.

Either Obama's an idiot or he thinks we are
August 13, 2015

Or both. The start of an article on 'President Obama has lost the argument on Iran'.[19]

> *When your best argument for an agreement is that the deal's opponents are "making common cause" with your negotiating partners, it's safe to say you've lost the debate.*

As for those who take his word for things being idiots, he was elected twice and the media still love him. Highly rational with a deep respect for the past, for freedom and the constitution is not part of their frame of reference.

~

Donald Trump – the inside story
August 23, 2015

I picked up from our local second-hand bookshop a copy of a hatchet job done on Donald Trump written in 1991 which goes by the name *Trumped: the inside story of Donald Trump – his cunning rise and spectacular fall*, a book written much too soon given his subsequent success. I cannot say I read every word, but as hatchet jobs go, what I came away with was a sense of someone who knew what he was on about, knew how to go about getting what he wanted, knew how to cut his losses when things did not work out, but was someone always in command of any situation, even as here, where he went in over his head in a series of deals on building casinos in New Jersey. But if you want a sense of who he is, the chapter headings are all quotes from Trump, and they reveal someone of substance even though they were not at all intended to be taken that way:

> *"Some people have a sense of the market and some people don't. I like to think I have that instinct.*
>
> *"People think I'm a gambler. I've never gambled in my life."*

---

[19] *The Washington Examiner*, 12 August 2015.

"We were selling fantasy."

"Despite what some people may think, I'm not looking to be a bad guy when it isn't absolutely necessary."

"Well, it's all a game."

"I want great promotion because it's great promotion."

"What I never anticipated was that we could win — and end up losing anyway."

"Life is very fragile. Anything can change, without warning, and that's why I try not to take any of what's happening too seriously."

"Sometimes your best investments are the ones you don't make."

"What separates the winners from the losers is how a person reacts to each new twist of fate."

"Good publicity is preferable to bad, but from a bottom line perspective, bad publicity is sometimes better than no publicity at all."

"In my life, there are two things I've found I'm very good at: overcoming obstacles and motivating good people to do their best work."

"I'm loyal to people who've done good work for me."

"Sometimes by losing a battle you find a new way to win the war."

For all his outward appearance, he is nobody's fool and gets things done. Meanwhile:

> TRUMP STADIUM RALLY IN ALABAMA…
> *Southern spectacle part of strategy…*
> THOUSANDS TURN OUT…
> *Senator Jeff Sessions Joins Donald Trump on Stage in Alabama* – IN TRUMP HAT!

And in other news that might also be relevant, from Drudge:

> *Dow Plunges 531 Points in Global Selloff: Signs of slowdown in Chinese economy pressure stocks, commodities*
> *World's Richest People Lose $182 Billion as Market Rout Deepens…*
> WEEKEND OF WORRY: APPLE UGLY…
> *Signs of panic-like selling…*

China blamed for free-fall…
Oil biggest losing streak in 30 years…
CURRENCY COLLAPSE…
CLAIM: Dow 5,000? Yes, it could happen…

We do live in interesting times.

~

What is the economic return on an unskilled migrant?

August 25, 2015

First there's this: 'EVERY DEPORTED ILLEGAL HOUSEHOLD SAVES TAXPAYERS MORE THAN $700,000'.[20]

Migrants, even the best of them, take a long time to pay off the resources they absorb when coming to a new country.

And then there's this: 'Sorry, Donald Trump: America needs birthright citizenship'.[21]

Fine. But tell me this, is there an upper limit on how many migrants we should take in or what sort of personal characteristics they should have?

~

Media lies and the parties of the left

August 31, 2015

The parties of the left depend on lies to get elected, and even more so depend on the news gathering organisations to suppress any news that might harm the left. Here is Andrew Klavan[22] making that point:

> Here is the first rule of "mainstream" news coverage in America: Whenever the prejudices and illusions of left-wingers are confirmed by an individual incident, the incident is treated as representative; when those prejudices and illusions are contradicted, the incident is considered an aberration — and treating it as representative is deemed hateful.

---

[20] breitbart.com, 24 August 2015.
[21] *The Week*, 24 August 2015.
[22] PJ Media, 30 August 2015.

You would think that everyone knew that, but not everyone does. You would think that everyone who does know that would discount any news source from the usual sources as tainted, but not everyone does that either. The left and the media are now as one. The media know the power they have and they are filled with those who are prepared to lie and distort every message they write and print to perpetuate the left in power

~

A very dark age coming
September 1, 2015

This is a long article by David Solway on 'Nine Signs of the Impending American Collapse'.[23] Written in an end-of-times style, but get past that opening if these are the kinds of things that put you off, and get to the secular version Solway has outlined. There are nine different harbingers for the descent that is about to visit us. Almost prosaically, I will list his very last, which is the presidency of Barack Obama, about which he said this amongst other things:

> Under Obama's nation-withering hand, the land of the free and the home of the brave is fast becoming the land of the hunted and the home of the suborned. Obama is like a Judas goat leading the sheep into the abattoir. If this ruthless minion of the left completes his term successfully according to his intentions, the United States will not recover. It will be fatally riven by internal dissension, infiltrated by avowed enemies and millions of so-called "undocumented workers" and queue-jumpers, drowning in unpayable debt, subject to judicial intimidation and repressive state control, and vulnerable to a host of hostile nations—China, Russia and Iran, to name only the most prominent. It will be game over.

Is it game over? Is all that will remain of the West, the Judaeo-Christian West, be a few enclaves that will need to defend their historic purpose and historic identity? Read Solway's article only because we are still, for the most part, in the best of times. It won't last, but for now we have the time and leisure to reflect on what is to come, although, as always, the future cannot be known.

---
[23] PJ Media, 31 August, 2015.

Hillary's rules for radicals
September 2, 2015

Why does no one even bother to mention that Hillary's senior thesis was on Saul Alinsky's *Rules for Radicals*. Once upon a time unavailable. Now, it is hardly worth a mention; it is, if anything, a feature and not anything she needs to hide. She has the same genealogy as Obama. If you are interested, you can read it www.hillaryclintonquarterly.com/documents/HillaryClintonThesis.pdf. You won't find anything you don't already know, which is in itself a large part of the problem.

~

Can he really be that stupid? Yes he can
September 3, 2015

Can he really have said this?

> *"If we do nothing, Alaskan temperatures are projected to rise between six and twelve degrees by the end of the century."*

Yes he did![24] It's four paras down after the picture, and I can only hope that this is another parody website I haven't picked up on. The only question I ask is why I had not heard this before. But it's not he who is deranged, although the possibilities are immense, but the media who cover his every action who have not said a word. Does anyone believe anything like this? Does no one in the media think it is outrageous that this can be said by a President of the United States at an international conference? There is no adult free press in the United States, and if there is, the media are as whatever as their president. I really honestly don't have the words to describe them or him.

---

[24] www.whitehouse.gov, 29 August 2015.

Why is Hillary electable?
September 6, 2015

It's not that Trump is ahead but that Hillary is close that is the most disturbing result. So far Trump is being given a free ride by the media, with almost no negative coverage. He is there to pulverise the established Republicans and then when he becomes the nominee all will change. The survey results,[25] which themselves may be a beat up.

> The poll by SurveyUSA finds that matched up directly, Trump garners 45 percent to Clinton's 40 percent.
>
> In other head-to-head matchups, Trump beats out Sen. Bernie Sanders (I-Vt.) by 44 percent to 40 percent; Vice President Joe Biden by 44 percent to 42 percent; and former Vice President Al Gore by 44 percent to 41 percent.

~

Ensuring the end of Western Civilisation
September 6, 2015

This is the title: 'Western Civilization: The Final Frontier?'[26] Here is what she said in her text, with the word "practically" inserted so as not to rule out divine intervention or some such thing:

> What is particularly appalling about the ill-informed Western elites is how their policies are practically ensuring the end of Western Civilization. They refuse to acknowledge the need for border security — sovereignty — and allow, if not encourage the wholesale influx of third-world immigrants (who do not wish to assimilate) into states with generous welfare policies.

I'm sure what comes next will be an improvement on what we have done. We obviously don't know what's good for us anyway. Here's another perspective: 'How Mainstream Media and Social Media Present COMPLETELY Different Views Of Syrian Immigrant Crisis.'[27] Its opening statement:

---

[25] *The Hill*, 4 September 2016.
[26] *American Thinker*, September 6, 2015.
[27] soopermexican.com, 5 September 2015.

> *The "Great Replacement" has begun, and social media is showing what the "refugees" from Syria are really all about.*

It's not the world I was born into so I wouldn't be expected to like it. But others are being born into this one so maybe they'll like it better. But it is amazing to be there at the end, although it may limp along for a bit longer still. Read *The Swerve*. Think about just how well this passage from a hostile review[28] fits the world we are on the threshold of entering:

> *It is possible for a whole culture to turn away from reading and writing. As the Roman Empire crumbled and Christianity became ascendant, as cities decayed, trade declined, and an anxious populace scanned the horizon for barbarian armies, the ancient system of education fell apart. What began as downsizing went on to wholesale abandonment. Schools closed, libraries and academies shut their doors, professional grammarians and teachers of rhetoric found themselves out of work, scribes were no longer given manuscripts to copy.*

The most haunting part of the book was the description of fifteenth century Rome, the centre of an empire a thousand years before. It was not until the middle of the 14th century, perhaps even the 15th, that living standards in Europe rose to where they had been in the 2nd. You think it can't happen until it does, and it does now look like it might.

~

The more news they watch the less people seem to know about the world

September 8, 2015

How is it even possible that a picture of a single drowned child could suddenly galvanise tens of millions around the world to open their borders and admit who knows who within their territories? And you know how? Because the newspaper readers and television-news watchers of the world have not been shown any of the horrors that have been routine over the past half decade in every war zone in the Middle East. For any of us who have been paying attention, the picture was so completely lacking in

---

[28] *Los Angelas Review of Books*, 1 December 2012.

newsworthiness that it has taken me by utter surprise to find that this one photo now has millions of people round the world ready to open their frontiers to just about anyone with a story to tell about their needs for refuge. Such ignorance is not an accident. It is the consequence of having come to depend on a media so singularly dishonest that it has given Barack Obama two terms as president.

~

Trump opposes the deal with Iran
September 9, 2015

Well, here's some news: 'Trump Storms Washington to Stop Iran Nuke Deal'.[29]

> *Donald Trump is coming to Washington with a message for Congress and the American people: Stop the nuclear deal with Iran.*
>
> *And he will be joined by a star-studded galaxy of conservative leaders.*
>
> *Appearing with the leading Republican presidential contender will be fellow candidate Sen. Ted Cruz, R-Texas, former Gov. Sarah Palin, R-Alaska, political commentator Glenn Beck, radio talk-show host Mark Levin and many others in what promises to be a huge rally to try stop the Iran deal at the Capitol on Wednesday.*
>
> *"This deal makes war a certainty," Cruz has charged.*
>
> *And, as he told WND, "If this deal is consummated, it will make the Obama administration the world's leading financier of radical Islamic terrorism."*

And with the photo of Trump and Cruz in the story, you might well be looking at the Repubican nominees for President and Vice President next November. As for Trump himself, the headline on the personal statement by Donald Trump reads: 'Donald Trump: Amateur hour with the Iran nuclear deal.'[30] It's not long so you can read it all. This is how it starts:

> *It is hard to believe a president of the United States would actually put his name on an agreement with the terrorist state Iran that is so bad, so*

---

[29] worldnetdaily.com, 7 September 2015.
[30] usatoday.com, 8 September 2015.

poorly constructed and so terribly negotiated that it increases uncertainty and reduces security for America and our allies, including Israel.

It was amateur hour for those charged with striking this deal with Iran, demonstrating to the world, yet again, the total incompetence of our president and politicians. It appears we wanted a deal at any cost rather than following the advice of Ronald Reagan and walking away because "no deal is better than a bad deal."

The US now has a Leader of the Opposition, and what a difference it makes.

~

Too stupid to survive
September 10, 2015

I do have to tell you I am surprised to find the disappearance of our Western civilisation being looked at as an opportunity to show our compassion. We are too stupid to survive, and we will not survive. We are about to have all the diversity anyone could ever have wanted. If you are of the view that open borders work for you, and one culture is equally as worthy as any other, everything will be great. But I am just that tad bit unsure of where all this will go, since if it made no difference, Damascus would look like Stockholm. So we shall see.

In the meantime, the only place I can find where the decline and fall of the West is being charted with any kind of recognition of what is overwhelming our cultural and historic home is at Andrew Bolt. Everywhere else in the media it looks like nothing of much significance is going on. While we still have time to think about things, reading this, also from Andrew, might be worth reflecting on: 'With more Syrians en route, Sweden struggles to maintain identity as country where refugees are welcome'.[31] It is from the Canadian *National Post* and therefore will inevitably look on the bright side of life:

Another point of division is language — most refugees have trouble mastering Swedish.

---

[31] nationalpost.com, 8 September 2015.

> *That helps explain what has happened in Rosengard, a suburb of Malmo, Sweden's third-largest city 80 kilometres from Astorp: more than 80 per cent of residents speak Arabic.*
>
> *"I love it here because it feels like the Middle East," said Taghrid, a young hijab-wearing Palestinian from Syria as she pushed a baby carriage past other women in similar attire. "It's special. You know, people in the streets, the smell of spices."*
>
> *Such segregated enclaves are part of the problem, said Jonczyk, who moves easily between Astorp's Swedish and Arab communities.*
>
> *"What they do at home, they want to do in Swedish society and they want Swedish society to accept that," he said. . . .*
>
> *With unemployment among refugees well above 40 per cent, finding them work was one of Jonczyk's major preoccupations. But to reach the point where they were employable was not possible if Sweden did not do a much better job of making them feel part of their new environment.*

The job will now be to make Swedes feel part of their new environment.

~

The US is "led by very very stupid people!"
September 10, 2015

You won't see it in the papers or on the news, but this is what Donald Trump said yesterday, in Washington, in front of the Capitol with no doubt one or two journalist about: "'Israel will not survive" with Iran nuclear deal in place'.[32]

> *Republican presidential front-runner Donald Trump warns Americans that "Israel will not survive" if the incompetence of the political class continues to dictate our foreign policy.*
>
> *Trump appeared Wednesday at the rally to stop the Iran nuclear deal in front of the U.S. Capitol. Preceded by Sen. Ted Cruz who called Trump his "friend," and entering to raucous applause against the backdrop of*

---

[32] breitbart.com, 9 September 2015.

> REM's classic hit "It's The End of the World As We Know It," Trump pulled no punches.
>
> "Never, ever ever in my life have I seen any transaction so incompetently negotiated as our deal with Iran," Trump said. "And I mean never."

I think he's going to be President.

~

Trump terrifies Wall Street
September 15, 2015

Sounds good to me:[33]

> The CEO of one large Wall Street firm, who declined to be identified by name criticizing the GOP front-runner, said the assumption in the financial industry remains that something will eventually knock Trump off and send voters toward a more establishment candidate. But that assumption is no longer held with strong conviction. And a dozen Wall Street executives interviewed for this article could not say what might dent Trump's appeal or when it might happen.
>
> "I don't know anyone who is a Donald Trump supporter. I don't know anyone who knows anyone who is a Donald Trump supporter. They are like this huge mystery group," the CEO said. "So it's a combination of shock and bewilderment. No one really knows why this is happening. But my own belief is that the laws of gravity will apply and those who are prepared to run the marathon will benefit when Trump drops out at mile 22. Right now people think Trump is pretty hilarious but the longer it goes on the more frightening it gets."

Trump is not going to be foxed by money manipulators and doesn't need their cash to run. Maybe, at last, a president who won't bail out the banks.

---

[33] *Politico*, 14 September 2015.

The single most important story of our times
September 19, 2015

But no one is paying attention.

> *GET OUT!*
> *EU nations pull welcome mats…*
> *Hungary Plans Longer Fence…*
> *35 MILLION heading to Europe?*
> *Munich faces collision of refugees and Oktoberfest…*
> *Top Iman: Muslim Migrants Should Breed With Europeans to 'Conquer Their Countries'…*

Does no one think this will matter?

~

Advice to Trump on what he should say about Obama
September 19, 2015

This is Steve Hayward's advice to Donald Trump on what he ought to say to someone who accuses Obama of being a Muslim.[34]

> *As far as I'm concerned, Obama's nationality and religious faith are a settled matter. But you can understand why many Americans might think otherwise from his words and deeds in office. He has strengthened our enemies seemingly on purpose, obviously hates Jews and Israel, and really doesn't appear to like America very much. If we did have a secret Muslim in the Oval Office, it would be hard to tell the difference from the actual Obama record. Instead of demanding my apology, the Democratic Party ought to apologize for foisting this plainly defective president on our once-great country.*

You can see what Hayward thinks but knows he cannot say.

UPDATE: Then there's this ridiculous article[35] attacking Trump for being somehow opposed to small government and Republican principles. Here is a reply in the comments that says pretty well what I think myself:

---

[34] *Powerline*, 18 September 2015
[35] PJ Media, 18 September 2015.

> *What the author, GOP Inc and the DC Establishment fail to grasp is 25 years of saying one thing and doing the opposite tends to make people question things. How could Trump be worse than the supposed leaders of the leaders of the GOP? They campaign on limited government, and then go to Washington and give away the store. And the most obvious example is the DC GOP wants desperately to give away the store again with amnesty to make the Chamber of Commerce donor class happy at the expense of middle and working class Americans. We're supposed to be upset because Trump isn't conservative enough, but the likes of Jeb and Grahamnesty are "true conservatives"? Without fixing immigration, none of it matters. And the idiots running the GOP do not grasp that. Trump, if nothing else, does. And without him no one else is even talking about immigration.*

Trump is the only one anywhere talking about America as a nation state while the rest are interested only in one form or another of open borders. If they really are unaware of what is going on across the world, where our way of life is being submerged by migrants who know nothing of the principles of a free society and personal responsibility, then there should be no surprise when some of us will make one last effort to preserve for the next generations what we were able to enjoy ourselves.

UPDATE: Here is what Roger Simon[36] thinks Trump ought to have said:

> *Although it's perhaps a bit too complicated, or even apocalyptic, for the campaign hustings, here's how Trump should have answered the man's question. Is Obama a Muslim? No, but he's something even worse — a transnational progressive.*

But he adds this, which is the Republican elite response of the moment to the challenge posed by Donald Trump:

> *On second thought, such complex ideological talk is obviously not Trump's style. But there is someone running for the presidency with the intellectual chops, guts and speaking clarity to explain something like this to the public — Carly.*

Fine and dandy, but what does she think about immigration, which is the real issue, not Obama's religious beliefs which no one will ever know while he is still president.

And then we may add this, which is the conclusion to 'It's Back: The

---

[36] PJ Media, 19 September 2015.

President's Religion Controversy':[37]

> *So, America, is Barack Obama a Christian or a Muslim? Wrong question, destined to lead to an insufficient answer. I suspect that we are presided over by a modern Marxist agnostic, holding our own historical foundations and culture in contempt, while he is sympathetic with and ready to enfold the culture of people who have sworn to slaughter us. I suspect he has no desire to make us Islamic, and that President Obama is more opportunistically taking advantage of Muslim upheaval to work anarchy and chaos against the America he wants to change. Because American government is indeed founded on the Judeo-Christian principles I stated above, he exhibits the same simmering hostility to Christianity that we see generally among the "progressive" American Left.*

Both of these have been taken from Instapundit.

~

What should Trump have said about Obama's religious beliefs?

September 21, 2015

This business about Obama's religion does go on with plenty of advice with what Donald Trump should have said, and now extending to the entire Republican field who are also being asked to answer what no one can possibly know, what religion does Barack Obama really follow in his heart of hearts. Mark Steyn has his own views which he has filed under the heading, 'Get Lost, You Palace-Guard Creeps'.[38] Naturally you need to read it all where he provides seven different possible answers, all good. This is number six.

> *As to whether he's a Christian, have you asked him whether he has attended even semi-regularly any church other than that of Jeremiah ("God damn America") Wright? A man is free to attend the Westboro Baptist Church but if he chooses to do so I'm not obligated to defend his Christianity. And frankly, whatever the President's personal faith, there is no dispute that his*

---

[37] virtualmilitia.com, 19 September 2015.
[38] steynonline.com, 19 September 2015.

leadership of the western world has been an utter catastrophe for Christians around the planet. Some of the oldest Christian communities on earth have been entirely extinguished on Obama's watch: in Mosul, Iraq, which was an American protectorate on the day he took office, not a single Christian remains. Every single one of them is dead or fled. So, instead of jumping through your preposterous hoops and speaking up for the most powerful man in the world, I would rather speak up for the powerless – for the Nigerian schoolgirls, for the Yazidi, for the Copts in Egypt, and for all the other beleaguered Christian communities in the world this feckless president has set alight and watched burn.

When you think about all this, what possible difference does it make what he believes when it is what he has done, or not done, that is what counts.

~

The first to say "racist" loses the argument
September 21, 2015

I came across a poster the other day that says the word "racist" was invented in 1927 by Leon Trotsky to give the communists some kind of rhetorical advantage in certain debates of the time. Looking around, this seems to be a widely held belief although I wouldn't know myself. Since he spoke Russian it's a hard one to confirm. Yet the point is clear enough. Those without an actual argument just say "racist" and then let the thought-police do the rest. As an example of almost an infinite number that might be found, I did come across this today on Drudge which is a story from last night's Emmy Awards in the US:

ATTACK: Trump Called 'Racist' in Opening Monologue…

Which is all related to Donald Trump's off-handed reply to a query from the stands the other day on what religion he thought Obama followed. In the wake of this non-story, which has, of course, become explosive in the hands of the American media, here is what we can also find on Drudge:

CARSON: A Muslim should not be president…

Video…
Stephanopoulos Grills Trump: Why Can't You Say That Obama Is Not Muslim?
FLASHBACK: Obama 'My Muslim Faith'…

This business about Obama's religion has led to plenty of advice over what Donald Trump ought to have said, and has now extended to the entire Republican field who are also being asked to answer what no one can possibly know, what religion does Obama really follows in his heart of hearts.

~

Maybe we should be frightened
September 23, 2015

This is the kind of story we are being spared by the media precisely so that we do not became terrified by what is going on in Europe. The basic premise of progressive internationalism is that every culture is basically the same and that civilised values are a universal. Maybe, but there are then stories like this one that make you ask what happens if that isn't true. The title is 'Germany's Migrant Rape Epidemic'.[39] Here's part of what it says:

> *A growing number of women and young girls housed in refugee shelters in Germany are being raped, sexually assaulted and even forced into prostitution by male asylum seekers, according to German social work organizations with first-hand knowledge of the situation. . . .*
>
> *Conditions for women and girls at some shelters are so perilous that females are being described as "wild game" fighting off Muslim male predators. But many victims, fearing reprisals, are keeping silent, social workers say.*
>
> *At the same time, growing numbers of German women in towns and cities across the country are being raped by asylum seekers from Africa, Asia and the Middle East. Many of the crimes are being downplayed by German authorities and the national media, apparently to avoid fueling anti-immigration sentiments.*

---

[39] breitbart.com, 22 September 2015.

The question is, if these are the kinds of people who are entering Europe, why wouldn't you want to fuel anti-immigration sentiments. The answer to this question I do not know, but there is much evidence that the authorities are conniving with the media to keep these stories out of the news. Everyone knows, of course, it's just not in the news so it is not officially true so no one officially needs to do a single thing. The reality is that the demographic shift in Europe may be the biggest story of our time yet is virtually never mentioned in the press.

Yet this is where some good could actually be done. By branding rapists as the barbarians they are, perhaps some kinds of social pressure could be brought to bear on such practices. By saying nothing in public we are, in effect, condoning behaviours that are disgusting to their very core. We must side up with the women being attacked, and do what we can to protect them from some of the most vile human scum who are found in their midst.

~

This is what we are told so you have to wonder what the real story is

September 24, 2015

Millions of people heading for Europe with no European language skills, and possibly no marketable skills of any kind, and read how the President of Hungary reacts:

> *Hungarian prime minister Viktor Orbán warned European life and its established laws were under threat from huge numbers of people heading through the continent from war-torn states in the Middle East.*
>
> *In a defence against criticism of the aggressive stance against refugees taken by the country, he said yesterday: "Our borders are in danger. Our way of life where we respect the law is in danger.*
>
> *"The whole of Hungary and Europe is in danger.*
>
> *"The migrants are blitzing us."*
>
> *Hungary and Serbia have constantly been at each others' throats over the issue, with Budapest urging its non-EU neighbours to do more to help*

tackle the growing neighbours migrants.

It is now sending troops armed with rubber bullets and tear gas to the border with Serbia to protect the country's frontier.

Pinter Bence, a Hungarian political journalist for the mandiner.hu website said the situation with growing tensions between nations was reminiscent of the international scenario from just over 100 years ago.

Leaders who don't love the countries they lead are becoming more common. The darkness of this century may yet overwhelm what we experienced in the last one.

~

Two articles on immigration
September 24, 2015

As everyone knows, open borders leads to a more harmonious happier more contented and prosperous world. Here are two articles published today that you might therefore read to confirm your views on how bizarre those who oppose immigration are. One is from the US by Ann Coulter. The second is from Australia by Peter Baldwin.

First Ann, whose article is titled, 'Useless Idiots'.[40] You'll have to read the article for yourself to see who she means, but she really does go over the top.

The second is titled, 'Migrant crisis: Europe must close borders to refugee influx'.[41] An obvious hysteric with no credibility. You'll again have to read the article for yourself to see just how off the planet he is.

AND LET ME JUST ADD THIS: Of course I'm a migrant and so the last thing in the world I would be against is migration. I was, however, amongst that first tranche in 1975 who needed a migrant's visa to move to Australia from Canada. This entailed an embassy official to come down to Toronto from Ottawa for an hour-long interview to which he brought a professor of economics from the University of Toronto to ensure themselves that I was up to the mark for teaching at the College in Bendigo. This is what I understand about migration. The country decides on who

---

[40] anncoulter.com, 23 September 2015.
[41] *The Australian*, 24 September 2015.

comes and who does not, and they also decide on how many in any given year, and they ensure as best they can that the migrant is likely to become a productive member of the community. However, what I do not accept is people just wandering in as they please where the host country does no sorting and assessing. That I don't get, which is why I was very keen to ensure that the boats were stopped, as was most of the country. These are not fine distinctions, but the very minimum requirement if we are to remain a nation state in a world of other nation states.

This is from Mark Steyn who never quits talking about migration and demographics. This one is called 'The Emperor's Moral Narcissism'[42] which even comes with a photo showing a crowd of sensible people holding up a sign reading "Refugees Welcome".

~

Not the six o'clock news
September 26, 2015

The world changing right in front of us but virtually none of it will be mentioned in any heated way by our journalist class. This is from Drudge:

> *EU chief fears union will collapse…*
> *Migrant stream shows no sign of slowdown…*
> *Rape, child abuse 'rife in German refugee camps'…*
> *Poll: Most U.S. Muslims would trade Constitution for Shariah*
> *Dem mayors ask Obama for more refugees…*

It is the first story[43] that is the oddest. It begins:

> THE European Union has lost control of its borders and risks total collapse if they are not sealed, a senior Brussels diplomat has warned.
>
> Donald Tusk, president of the European Council, warned the EU was now facing a "critical point" and that the migrant crisis hadn't even reached its peak.
>
> As he chaired an emergency meeting of EU leaders in Brussels last night Mr Tusk painted a bleak picture of the EU's future, saying the

---

[42] steynonline.com, 24 September 2015.
[43] *Express*, 24 September 2015.

28-member bloc was on the verge of breakdown with "recriminations and misunderstanding" pitting nations against one another.

The future of free movement was at stake, he said, as the continent had lost control of its borders as well as a "sense of order".

He added: "The most urgent question we should ask ourselves…is how to regain control of our external borders.

"Otherwise, it doesn't make sense to even speak about common migration policy."

He appeared to lay much of the blame with Germany, accusing Chancellor Angela Merkel of exacerbating the problem by sending the signal to desperate Syrians fleeing their war-torn homeland that Germany had no limit on the number of migrants it would accept.

It's not "the EU" that is on the point of collapse but European civilisation. The narrowness of the perspective is what gets me, not to mention the madness of Merkel's policy of open borders. Do they have any idea at all what they are doing?

~

The stupidest generation in history that has brought down the Western world, that's who they are

September 26, 2015

There is an article posted at Powerline from *National Review* in 1967 with the title, 'Who are the Hippies?'[44] Having been one amongst them, I know only too well who they are. They are the same people, now all grown up, who have opened up Europe to a barbarian horde that Europeans had been able to keep out for 1500 years. They are the idiot last generation of a Europe of Europeans. Next time you go to Europe, drop by St Sophia in Istanbul to see the future of Notre Dame.

As to the article, I was personally more New Left than Hippy but I was both. If anyone has ever repudiated an earlier incarnation of themselves, that person is me. But I have also always thought that if there had to be such a

---

[44] *National Review*, 25 February 2015.

time and place, I was glad to have been part of it, for no other reason than just because. The article – and you must keep in mind that this is from the famously right-wing *National Review* – compared these people to a second century small Christian sect known as the "Adamites". This really is how they were portrayed, and this is not intended to show what a dangerous and unworldly crew of dimwits they were, but to criticise them for their misunderstanding of the proper ethos of love. If you don't believe me, read the article from which these come.

1. *A sense of primal innocence, without "knowledge of good and evil."*
2. *Antinomianism, rejection, in principle, if not always in practice, of all restrictive law imposed from the "outside."*
3. *Hostility to all authority, as in fringing upon their paradisal freedom.*
4. *Pacifism, since there can be no hurt in Paradise.*
5. *Sexual freedom, and no sense of shame, like Adam and Eve in Paradise.*
6. *Community of goods.*
7. *Free-floating fantasy-thinking: impatience with critical thinking as the product of man's fall.*
8. *Emotional self-indulgence: resentment at demands for inner restraint and emotional self-discipline.*
9. *A comprehensive cult of love, as appropriate to the sinless life in Paradise.*

For myself, I was there because I was genuinely unsure how I should lead my life. I was not prepared to embark on a career unless I felt those early steps were in the direction I truly wished to travel. If you were there then, the one thing that was open to all was a marriage, job and family, more or less as a carbon copy of the generation that came before. I now know that there is little else to life, but it looked too easy for those of us there at the time. The result has been that every possible obstacle has been placed in the way of each of these by a society that seems to have a death wish. What looked easy in 1967 now feels difficult beyond imagination.

Progressive internationalism
September 29, 2015

The deadliest enemy we have is that marriage of the left in general and the libertarian right in particular, best described as progressive internationalism. We few still seeking sanctuary within the nation state are being overwhelmed by these progressive internationalist policies, represented here in this article by George Soros, 'Europe mired in crisis without a common asylum-seeker policy'.[45] A pretty nondescript title, but let me take you to the six recommendations Soros provides:

> *First, the EU has to accept at least a million asylum-seekers annually for the foreseeable future.*
>
> *Second, the EU must lead the global effort to provide funding to Lebanon, Jordan, and Turkey to support the four million refugees in those countries.*
>
> *Third, the EU must immediately start building a single EU Asylum and Migration Agency and eventually a single EU Border Guard.*
>
> *Fourth, safe channels must be established for asylum-seekers, starting with getting them from Greece and Italy to their destination countries.*
>
> *Fifth, the operational and financial arrangements developed by the EU should be used to establish global standards for the treatment of asylum-seekers and migrants.*
>
> *Finally, to absorb and integrate more than a million asylum-seekers and migrants a year, the EU needs to mobilise the private sector — NGOs, church groups, and businesses — to act as sponsors.*

Got it? Once we have been overwhelmed by their numbers, nothing of what we built will remain other than the technologies we were able to develop. The rest will be utterly swept away in a sea of barbarism. The only part I have never understood is why, other than hatred and envy, would anyone wish to see these changes taking place.

---

[45] *The Australian*, 29 September 2015.

Syrial killers
October 1, 2015

WAR: RUSSIA BEGINS AIRSTRIKES IN SYRIA; WEST DISPUTES TARGETS

USA DISARRAY

Both from Drudge. From the first story:

> *Russia launched airstrikes Wednesday in Syria, sharply escalating Moscow's role in the conflict but also raising questions about whether its intent is fighting Islamic State militants or protecting longtime ally, President Bashar Assad.*

If ISIL is fighting Assad, and the Russians are trying to protect Assad, then who are the Russians bombing if not ISIL? And then from the second story which is essentially that Putin treats Obama as a no-account nonentity:

> *This would be a plain victory for Assad, who invited the Russians to join his battle to cling on to power, and a defeat for the United States, which has demanded he step down.*

> *The attacks came despite President Barack Obama sitting down with Russia's Vladimir Putin on Monday at the United Nations for 90 minutes of what both camps called "business-like" talks.*

Seriously, who would trust Obama or Kerry on anything? This is no longer the cold War so I no longer have any kind of reflex anti-Soviet bias in thinking about Russia, authoritarian state though it may well still be. Who any longer knows who's on whose side in the Middle East. But my enemy's enemy is my friend, in this business with ISIL that is more than ever the bottom line.

You can't tell the players without a program
October 2, 2015

This is the story as I understand it, but really I don't understand it at all. Russia, it seems, attacked America's anti-Assad allies in Syria who are themselves enemies of ISIS but are also the remaining forces of al Qaeda! The US can do nothing to defend its allies, not that they should be its allies, but is in any case without any genuine ability to enforce its will. *The Wall Street Journal* provides a rough guide to the various major parties and what they are seeking out of the conflict. Meanwhile Europe is submerged in new migrants from alien cultures which has changed Europe forever.

The American reaction is all spelled out here: 'US urges Russians to focus airstrikes on Islamic State'.[46] But in the midst of it, there is a passage that highlights to me, and probably others, the profound lack of seriousness in American foreign policy:

> *"We are not yet where we need to be to guarantee the safety and security" of those carrying out the airstrikes,* Kerry said, *"and that is the discussion that is taking place today,"* referring to the US-Russia military talks. *"And it will take place even more so over the course of the next few days depending on the outcome today."*

> *"It's a way of making sure that planes aren't going to be shooting at each other and making things worse,"* the secretary said in an interview late Thursday on CBS' *"The Late Show with Stephen Colbert."*

Colbert is the replacement for Jon Stewart on Comedy Central. You cannot parody these people and satire is now impossible.

---

[46] bigstory.ap.org, 2 October 2015.

Something we can all agree with Trump about
October 13, 2015

I'm not sure if you are being diplomatic that you're supposed to say it just because you think it. From the Donald: 'Trump: Merkel Insane'.[47]

> German Chancellor Angela Merkel's invitation to migrants to come to her country has been described as "insane" by U.S. Presidential candidate Donald Trump, who has predicted more violence will follow in the country as a result.
>
> Donald Trump, the Republican Party presidential front-runner, was talking about Mrs. Merkel's invitation to migrants on the American political interview show, 'Face The Nation'.
>
> Mr Trump said: "I do not like the migration. I do not like the people coming". Instead he favours "a safe zone for people", an idea on which he expanded.
>
> He said: "Frankly, look, Europe is going to have to handle — but they're going to have riots in Germany. What's happening in Germany, I always thought Merkel was like this great leader. What she's done in Germany is insane. It is insane. They're having all sorts of attacks."

It will be hard to keep this out of the news but the media will no doubt find a way.

~

Their vision of our future
October 14, 2015

You antediluvian reptile, you. You reactionary, backward neolithic barbarian, locked into your out-dated twentieth-century mindset. This is what our elites believe, and this is the world they are making for us from inside their gated communities. From *The Atlantic*: 'The Case for Getting Rid of Borders—Completely.'[48] This is the conclusion:

> Closed borders are one of the world's greatest moral failings but the opening

---

[47] breitbart.com, 12 October 2015
[48] *The Atlantic*, 10 October, 2015

of borders is the world's greatest economic opportunity. The grandest moral revolutions in history—the abolition of slavery, the securing of religious freedom, the recognition of the rights of women—yielded a world in which virtually everyone was better off. They also demonstrated that the fears that had perpetuated these injustices were unfounded. Similarly, a planet unscarred by iron curtains is not only a world of greater equality and justice. It is a world unafraid of itself.

Merkel's not insane. She, like others of her kind, just thinks that everyone should be allowed to go wherever others have been successful in creating wealth so that they too can have their fair share as well. What could possibly be wrong with that? What could be more just? A hundred years from now they will all look back at us and think how primitive we must have been.

~

Trump was worried about terrorists a year before 911
October 20, 2015

The article is titled, 'Over A Year Before 9/11, Trump Wrote Of Terror Threat With Remarkable Clarity'.[49] This is from his 2000 book, *The America We Deserve*, that is, a book written while Bill Clinton was still president. This is part of what he wrote then:

> *"I may be making waves, but that's all right," wrote Trump. "Making waves is usually what you need to do to rock the boat, and our national-security boat definitely needs rocking.*
>
> *Let's point fingers. The biggest threat to our security is ourselves, because we've become arrogant. Dangerously arrogant. It's time for a realistic view of the world and our place in it. Do we truly understand the threats we face? And let me give a warning: You won't hear a lot of what follows from candidates in this campaign, because what I've got to say is definitely not happy talk.*
>
> *There are forces to be worried about, people and programs to take action against. Now."*
>
> *"We face a different problem when we talk about the individual fanatics*

---

[49] buzzfeed.com, 20 October 2015.

who want to harm us," The Donald continued, discussing the threat from individual terrorist organizations that despised American culture.

Trump said such people were determined to attack us.

"We can kid ourselves all we want by mocking their references to the Great Satan, but also keep in mind that there is no greater destiny for many people than to deal the Great Satan a major kick in the teeth," he wrote, adding they despised the U.S. support for Israel.

"Our teenage boys fantasize about Cindy Crawford; young terrorists fantasize about turning an American city (and themselves) into charcoal," Trump wrote.

Other than not being old school tie, just exactly what is wrong with him as President? I guess the way things are heading, we are going to find out in real time.

~

Trump is not "fading" as the left seems to hope – he is getting better
October 31, 2015

I could just keep quoting Rush forever because each sentence makes you want to read the next. This is about the news-meme that Trump is supposedly fading.[50] This is part of Rush's take:

So I checked the e-mail during the break, and there was a fairly decent point. "Rush, you're ripping into Jeb's campaign people. But don't you realize, if it weren't for Trump, Jeb would probably be the guy with 20 points right now and this thing would be over?" Well, there that word is again: "If." Yeah, well, "if" a lot of things, then things would be different. But that actually kind of buttresses my point. You say, "If it weren't for Trump…" Well, it is for Trump. Trump is there. You'd better be able to adapt to it and you better be able to figure out why Trump is doing well.

And if the only ammo you've got with Trump is, "He's gonna blow it, he's gonna fade, he's gonna step in it, he's not gonna last, he doesn't really mean it, he's gonna get out," and that's all you can do, then you're not doing your

---

[50] rushlimbaugh.com, 29 October 2015.

job. It's not hard to explain Trump's success. It's really rather easy. That's why when I see The Politico story, "The Incredible Shrinking Trump." In their dreams. They haven't the slightest idea what they're talking about. "The Incredible Shrinking Trump — The usual blustery billionaire offered a downright demure performance at the third GOP debate."...

If these hacks in the media were not Democrat Party activists, this story could just as easily be written as, "Donald Trump Shows More Maturity as Campaign Evolves." But, no, because the Democrat media does not see Republicans and conservatives in any way anywhere near a favorable, fair, even almost human way. It's not possible for them. Trump is a cartoon character to all of them, not just Harwood. He is a cartoon character to all of who they hate.

So Trump, who many people might say was behaving a little bit more serious. Less bombast, less personal assault and attack last night. They might say Trump is becoming more serious. Trump is becoming more mature, whatever. But, if you're not inclined to note anything positive or synonymous with what you would say is growth in a human being or candidate, if all you can see is somebody's a cartoon character and a buffoon, and if you think the Republican electorate is so stupid — which they do...

Remember, you people are a bunch of mind-numbed robots to the Drive-By Media. You are incapable of thinking on your own. Your public opinions are nothing but the result of whoever it is influencing you. Me, Fox News, whoever. You're incapable of independent thought, critical thought, what have you. You put these two things together and Trump's where he is precisely because he's a cartoon character, and you people are so shallow and so dense that that's what you want in a president.

The left assumes everyone else is like they are, that there is a single acceptable position on every issue and therefore once it is proclaimed there is no further thought required. That is not how it is on this side. That they are not embarrassed that Hillary will be their candidate come what may is as sure a sign of the decadence of the American left as there ever has been. Why aren't they embarrassed that not only is she out of her depth on every issue, but that no one else is being allowed to stand in her way even if there were anyone else who could.

C'mon, seven days from now it will all be last week's news

November 18, 2015

Everyone lives at a moment in time which vanishes even as a new present arrives. Don't worry. Be happy. This is today.

> *TERROR SCARE HITS GERMANY: COPS WARN 'NOT TO WALK IN GROUPS'*
> *MERKEL DEATH KNELL: RISE OF THE ANTI-IMMIGRATION PARTY...*
> *'420 DANGEROUS ISLAMISTS LIVE IN GERMANY'...*
> *Video: Turkey fans boo moment of silence for Paris attacks, then chant 'Allahu Akbar'...*
> *Syrian 'Refugee' Already MISSING IN LOUISIANA...*
> *Resettlement group admits: We don't track them...*
> *WHITE HOUSE WON'T TELL GOVS WHERE SENDING REFUGEES...*
> *Planeload arrives in Britain...*
> *Speaker Ryan calls for 'pause' on program...*
> *CZECH PRESIDENT ADDRESSES RALLY AGAINST MUSLIMS...*
> *Israel Outlaws Domestic Islamic Movement as Police Raid Offices...*
> *WASH TIMES WEDS: FBI FEARS HOLIDAY SEASON...*
> *Extensive ISIS plotting, political indifference from Obama raises concerns...*

Is this tomorrow?

> *REUTERS 5-DAY ROLLING POLL: TRUMP 36%, CARSON 14.6%, RUBIO 11.2%, CRUZ 7.9%... MORE...*
> *Trump Rides Blue-Collar Wave...*

Bill Clinton was advocating open borders while in Australia on 911

November 22, 2015

To understand the problems we face with ISIS it is essential to understand the mindset of those who lead the parties of the left, and now even some parties of the conservative right. This is from *The Age* on September 11, 2001: 'Open borders to all: Clinton'. Here are the relevant parts of the article.

> *Bill Clinton believes Australia should not shut its borders to immigrants and those genuinely seeking asylum but should open its arms to cultural diversity.*
>
> *Free trade and an open-door policy would bring prosperity, the former US president told a meeting of 35 Australian business leaders in Melbourne yesterday.*
>
> *"He discussed the immigration issue in Australia and he took a position on it," said Tom Hogan, president of Vignette Corporation, host of the exclusive forum.*
>
> *"The (former) president believes the world will be a better place if all borders are eliminated – from a trade perspective, from the viewpoint of economic development and in welcoming (the free movement of) people from other cultures and countries," Mr Hogan said.*
>
> *Mr Clinton showed an understanding of the political problems Australia faced, but said he supported the ultimate wisdom of a borderless world for people and for trade.*
>
> *He spoke for 45 minutes on topics ranging from the urgent need to combat AIDS to global economic issues. He spent another 45 minutes answering questions.*
>
> *Mr Clinton said he believed the US was a better place for having opened its borders to a diversity of peoples and cultures.*
>
> *Of the global economic downturn, he said half the problem arose from real economic issues and half of it was due to self-fulfilling prophecies. If people talked gloom and doom long enough and often enough, he said, what they feared generally came to pass.*

This is the progressive internationalist creed[51] and no event in the modern world will change their views. And they have the power to cause our borders to open and remain open no matter what the rest of us think or wish.

Ironically, Bill Clinton was in Australia on 911 while at the same time John Howard was in Washington.

~

That's got to be a political asset
November 25, 2015

This is a story about Donald Trump[52] campaigning with his wife and children. The caption at the bottom of the picture of Trump with his family reads:

> *Republican presidential candidate Donald Trump, middle, speaks near his wife, Melania, left, son Baron, daughter Ivanka, second from right, and daughter Tiffany during a campaign event at the Myrtle Beach Convention Center on Tuesday, Nov. 24, 2015, in Myrtle Beach, S.C.*

Having watched both the press and the polls suggest that Mrs Trudeau was a reason for Justin's success, shows again how different North American politics is from everyone else's. Here, however, is the bit at the end of the story that Trump must have repeated a dozen times for the journalist even to have mentioned it:

> *Trump denounced the media for focusing on the protesters rather than his popularity at campaign appearances.*
>
> *"Seventy percent of those people back there are absolutely total scum," Trump said Tuesday, gesturing to the press area at the back of the arena, getting a roar and applause from the crowd.*

You really do have to wonder why they were applauding.

---

[51] Catallaxy Files, 30 September 2015.
[52] South Carolina Is a Family Affair for Trump, *US News*, 25 November 2015.

The corruption of the fourth estate
December 4, 2015

This is Pat Buchanan on 'Why Liberal Media Hate Trump'[53] but it is more than that. It has a history lesson worth thinking about.

> *In the feudal era there were the "three estates" – the clergy, the nobility and the commons. The first and second were eradicated in Robespierre's Revolution.*
>
> *But in the 18th and 19th century, Edmund Burke and Thomas Carlyle identified what the latter called a "stupendous Fourth Estate."*
>
> *Wrote William Thackeray: "Of the Corporation of the Goosequill – of the Press … of the fourth estate … There she is – the great engine – she never sleeps. She has her ambassadors in every quarter of the world – her courtiers upon every road. Her officers march along with armies, and her envoys walk into statesmen's cabinets."*
>
> *The fourth estate, the press, the disciples of Voltaire, had replaced the clergy it had dethroned as the new arbiters of morality and rectitude.*
>
> *Today the press decides what words are permissible and what thoughts are acceptable. The press conducts the inquisitions where heretics are blacklisted and excommunicated from the company of decent men, while others are forgiven if they recant their heresies.*

Now do read on how this is affecting us today and especially how the media is aiming to prevent, if it can, the election of Donald Trump.

~

The left seeks only plausible liars to lead them
December 4, 2015

There is no point in arguing that Hillary is being inconsistent, or that those who have accused her husband of rape have made a case that needs to be answered. Same with everything else about the lies that surround Clinton. No one believes her unless they desperately want to. But many of those who vote for the left now understand somewhere deep inside that everything they believe is wormeaten and rotten. If they are therefore to go

---

[53] worldnetdaily.com, 3 December 2015

on as before, they must find ways to shield themselves from the truth they will not confront. So they look for liars, and the better they are the more they seek them out. Clinton to Obama and to a different Clinton, with the media there to protect them at every turn. America and the West may crash and burn but they will keep their illusions at all cost. There are some who will never allow reality to intrude, but seeing how muted the applause she receives has become underscores how even among those who show up at Clinton event know that she is lying and her husband is as well. What she represents remains an unknown to me, but she is 50-50 to be the next president of the United States.

~

The media and Mr Trump
December 9, 2015

As big a problem as anything that now exists for the United States and the West in general is the far-left media who work hand and glove with the politicians of the left to pollute political debate. The genius of Donald Trump is that he is able to transcend the media and get through to the actual population in a way that no one else has previously been able to do.

Trump said it himself, the media are "unbelievably dishonest". He says things that are so outrageous from the perspective of the left that they made him the formidable presence he is by publishing everything he said on the assumption that telling people what he says will be instantly discrediting. Yet finding out that Katrina Pierson, Donald Trump's new press secretary, is a black Tea Party activist,[54] is quite astonishing and revealing.

> *Pierson says her alliance with The Donald is "perfect."*
>
> *"This is a nontraditional campaign," the outspoken Republican and Dallas tea party activist said. "I can be a little bit more who I am. That's what I mean when I say it's like a perfect fit. [Trump's] sort of not politically correct. He sort of calls it like he sees it. I'm kind of that way, too."*

Rush Limbaugh discussed all of this yesterday: 'How Donald Trump

---

[54] rushlimbaugh.com, 8 December 2015.

Plays the Media'. If Trump is unique in what he is doing, non-transferable to anyone else for whatever reason, then it is a serious problem. But in the meantime he is changing the rules of the political process.

> *You Republicans, you can denounce Trump all day, all week, all month, and the Democrat Party and the media are still gonna say you laid the table for it. You can condemn Trump all you want, but it is not going to buy you any love or respect or admiration from the Drive-By Media and the Democrats. Now, folks, the conventional wisdom is that Trump is scum, that Trump is a reprobate, that Trump is dangerous, that Trump is obscene, Trump's insane, Trump's a lunatic, Trump's dangerous, Trump's got to go. Why join in with that phrase? Why join that crowd? We never fall in with conventional wisdom here. . . .*
>
> *Meanwhile, I've never said anything like anything Trump says. But despite it all they can't take him out. They can't stop covering him. They can't humiliate him. They can't embarrass him. They can't diminish his support. They're powerless, and this has them in a panic. The media that can make-or-break anybody cannot touch Trump, and every time they try, all they do is make him bigger. They can't explain this. They are frustrated to no end, and so are both political parties who rely on the media to be the great equalizer in all of this.*
>
> *Nothing's working. No matter what Trump says, the media is there, and every member of the media is there. Every network, every camera, every microphone is there. Last Friday night Trump was in Raleigh, North Carolina. Reuters lied. Reuters even tried lying to destroy Trump. They ran a story claiming that Trump's performance and his appearance were shut down by Black Lives Matter protesters. MSNBC ran with it. . . .*
>
> *Donald Trump is condemning ISIS. Donald Trump is condemning illegal immigration. Donald Trump is condemning a weak, stupid United States leadership. Over here, everybody else is not. They are condemning Donald Trump. In a political sense, Donald Trump, leading the presidential campaign, is the sole occupier of his position. He has no competition for it. Just in a political sense, that's pretty brilliant positioning to me. He owns the media. They can't stop talking about him.*
>
> *And what's it costing him?*
>
> *Zero.*

The knives are coming out for Ted Cruz
December 10, 2015

Here's a story reprinted in *The Australian* from *The Times* in London: 'Ted Cruz, the man more dangerous than Donald Trump'.[55] Why is he more dangerous? Because he doesn't look as dangerous to those rubes known as voters and citizens. This is the subhead of the article which spells it out, "Senator Ted Cruz is the acceptable face of right-wing Republicanism — which is why he's scarier than The Donald." This is from the article itself.

> One leading Republican did not join the anti-Trump chorus, however. He is the man that many in the Republican establishment fear is more likely to become their presidential candidate than Trump: the Texas senator Ted Cruz. Cruz moved to the top of the polls this week in Iowa — the first state to vote in the presidential nomination race. At a press conference given by Cruz on Tuesday I waited and waited for a repudiation of Mr Trump but none came. He did say that he disagreed with the specific "no Muslims" policy idea but praised Trump's contribution to the debate. Cruz will undoubtedly be aware that 78 per cent of Republican voters think Islamic values are somehow un-American.
>
> Cruz has been the most consistently pro-Trump of all of the Republicans running for the White House. He has already said that he'd happily give Trump the job of building that US-Mexico wall if he became president. Cruz has also said that he'd consider putting Trump in charge of renegotiating America's trade arrangements with China.

What scares me, of course, are authors as obtuse as this one. No clue what really does concern the rest of us.

Meanwhile.

> Congress to vote on right of Muslims to migrate...
> Muhammad Ali Hits Trump and 'Misguided Murderers' Sabotaging Islam...
> DONALD'S RIGHT — UK HAS MUSLIM NO-GO AREAS, SAY POLICE...

The actual headline of that first posted article is 'Congress to Consider Easing Passage into U.S. for Immigrants'[56] which gives a much different sense of what's in mind than the headline at Drudge.

---

[55] *The Australian*, 10 December 2015.
[56] *The Washington Free Beacon*, December 9, 2015.

Jihadists seize Roman city of Sabratha and the West does nothing
December 13, 2015

Just a line item at Drudge and nowhere else to learn about it either: 'ISIS to raze another ancient city: Priceless landmarks at risk of destruction as jihadists seize Roman city of Sabratha in march towards Tripoli.'[57]

> *Fears are mounting that Islamic State terrorists could destroy an ancient Roman site in Libya which they have seized in their march towards the capital Tripoli.*
>
> *ISIS fanatics travelling in 30 pick-up trucks stormed the coastal city of Sabratha on Wednesday night after three of their men were captured by a rival militia.*
>
> *Black-clad militants overpowered residents and set up checkpoints in the city, which is just 50 miles from Tripoli, before successfully retrieving the three men.*

And in unrelated news, also at Drudge:

> REUTERS ROLLING: TRUMP 35.4%, CARSON 12%, RUBIO 10.5%, CRUZ 9.7%
> Fresh-Faced Star of France Far Right Is Candidate of Steel...
> Le Pen vows to 'ruin Hollande's life'...

~

Well then, who should we vote for?
December 15, 2015

First this about Mr 41%: 'Trump Is Going To Break Your Heart'.[58] The central point:

> *When he dumps you, when he goes back to the New York liberal roots that are at the core of his being and starts talking about how he's decided to switch back to his old positions, that it's reasonable to take your guns, to liberalize immigration, and to keep Obamacare, you're going to feel like fools. You're going to be humiliated. And the GOP establishment, which is terrible, is going to be looking at you saying, "I told you so."*

---

[57] *The Daily Mail Australia*, 11 December 2015.
[58] townhall.com, 14 December 2015.

Then there is this about Ted Cruz: 'Ted Cruz: The Anti-Reagan'.[59]

> *Like many of his rivals for the Republican nomination, Ted Cruz has embraced the mantle of Ronald Reagan. He regularly cites the Gipper as an inspiration, and last week gave a foreign policy address at the Heritage Foundation that was laced with tributes to him: "As Reagan knew well, the best way to project America's leadership is by protecting and promoting America's strength and this principle should always guide our actions." I didn't know Ronald Reagan (neither did Cruz), but I do know a lot about him. And from what I know, it's fair to say that Ted Cruz is no Ronald Reagan. In many ways, he is actually an anti-Reagan.*

That is, he criticises fellow Republicans, is unreliable on foreign policy and cannot get on with anyone. Trump feels like the emergency bailout position if there was no one else around, that is, if the next Republican President fails to deliver balanced budgets, a freer economy and a sound immigration policy.

~

Hillary Clinton plays Princess Leia
December 21, 2015

In the latest Star Wars, Princess Leia looks just like Hillary Clinton. I don't know if it was intentional, but it hit me around three quarters of the way through the film that it's the same person.

~

And now the heavyweight division
December 22, 2015

Republicans have been very reluctant to attack Obama for the whole of the past seven years. Whether it is the courtesies of the American system or Obama has the photos I don't know. But now we shall see since he has moved to attack Donald Trump himself. This is from the NYT and featured

---

[59] realclearpolitics.com, 14 December 2015.

at Drudge: 'Obama Accuses Trump of Exploiting Working-Class Fears'.[60]

> President Obama said in a radio interview airing on Monday that Donald J. Trump, a leading contender for the Republican presidential nomination, is exploiting the resentment and anxieties of working-class men to boost his campaign. Mr. Obama also argued that some of the scorn directed at him personally stems from the fact that he is the first African-American to hold the White House.

That Obama reached for the race-card is disgusting and despicable but par for the course. Since nothing anyone in any leading position has said has referred to the President's racial background – half white, half black – that he grabs for it in every controversy he is part of has degraded the American political system since it allows him to ignore the substantive parts of any criticism. But lets get to this business about resentment and anxieties, which are not just held by men, and not just held by members of the working class. Let us go on to what he had to say:

> "If you are referring to specific strains in the Republican Party that suggest that somehow I'm different, I'm Muslim, I'm disloyal to the country, etc. — which unfortunately is pretty far out there, and gets some traction in certain pockets of the Republican Party, and that have been articulated by some of their elected officials — what I'd say there is that that's probably pretty specific to me, and who I am and my background," Mr. Obama told Steve Inskeep, an NPR correspondent. "In some ways, I may represent change that worries them."

I just think he's a far-left loon, and that pretty well covers the kinds of change he represents. If his standard of concern is whether something might "destroy the United States", as he says below, I'm not sure short of a nuclear war what he would include. This is truly disturbing:

> "This is a serious challenge — ISIS is a virulent, nasty organization [!!!!!] that has gained a foothold in ungoverned spaces effectively in Syria and parts of western Iraq," Mr. Obama said, referring to attacks the group organized in Paris and apparently inspired in San Bernardino. "But it is also important for us to keep things in perspective, and this is not an organization that can destroy the United States."

---

[60] nytimes.com, 21 December 2015.

As for destroying the United States, there are other nations along the pathway to the US that might find things have deteriorated to a very considerable extent because of the American President. Think about this, a reminder of where things have gone with Iran:[61]

> The Iran deal isn't merely sub-par diplomacy, it is a scandal. I don't see how a president who took seriously his duty to preserve American security could have entered into it. There is another scandal, too: a journalistic one. Here, as in so many instances, reporters have covered up for the Obama administration by deliberately failing to report the facts surrounding the Iranian nuclear debacle. It would be interesting to compare the number of minutes that network news broadcasts have devoted, over the last few months, to the fulminations of Donald Trump with the minutes they have devoted to the crumbling of the Iran agreement. Likewise with column inches in our supposedly sophisticated newspapers.

But Obama has now taken on Donald Trump who will or will not react and will or will not reply directly to what has been said. This really is a moment of truth. I don't know why it has taken so long for such a showdown to have occurred, but the time has now arrived. Is Trump up to it? We are now about to find out.

~

Obama attacks Trump to help Hillary so they say
December 22, 2015

This is the story 'Obama, Clinton may be setting up Trump to win Republican nomination'[62] and who knows if it's true. Here is the heart of it:

> In a head-to-head matchup, the RealClearPolitics average of national polls show Mrs. Clinton beating Mr. Trump by an average of 6 percentage points, significantly higher than other Republicans such as Sen. Ted Cruz of Texas and Sen. Marco Rubio of Florida, who trail Mrs. Clinton by 1.5 percentage points and 2.5 percentage points, respectively. All the other Republican contenders fare better in matchups with Mrs. Clinton than Mr. Trump in the average of national polls.

---

[61] powerlineblog.com, 20 December 2015.
[62] *The Washington Times*, 21 December 2015.

It's a theory and a strategy. Personally, I think if Trump wins the nomination he will win the election in a walk.

~

Trump v Clinton head to head
December 22, 2015

So far as any reports I have seen, Trump has not replied to Obama in spite of the opening Obama provided by criticising Trump. I find that inexplicable, but I am not going to go around telling him how to run a campaign, since he seems quite capable of doing things on his own. Where Trump did go head to head is here: 'Presidential Front-Runners Donald Trump and Hillary Clinton Face Off'.[63] And the issue is this:

> The crossfire between the two leading presidential candidates intensified Monday, as Democrat Hillary Clinton's campaign stood by her claim that Republican front-runner Donald Trump's rhetoric is being used as propaganda by terrorist groups, though there is no evidence Islamic State has put him in videos.
>
> Mrs. Clinton said in Saturday's Democratic debate that Mr. Trump "is becoming ISIS's best recruiter," and that he was being used in videos. Mr. Trump angrily denied the former secretary of state's charge and demanded an apology from her. The Clinton campaign refused to provide one, pointing to comments from several counterterrorism experts and social media posts by terror groups to support the claims.

That she didn't have evidence for what she said is the way of the world, not that the American media will ever mention it. But Gateway Pundit has a posting on Somebody Tell Hillary… ISIS Recruitment Video Featured Bill Clinton the "Fornicator" (VIDEO).[64] It also shows John Kerry and Obama himself. The video has quite some production values, and is interesting as an artefact of our own times. It obviously will only repel, and I hope frighten the likes of us. So on the narrow issue of who can be used as part of an ISIL recruitment drive, Hillary is lying again. But the wider and more important

---
[63] *The Wall Street Journal*, 21 December 2015.
[64] thegatewaypundit.com, 21 December 2016.

issue is that only you and I will even know of such videos that expose Hillary as dangerously and badly informed. This is part of the sickening nature of the modern political process, where to find out the kinds of things you might wish everyone to know requires you to move beyond mainstream sources of news and make the effort yourself to see what's going on, assuming it is now even possible to find out what is going on.

And as an afterthought, there is this to consider as well: 'Obama, Clinton may be setting up Trump to win Republican nomination'[65] because they think he would be the easiest one among the Republicans to beat.

> *President Obama and Hillary Clinton have intensified attacks on Republican presidential front-runner Donald Trump, accusing him of manipulating voters' "fear and ignorance" and using anti-Muslim rhetoric that helps recruit Islamic State terrorists — jabs that appear to be energizing his supporters and strengthening his campaign.*
>
> *But campaign strategists say the attacks are not aimed at knocking down Mr. Trump. Instead, the smears are part of a calculated ploy by Democrats who want to help him win because they are convinced the billionaire businessman will lose in the general election.*

That Hillary might be president makes you wonder how this is even possible in a country of 300-million-plus people: Bush-Clinton-Clinton-Bush-Bush-O-O-Clinton?

~

Rush to judgment
December 23, 2015

This is Rush Limbaugh explaining why 'He is Amazed by How Few Understand Obama and the Movement He's Mobilized'.[66] There is nothing well-meaning or altruistic about the left. Their views are overwhelmingly parasitic and harmful. I can hardly recall a single instance when some policy of the left actually led to an improvement in our economic or social relations – think Stalin in the 1930s or Venezuela today. The left has

---

[65] *The Washington Times*, 21 December 2015.
[66] rushlimbaugh.com, 21 December 2015.

invariably focused on genuine problems but almost no solution proposed by a government of the left has ever succeeded. If you know what the left is up to, you never wish them success. Which brings me to the start of what Rush had said:

> *You remember back on January 16th, 2009, a few days before Obama was to be inaugurated, I mentioned on this program the Wall Street Journal had asked me (along with a lot of other people) to write 400 words on my hopes for the administration, the first African-American president, Barack Hussein O. And I told you what I told them, 'cause I wrote back and I said, "I don't need 400 words; all I need is four words: 'I hope he fails.'"*

Obama has sadly not failed. He has achieved many of the destructive aims that he had from the start. To wish that a far-left President fails is not to wish that America fails. It is to wish that the President does not achieve what he has set out to achieve. He goes on:

> *I thought after two years of an intense campaign that the people on our side, the people opposing Obama had learned what I had learned about Obama, had learned how truly radical he was.*
>
> *And not just in the Alinsky mold, and not just in the Reverend Wright mold, but I mean literally radical, radical. The most radical leftist Democrat ever elected to the White House and maybe by a long shot. And I was under the impression that people on our side understood the danger, the real danger to the country.*

The focus of the post is on Dinesh D'Souza's new book, which is about how D'Souza had thought that Obama was merely a left-liberal until he ended up being railroaded into jail by Obama for a non-crime that no one had ever previously been jailed for. Limbaugh is astonished, and I am as well, that someone who has paid such close attention to Obama and what he has said and clearly stands for, didn't get it.

> *Up until now, Dinesh D'Souza admits that he thought all this time that Obama was just a liberal, a Democrat, another in a long line of Democrats.*
>
> *And that the liberalism of Obama was just an intellectual exercise against which we must debate. There was nothing inherently destructive about Obama. He was just a liberal, and it was an intellectual challenge for us on the right to*

go up against Obama and to see if we could win the argument in the arena of ideas. I was stunned. I have to tell you, I was stunned that it took being put in jail for Dinesh D'Souza to admit that he didn't know what Obama and the modern day Democrat Party was really all about.

The thing is that I have the same problem as Rush. I was introduced to someone right at the start of the Obama era because he was also, I was told, against Obama. So I spoke to him in the way that I might when I am with someone who is on the same side of the fence as I am. And to my shock – and I have seen him many times since but will not talk politics with him such an idiot he is – he began to defend Obama since I was going way too far. I do always say that you have to have been on the left to understand really how evil these people are, unprincipled and with no aim other than the accumulation of personal power. Not the cannon fodder, of course, their foot-soldiers and deluded supporters, but a very high proportion of those who get to the top. So let me finally bring you to Rush's conclusion:

This is the first time in our country's history that such a leftist radical has been elected and has proceeded unopposed for seven years in erasing the origins of this country, under the guise of fixing it, under the guise of fixing the never-ending racism and bigotry and racism and homophobic, all these other things that in Obama's world define this country. I think it's one of the things that explains this budget deal. I think it explains a lot. The Republican Party is not pushing back, not wanting to disagree. If they do recognize what I recognize, it must have been pretty daunting to say so and stand up and fight against it, which maybe they don't want to do, I guess.

It is across the West. I am part of the worst generation, that sensationally ignorant stupid New-Left hippy group-think idiocracy that has created the political world we now inhabit. If you think a centuries long Dark Age could not possibly lie before us, you really haven't done your sums.

The media and constitutional government
December 24, 2015

I am like many in seeing the dangers of a President Donald Trump, but I am also like many others in thinking he is the only cure for what is wrong with the American political system. The rush from constitutional government to government by executive decree has been astonishing. Obama decides what he wants and does everything he can to impose the outcome by executive order. The fear expressed below is that Trump will continue the approach that has been driven by Obama:

> *Cruz believes our constitutional arrangements are basically sound but that the leadership class that manages those arrangements has got to go. Trump, on the other hand, seems to reject those arrangements altogether – Rich [Lowry's] "post-constitutional" label, or even "post-republican" (small-r).*
>
> *Trump's support comes from people who have given up on our existing "regime," in the political science sense of the word. The Tea Party's efflorescence of constitutionalism was, as Rich writes, "a means to stop Obama" – in other words, to stop lawlessness and rule by decree, which is what constitutions are for. But, as Rich continued, constitutionalism "has been found lacking" – Obama, and the Supreme Court, have pursued extra-constitutional (i.e., illegal) tactics and prevailed. Repeatedly. On momentous issues that immediately affect every American.*

As I have written before, politics is what you can get away with. In the US, you can get away with whatever the media allows you to. If it does not call a president out in a prolonged and intensive way, there is nothing, it seems, a president cannot do. The only limits are what can actually be done, not what can be attempted. Some things fail because they go so far against the grain of society that no writ will run no matter what a president might wish to do. But for most – such as the wrecking of the medical system in the US, or the effective introduction of open borders – the absence of a watchdog media has permitted every illegal action and inaction to occur.

This will never happen under a Republican president. The media will never give a President Trump the pass. Look at CNN where it is fine to attack Trump (R) but not Clinton (D).

If Americans want a constitutional presidency, they need to elect Republicans. It's as simple as that, although simple it definitely is not.

~

Donald Trump may already be a conservative
December 26, 2015

The picture of Donald Trump was taken by me at his very first public presentation that has taken him to the edge of the Republican nomination for president. This was at Freedomfest in Las Vegas last July. And what was notable about this presentation was that he sought out the invitation to speak. He was not on the program until he asked that he be included. And he perfectly well knew that Freedomfest is the most important annual meeting of conservatives and libertarians in the United States. What's more, he gave one of his free wheeling speeches off the top of his head that had half the audience on its feet at the end. My feeling at the time was that in speaking to that audience he was in home territory among people who understood what he was about and about whom he understood what they were about. I live blogged his presentation and in re-reading it now, I can again see his vast appeal.

There is a post at Instapundit by Roger Simon, IT'S A CHRISTMAS

MIRACLE! Roger Simon: 'How I Stopped Worrying and Learned to Love The Donald for Xmas.'[67] This is the passage quoted:

> *All the Republican candidates have their flaws, as does, in spades, the woman far at the front of the Democratic pack, described almost twenty years ago by William Safire in one of the most prescient op-eds ever as a "congenital liar."*
>
> *But my interest here is not in detailing everyone's weaknesses – I like to remain friends with people – but, as a Christmas present to the angst-ridden, to try to explain how Trump's flaws can be turned to the advantage of Republicans and conservatives. This is particularly important if, as appears highly possible, he wins the nomination. What do we do about it?*
>
> *The answer is obvious. The solution to conservative angst over Trump is simple: stop criticizing him, co-opt him.*

You don't have to co-opt him. He is with us. Nobody understands all of the issues and everyone needs input to find their way. But what seems apparent on the evidence so far is that Trump is already onside with most of what we conservatives believe and would like to achieve. Marco Rubio had spoken the day before and left no impression other than he was too callow for the job. Given that it was Freedomfest, the libertarians there were largely ready to support Rand Paul. But it was only Trump who actually made fixing things seem possible. It may be a mirage. He may in the end not have what it takes. But unless he is the greatest charlatan in political history – putting even Obama into the shade – what you see is what you get, and what you get is possibly the most conservative candidate we have seen since Ronald Reagan. What constitutes a conservative in the era of Obama and Clinton is something different from what it was in 1980. Donald Trump may be as conservative as it is possible to be at the present time and still get elected in the United States.

---

[67] pjmedia.com, 25 December 2015.

The war on hypocrisy
December 27, 2015

There are swamps in the American political system so fetid that no one will even try to clear them out, with the one exception being Donald Trump. The article is naturally pro-Hillary but with Trump the way he is, they cannot avoid bringing the issue into the light. 'Trump campaign: Hillary bullied women to hide Bill's 'sexist secrets'.'[68] No doubt there is more to come.

~

Anti-anti-Trump
December 29, 2015

The world remains a place of mystery: Clinton vs. Trump: Still A Dead Heat.[69] Half of the American voting public would vote for Hillary. Who can make sense of such things, but there you are. More intriguing, we have William Voegeli writing The Reason I'm Anti-Anti-Trump.[70]

> *The fact that Trump has become a credible contender despite, or even because of, his obvious faults argues, however, for taking his followers' concerns seriously rather than dismissing them. It is not, in fact, particularly difficult to explain the emergence of Trumpismo in terms of legitimate concerns not addressed, and important duties not discharged. That such a flawed contender could be a front-runner tells us more about what's wrong with the country than about what's wrong with his followers. People have every reason to expect that their government will take its most basic responsibilities seriously, and every reason to be angry when, instead, it proves more feckless than conscientious. Governments are instituted among men to secure their inalienable rights, according to the Declaration of Independence. This means that when we and our rights are left avoidably insecure, government has failed in its central mission.*

A government that worries about global warming more than

---

[68] thehill.com, 24 December 2015.
[69] rasmussenreports.com. 28 December 2015
[70] claremont.org/crb, 28 December 2015

immigration is a failed government and will in the fulness of time ruin the country it supposedly governs. And with the imperative for anyone to overcome the problems facing us being able to overcome the power of the media, there is no one other than Donald Trump who has found a way to do it. Voegeli concludes:

> *The best way to fortify Trump's presidential campaign is to insist his followers' grievances are simply illegitimate, bigoted, and ignorant. The best way to defeat it is to argue that their justified demands for competent, serious governance deserve a statesman, not a showman.*

Fine, bring on the statesman or stateswoman. Meantime, if Hillary is the alternative, no one could look more statesmanlike than Trump.

~

Americans are so stupid – their country has become a dumping ground
January 4, 2016

Actually, I don't think this way at all about Americans who are among the most generous and sensible people on the planet. But America is being taken for a ride by its political elites, and in this heading I am only echoing Donald Trump's own concerns. This is a story from the *Washington Post* on Donald Trump's first paid ad[71] where the above sentiment is found:

> *In an interview Sunday with The Post, Trump said that he has six to eight ads in production and that his was a "major buy and it's going to go on for months." He said he hopes the spots impress upon undecided voters that the country has become "a dumping ground."*
>
> *"The world is laughing at us, at our stupidity," he said. "It's got to stop. We've got to get smart fast — or else we won't have a country."*

It is America's elites that are not quite there.

Obama describing foreign leaders as "insane"[72] is the most perfect example of projection I have ever seen.

---

[71] *The Washington Post*, 3 January 2016
[72] Deadline Hollywood, 31 December 2015.

Terminal decline
January 5, 2016

There is a picture of The Fall of Rome comes with this story, 'Our spoiled, emasculated, de-spiritualised societies in the West are in terminal decline'.[73] We live in a complete bubble of vacuousness, and when the barbarians finally break through it will be brutal. You can see our future in the far off Middle East even as we let these invaders enter within our walls. Do the inhabitants of our former Christian civilisation really believe they have anything to offer other than a bit of technology which will be scooped up with the rest of the booty? The story is by Christopher Booker and this is how he concludes:

> The reason why we do not see just how far our spoiled, emasculated, de-spiritualised societies in the West have lost the plot is that they are the bubble we live in. But these days there is a great big world out there, much less sentimental and much tougher than what we have become used to. Over the coming years, our world is going to change more than we can imagine.

It always changes more than we can imagine but this time it will be a change for the far worse. The picture, you see, is us.

This, too, might help to see where we are headed: 'Islam v. Free Speech: Twitter Surrenders'.[74]

> The top agenda item of Islamic supremacists has long been the imposition of sharia blasphemy standards on the West. This campaign is not waged exclusively or even primarily by violent jihadists. Instead, its leading proponents are the Muslim Brotherhood's network of Islamist activist groups in the West and the Organization of Islamic Cooperation (a 57-government bloc of, mainly, majority-Muslim countries).

> The West should be fighting these anti-Western Islamic supremacists in defense of our core principles. Instead, the Obama administration — particularly the president and his former secretary of state, Hillary Clinton — has colluded with them. So have other left-leaning governments and institutions that are naturally hostile to free speech and open debate. One prominent result is U.N. Human Rights Council Resolution 16/18. This

---

[73] *The Telegraph,* 31 December 2016.
[74] nationalreview.com, 4 January 2016.

blatantly unconstitutional provision, co-sponsored by Obama, Clinton, and OIC members, calls on all nations to ban speech that could promote mere hostility to Islam. Essentially, this is a codification of sharia, which prohibits all expression that subjects Islam to critical examination.

We are being sold down the Tiber and it is almost certainly too late to do a thing about it. If you still have doubts, then contemplate this: 'Germany stunned by rash of New Year's sex assaults'.[75] The refusal to face reality in the opening para is borderline insane and if you want to read more, you can look up the article online.[76]

The German government Tuesday condemned dozens of apparently coordinated sexual assaults against women on New Year's Eve in the western city of Cologne blamed on Arab men but warned against anti-migrant scapegoating.

Today's migrant is tomorrow's European. Just as after 476 AD, the barbarians became the new Romans. The subsequent Dark Age lasted almost a thousand years.

~

Ted Cruz on border control
January 7, 2016

There is a Ted Cruz ad warning about illegal immigration which his polling must show will be effective in the constituency he wishes to reach.

But let me add this. Trump has started down the path of doubting Cruz's eligibility for the presidency since he was born in Canada of an American mother and a Cuban refugee dad, similar to Obama having been born of an American mother and a Kenyan dad, even though within America. Whatever else may have made Obama unfit to be president, it was not where he was born or who his parents were that mattered. John McCain, so far as that goes, was born in the Canal Zone of an American mother and father which also would not have disqualified him. Trump is already a loose

---

[75] Yahoo News, 6 January 2016.
[76] pjmedia.com/instapundit, 5 January 2016.

cannon without obvious impulse control and not everyone's first choice for President, even in a post-Obama era. If he wins on policy, that's one thing, but if he tries this kind of shoddy nonsense, then he will have difficulty holding his constituency together since he will have alienated a substantial proportion of those whose support he will need.

I am now interested to see that Obama has joined in: 'Team Obama Joins Donald Trump's Attack On Ted Cruz's Citizenship'.[77] Is there now an Obama-Trump axis trying to defeat Ted Cruz? It's getting as hard to follow as the battle lines in Syria.

~

You want crazy, I'll give you crazy
January 8, 2016

Trump's protectionist beliefs are old news but this has shown up on Instapundit today: 'Trump wants a 45 percent tax on Chinese imports'.[78]

> *"I would tax China on products coming in," the Republican presidential front-runner told the New York Times. "And the tax, let me tell you what the tax should be … the tax should be 45 percent."*
>
> *The savvy [!!!] New York businessman released a policy paper on U.S.-China trade reform in early November that detailed his plans, as president, to take action against China's currency manipulation and intellectual property theft, and to strengthen America's negotiating position with the potential U.S. adversary.*
>
> *Until now, however, none of Trump's rhetoric on U.S.-Chinese relations has included any mention of a 45 percent tariff on Chinese exports to the U.S.*

I know history is bunk and all that, but do we really want to bring back Herbert Hoover and the Great Depression? The story inserts the mildest, virtually non-existent criticism of such an idea, that makes you worry that this may well be an idea whose time has come, even if it will be an idea whose time will have gone a year after it would be put in:

---

[77] breitbart.com, 6 January 2016
[78] *Washington Examiner*, 7 January 2016.

> *According to David Dollar, a senior fellow in the Brookings Institution's China Center, Trump's suggested tariff could open the door to negative implications for both countries, if instituted.*

"Negative implications" – that's really nailing it. On top of everything going on already, to stop international trade in its tracks would be a policy as devastating as it is possible to have. Even the comment at Instapundit – "As Tom Nichols tweets, 'I bet this sounds awesome to people who have no idea how much stuff they buy from China.'" – gives the impression that they have little idea what the effect would be. In so many ways, this is the 1930s all over again.

~

Women and Muslim migration
January 9, 2016

What are the advantages Muslim societies have in dealing with others? This is how it is explained by John O'Sullivan: 'Europeans Studiously Ignore Muslim Mobs',[79] but most importantly, what he shows is the effect of Islam on the subjection of women and the state of mind it creates. His final para, though, is the one that matters. It is the one that everyone migrates to if they are thinking about the preservation of our Western way of life.

> *Which brings me finally to Donald Trump. His policy of simply halting Muslim immigration has been denounced all around. It is, of course, discriminatory and thus a mortal sin in today's politics. Fine. Let's rule it out. But if his critics don't want a blanket moratorium on all immigration — which I assume they don't — and if they don't want to repeat the experiences of France and Germany in 30 years' time — which I also assume they don't — shouldn't they tell us what they will do?*

He, of course, does not mean let us rule it out. He means, if you are serious about an end, you must be serious about finding the means. And to understand either, you have to have some idea of what you are up against. This is what we are up against.

---
[79] *National Review*, 8 January 2016

If we exclude divine favor as an explanation of this long advance, as Christians and post-Christian secularists presumably should, the rules that explain it include capital punishment for leaving Islam (a.k.a. apostasy), which is presumably a disincentive to doing so; strict rules for regular public prayer, which strengthen group solidarity; a privileged position for men over women, amounting in practice to ownership of them as either wives or concubines; a hierarchical structure within Islamic society that places Muslims in a position above non-Muslims in law, government, and social life; and a religious orthodoxy that endows Muslims with a general superiority (and sense of superiority) over others in non-Islamic societies.

Taken together, these rules help to shape a Muslim community that is cohesive, conscious of its separation from the rest of society, resistant to influences likely to undermine its cohesion, self-policing through its male members, and — because its sense of superiority is not reflected in its actual status either locally or globally — prey to resentment and hostility toward those whom it blames for its unjust subordination...

The minority that supports aggressive jihadism (or is simply contemptuous of non-Muslim society) is not just larger but, as opinion polls show, far larger than similar tendencies in other religions and ideologies. That minority seeks to impose its rules both on fellow Muslims and on the wider society. And it has had remarkable success in areas where Muslims predominate locally, making U.K. state schools conform to Islamic teaching and practices, including the separation of the sexes; establishing "no-go areas" of European cities where police go only by agreement and where in their absence Muslim rules on alcohol and modest female dress are enforced by violence; and turning local governments into reliable Muslim fiefdoms through levels of voter fraud not known in England since the mid-19th century. But the most disturbing effects occur when the Muslim sense of superiority over non-Muslims combines with the Muslim males' sense of superiority over women.

This is why Jamie Briggs and Chris Gayle stories are such evasions of the genuine issue that confronts us. The left is full of excuses and refuses to recognise a problem.[80] So does much of the right. This is where Donald Trump comes in. There may be a million problems that come with him as president, but if he is the only one that gets the one big thing right, then he

---

[80] breitbart.com, 8 January 2016.

will be president and everything else will just have to take care of itself.

UPDATE: This is Roger Simon on the same subject: 'In Your Heart, You Know He's Right: Trump and Muslim Immigration'.[81] This is the conclusion:

> *The doctrines of Islam are virtually entirely inconsistent with the founding principles of our county. And yet, per Pew, we are not-so-gradually being inundated with its adherents. Unchecked, the character of the USA will change, possibly to the extent of being unrecognizable, I doubt this is what the majority of Americans want. But it is happening nevertheless — and we have a living, breathing illustration of the results just across the Pond. (Illustrative of how self-immolating European elites have become was the advice the female mayor of Cologne gave women of her city for dealing with the sexual assaults — they should stand further away.)*

And then, from *National Review*, 'Is the Left Even on America's Side Any More?'[82] where we find:

> *Leftists and Democrats have also joined the Islamist propaganda campaign to represent Muslims — whose co-religionists have killed hundreds of thousands of innocents since 9/11 in the name of their religion — as victims of anti-Muslim prejudice, denouncing critics of Islamist terror and proponents of security measures as "Islamophobes" and bigots. But in truth, 60 percent of religious hate crimes are directed at Jews, with a small minority directed a Muslims.*

> *Exploiting the myth of Muslim persecution, progressives oppose scrutiny of the Muslim community, including terror-promoting imams and mosques. They immediately denounce proposals to screen Muslim immigrants as religious bigotry, and thus close off any rational discussion of the problem. Led by Hillary Clinton and Barack Obama, Democrats have enabled the Islamist assault on free speech, which is a central component of the Islamist campaign to create a worldwide religious theocracy.*

> *Most notoriously the president and his operatives cynically spread the lie that an obscure Internet video about Mohammed was behind the Benghazi terror attack. Speaking like an ayatollah before the U.N. General Assembly, shortly after the attack, Obama declared: "The future must not*

---

[81] PJ Media.com, 8 January 2016.
[82] *National Review*, 8 January 2016.

belong to those who slander the prophet of Islam." What an American president should have said is: "The future must not belong to those who murder in the name of Islam."

FURTHER UPDATE: This thing seems to be catching on: 'To Save Europe, Stop All 'Migrants,' Says Hungary's Orban'.[83]

~

In politics as well, you go to war with the army you have
January 12, 2016

Not ideal, but lots of things are not ideal. This is Kurt Schlichter at *National Review* summing up an article in which he assesses the future probabilities on President Trump: 'Taking The Donald Seriously'.[84]

> *Trump can win the nomination. I don't like that, because I don't think he's a conservative. He can also win the general, and I do like that because this country can survive a Donald Trump administration intact, assuming he learns what the nuclear triad is. But a Hillary Clinton presidency? A presidency for a woman who has not mere contempt but active hatred for the half of the population that she labels as her greatest enemy, and who aspires to restrict every amendment in the Bill of Rights that doesn't keep her from having to testify to her own crimes? A slave to her unique homebrew of hatred, undue self-regard, and foolishness, her lawless reign will rip this country apart. If it's Donald Trump versus Hillary Clinton, Trump all the way – and, thankfully, he absolutely could win.*

And then there is this, 'What Bernie and The Donald portend'.[85] A year ago Bernie Sanders v Donald Trump was on no radars anywhere at all. Now it is as likely as anything. And as for "The Donald", this is how the article concludes:

> *Nominating Trump is by no means a guarantee of GOP defeat. But beyond politics, what do the successes of Sanders, Trump and Cruz portend?*

---

[83] pjmedia.com, 8 January 2016.
[84] townhall.com, 11 January 2016.
[85] wnd.com, 11 January 2016.

> *Well, Sanders and Trump both opposed the war in Iraq that the Bush Republicans and Clinton Democrats supported.*
>
> *Both Sanders and Trump oppose NAFTA and MFN for China and the free-trade deals that Clinton Democrats and Bush Republicans backed, which have cost us thousands of lost factories, millions of lost jobs and four decades of lost wage increases for Middle America.*
>
> *Trump has taken the toughest line on the invasion across the U.S.-Mexican border and against Muslim refugees entering unvetted.*
>
> *Immigration, securing the border, fair trade – Trump's issues are the issues of 2016.*
>
> *If a Trump-Clinton race came down to the Keystone State of Pennsylvania, and Trump was for backing our men in blue, gun rights, securing America's borders, no more NAFTAs and a foreign policy that defends America first, who would you bet on?*

For myself, how Hillary even remains in the equation can only be understood as a product of media corruption in the US, and indeed, across the West. Trump has that one massive advantage, he no longer needs the media, and the more they criticise, the more others find in Trump just exactly what they like. The question at the article's end answers itself.

~

Ted Cruz and the Republican establishment
January 12, 2016

To the Republican establishment, Donald Trump may be the second worst outcome. The worst outcome may be Ted Cruz. It is why suddenly the Republicans, including John McCain, Rand Paul and plenty of others, have suddenly raised his citizenship as an issue. Roger Kimball brings this forward, 'Why the Sudden Love Among Establishment Republicans for Trump?'[86]

> *What you hear people say is that "Donald Trump may have the best chance of beating Hillary Clinton." But what does that means? "Maybe Trump*

---
[86] pjmedia.com, 11 January 2016.

can beat Hillary, assuming she is the Democratic candidate, but anyway, despite his bluster, he really is deep down a pay-to-play kind of guy, just like us. Ted Cruz, on the contrary, really means all that stuff about ending the 'Washington Cartel' and restoring Constitutional restraints on government. It's OK to say that in election years, but we don't want to elect someone who will actually try to do it."

The problem for them is that Cruz would do it. With Trump, you have no idea at all what he would do about anything.

~

If Trump is the answer what is the question?
January 29, 2016

How do we get back the America we had in the 1950s?

It's the wrong answer, but that's the question.

It may still, nevertheless, be the best answer available.

~

Why isn't this the Huma Abedin scandal?
January 30, 2016

Here is the story in *The Oz* reprinted from *The Times*: 'Sex scandal dogs Hillary's 'surrogate daughter' Huma Abedin'.[87] A big Hillary problem, it seems, in the movie that is being released on Huma's marriage to former Congressman, Anthony Weiner, who became notorious for exposing himself on the internet. Weiner is a Jew, so the following ought to be more than of passing interest, which comes as a throw-away in paragraph 22:

> *Abedin's mother is Pakistani; her late father was Indian. She was born in Michigan but when Abedin was two her family moved to Saudi Arabia, where her father established a think tank, the Institute of Muslim Minority Affairs. Some alleged the family had connections to figures inside the Muslim Brotherhood, which has fuelled conspiracy theories.*

---

[87] *The Australian*, 29 January 2016.

They certainly have "alleged" these connections. Here's just one example: 'Huma Abedin's Muslim Brotherhood Ties'[88] which are a good deal more significant, you would think, than her marriage ties. It is the absence of controversy about her background that needs to be accounted for. From the story, which appeared in *National Review*:

> *Huma Abedin's mother, Saleha, who is a member of the Muslim Brotherhood's female division (the "Muslim Sisterhood"), is a major figure in not one but two Union for Good components. The first is the International Islamic Council for Dawa and Relief (IICDR). It is banned in Israel for supporting Hamas under the auspices of the Union for Good. Then there's the International Islamic Committee for Woman and Child (IICWC) — an organization that Dr. Saleha Abedin has long headed. Dr. Abedin's IICWC describes itself as part of the IICDR. And wouldn't you know it, the IICWC charter was written by none other than . . . Sheikh Qaradawi ["the Muslim Brotherhood's chief sharia jurist"], in conjunction with several self-proclaimed members of the Muslim Brotherhood.*

What may be the most interesting thing about the times in which we live is that everything is known but nothing seems to matter.

~

Hillary – the worst imaginable successor to Obama
January 30, 2016

That there has been more controversy around Donald Trump than around Hillary Clinton is further evidence, if more were needed, of the deeply corrupt nature of the media, and the American media in particular. Hillary should go to jail. She illegally used a personal server for her correspondence as Secretary of State because in this way nothing she wrote could be subpoenaed by the American Congress. Instead, every email she sent could be read by governments around the world. Just think of this:[89]

> *The ex-CIA official said there is "zero ambiguity — none" about the impropriety of SAP-level intelligence being housed on an unsecure private email server. Faddis added that the very existence of that information on*

---

[88] *National Review*, 26 July 2012.
[89] PJMedia.com, 22 January 2016.

> her server means that highly classified information must have been moved off of a "completely separate channel" under a process that is "specifically forbidden." If you had done this while working at the CIA, Hemmer asked, what would've happened to you? Faddis' response: "My career's over, I lose my clearance, I lose my job, and then I go to prison, probably for a very long time." Faddis explained that the "consequences are enormous" when information at this level of secrecy is made vulnerable to foreign penetration. "The reason this stuff is in this channel is because it's going to do incredible damage to US national security if it gets out in the open. That's why we protect it this way." When Hemmer inquired whether Hillary's conduct could have cost lives, Faddis didn't hesitate. "Absolutely. Without question," he asserted.

That she protected her husband from harassment charges and highly plausible accusations of rape in order to protect Bill's presidency and her own political prospects is known to everyone without it becoming the impediment to ought to be. It's not that Abedin is a close friend and confidant, but that she is Hillary's closest political advisor that should make you think about what is going on in the US. The media is the fourth estate, more powerful than whatever might be classified as numbers two and three. What makes Donald Trump so important is that he is able to say things the media would murder anyone else for saying and remain viable. Anyone who thinks of Hillary as anything other than near enough the worst imaginable successor to Obama really has nothing to add to a conversation about the politics of the United States.

AND IN NEWS JUST TO HAND: Former House Oversight chairman: 'FBI director would like to indict Clinton and Abedin'.[90]

> *California Congressman Darrell Issa, who previously led an investigation into Benghazi as former chairman of the House Oversight Committee, says the FBI "would like to indict both Huma [Abedin] and Hillary Clinton" for conducting sensitive government business on an unsecure, private email server.*
>
> *"I think the FBI director would like to indict both Huma and Hillary as we speak," the Republican heavyweight told the Washington Examiner Thursday, during a debate watch-party at Florida Sen. Marco Rubio's New Hampshire campaign headquarters.*

---

[90] *Washington Examiner*, 29 January 2016.

"I think he's in a position where he's being forced to triple-time make a case of what would otherwise be, what they call, a slam dunk," Issa said, referring to FBI Director James Comey, who previously told the Senate Judiciary Committee he would conduct a "competent," "honest" and "independent" probe into Clinton's handling of classified information during her tenure as secretary of state.

~

Is Trump a "conservative"?
January 31, 2016

I don't vote according to labels but there is no doubt that so far as modern political labels go, conservative is the closest it gets. This is from an article on 'Why I Support Donald Trump and Not Ted Cruz'[91] which begins by addressing what does it mean to be a "conservative":

"Conservatism," as [Russell] Kirk explained it, encompassed an inherent distrust of liberal democracy, staunch opposition to egalitarianism, and an extreme reluctance to commit the United States to global "crusades" to impose American "values" on "unenlightened" countries around the world. Conservatives should celebrate local traditions, customs, and the inherited legacies of other peoples, and not attempt to destroy them. America, Kirk insisted, was not founded on a democratic, hegemonic ideology, but as an expression and continuation of European traditions and strong localist, familial and religious belief. Indeed, Kirk authored a profound biography of Senator Robert Taft, "Mr. Conservative," who embodied those principles.

It's a long article and well worth reading through. Here, however, is the core point on why Trump is preferred to Cruz:

What is needed in this nation now is dramatic, even radical change. What is needed is not someone who will simply raise Hell, but someone who will be more like a bull loosed in a terrified china shop. Half measures and regular politicians, "mainstream conservatives" like Ted Cruz, I don't think can pull it off. Trump, I believe, just maybe can.

"Just maybe can" is a better probability statement than is attached to

---
[91] unz.com, 25 January 2016.

any other candidate at the present time. Interestingly, and by no means a coincidence since this is a central issue in this election, Byron York has asked Trump what makes him a conservative.[92] Here is the Q and A:

> **Conservatives are very worried about you. They concede that you've brought attention to issues that are important to them, like immigration or radical Islamic terrorism. But they don't believe you're one of them. Are you a conservative?**
>
> *I am, and I'll tell you what will happen, I think, is they'll maybe see it more and more as time goes by.*
>
> *If you think about it, if you take a look at what I've done, I've brought millions and millions of people to the Republican Party, and to the conservative party, because, as an example, the debate had 24 million people. If I wasn't in the debate, would it have had three, or four, or two, or what would it have been? And you look at the kind of numbers that they're doing on television, where every one of the stations, the networks that are covering us, and honestly in particular covering me, because I do seem to get a lot more coverage than anybody else, but their ratings are through the roof. So that focus is a very important focus because other people are allowed to take advantage of all of the eyeballs that I'm bringing to the screen.*
>
> **But what makes you a conservative? What does being a conservative mean to you?**
>
> *Well, I think it's just a conservative value. I'm very conservative fiscally. I mean, we owe $19 trillion, this is going to destroy our country, we're going to be destroyed by what's going on fiscally. And in terms of the economy, in terms of jobs, we're losing our jobs to everybody. You take a look at the kind of numbers that we're talking about with the closures and just pure and simple the number of jobs that have been lost, it's incredible. To places like China, Vietnam is the new hot one, they're taking our jobs. Mexico, always. They're outsmarting us at every turn, and we don't seem to be able to do it. I mean it's an incredible thing.*
>
> *I will say this. In terms of conservative, I've had tremendous polling numbers with conservatives, I think to a large extent because of the border. Nobody has that issue like I have it, whether it's building the wall or closing the*

---

[92] *Washington Examiner*, 13 January 2016.

border and letting people in but they have to come in legally.

So why have you so many conservative leaders — the Wall Street Journal, Weekly Standard, National Review, lots of them don't think you're a conservative. They would look at what you just said about trade — they would say protectionism and tariffs, that's not conservative.

No, no, not protectionism — fairness. China is making hundreds of billions of dollars a year with us. At some point, we have to say, look, you can't do that. I mean we have rebuilt China virtually. Now, I am a free trader, 100 percent. But we can't continue to lose tremendous amounts of money to these countries. We're losing with virtually everybody, everybody that we do business with. The fact is, our leaders have been outsmarted at every step of the game. And we just can't do that.

Much more again at the link. But if conservative means to preserve what is good while allowing positive change to occur, the Donald may well be the most conservative candidate in this election. It is also what I liked about Tony Abbott even though no two people may be as far apart personally from each other than he and Donald Trump.

~

Megan McArdle - You have to be kidding
February 1, 2016

If you would like to see an example of unpersuasive, this one is near the top of the line: 'How can Trump voters possibly trust this guy?'[93] It's a short article that focuses on how we cannot be sure what a Donald Trump will do as president. I am happy to concede exactly that if she will concede you cannot say what any of the others will do either. And a large part of the reason is that while we ask people running for office what they would do in known circumstances and deal with already existing problems, when they arrive things suddenly spin out of control as entirely new problems spring up from nowhere. But let us look at the issues of the moment through her eyes. She starts by characterising people who lean towards Trump in the

---

[93] nypost.com, 30 January 2016.

following way:

> You are sick to death of well-paid folks in Washington and New York and California calling you bigots because of your stance on immigration, trade or foreign policy.

If they did so, I would be offended and such people would have no influence on me. But then writes in the very next sentence:

> I don't happen to agree with you on immigration policy.

Well that's that. You can now take your snooty condescension and be on your way, you buffoon. And then she concludes with this:

> Trump voters seem eager to ignore the fact that their candidate is theirs only until he doesn't need them.

Well listen, Megan. It is still a political system that needs to work through Congress and the public service. Although Obama may have given you this impression, you are not electing a king, but an administration. There is plenty of politics after an election. And with the media filled with shrews and scolds like yourself, doing things, even the kinds of things people would like done on immigration, will not be as easy as all that.

~

The Trump phenomenon has changed everything in American politics
February 1, 2016

An unusually acute examination of the American election from *The Wall Street Journal*[94] by John O'Sullivan, *Quadrant*'s interim editor. It is now almost universal among elite opinion on the right that Donald Trump is a disaster in the making, with an anyone but Trump the standard response. That there are people who classify themselves as Republican who would vote for Hillary over Trump only proves how empty their views must be about the nature of the problems that must be solved. If they really cannot see the certainty that Hillary would be the final nail in an American decline then it is beyond me

---

[94] *The Wall Street Journal*, 29 January 2016.

why anyone should listen to a thing they say.

> It is almost an understatement, at this point, to say that the Trump phenomenon has changed everything in American politics, but it has. Here's a brief laundry list:
>
> **Immigration.** *From the start of this century, both Democratic and Republican elites have wanted to pass "comprehensive immigration reform" of a broadly liberal kind. Popular opposition prevented this, but the party elites headed off any movement toward a more restrictive approach. Mr. Trump, encouraged by the European migrant crisis, picked up the issue, made it the booster rocket of his campaign and now advances a policy that would reduce immigrant numbers overall. Comprehensive immigration reform is not quite dead, but it is collapsing.*
>
> **Libertarianism.** *Young people were said to see it as a respectable modern version of conservatism. But libertarianism and its prophet, Sen. Rand Paul, have been pushed aside by the rush of popular support to Mr. Trump, who represents, if anything, a movement from libertarianism to activist government.*
>
> **Isolationism versus interventionism.** *This was going to be the debate between Sen. Paul and Sen. Marco Rubio to determine the future direction of the GOP's national security policy. Instead, despite remarks on Vladimir Putin that are silly and worse, Mr. Trump has swept aside this debate. He plays to a widespread mood in American life that is perturbed about Mr. Obama's failing foreign strategy and responds, in effect, that the U.S. should fight "no more unwinnable wars." Mr. Trump promises that he won't pick fights but will definitely win those fights he gets into while pursuing a fairly narrow version of America's national interest.*
>
> **Reforming the welfare state.** *Walter Russell Mead, writing in the American Interest, has called for the reform of what he labels the "Blue State Model"—that is, the fiscally failing American welfare state of entitlements and urban programs, resting on budget-busting public sector salaries and pensions. Mr. Mead and others have advanced serious schemes for cuts that would make the system sustainable in the long run. Again, Mr. Trump has sweepingly promised to preserve entitlements against such reforms, discouraging other Republicans from making this tough case.*

All this is true, but for myself, the most important change Trump may bring is a weakening of the media's narrowing the range of acceptable opinion and some lessening of the grip that political correctness has on policy and public discourse. America is heading for the rocks and we will join them if nothing is done to turn things around. It is this most of all that O'Sullivan sees and understands making him alone of all of the major commentators to have accepted that Trump is not an unmitigated bad.

~

Trump has been talking about illegal immigration since 2013

February 1, 2016

This is from Ann Coulter's latest column:[95]

> *In more than a dozen tweets that year — the very year that Marco Rubio nearly destroyed the nation with his amnesty bill, as the "conservative" media cheered him on — Trump repeatedly denounced the maniacal push for amnesty:*
>
> *— "Immigration reform is fine — but don't rush to give away our country! Sounds like that's what's happening." (Jan. 30, 2013)*
>
> *— "Amnesty is suicide for Republicans. Not one of those 12 million who broke our laws will vote Republican. Obama is laughing at @GOP." (March 19, 2013)*
>
> *— "Now AP is banning the term 'illegal immigrants.' What should we call them? 'Americans'?! This country's political press is amazing!" (April 3, 2013)*
>
> *— "TRUMP: IMMIGRATION BILL A REPUBLICAN 'DEATH WISH'" (June 4, 2013)*

You may not like what he says, but he is certainly consistent. He may even be right, and just think what it means if he is.

---

[95] anncoulter.com, 27 January 2016.

Who do you support for President?
February 2, 2016

I did an online questionnaire and these were my results.

Candidates		So far as the parties went:
Trump	*94%*	*Republicans 98%*
Rubio	*91%*	*Constitution Party 93%*
Cruz	*90%*	*Libertarians 74%*
Santorum	*87%*	*Democrats 30%*
Carson	*86%*	
Paul	*84%*	
Bush	*79%*	
Clinton	*15%*	
Sanders	*13%*	

Not much of a surprise to me.

I might just mention here Conrad Black's assessment, 'Donald Trump knows how to make a deal'[96] in which he writes:

> *In fact, Donald Trump is reasonably conservative. He opposes tax breaks for the rich and back-handers for rich cronies, if not as histrionically as Warren Buffett does (though Buffett has often been a beneficiary of them). Moreover, he spares the country the tedious spectacle of politicians ambling about with begging bowls or cupped hands asking for money, because Donald is paying his own way. His presentational methods grate on the nerves of sophisticated people, but it is an Archie Bunker approach by a man who is a successful businessman rather than, like Archie, a blue-collar clock-puncher. And the approach works: He is leading the polls. In a democracy, the people are always right, and if he wins, it will be because an impatient and disserved people wishes it so.*

It's just an opinion, of course, but I do see his point.

---

[96] *National Post*, 30 January 2016

Rubio would be a disaster
February 6, 2016

The Republican establishment is now backing Marco Rubio to the hilt against Donald Trump and Ted Cruz. I actually saw Rubio speak in Las Vegas the day before Trump and I could not believe how weak and ineffectual he came across. The words were all right, but the lack of conviction was palpable. No one came away fired up about his prospects, unlike my experience when I had listened to Rand Paul (the year before) or Donald Trump. Hillary will eat Rubio for lunch.

But what makes Rubio likely poison is his lack of creds on border protection. This was published just two months ago, in December, 'The Ugly Truth About Marco Rubio And His Gang-of-Eight Amnesty Bill'[97] and represents a very strong attitude among Republicans:

> *Rubio was a Jeb Bush acolyte who embraced the Tea Party and ran for senator in Florida against Charlie Crist. Crist was the popular sitting governor in the state and Rubio was thought to be a huge underdog. However, the grassroots embraced Rubio. Just to give you an example, very early on I organized a coalition that endorsed Rubio and encouraged people not to give money to the NRSC over its endorsement of Crist. I even called for NRSC chairman John Cornyn to RESIGN over his decision to get involved in the race on Crist's behalf.*
>
> *Back then, Rubio was talking very tough on immigration by necessity. Although Rubio is significantly more conservative than Crist, the conservative base would have never rallied to his side if he had supported amnesty; he would have lost in a landslide. In other words, Rubio's anti-amnesty position was one of the central promises of his campaign. In fact, Rubio slammed Charlie Crist for being pro-amnesty and very specifically said he opposed giving illegal aliens citizenship. Back then, Marco Rubio sounded like Jeff Sessions on immigration. . . .*
>
> *Unfortunately, even though Marco Rubio is only in the Senate today because he claimed to be in favor of securing the border and stopping amnesty, his position shifted 180 degrees and he became the front man for the Gang-of-Eight amnesty bill. . . .*

---

[97] townhall.com, 19 December 2015.

> *Getting beyond the Gang-of-Eight bill, as late as June of this year, Marco Rubio was openly saying that he wanted to make illegal aliens citizens. However, today he tries to muddy the waters about the subject by merely saying he thinks illegal aliens should eventually be able to get green cards. Of course, people who have green cards are allowed to apply for citizenship; so it's the same difference over the long haul.*

I don't think Rubio can win – he is no JFK – but really what difference would it make if he did. As noted in the article:

> *If Rubio's lying, it doesn't really make much of a difference over the long haul whether you elect him or Hillary because his immigration policies would permanently cement liberals in power without securing the border or doing anything of significance to stop illegal immigration.*
>
> *If Marco Rubio becomes the President of the United States, the future of our republic depends on Rubio telling the truth this time after he already lied about the same thing to people who walked over broken glass to get him elected.*
>
> *So now, are you ready to walk over broken glass to get Marco Rubio elected? Choose wisely because if Rubio becomes President and he's lying about immigration again, it will be the end of the road for conservatism in America.*

All you need to know is that Rubio is the choice of the Republican establishment who have been trying to get amnesty passed over the massed opposition of the people who actually vote for Republicans. Rubio would be a disaster as president but why worry? He would anyway almost certainly lose to Hillary if he became the nominee. It is either Trump or Cruz. Rubio is no answer, which is why the media is now doing everything it can to help him along.

MORE ALONG THE SAME LINES: This time from Phyllis Schlafly, as iconic a conservative as there is to be found anywhere: Schlafly unloads on Rubio: 'He betrayed us all'[98] with the sub-head, "Conservative icon calls media favorite 'lackey for the establishment'". She writes:

> *"When Marco Rubio ran for the Senate in Florida, I think I was the first one to endorse him," said Phyllis Schlafly. "I made a trip down to Florida*

---

[98] wnd.com, 5 February 2016.

in 2009 just for the purpose of helping him."

But Schlafly, a legendary conservative activist, author and WND columnist, now says she is bitterly disappointed by Rubio's record.

"Once he got elected, he betrayed us all," she told WND. "He said he was against amnesty and against the establishment. And once he got in, right away, he became an agent of the establishment. And now, of course, he's big for amnesty and letting all the illegal immigrants in. He betrayed us a number of times on that issue."

Schlafly said she was startled at the magnitude of Rubio's "betrayal" on amnesty.

"It was so public," she said.

"He's a lackey for the establishment now," she said. "There's no question they're picking up as Plan B – or maybe Plan C in this election cycle, or whatever we're on now – but he certainly is an establishment agent."

~

The selling of Marco Rubio
February 7, 2016

We don't vote in American elections so it is all academic in a way. But it is worth having some sense of who's doing what and where things are heading. A Malcolm-led Liberal Party may be the best there is across the world, so think about that. This is Mickey Kaus on 'The Rubio Menace'[99] which more or less says the same as I did in my post yesterday on 'Rubio Would be a Disaster'. This might bring out the extent to which the American election cycle is a charade which, given the unstoppable success of Hillary, we knew already. This is Rubio who has taken up the mantle that was supposed to fall to Jeb Bush.

> *Bush is explicit about his support for mass immigration and amnesty. Rubio has now effectively wormed his way into a position where championing mass immigration and amnesty would involve breaking what seems to be an explicit policy pledge. But anyone who has followed Rubio knows that's*

---

[99] kausfiles.com, 5 February 2016.

exactly what he'll do.

a) He's done it before, having opposed amnesty when seeking his Senate seat only to become its front man on arriving in Washington;

b) He dissembled when necessary to push the Gang of 8 bill, why not dissemble now?

c) The GOP establishment thinks that's exaclty what he'll do;

d) His retreat from the Gang of 8 has been grudging and weaselly, always giving as little ground as he thinks he can get away with until he discovers he has to give a little more;

e) He still hasn't repudiated the bill, let alone apologized for it; and most important,

f) actually achieving an Enforcement First solution would mean standing up to the Democrats, who will demand quick legalization, and the bulk of the GOP Congressional caucus, who will be happy to settle for a fig-leaf of enforcement they can try to sell their voters (not unlike the fig leaf added to the Gang of 8 by the for-show-only Corker-Hoeven "double the border patrol" amendment). The current flash mob of GOP representatives streaming into Rubio's camp suggests they recognize him as someone who won't make their lives difficult — when that's exactly what is required.

Rubio's not going to drive Jeff Sessions from the capital. But you can count on the combination of President Rubio and Speaker Ryan to quickly pass an amnesty bill that (like the Gang of 8) contains only the most chimerical guarantees of new enforcement measures. You can also expect them to promote and defend trade, including "trade in services" that involves foreign workers performing those services on American soil. And what about the Sessionsesque suggestion that immigration levels actually be lowered? As one Senate immigration advisor said, "We have a better chance of discovering time travel than getting Rubio-Ryan to take up immigration-reduction bill."

And on the off chance you are of the opinion that Rubio has that spontaneous human touch, you might like to look at this.[100]

Marco Rubio is running a presidential campaign marked by precision, caution and discipline — so much so that the Florida senator delivers the

---

[100] CNN Politics, 5 February 2016

exact same speech, jokes, quips and one-liners wherever he goes.

When he addresses the media, his aides select the reporters who can ask questions, often shutting down follow-ups. During media interviews and presidential debates, Rubio is quick to fall back on the same script that he often delivers before GOP audiences in New Hampshire and Iowa.

His campaign makes sure every room is packed. Lately, that's because an overflow audience is interested in hearing from the surging candidate. But other times his aides have cut the room in half with drapes, ensuring it's a standing-room-only crowd.

It's great theatre, but is it politics?

~

Feeling the Bern
February 10, 2016

REVOLUTION!
*SANDERS 60% CLINTON 39%
*TRUMP 35% KASICH 16% CRUZ 12%

Which comes with this additional detail:

Clinton Horror Deja Vu…
NH Brings Rumors of Campaign Implosion…
Biden ruling nothing out…
She lost every demo except 65+…
DICK MORRIS: Falling Apart…
B Team Deployed to Smear…
MOOK SPOOKED: 'VICTORY' MEMO…
Backer Urges Campaign: Keep Steinem and Albright Away!
Photo shows American flags crumpled up on HQ floor…
RESULTS: DEM REPUBLICAN…
LIVE: MAP…

It really is gruesome. Neither side has a solid grounding in common sense and sound economics. But half of America would now vote Socialist, on the Democrat side whether Hillary or Sanders it makes hardly a difference.

In 2008 I used to say Anyone But Clinton so I learned a tragic lesson. Now it's Anyone But Any of the Ones who are Running for the Democrats. Just remember, democracy is the worst system except for all the others that have been tried from time to time.

~

Donald Trump in 2013
February 11, 2016

This video (youtube/2AZaPhCA_-U) is Donald Trump receiving an award from the *American Spectator* in 2013, long before he was running for President. Listen to not just what he says – which are themes he has been discussing since entering the race – but also how he says it – which is temperate, balanced and filled with common sense. And he knows a thing or two about budgets, deficits and getting value for money. There is no doubt in listening to this that he is not a Democrat and is a Republican, but of a kind not hitherto seen. From this point on, for me it is Donald Trump for President. America's problems may be too large to fix, but if they can be fixed, he is the only person in public life who has the potential to do it.

~

Trying to save America
February 13, 2016

This is the conclusion from someone who has written a book with the title, *9 Presidents Who Screwed Up America–and Four Who Tried to Save Her*. The article is titled, 'Which candidate will screw up America the least',[101] and this is what he said at the end:

> *Trump may not be able to "make America great again" on his own, but he would be the one who would screw it up the least. The others would eventually have to be added to a Volume 2 of my 9 Presidents Who Screwed Up*

---

[101] breitbart.com, 8 February 2016.

America. Trump, at least, would have a chance to be considered for the "Four Who Tried to Save Her."

If you're the sort of person who thinks that Obama has had his good points and his bad points, you are not the sort of person who will see how necessary Donald Trump is. But he is. In a normal world Hillary would have zero chance of being president but this is not that world. If you don't want Hillary to win, Trump is the only candidate who might stop it from happening.

~

You go to war with the army you have
February 14, 2016

I read the comments on Donald Trump in 2013[102] with some dismay. We are now down to seven people who might become President of the United States:

Jeb Bush, Hillary Clinton, Ted Cruz, John Kasich, Marco Rubio, Bernie Sanders, Donald Trump

Maybe Joe Biden might get into this at some stage, or Michael Bloomberg, or Ben Carson may come back into it, but that's all that's left. That's it. No one else. It is one of the above and no other.

Then there are the problems the United States now confronts – the US being our last hope for a defence of the West – problems from open immigration, a rapidly descending economy and a clueless millennial generation who you could easily imagine voting in a Hugo Chavez. And so I said, after watching the video of Trump in 2013, that Trump is the best of the lot. He not only has sentiments that match my own [94% as it happens] but he has the force of personality that might actually bring it off. He is our Churchill circa 1940.

I can see just as easily as anyone else that he is not your standard issue highly polished product of the elite establishment in the US. He is crass and loud and bumptious and vulgar. All true, but he is also smart, and shrewd, and tuned in and hard edged. But most of all, the things he wants are the

---

[102] catallaxyfiles.com, 12 February 2016.

things I want, the most important ones being the preservation of the United States as the land of the free and the defender of our values. He also has the one element none of the others on the Republican side have, a fighting will that will not be pushed around by the media and the left.

And I am not even going to say something like he's not perfect, because, for all I know, given the way things are and what now needs to be done, he may well be exactly what is needed. He may exactly suit the times we are in.

There's the list above. If it's not Donald Trump then who among that list should it be instead? If you think it's any of the others, then we will just have to agree to differ. But in my view, it will be a tragedy if he does not become president because all other choices will either hasten the ruin of the US or at best delay the now almost inevitable by a year or two. He may end up unable to stem the tide of history, but given the moment we find ourselves now in, Trump is the only candidate who has even a ghost of a chance to pull it off. Why others cannot see the same is absolutely beyond me. First, though, he has to win. Then we can worry about the rest.

~

It's enough
February 15, 2016

The choice of who to support for president has never been more difficult. Trump is wildly different from the norm – another Andrew Jackson. He will be hated by everyone on the left, but he also is not liked or respected by many within the Republican establishment and those whose support he will need.

He may have had what is required but he may also not have the mental discipline, never mind the background knowledge, to do what's needed. Trump might have been able to do what's needed but you can't do it by alienating everyone in your path. A leader brings people together. A businessperson makes everyone do what they want because a decision has been reached. And his sensational thin skin is a massive worry. And now with the death of Antonin Scalia, only one of a number of Supreme Court justices who might end up being chosen in the next 4-8 years, the stakes are extraordinary. You might be willing to compromise on a less adventurous president if it raises the probability that a Republican gets to choose.

With the appointment to the Supreme Court right there in the mix, there will be no doubting in anyone's mind, that this is not just a decision for the next four years, but for the next 20-30 years. Everything about the future of the US will be in the mix. And while I think the Republican establishment is bizarrely out of touch – Jeb Bush is their chosen vehicle, for heaven's sake! – I am hopeful that there will be a coming together among the candidates about what must be done.

The major impression I received in listening to Donald Trump at the debate in South Carolina was that he has spent too many years reading *The New York Times*. It is what Ted Cruz has said, about Trump being infused with "New York values".[103] I'm not sure it was the best way to put it, but I knew what he meant. There is a smarmy left-liberal condescension towards any other way of thinking that is tearing down the world we have built. We live in the freest, most tolerant society that may ever have been, but that freedom is being ground to dust by a liberal intolerance that if left unstopped will be our ruin. I thought Trump might have done something to stop it, but I am becoming less sure he can. I don't think anyone else can, so I will just have to wait on events.

~

So where now?
February 16, 2016

I have often thought of this post of mine, Obama in the lead 68-7 – in Australia.[104] It is the results of a round-the-world survey conducted by the BBC on how different countries would have voted in the American presidential election in 2012. The results were published right at the end of the campaign. And in Australia: Obama 68% – Romney 7%. They still look as gruesome as any set of data I have ever seen.

This, mind you, was after Obama had been president for four years.

---

[103] Time.com, 25 January 2016.
[104] catallaxyfiles.com, 25 October 2012.

The world was disintegrating, but nowhere near the level it has reached today (see the story on The Obama Legacy[105]). Yet, I doubt that were the question raised again that there would be much regret among the 68%. Obama would still win an American election in Australia, perhaps he would even still win in the US.

My point. I seem to see political issues in a different way from most Australians. I regret Donald has not got quite the needed polish to go all the way, but no one else can make the difference he could. He ruined himself in his criticisms of George Bush and the Iraq war in the debate on the weekend. He is a New Yorker who inevitably reads *The New York Times* and watches NBC. Ted Cruz is right that Trump has "New York values".[106] He has seen how colossal his mistake has been[107] but it's now, I think, too late. If he wins the nomination, which he still might, although the odds have lengthened a long way, he will no longer have the support of the *bien pensants*, many of whom would vote for Hillary or Bernie instead.

And while we don't elect presidents in 2016 to deal with the problems we faced in 2001, the continuity is crucial. He may even have opposed the war in Iraq, and given how things have turned out, he may even have been right to do it. No one contemplating on what to do after 911 could possibly factor a Barack Obama presidency into a Middle East policy from 2009-2017. Everything achieved has been thrown away, and matters made infinitely worse. The world I grew up in is disappearing. Something different is emerging. There will always be an elite – go to the poorest nation on the planet and there you will find an elite living extremely well – but for the rest, neither peace nor wealth nor freedom.

But who knows? Nothing is certain. 2030 is as far from us now as we are from 2001 so maybe things will turn around. I'm sure serfdom didn't look all that bad to the serfs.

---

[105] lawofmarkets.com, 16 February 2016.
[106] Time.com, 25 Janyary 2016
[107] *Washington Examiner,* 14 February 2016.

The Obama legacy – international division
February 16, 2016

There is nothing, either domestic or international, that has not been made worse by the Obama presidency. This is from *The New York Post* that deals with the international side: A world aflame: Obama aides debunk the boss's happy talk.[108] There is much more than this, but this is quite good enough:

> *"Violent extremists are operationally active in about 40 countries. Seven countries are experiencing a collapse of central government authority, 14 others face regime-threatening or violent instability or both, another 59 countries face a significant risk of instability through 2016," Clapper said.*
>
> *"There are now more Sunni violent extremist groups, members and safe havens than at any time in history."*

That's quite an achievement. We can talk about the domestic stuff some other time.

~

The Donald Pro and Con
February 17, 2016

There is little doubt that Donald Trump is a high-risk choice for president, but there is equally little doubt that the American enterprise is at a very dangerous crossroads. He's not the obvious choice that Romney was in 2012, although to hear the story told today you would think Romney was about on par with Obama in his negatives. So let us do a bit of weighing up the two sides of the question.

Pro

- His central slogan is "Make America Great Again", the very antithesis of the Obama creed.
- He wants to protect the integrity of America's borders.
- He wants to strengthen America's national defence.
- He understands that not all potential migrants are equal.

---

[108] *New York Post*, 13 February 2016.

- He understands the importance of balancing the books and is more likely than any other candidate to bring fiscal sanity back into the American economy.
- He is non-politically correct and is unafraid to say things no one else will say.
- He is unafraid of the media and gives back better than they dish it out to him.
- He can do through force of personality things that no one else could do in his place.

Con

- He is half (three-quarters?) crazy.
- He is vulgar and intemperate.
- He knows little history.
- He is unanchored to the Republican Party.
- He has had no experience in dealing with foreign policy issues.
- No one knows, least of all him, what he would really do if he won.
- His background is in business which is among the worst places for anyone in politics to try to learn the trade.
- He may make either Hillary or Bernie more electable than they otherwise would be.

You would prefer that he were more like a Tony Abbott or a Stephen Harper, but then again, where are they now, pushed aside as they were by flea-weights.

UPDATE: I don't know if this connects with you, but it does with me.[109]

> *President Obama said today that he does not believe GOP frontrunner Donald Trump will make it to the White House, but the real estate mogul took the remark as a compliment, saying Obama has done a "lousy job."*
>
> *"I continue to believe Mr. Trump will not be president," Obama said while speaking at a press conference in Rancho Mirage, California. "And the reason is because I have a lot of faith in the American people."*

---

[109] ABC News, 16 Feburary 2016.

> *Obama told reporters he believed Americans still see the presidency as "a serious job."*
>
> *"It's not hosting a talk show, or a reality show. It's not promotion, it's not marketing," Obama said. "It's hard and a lot of people count on us getting it right."*
>
> *Obama did not, however, answer whether he believed Trump was capable of securing the GOP nomination.*
>
> *The president also took a shot at the rest of the GOP field, saying "foreign observers are troubled" by the GOP's rhetoric, specifically the doubting of climate change and proposals to ban Muslims from entering the U.S.*
>
> *Trump, speaking at a campaign event in South Carolina, immediately hit back, saying Obama is doing a "lousy job."*
>
> *"He has set us back so far, and for him to actually say that is a great compliment, if you want to know the truth," Trump said.*

That Obama can still show his face in public is what makes me most fearful about the future of the US and our way of life. Sanders is not a more extreme version of what Obama stands for, only someone who is more explicit and willing to say just what he thinks.

~

Donald Trump passes the Jeff Sessions test
February 17, 2016

This is the headline 'Jeff Sessions Praises Donald Trump's Answers to 'Sessions Test'[110] and this is the story:

> *Alabama Senator Sen. Jeff Sessions (R-AL) praised GOP frontrunner Donald Trump's responses to his GOP candidate questionnaire.*
>
> *Sessions noted that to date Trump is the only candidate who has "answered to my satisfaction."*
>
> *On February 5th, Sessions, the intellectual thought leader of the conservative*

---
[110] breitbart.com, 16 Feburary 2016.

nation-state movement, issued a questionnaire to all candidates seeking the Party's nomination. The Sessions test consisted of five straightforward questions addressing immigration, trade, and crime in the United States. In his response, Trump wrote, "After my inauguration, for the first time in decades, Americans will wake up in a country where their immigration laws are enforced."

On Monday's program of the Mark Levin Show, Sessions said:

The American people need to be alert. This is a very, very critical election. I think if they care about immigration issues and trade issues, they need to be sure about where their candidates stand. And I've asked them questions about trade and immigration and one question on crime. And Trump has answered to my satisfaction, but the others haven't yet. So I think these candidates need to be specific about where they stand before Americans start giving them their vote.

"I'm a fan of Trump," Sessions said. "He's been clear on immigration, he's been clear on trade, and he's talking directly to the American people."

Sessions said that he was similarly impressed with Trump's picks for the Supreme Court. During Saturday night's GOP debate, Trump was the only candidate to list his potential picks: Bill Pryor and Diane Sykes.

Sessions, who sits on the Senate Judiciary Committee, said "Trump really hit a home run with me when he mentioned [Pryor]."

"Sykes and Pryor are conservative federal judges," Business Insider reports. Because Pryor is adamantly pro-life, "Senate Democrats tried to block Pryor's nomination to the 11th Circuit court, saying that he had described Roe v. Wade as 'the worst abomination in the history of constitutional law.'"

In recent days, Trump has been hitting Cruz for his prior support of John Roberts. In 2005, Cruz penned an op-ed in favor of Roberts' confirmation, declaring: "John Roberts should be a quick confirm" for the Senate.

Trump comes across less serious than he is but those with an agenda can see he has been thinking about the questions and has some seriously sensible answers.

David Horowitz on Trump and the War in Iraq
February 18, 2016

This is from a post by David Horowitz at FrontPageMag which he titles, 'Election Fog'.[111] And what was important to me was that he sees past the lack of knowledge and historical understanding to the core motivations of Trump's run for president.

> *Trump showed himself recklessly ill-informed on the causes of the Iraq War during the South Carolina debate. George Bush did not lie to lead us into war – that is, in fact, a Democrat lie. The Iraq War was about Saddam's defiance of a UN Security Council ultimatum to disclose and destroy his Weapons of Mass Destruction. Contrary to an enormously destructive political myth, the WMDs did exist – including 2250 Sarin-gas-filled-rockets and chemical weapons in storage tanks that Saddam buried and are now in the possession of ISIS. Finally, the destabilization of Iraq and the Middle East are entirely a consequence of Obama's policies not George Bush's as Trump falsely maintained. Trump's misreading of the Iraq War is a serious political fault. But it is the result of ignorance rather than malice against his country, which is what motivates the left. Whatever one thinks of Trump, he is justly hated by the Sanders radicals, who understand that his intentions make him their nemesis not their twin.*

It's not something you can pass over lightly since understanding history is crucial to political judgement, but history can be learned. The will and judgement to do the right thing is what matters in the end, and the question that does still remain open is whether Trump does have the judgement to succeed. I think he does, and more so than any of the others, but that still remains the question after all of the other issues have gone by.

---

[111] frontpagemag.com, 15 February 2016.

Isn't it obvious that Obama is on the other side?
February 18, 2016

Eight years is a long time for a political mistake to continue. Victor Davis Hanson looks at Obama and the Middle East in a post on 'Speak Loudly And Carry A Twig'.[112] That Obama has continually sought to aid and abet the most radical of the Islamists in every one of the theatres of war ought to make clear whose side he's on. Yet it remains merely a series of errors and examples of poor judgement. No one in Israel or Egypt misunderstands even in the slightest, but it still cannot be said that Obama sides with the Muslim Brotherhood. Here is one of the examples Hanson gives.

> *The Egyptian military junta tried to explain to the Obama administration that it had no choice but to abort the one-election/one-time Islamization efforts of Mohamed Morsi's Muslim Brotherhood. President Abdel Fattah el-Sisi is baffled that Egypt's opposition to radical Islam has not softened American anger, but apparently only cemented the estrangement.*

The only thing that baffles him is that Obama could get elected and that his policies have not brought the house down on his head. It's now just about waiting it out since whoever is next is bound to be better. But then again, it might be Hillary Clinton or even Bernie Sanders so "better" might need to come with the modifier "slightly". And even if it's not, everyone now understands that the US cannot be the long-term anchor. Security must be found elsewhere. As Hanson says:

> *The only upside is an emerging de facto alliance between Israel and the so-called moderate Arab monarchies. That odd coupling assumes that Iran threatens both more than they do each other, and that the United States is no longer a reliable patron to either.*

The US under Obama has not been "unreliable", it has been positively hostile. This is a lesson learned, but we are not living in a better world as a result.

---

[112] hoover.org, 16 February 2016.

The Democrats could still win
February 18, 2016

Meaning,[113] no matter who the Republicans put up, the Democrats, even with Hillary and Bernie, might actually win. It's the 12-13% still unaccounted for who will now decide the fate of the American Republic and much else.

Against Hillary:	Against Bernie:
Trump wins 45% to 43%.	*Trump wins 44% to 43%.*
Cruz wins 45-44%	*Cruz loses 42-44%*
Rubio wins 46-42%	*Rubio wins 46-42%*

The question remains, who would **be** the best president, although to be the best president you also have to be the winner of the election. Meanwhile, you have this kind of nonsense from *The Wall Street Journal* to contend with: 'Donald Trump's hostile takeover of the Republican party'.[114] And when we are talking about voting Democrat, we are talking about putting either Hillary Clinton or Bernie Sanders into the White House, not some anonymous person unknown. So you tell me what sense there is in this?

> *The Trump phenomenon offers a moral challenge not only to evangelicals, but to the entire Republican leadership. Nine months ago I couldn't imagine a scenario in which Mr. Trump would receive his party's nomination and go on to win the presidency. Now I can. If he wins in South Carolina, conscientious Republicans will have to ask themselves whether they can be complicit in a course of events that hands the Oval Office to a man so manifestly unfit for the presidency. It is hard to decide which is a greater threat to the republic — Donald Trump's pervasive ignorance or his deep-seated character flaws.*
>
> *Some leading Republicans have quietly told me that they would break ranks if Mr. Trump wins their party's nomination. A few have said so publicly. Unless a viable alternative emerges soon, every Republican will face the same dilemma.*

The same kind of idiocy that found itself walking away from Romney in 2012. I cannot think of two more extreme possible representatives of the Republican Party than Trump and Romney, businessmen though they both may be. I will merely add this comment from *The Australian* thread

---

[113] breitbart.com, 17 February 2016.
[114] *The Australian*, 18 February 2016.

following the article:

> *It seems clear to me that Trump's critics have got him completely wrong.*
>
> *Many Americans are looking for the one man they believe can fix the problems created under Barack Obama. They know it's Donald Trump.*
>
> *Trump's supporters already know what he plans to do as President. They know what he will do, why he will do it, how he will do it, and how he will pay for it. It's all set out in Trump's two books "Time To Get Tough: Making America #1 Again" and "Crippled America: How To Make America Great Again".*
>
> *Trump's critics haven't bothered to find out his plans ... they prefer to pander to the tabloid sound-bites.*
>
> *If Trump can win South Carolina, it will send shock waves through the republican party. You see, while New Hampshire has produced the republican nomination 15 out of 17 occasions, South Caroline has a perfect record in picking the eventual republican nomination.*

Anyone who thinks that it ought to be a toss up between Hillary Clinton and Donald Trump should never be allowed to comment on politics again. You may not think he is the best among the Republicans, but if you vote Democrat because Trump is the nominee then you are too stupid for words.

~

How many divisions has the Pope in joining the campaign against Trump?
February 19, 2016

POPE PICKS FIGHT WITH TRUMP – ENTERS U.S. ELECTION BATTLE[115]

Mom of Son Tortured to Death by Illegal Endorses Trump…
'Pope Doesn't Care About Me'…
VATICAN SURROUNDED BY WALLS…
Has most restrictive immigration, citizenship policies of any nation in world…
SESSIONS: Lord Commanded Nehemiah to build wall…

---
[115] *New York Times*, 19 February 2016.

If they are so worried about Hillary why don't they start being positive about Trump
February 19, 2016

It is not hard to see that our Republican elites are unable to accept that Donald Trump could win the nomination. The highest risk candidate imaginable, but also the only one who, if elected, could make a genuine difference in the right direction. Here is Paul Miringoff at Powerline, 'FOX NEWS POLL HAS SANDERS AHEAD OF CLINTON NATIONALLY, AND BOTH AHEAD OF TRUMP'.[116] About this, he concludes:

> *Anyone frightened by the prospect of a President Hillary Clinton or a President Bernie Sanders should also be frightened by the prospect of Donald Trump as the GOP nominee.*

Trump is not impossibly behind in any of these polls and others have him ahead. But the extreme negativity about Trump's policies among establishment Republicans will end up settling the issue in Hillary's favour. If you are really worried about a Democrat win, why don't you start looking for some of the virtues in Donald Trump as president. It is the lack of imagination on the right side, who looks for a kind of French polish on its candidates, rather than the rough and tumble fighters that we truly need, that is going to pull the West into oblivion.

~

So it's all but settled then: Trump v Clinton
February 21, 2016

With Donald Trump's convincing win in South Carolina and Hillary Clinton's win in Nevada, the dust has settled early this time on the respective party nominees. You must not think of this as carrying a great deal of satisfaction on my part in relation to Trump. He is the only candidate who had a chance to beat Hillary and even do some good if elected. More than ever do I see how the 2012 election was the one that mattered. But he remains a high risk candidate who will change the nature of politics in the US and across the world.

---

[116] powerlineblog.com, 18 February 2016.

Perhaps to help us all see clear of what's involved is an article by Jacob Heilbrunn, editor of the right-side *National Interest*, on 'Trump Is Trampling Over the GOP's Corpse.'[117] He has no more satisfaction in seeing this outcome than I do, but also has something else to say about how out of touch the Republican establishment had become. I might say that the comparison in my own mind has been to Andrew Jackson, which you'd have to know a bit about American history to see the parallel. This is his conclusion but there's lots more at the link.

> *Militaristic unilateralism is fine for a conservative nationalist like Trump who displays a macho Jacksonian attitude about American honor—calling Iran's seizure of American sailors an "absolute disgrace" that evinced a "lack of respect for our country and certainly our president." But he's also made it clear that he's ready to give Russian president Vladimir Putin a free hand when it comes to Ukraine. And when it comes to Syria he's cast doubt about the rebels by implicitly backing Bashar al-Assad — "we have no idea who these people [are] and what they're going to be, and what they're going to represent." Trump's intense repugnance for allies is deeply rooted in the GOP and in American history. Trump's truculent stands prompted the historian Max Boot, an adviser to Rubio, to complain in the February Commentary that both Trump and Cruz are turning "their backs on decades of Republican foreign policy, which has been internationalist, pro-free trade, pro-immigration, pro-democracy, and pro-human rights."*
>
> *It's not quite that simple—Republican foreign policy has veered between the pragmatism of Ronald Reagan and George H.W. Bush to the truculence of George W. Bush—but Boot is definitely onto something: like it or not, Trump and Cruz do represent a return to the party's older traditions. Republican grandees are responding by trying to paint Trump as some kind of closet leftist for having the temerity to question the Bush war on terror. On Monday, Sen. Lindsey Graham called Trump "the Michael Moore of the Republican Party," and poor Jeb Bush echoed him. "I don't get it," Jeb said.*
>
> *You hear a lot of leading Republicans use that phrase nowadays: "I don't get it." That's because they don't get it. All Trump is doing is simply telling the truth as Trump sees it, and what he says is resonating because while it may be wrong at least it is new, and other Republicans are pretending the old*

---

[117] politico.com, 16 February 2016.

bromides still work. All of which is why the GOP is becoming unmoored by his candidacy.

What worries me is that we will find, yet again, "Republicans" sitting the election out, or even worse voting for Hillary. I can only think that people don't read the news or cannot see what's happening with the borderless world that is being created. Trump says he will return us to a world of nation states and close the American border to all who cannot become Americans. I have no idea whether it can at this late stage be done, but I definitely want someone to try. But with Donald and Hillary selected, the big guns of the media will now turn on Trump. One of the parts about Romney that made a difference was that he was so clear of scandal that ultimately the only blemishes that could be found was that he had driven from Boston to Montreal with his dog on the roof, and when he was sixteen had been mean to some other kid at summer camp. Trump no doubt has much more scandal (but then so does Hillary in spades!), but on the other side, he will take none of this lying down, as the Pope himself recently discovered.

We shall see. I think it's largely too late, but if there is any way to ensure the collapse of the West, it is to elect Hillary Clinton president. Although I imagine no newspaper you will read between now and November will say so, Trump is the only one who might, just possibly, bring some order back into our world which is now disintegrating at every turn.

~

Donald Trump and international trade
February 22, 2016

A comment from the thread in this case dealing with Donald Trump on free trade:

> Heads explode all over these days. Note the outrageous claims, lots of personal invective and total lack of balance. Lowenstein was (is?) in the employ of the ferociously anti-Trump Murdoch vehicle, the WSJ. The same outfit who love their cosy relationship with the current political apparatus, and who run bogus 'agenda polls' to undermine Trump. RL is a shock jock journo. So think of this:[118]

---

[118] forbes.com, 21 February 2016

'As someone who lived 27 years in East Asia, I know what a rich seam Trump is tapping into as he focuses on America's trade disaster. For two generations already, increasingly pathetic American trade officials have turned a blind eye to the blatant barriers facing American exports in key foreign markets. One result has been a tragic roll-call of factory closures in the American heartland. Another result, as Trump has insistently pointed out, is that other nations literally laugh at the United States. They think of the U.S. government as idiotic where it is not corrupt.

The problem with free trade is not just that other countries cheat but that they see no reason not to cheat. Cheating confers several key benefits that American officials and commentators consistently sweep under the rug: just the most obvious is that it forces the transfer of American production technology.

Perhaps the most telling evidence of how formidably the Japanese car market is protected has been the performance of the Korean auto industry. At last count the Koreans had less than 0.02 percent of the Japanese car market.

Even Hyundai, Korea's largest auto maker, sold a mere 1,700 cars a year in Japan in the first decade of the twenty-first century. Repeated efforts to surmount Japanese trade barriers yielded so little that in 2009 Hyundai shut down its Japanese car sales division.'

I post regularly on this subject since I check out each of DJT's claims. Technology theft from the engine of innovation is extremely well documented as are the methods of coercion in US-China trade relations.

I suspect Trump knows a good deal more about the realities of business dealings national and international than virtually any of those who comment in the press.

~

Trump's kitchen cabinet
February 23, 2016

Naturally not in the American press but from *The Daily Mail Online*: Rudy Giuliani says Trump is smarter than he looks as The Donald consults with former NYC mayor and other 'kitchen cabinet' advisers.[119] Here are the

---

[119] *Daily Mail Australia*, 23 February 2016.

sub-heads for your delectation:

- *Donald Trump is assembling a 'kitchen cabinet' advisers*
- *Former NYC mayor Rudy Giuliani, former Education Secretary Bill Bennett, economists Art Laffer and Steve Moore rumored to be involved*
- *Trump promised in South Carolina that he would soon unveil a foreign policy advisory team*
- *He has an exceptionally good understanding of how the economy affects our foreign policy,' Giuliani said of Trump*
- *'This idea that he's only familiar with slogans, it's not accurate at all'*

And the opening paras of the story:

> *Former New York City Mayor Rudy Giuliani and a handful of policy wonks are casually advising Donald Trump as the Republican front-runner prepares for the kind of scrutiny he has yet to face.*
>
> *But Giuliani says The Donald is up to the task.*
>
> *'You know, he's very good,' Giuliani told The Washington Post on Sunday, when a reporter asked whether the Republican front-runner has a decent grasp of complicated public policy issues.*
>
> *'It's clear that he has an exceptionally good understanding of how the economy affects our foreign policy,' he said of Trump.*
>
> *'He understands what's happening with China, how they could stop North Korea in a heartbeat. This idea that he's only familiar with slogans, it's not accurate at all.'*

A kitchen cabinet that includes Giuliani, Bill Bennett, Art Laffer and Steve Moore! This is the Dream Team of conservative political economy. And he's anti-PC, and he knows his way around politics. And he can beat Hillary Clinton in a way no one else can even come close to trying. If you don't see Trump is the closest answer there is to the problems we now face then you should renew your subscriptions to *The Age* and *New York Times* and be done with it.

Mark Steyn Update: Steyn, presently in Australia, casts his eyes back home to the election. Here[120] he explains the formidable problems facing

---

[120] steynonline.com, 22 February 2016.

any Republican and concludes:

> *Long term, two things have to happen: America has to restore the integrity of its borders, and conservatism has to get a piece of the action in the schools and the culture. Short term, the GOP has done a grand job of screwing itself out of electoral viability.*

The problem has been that many on the right side of politics believe it has to win over the left, hence Malcolm Turnbull, PM. Being a veteran between-the-lines-reader as I am, Steyn is saying it is Trump or no one. Alas, no one on the respectable right is permitted to say a good word about Trump, so he doesn't either. But if the article doesn't manage to set out for you where things are and how dire it is, then just wait till the campaigns start for real.

~

"A narcissistic, fearmongering authoritarian peddling a destructive, fascistic policy agenda"
February 24, 2016

The quote is from an article at Reason.com aimed at Donald Trump. But in spite of the author's aversion to common sense, the article is quite interesting, coming as it does with the following title, 'How Political Correctness Caused College Students to Cheer for Trump'.[121] You are advised to read it all, but this gets to the essence of the matter. I will say here that the author seems blinded by his own prejudices but notwithstanding any of that, he was still able to work some of this out:

> *College students and Trump supporters, have at least something in common: both groups are plagued by legitimate economic anxieties: middle-class job losses and burdensome loan debt, for example. But the argument can certainly be made that these concerns are trumped (pardon the pun) by cultural issues, at least as evidenced by the priorities of both groups. And when it comes to the culture wars, they are on opposite sides.*
>
> *The masses of people who show up at rallies for Trump—and have propelled*

---

[121] reason.com, 23 February 2016.

> *him to Republican frontrunner status—are thought to be uneducated, coarse, and intolerant of immigrants [zero out of three in my case]. College students, on the other hand, are so tolerant their tolerance is borderline oppressive. Trump's backers despise the political correctness of liberal elites: students think liberal elites are closet reactionaries who disdain leftist goals and refuse to nominate black actors and actresses for Oscars. The two groups might possess a shared distrust of social progress—Trump people, because it's happening too quickly, and student protesters, because it's not happening quickly enough—but they are on opposite ends of that fight, and virtually all others.*

Not every college student is a SJW, and libertarians and conservatives least of all. Trump does have policies that make sense, although if you start from the standard presuppositions of our present much deformed age, you will have no idea what they are or how much sense they make. But it is very nice to see that even on an American university campus, Donald Trump's message is able to get through at least to some.

Via Instapundit[122] who, by the way, chose the following quote to highlight the article:

> *"For these students, Trump is not the leader of a political movement, but rather, a countercultural icon. To chant his name is to strike a blow against the ruling class on campus—the czars of political correctness—who are every bit as imperious and loathsome to them as the D.C.-GOP establishment is to the working class folks who see Trump as their champion."*

We working class folk have got to go somewhere, and to Trump we are now going, along with the occasional anti-PC student, and then some others like Rudy Giuliani and Art Laffer.

---

[122] pjmedia.com/instapundit, 23 February 2016.

The promise of Donald Trump
February 24, 2016

TRUMP WINS NEVADA

Now read below why it matters.

The title only one quarter gets what the story actually says: 'The Anti-Establishment Vote'.[123] If Trump represented "the establishment" I would be very happy to support the *status quo*. The following bits of an article you should read from end to end exactly picks up what I would say myself:

> *Trump supporters variously favor him because he is not of the Washington establishment, because he is politically incorrect, because he is unafraid to call it as he sees it, and because he is beholden to no one, to no Republican, to no Democrat, to no media icon, and to no conservative intellectual. Trump supporters reject groomed politicians who, together with their advisors, weigh the meaning of every word spoken and fear offense.*
>
> *Trump supporters do believe in limited government, a strong national defense, and free enterprise. They reject government solutions to economic problems and favor a restoration of a vibrant, free enterprise economy unfettered by excessive government regulation. They reject a foreign policy stymied by advocates of social justice who will not allow this nation to annihilate its terrorist enemies, to revoke the appeasement deal with Iran, and to rebuild American military might and alliances. They reject international trade bargains built on concepts of "managed trade" where select industry insiders with political clout are favored in lieu of a true free trade arrangement. They want to secure America's borders and ensure that the United States does not become a haven for terrorists. . . .*
>
> *Fundamentally Trump's supporters are fed up with all things characteristics of the Washington establishment. They do not want a candidate who can eloquently articulate viewpoints pleasing to their ears because they have watched politician after politician do that, then assume elected office only to betray the promises made. They want someone who has neither financial nor political ties to those in power, who will restore American greatness by courageously and unrelentingly breaking down all barriers to that greatness erected by those now in power and their cronies in the market.*

---

[123] newswithviews.com, 22 February 2016.

> *In short, they mean to take down the protectionist government that is, unleash the power of the private sector to restore American greatness, erect immigration limits and border security capable of stemming the flow of illegal aliens and terrorists, and rebuild American military might and power in the world. For that revolution, they seek a private sector titan not beholden to the Washington establishment. Trump perfectly fits that bill.*
>
> *In Trump, they find a person who speaks his mind fearlessly; who stands toe to toe with those tied to the Washington establishment and has no problem directly exposing their duplicity and weakness; who promises to shake things up in Washington such that barriers to economic growth, border protection, and a strong national defense are eliminated; who promises lower tax rates for corporations and individuals; and who plans to free the market rather than regulate it in politically preferred directions.*
>
> *. . .*
>
> *Trump is viewed as unapologetic, strong, and sincere, a man who gets things done rather than prattles on about what he will do without a sincere interest in doing what he says and without the stamina required to withstand stiff opposition. Trump is the antithesis of political correctness. Trump supporters are fed up with groomed politicians who profess to be possessed of an elite knowledge and skill but who do nothing consequential in office. They want to remove government from the control of the political class and vest it in those who are from outside the realm of politics, who are citizen politicians. They do not accept the legitimacy of the campaigners who hail from the political class and, so, they place little credence in the attacks they level against Trump.*

We may be wrong in believing that Trump can and will do the things that he has undertaken to do, but there is only one way to find out. The one certainty is that no one else would even try.

Time to embrace the inevitable
February 25, 2016

Here's the best advice from Roger Simon: 'The Republican Establishment Needs to Stop Worrying and Love the Donald.'[124]

I will highlight the particular para that is most to the point:

> *Now that Donald Trump has wiped the floor yet again with the other Republican candidates in the Nevada caucuses, it's time for the GOP to face reality — barring force majeure, they have a presidential candidate, like it or not.*
>
> *The so-called establishment has a choice: Get on the Trump bandwagon or try some desperate maneuver to stop him. But what would that be? A Rubio-Cruz ticket, assuming they would do it? At the time of this writing, the two men added together don't equal the Trump vote in Nevada — and that's even assuming their voters would hold, which is a risky assumption, given the current momentum. I mean — Donald won 46% of the Hispanics! Enough already.*
>
> *A lot of my Republican friends are depressed about this situation. They worry that Trump is not a real conservative. They cringe at his vulgarity. They are concerned he's a bully, even totalitarian.*
>
> *I'm not. And I am not depressed, even though I admire many of the other candidates in the race. Given the gravity of the situation, what Obama has done to this nation and the candidates being offered by the Democrats, a world class liar and a Eugene V. Debs retread, a personality as large as Donald may be necessary to revive our country. In fact, I think I'll take the "may" out of that.*

This is what I think the electorate senses and what the Republican establishment fears. Rather than being afraid that Donald will lose, many establishment folks, I suspect, are afraid he will win. It will not be business as usual and most human beings seek business as usual, especially successful ones. What, for example, is more conventional and unchanging than the Democratic Party? They have patented stasis under meaningless junk terms like "liberal" and "progressive." Nothing ever changes. Republicans

---

[124] pjmedia.com, 23 February 2016.

are at risk of doing the same thing with the word "conservative." If I hear another candidate claim to be the most "conservative," I think I'll bang my head against the table. I can't be the only one who feels that way.

So if I were a member of the Establishment, whatever that is, I would quit bellyaching, embrace Donald and make him my friend. He's ready and willing. If you bother to check that ultimate news source the Daily Mail, you'd see that already he is hobnobbing with such Republican stalwarts as Rudy Giuliani, Arthur Laffer and Steve Moore. Unless I missed it, I didn't notice the article mentioning David Axelrod or James Carville.

And listen to what Trump is actually saying. He's for lower taxes and a strong defense and he's not really against free trade. He just wants a better deal. Who wouldn't and who wouldn't assume he'd get a better one than the Obama crowd? Or the Bush crowd for that matter, on just about anything. He's also pro-life, despite soreheads like Erick Erickson screaming that Trump supports Planned Parenthood when he has said explicitly he does not support what they do on abortion, only on other women's health issues. Does Erickson oppose pap smears for cervical cancer? (Frankly, I don't want to know.)

People like Erickson and pundits far more sophisticated suffer from Trump Derangement Syndrome. Because he's not part of "Their Crowd" they can't really grasp what he's saying. Time to end that. Don't fight Donald. Be smart, co-opt him. Or, as we used to say, be there or be square. Next November depends on it.

And this comes via Ed Driscoll at Instapundit[125] so it's time the rest of you got with the program.

~

What if he's just as good as he thinks he is?
February 26, 2016

This is Scott Adams – the Scott Adams who draws Dilbert – explaining How to Spot a Narcissist (Trump Persuasion Series).[126] The caricature drawn here should be compared with the greatest Walter Mitty character of all time, the

---
[125] pjmedia.com/instapundit, 24 February 2016.
[126] blog.dilbert.com, 24 February 2016.

One who is president of the United States at the moment, a narcissist who may have broken the mould. Now for contrast.

> *Donald Trump is the most famous narcissist in the world. That fact probably seems obvious to you, given Trump's continuous self-promotion. Mental health experts agree with your assessment. Trump hits most of the checkboxes for the diagnosis.*
>
> *The biggest tell for narcissism is a belief that you are better than other people. For example, if Trump believed he could run for President – with almost no political experience – and dominate the Republican party in only a few short months, that would be an example of…*
>
> *Okay, wait. That one doesn't work. Apparently his self-image was spot-on in that one specific case. It was the rest of us who got that one wrong.*
>
> *But still, Trump obviously has an inflated self-image. For example, there was the time he thought he could transition from being a real estate developer to being a best-selling author of a book about negotiating, but then…shit. Okay, that example doesn't work.*
>
> *Okay, how about this example: Remember when Trump thought he could transition from developing real estate and being a best selling author to becoming a reality TV star and then…okay, forget that one. That sort of worked out for Trump.*
>
> *Um…okay, I have one. Remember all of the Trump real estate and casino businesses that failed? I think there were a handful of big failures. That's a terrible track record when you consider Trump's hundreds of successful projects that…shit. Okay, that example doesn't work when you put it in context.*
>
> *But the ego on that guy. For example, Trump thinks models are attracted to him. Models! Ha ha! And they are, but my point is that I forget what my point is. Something about his ego? Yes, that's it.*
>
> *Anyway, Trump thinks he is smarter than most people just because he has a high IQ and went to great schools. Usually that does mean you are smarter than 98% of the public, but in this case it was probably just luck, because obviously all of us are smarter than Trump. I mean, look at his haircut!*
>
> *Narcissists also seek attention from others. That is Trump all over! Compare his attention-seeking ways to other people who license their brands for a living. Those other people like to stay quiet or maybe say their brand is not so good. That is what good mental health looks like. But narcissist Trump*

actually promotes his brand every chance he gets, which is gross. Sure, it makes him a lot of money, but capitalism is about more than that. For example, something about the Fed.

Anyway, unlike Trump, the other candidates for President of the United States do not seek attention. Okay, technically they are seeking it as hard as they can, and failing. But to me, that seems exactly the same as not trying.

Narcissism is more than having an over-inflated ego and a need for attention. Narcissists also lack empathy. That's Trump all over. He has no empathy whatsoever. Sure, he says he loves wounded veterans, underemployed Americans, and even the undereducated. But you know all of that is lies.

How do you know? Simple! You know because you are far smarter than normal people. You might be an unrecognized genius, given your modesty. Maybe you're not the test-taking kind of genius, but you are definitely a beacon of common sense. For example, you know for sure which candidate would be the best president while idiots like me can only guess. In fact, you are so smart that you can peer into Trump's soul from a distance and see his lack of empathy. Impressive! And, I might add that you are an ace at diagnosing mental conditions despite your total lack of training in the field. You, my friend, are indeed better than other people because you see Trump for the over-inflated, uncaring buffoon that he is. And unlike Trump, you do not seek attention. So don't leave a comment below to showcase your brilliance.

Narcissism is definitely a thing. But we also need a name for the mental condition in which you believe you are so smart you can diagnose narcissism from a distance.

I won't call you a narcissist unless you state your opinion in a public comment forum and insult other voters and commenters as if you have no empathy. So don't do that.

"The most Australian-like presidential candidate in modern US history"
February 27, 2016

This is from the Steve Sailer open thread[127] on the Republican debate from someone commenting under the name "unpc downunder".

> Steve, you'll love the irony/national self-loathing in this one – Australian progressives are starting a petition to ban Trump from visiting Australia.
>
> Why is this ironic? because Trump is the most Australian-like presidential candidate in modern US history.
>
> Brash, blond, economic moderate and nationalist, tough on illegal immigration, concerned with pensions for veterans and little time for PC. He would probably be more at home in Queensland than Queens.

There was also this one which I found quite to the point, from "boomer expat".

> I live in Asia and when an Asian asks me about why Trump is popular, this is a way I use to explain it.
>
> If you really want to understand Trump's appeal, just look at the fact that 45% of US citizens don't pay taxes because they don't make enough due to jobs increasingly being low-level service work with many of the higher level jobs being taken by H1B.
>
> Then combine it with this scenario – imagine the head of Japan announces:
>
> 1. Japan is opening its borders and plans to make the majority of the country Chinese and Muslims
> 2. Japanese privilege classes will begin in all schools to combat Japanese racism and the country will begin eliminating Japanese cultural events as non-inclusive
> 3. Japanese will pay more taxes to subsidize these workers who for the most parting won't be pay taxes
> 4. Crime and terrorism will go up but that is unavoidable and Xenophobic to mention
> 5. When any business employs a majority of Japanese ethnics, there will be a discussion of the "Japanese problem"

---

[127] unz.com, 25 February 2016.

6. Preferences will be given in hiring to the newcomers

7. Any negative comments about what is going on will be clamped down on because if you don't like this cultural cleansing you are Hitler.

Now, honestly ask yourself how the Japanese would react to this plan? Add those two together and it gives you an idea of why people are backing Trump.

After that, they all say they understand his appeal and would never let that type of scenario develop in their own country.

I'm sure there is something wrong with the analogy but will have to dwell on it for a while to see if I can work it out.

~

They're beginning to get the point
February 28, 2016

There is now talk of Newt Gingrich as Trump's Chief of Staff. And Chris Christie has endorsed Trump for President. So slowly – very, very slowly – there is a drift towards seeing the point. How abysmal every alternative is.

This is from Peggy Noonan via Instapundit.[128] The last time she wrote something I truly agreed with may have been when Ronald Reagan was still president. But here I think she gets it. I am part of that buffered few but I also have a sense of how things change rapidly and I worry endlessly, and probably fruitlessly, about how things may end up. It may be too late, but then again maybe not.

> There are the protected and the unprotected. The protected make public policy. The unprotected live in it. The unprotected are starting to push back, powerfully.
>
> The protected are the accomplished, the secure, the successful—those who have power or access to it. They are protected from much of the roughness of the world. More to the point, they are protected from the world they have created. Again, they make public policy and have for some time.
>
> I want to call them the elite to load the rhetorical dice, but let's stick with the protected.

---

[128] pjmedia.com/instapundit, 27 February 2016.

They are figures in government, politics and media. They live in nice neighborhoods, safe ones. Their families function, their kids go to good schools, they've got some money. All of these things tend to isolate them, or provide buffers. Some of them—in Washington it is important officials in the executive branch or on the Hill; in Brussels, significant figures in the European Union—literally have their own security details.

Because they are protected they feel they can do pretty much anything, impose any reality. They're insulated from many of the effects of their own decisions.

One issue obviously roiling the U.S. and Western Europe is immigration. It is the issue of the moment, a real and concrete one but also a symbolic one: It stands for all the distance between governments and their citizens.

It is of course the issue that made Donald Trump.

Britain will probably leave the European Union over it. In truth immigration is one front in that battle, but it is the most salient because of the European refugee crisis and the failure of the protected class to address it realistically and in a way that offers safety to the unprotected.

If you are an unprotected American—one with limited resources and negligible access to power—you have absorbed some lessons from the past 20 years' experience of illegal immigration. You know the Democrats won't protect you and the Republicans won't help you. Both parties refused to control the border. The Republicans were afraid of being called illiberal, racist, of losing a demographic for a generation. The Democrats wanted to keep the issue alive to use it as a wedge against the Republicans and to establish themselves as owners of the Hispanic vote.

Many Americans suffered from illegal immigration—its impact on labor markets, financial costs, crime, the sense that the rule of law was collapsing. But the protected did fine—more workers at lower wages. No effect of illegal immigration was likely to hurt them personally.

It was good for the protected. But the unprotected watched and saw. They realized the protected were not looking out for them, and they inferred that they were not looking out for the country, either.

The unprotected came to think they owed the establishment—another word for the protected—nothing, no particular loyalty, no old allegiance.

> *Mr. Trump came from that. . . . You see the dynamic in many spheres. In Hollywood, as we still call it, where they make our rough culture, they are careful to protect their own children from its ill effects. In places with failing schools, they choose not to help them through the school liberation movement—charter schools, choice, etc.—because they fear to go up against the most reactionary professional group in America, the teachers unions. They let the public schools flounder. But their children go to the best private schools.*
>
> *This is a terrible feature of our age—that we are governed by protected people who don't seem to care that much about their unprotected fellow citizens.*

These are the progressive internationalists who are ruining the world on behalf of their one-world open borders ideology. Europe is now the most advanced experiment with Southern California a close runner up. But unlike some experiments, this only goes in one direction. If it turns out not to work, there is nothing you can do to fix it.[129]

~

The party of closed borders will win the election
February 29, 2016

First there's what Glenn Reynolds wrote[130] and he would know:

> *The GOP establishment has an almost-religious attachment to open immigration. It appears to be their only firm principle. It's what led to Trump's rise.*

And then there are the three top rated comments. First:

> *"It appears to be their only firm principle."*
> *GOP principles:*
> *1. Have contempt for conservative voters.*
> *2. Go after conservative members of Congress ruthlessly, but treat Democrats with respect.*
> *3. Do whatever it takes to win the love of the main stream media.*
> *4. Always believe in more government.*
> *5. Immigration, immigration, immigration.*

---

[129] breitbart.com, 27 February 2016.
[130] pjmedia.com/instapundit, 27 February 2016.

Second:

> *Get replaced by a foreigner brought in to do your job and see how you feel. You expect people to vote to give their jobs to cheaper immigrants?*

And third:

> *I dislike Trump, and I distrust whatever his politics are. That said, I believe him on the immigration issue, which as we are seeing in Europe, is existential.*

That's it. Says it all. The party of closed borders will win the election but if it weren't for Trump, no such party would exist.

~

Super Wednesday
March 1, 2016

As it will appear to us who live just this side of the dateline – Tuesday in the US is already Wednesday here. This is the lay of the land:

> *CNN: TRUMP AT 49%...*
> *Finds Ally in Delegate Selection System...*
> *Small Biz Owners Say Donald Top Choice...*
> *VIDEO: Reporter Grabs Secret Service Agent Throat at Trump Rally...*
> *ICE Union On Gang of Eight: 'It's as if criminals wrote it themselves'...*
> *Rubio Doesn't Realize Energy Policy He Supports Already Been Enacted...*
> *INGRAHAM: The GOP Establishment Suicide...*
> *Republican Senator Believes More Candidates Will Enter...*

And for those who are wondering what Hillary is up to:

> *Clinton Rape Accuser Thanks Lady Gaga For 'Overwhelming Performance'...*
> *WASH POST LEAD TUES: Hillary prepares to take on Trump in general election...*
> *NYT PAGE ONE: Plan to Defeat Him...*
> *HILLARY HEADACHE: AIDES IN CROSSHAIRS AFTER LAST DOC DUMP...*
> *Cheryl Mills still has top-secret status despite FBI probe...*
> *GOVT WITHHOLDS MORE EMAILS, INCLUDING OBAMA CORRESPONDENCE...*

1,800 Reasons Why Controversy Is Far From Over…
STILL IGNORING TRAVELING PRESS…
What if Hill is indicted?
BEGALA: Enthusiasm gap 'keeps me up at night'…

And what amazes me more than anything else are the number of people supposedly on the right who would vote for Hillary ahead of Trump. And for added interest, there is this Why they hate Trump[131] written by someone who doesn't much seem to like Trump either. But he does include this which is much to the point about a lot of things:

"BLITZER: *You said this about the ongoing conflict between the Israelis and the Palestinians – I'm quoting you now: 'Let me be sort of a neutral guy. I don't want to say whose fault it is, I don't think it helps.'*

"TRUMP: *Right.*

"BLITZER: *Here's the question. How do you remain neutral when the U.S. considers Israel to be America's closest ally in the Middle East?*

"TRUMP: *Well, first of all, I don't think they do under President Obama because I think he's treated Israel horribly, all right? I think he's treated Israel horribly. I was the grand marshall down 5th Avenue a number of years ago for the Israeli Day Parade, I have very close ties to Israel. I've received the Tree of Life Award and many of the greatest awards given by Israel.*

"*As president, however, there's nothing that I would rather do to bring peace to Israel and its neighbors generally. And I think it serves no purpose to say that you have a good guy and a bad guy.*

"*Now, I may not be successful in doing it. It's probably the toughest negotiation anywhere in the world of any kind. OK? But it doesn't help if I start saying, "I am very pro-Israel, very pro, more than anybody on this stage." But it doesn't do any good to start demeaning the neighbors, because I would love to do something with regard to negotiating peace, finally, for Israel and for their neighbors.*

"*And I can't do that as well – as a negotiator, I cannot do that as well if I'm taking … sides.*"

Whatever it is, it is not anti-Israel and does sound like someone who

---
[131] original.antiwar.com, 29 February 2016.

might know a thing or two about negotiation. But the last word will go to Steve Hayward at Powerline, 'Apologia Pro Vita Trump'.[132] He really is sorry that it has come to this, but this is what it has come to:

> *I'm sure lots of voters don't think Trump has what it takes to be a great president. But he is the ideal person to disrupt a political class that deserves a hard smash in the mouth. This is why Trump is going to win.*

And then, of course, there are others who do think he has what it takes to be a great president indeed. I can only hope we are going to find out for ourselves over the next eight years.

~

Know thine enemy
March 3, 2016

There is now a battle for the soul of conservatism, whether our Western way of life can be maintained, or whether we are going to be swamped by ideologues and profiteers at the cost of how we have lived. I keep using the image of progressive internationalists as the enemy, you know, the one-world, open-borders, the-nation-as-a-bus-depot sort of people, and it is a shared vision of both sides of politics, the Democrats more openly, with the Republicans the ones who shout, whatever you do, don't throw us into the briar patch. Which is why we find How the GOP Insiders Plan to Steal the Nod from Trump.[133]

> *Despite a growing string of victories in the Republican primaries, the DC-Wall Street cabal that has dominated the GOP since 1988 has no intention of letting the billionaire real estate mogul be nominated. None other than Karl Rove has insisted the stop-Trump effort is not too late and can succeed.*
>
> *A new superPAC has dumped $10 million dollars into blistering negative TV ads against Trump in the last three days. The Koch brothers and their associates deny funding the effort but they denials are questionable at best. The New York Times reported Sunday that the Rubio and Kasich campaigns are now openly planning on a 'brokered convention" to stop*

---

[132] powerlineblog.com, 29 February 2016.
[133] breitbart.com, 1 March 2016.

> Trump in the back rooms in Cleveland. The New York Daily News reported that Barbara Bush has vowed revenge against Trump for ending the "low energy" campaign of her son Jeb, the anointed one and that the Bush clan is all-in in the effort to stop Trump. The News reported that Jeb may transfer the $25 to $30 million in SuperPAC funds he has left to an anti-Trump effort.

Trump thus not only must campaign against the Democrats, he will have to campaign against many in "his own" party who do not seem to be interested in backing someone who really could win it all in a big way. There is a realignment of politics happening, as many of us are finally waking up to the fact that the water has continually been heating and is almost on the boil.

UPDATE: If you are interested in a true understanding of Donald Trump, read 'The Donald Trump Playboy interview'[134] from 25 years ago. Long but brilliant. You will learn a lot, and not just about him. Here is a sample, but you owe it to yourself to read it all.

> *Sometimes you sound like a Presidential candidate stirring up the voters.*
>
> *I don't want the Presidency. I'm going to help a lot of people with my foundation-and for me, the grass isn't always greener.*
>
> *But if the grass ever did look greener, which political party do you think you'd be more comfortable with?*
>
> *Well, if I ever ran for office, I'd do better as a Democrat than as a Republican-and that's not because I'd be more Republican-and that's not because I'd be more liberal, because I'm conservative. But the working guy would elect me. He likes me. When I walk down the street, those cabbies start yelling out their windows.*

He wasn't running for a thing but described himself as a conservative. What more could anyone want?

---

[134] filthy.media/donald-trump-playboy-interview

Why does no one know this about Donald Trump?
March 8, 2016

Here's the heading: 'Trump insisted on including Jews and blacks at Palm Beach golf course in 1990s'[135] and here's what it says:

> *"When Donald opened his club in Palm Beach called Mar-a-Lago, he insisted on accepting Jews and blacks even though other clubs in Palm Beach to this day discriminate against blacks and Jews. The old guard in Palm Beach was outraged that Donald would accept blacks and Jews so that's the real Donald Trump that I know."*

Is there more to the story? There always is, but not a bad place to start. Read the full article, but it's the kind of principled position that makes him so unusual in the world of politics as it has become.

~

Obama is beginning to see how his legacy will be written and he doesn't like it
March 11, 2016

A couple of stories, mostly straws in a wind that will become more hurricane-like after January 2017. First this one, 'Obama: Trump's rise not my fault'.[136] A Trump presidency will be due to Obama, worst president in American history that he is. But the whiny sot is already recognising that the history books may not end up treating him all that well:

> *Some well-known Republicans have said, however, Obama bears responsibility for voters' affinity to Trump.*
>
> *"After seven years of the cool, weak and endlessly nuanced 'no drama Obama,' voters are looking for a strong leader who speaks in short, declarative sentences," Louisiana Gov. Bobby Jindal (R) wrote in a Wall Street Journal op-ed this month.*
>
> *"Middle-class incomes are stagnant, and radical Islam is on the march across*

---

[135] netrightdaily.com, 3 March 2016.
[136] thehill.com, 10 March 2016.

the Middle East," the former 2016 candidate wrote. "No wonder voters are responding to someone who promises to make America great again."

But the more interesting story is how difficult it is to be in public life and criticise Obama. This story is noteworthy because someone actually tried to say what they really thought: Mike Ditka is replaced on ESPN Sunday NFL Countdown one week after calling Obama the 'worst president we've ever had'.[137] You have to appreciate that he is one of the greatest football players in American history but not even someone with his name and background could withstand the instant blowback:

> *Mike Ditka will be replaced as a panelist on ESPN's Sunday NFL Countdown, it has been revealed.*
>
> *The announcement came less than a week after Ditka, both a former player and coach for the Chicago Bears, revealed he believed Barack Obama was the worst president 'we've ever had'.*
>
> *Ditka, who has been a main panelist for the ESPN show since 2006, said Obama was a 'fine man' but not a leader when he went on WABC'S The Bernie & Sid Show last Thursday. . . .*
>
> *'He's not a leader. This country needs leadership. It needs direction. It needs somebody that steps up front.'*

You cannot say this now in the United States but soon you will be and everyone will be saying it. Worst president in history, and this is even said by people who remember Jimmy Carter.

And now we can add this which is almost definitive, although it is only about Obama's one and only "accomplishment": NPR and Harvard say Obamacare is a complete failure.[138] Add that to the debt, deficits and unemployment and you have pretty well summed up the domestic disaster he has overseen.

---

[137] *Daily Mail Australia*, 10 March 2016.
[138] powerlineblog.com, 9 March 2016.

Sarah Palin on Ted Cruz – she doesn't seem to like him

March 11, 2016

It's from Sarah Palin's Facebook Page[139] where you can find all of the links to the points she makes.

> *GOP Majority Voters in Primary are Wayyyyyy Beneath Cruz, So Says Cruz.*
>
> ** Calling GOP frontrunner supporters "low information" disengaged voters, Ted Cruz's insinuation reeks of all the reasons America knows "the status quo has got to go." The arrogance of career politicians is something at which the rest of us chuckle, but Cruz's latest dig strays from humorous into downright nasty. Cruz is right, though – independent, America-first, commonsense conservatives supporting Donald Trump ARE "low information" when it comes to having any information on Cruz's ability to expand the conservative movement, beat Hillary Clinton, unify and lead the nation.*
>
> ** Where's information on any Cruz success whilst in his short, half-term U.S. Senate seat, proving his resume's advantage over another career politicians's lawyerly executive inexperience that includes never having created a single private sector job, but boasting of his constitutional law teacher creds? (Remember America experimented with that resume before; how'd that work out for the country?)*
>
> ** Where's info on his reasoning in inviting more illegal aliens to flood our porous borders by enticing families with benefits and literal gifts (like teddy bears and soccer balls)?*
>
> ** Any info on why he won't denounce his highest-profile campaign buddy, despite Glenn Beck's proclamation that he "hates" America's innocent victims of 9/11 and calls the families crybabies? nor hold accountable his campaign manager for abhorrent tactics that mirror Alinsky's Politics of Personal Destruction?*
>
> ** Info on why he continues to stand on stage with that most prominent supporter who slurs millions of patriotic Americans supporting the GOP frontrunner, calling them Nazi "brown shirts"?*
>
> ** Info on consistency with his big endorsement this week, as Carly tells it*

---

[139] www.facebook.com/sarahpalin, 11 March 2016.

like it is so very recently?

"Ted Cruz is just like any other politician. He says one thing in Manhattan, he says another thing in Iowa. He says whatever he needs to say to get elected, and then he's going to do as he pleases. I think people are tired of a political class that promises much and delivers much of the same." – Carly Fiorina 1/2/16

* Info on his support for his crony capitalists' insistence that he fast-track Obama's unbalanced trade agenda, then lied about it?

* Info on why he's fine with increasing U.S. debt?

*Info on how it helps make America great again by arrogantly disenfranchising this Primary season's majority voters who are fed-up, inspired, optimistic, and engaged? How does it help unify the party or the nation when that holier-than-thou narcissism manifests itself through negative, biting, deceptive tactics… when he's had so many opportunities to disavow his campaign's shenanigans and apologize for his own?

The information we've sought is nonexistent, thus "low information voters" comprising the GOP majority support Cruz staying in the Legislative branch, while hopefully gaining understanding of the private sector's need to reduce the big government he's a big part of.

Trump's energized, positive campaign has led to this record setting stat: of all 24 states that have voted so far, ALL smashed previous GOP turnout records! 4,347,317 votes nationwide for Trump already. Now THAT'S "enlarging the tent." Any info, Ted, on where you think that "disengaged" momentum will take us?

~

#NeverTrump
March 11, 2016

Apparently this is becoming a common hashtag among Republicans who will vote Clinton before they let a Donald Trump become President. The article is titled, 'What Would Hamilton Do?'[140] which is based on a request among established Republicans to answer the question, What's Wrong with Donald Trump? Before I continue, I will note that hundreds of emails is a

---

[140] weeklystandard.com, 21 March 2016.

drop in the ocean, but this is what we have:

> *Hundreds emailed; the breadth of response — across all regional, social, professional, and class divides and every conceivable wing of the party; and the depth of feeling, with her correspondents being "appalled, repulsed, afraid, and dismayed" at the prospect of Trump being either nominee or president. Their concerns included his authoritarian conduct, his lack of principle, his racism, his conduct toward women, his erratic behavior, and his potential access to the nuclear arsenal. They were party stalwarts who had voted Republican on a regular basis, served in Republican administrations, and raised money for and volunteered in campaigns.*

Out of which a profile emerged:

> *"I'm a 40-year-old National Review and Instapundit-reading conservative who has voted for the Republican in every election since 1996. I intend to vote for Cruz in the primary and would be happy to vote for Cruz or Rubio in November. My opinions about Hillary Clinton are about what you would expect, and if it's Hillary vs. Trump, I'll most likely vote Libertarian. I've spoken with many of my friends from my College Republican days and it seems they all have the same thoughts. I will never vote for Trump. Ever. And if that brings about the end of the GOP, so be it. Any party that picks Trump as its voice is not a party I want to be affiliated with. He has no moral compass and no abiding principles except for self-promotion. Being in the wilderness, politically speaking, is preferable to being complicit in the election of Donald Trump, and with it the destruction of the party I have supported my entire adult life."*

Well, let us get down to it then. First, nothing would give me greater pleasure than to destroy the Republican Party as it now is. As useless at protecting what matters to me as the Democrats. I will happily exchange your aimless and worthless hides for the millions who are seeking a refuge from the mess you have made of the United States.

Second, if Hillary Clinton President does not fill you with horror then you are dead from the neck up. Your views and your values are dead to me. You have nothing you can say that will get us to agree. Off you go, you Democrat numbskull.

Third, if you are looking for a moral compass, you will not find it looking inside your own misbegotten souls. You cannot see what is at stake and care little about preserving your own society as it was and as millions wish it to be. Every new refugee hostel should be put up within princincts that have voted Clinton in the next election and then we will see how things go in 2020.

Fourth, you have no idea what democracy means. One vote per person, and no more than one vote per person. If you really do side with those who seek a borderless USA, then you have no clue what a nation state is and why there really is value in a continuity between something called America in 1816 and that entity with the same name in 2016. What exactly you are trying to preserve by voting Clinton escapes me since absolutely nothing that truly matters will survive eight more years like the last eight have been.

Fifth, speaking about those last eight years, where have you been? The clamour you have been making about Obama all this time has been so quiet that I am not sure it could even have been detected. You have been given votes and seats year after year and have achieved nothing at all. So something else is going to be tried, and you can sit there with your hands covering your eyes but this is your fault since you allowed the system to break and did nothing to fix it.

So be off with you, you useless cowards. There is a new American about to be made, which we hope will be more like the old one you have been so willing to see go by.

~

Donald Trump's views on global warming
March 14, 2016

To run for high office you have to at least pretend to care about global warming. There are too many voters on both sides, even on the Republican side, who would make disbelief in AGW the single issue that determined their vote. For me, belief in global warming is as clear a sign of feeblemindedness as I would care to choose. It may be a reality, but it is one for which the evidence is virtually non-existent while the costs of trying to contain our carbon footprint so immense that skepticism is the only answer that makes sense. I therefore googled "Donald Trump and Global Warming" and the following article, from MSNBC, seems to be representative of his views.[141] And what makes this article so fascinating is that the article is trying to prove that Trump really thinks acceptance of AGW is utterly without merit although he is now beginning to pretend that he actually thinks it is important even though he doesn't really think so. The article was published in February. Here's the start.

> *Something unexpected is happening in the Republican presidential field.*
>
> *Leading GOP candidates once denied the reality of manmade climate change, but now they seem to be softening their posture and subtly embracing it.*
>
> *Democratic candidates Hillary Clinton and Bernie Sanders have long pledged to deepen President Obama's climate commitments if elected to office. The Republican candidates are still far from believers or political backers of the president's agenda. But a close parsing of their comments suggest the party of no is becoming the party of maybe – or perhaps even the party of yes.*
>
> *Take the case of Donald Trump, the billionaire contrarian and big winner of the New Hampshire primary on Tuesday. His denial of climate change has been a centerpiece of his act for years.*

Naturally, this is taken as a sign of ignorance and a lack of seriousness about dealing with one of our most important contemporary problems. But even though he is now trying to be more political in how he expresses his views, the folks at MSNBC are not going to be caught out in accepting his more recent statements as his real beliefs.

> *In tweets between 2012 and early 2015, he called climate change a "con job," a "canard," a "hoax," "bulls**t," and a concept "created by and for the Chinese in order to make U.S. manufacturing non-competitive."*

Now, however, Trump wants to be president so has begun to reverse course.

> *But as his political star has risen, he's changed his tune on global warming.*
>
> *He's walked back his wildest conspiracy theories and toned down his claims that cold weather somehow disproves global warming. He's also retired some of his most incendiary language ("con job," "canard") and wrapped what

---

[141] msnbc.com, 10 February 2016

remains in strong qualifiers.

In January, for example, after relentless mockery from the Sanders campaign, Trump told "Fox & Friends" that his tweet about climate change as a Chinese plot was a "joke."

So what does Trump say now?

"Obviously, I joke," he said. "I know much about climate change. I'd be — received environmental awards. And I often joke that this is done for the benefit of China."

The Republican front-runner still uses the word "hoax," deploying it on December 30 at a rally in Hilton Head, S.C. But he bookends it in un-Trump-like uncertainty. "A lot of it is a hoax," he said, according to ThinkProgress, a left-leaning news site "I mean, it's a money-making industry, OK? It's a hoax, a lot of it."

You can trace the change to September, when Trump delivered his most expansive comments on climate change. Speaking with conservative radio host Hugh Hewitt, he criticized Obama for trying "to solve a problem that I don't think in any major fashion exists."

And that is their last word on Trump. The rest of the article shows similar lack of belief on climate change by the other leading Republicans. Trump, however, has been the most consistent and hardline of the lot. Whatever he ends up saying from this point on, you may be sure what he really thinks is what he has most consistently said. If he thought global warming was a con job and bulls**t a year ago, there is nothing that has happened since to have changed his mind.

~

Dear Nick, Trump's appeal is not all that hard to see
March 15, 2016

Nick Cater has an article in *The Oz* today on Donald Trump's primary appeal is that he's not a politician.[142] This is his point:

The inconvenient truth for the political class is that in so far as Trump

---

[142] *The Australian*, 15 March 2016.

exploits hate, the principal object is not Hispanics, Muslims or homosexuals but them. The anger welling up from below is anger directed at urban sophisticates like themselves.

Americans regularly elect presidents who are not part of the political class. Eisenhower was the last, and military leaders are a consistent theme. It is executive experience that is valued, of which Obama has none at all while Trump has a lifetime of running things behind him. So for those who still don't get it, here's the list of **policy** issues that matter.

First border protection. Here's an article by Victor Davis Hanson, who because he works for *National Review*, cannot actually say he supports Trump (similar to working for Murdoch), but read the article and imagine him voting for anyone else: 'The Weirdness of Illegal Immigration.'[143] Note the word "if" that runs through the para:

> *If the border were to be closed, if immigration laws were enforced, if there were some reduction in legal immigration, if entry were to be meritocratic, if we reverted to the melting-pot ideal of assimilation, if we cut studies courses and jettisoned therapy and ideology for hard science, math, and English language, in just two decades one's particular ancestry would become irrelevant — the image of Oaxaca would be analogous to having a grandfather from Palermo or cousin from the Azores. In other words, things would work out fine.*

Second, the economy. Trump has spent a lifetime creating value for money. The American economy, like so many others, is being ruined by Keynesian Crony Capitalism, where the government decides how to use large proportions of our national savings and determines what ought to be built. The US is heading for a $20 trillion debt if it hasn't reached it already. Is there seriously anyone else within a thousand miles of being electable who has a greater likelihood of getting the American economy on the right track?

Third, foreign policy. Trump wants to rebuild America's national defence but is not in the business of nation building in third world countries. He will defend our interests, but with the additional thought that maybe those who America has been defending might chip in a bit in their own defence.

Fourth, he would get to choose the new justices for the Supreme Court.

---
[143] pjmedia.com, 13 March 2015.

Fifth, he not taken in by global warming. Sixth, has the ability to achieve his agenda because he knows how to get things done. Seventh, represents a return to traditional American values. Eighth, he opposes the thug tactics of the left. Ninth, he is the most non-politically correct politician in years and is unafraid of the American media.

Tenth, he is far and away more likely to win than any other Republican who might be nominated. Ted Cruz would lose to Hillary in a landslide and he is the only alternative. Trump is reconfiguring politics in a way that could renew the American system for a generation in the direction that might actually appeal to a conservative.

If you don't get it, you don't get it. But it really should not be that hard to see his appeal.

~

It could be worse, it could be a lot worse
March 16, 2016

Trump took a big step towards the nomination today in winning Florida and other states. This is by Victor Davis Hanson, 'Time to Calm Down about Trump'.[144] It's more than that. It is time that the Republican Party took him in and gave him their kindness and attention. The sub-head makes the point:

> *Trump is crude and politically clueless, but no more so than the Clintons, Sanders — or Obama*

I will merely add that working for the Chamber of Commerce I met many like him. They knew everything, and when you have a billion dollars and a boat that's bigger than my house, it's not hard to think that way. But I also always knew how wary they were of me. My job was to make their vague capitalist notions fit into a wider economic and social narrative. Few of those at the top of a business conglomerate would have been able to carry on a conversation at Treasury or with the Fair Work Commission. That is what I did. And we were the most free market, anti-Keynesian

---
144 *National Review*, 15 March 2016.

operation in the whole of employer politics.

Trump is at the top of the league as a business strategist, and has a number of ideas that are sound and others which are not. But his core message works for me. He would have been the perfect Chairman of my Economics Committee. He won't be a perfect president, but he will be better than any of the others who have sought the nomination on either side. Here is some sound advice from VDH:

> *I agree that it is disturbing that Trump does not grasp the nature of the nuclear triad, but so far he has not, as has Vice President Biden, claimed that a President FDR went on television in 1929 or, as has President Obama, that the Falklands are better known as the Maldives. His Trump vodka and steaks and eponymous schlock are a window into his narcissistic soul and his lack of concern with integrity; but I'll say more about the size of his ego when he says he can cool the planet and lower the seas, and that he is the one we've all been waiting for — accompanied by Latin mottos and faux-Greek columns. Trump has no team to speak of. Is that because the ego-driven Trump fancies himself a genius in the manner of "I think I'm a better speechwriter than my speechwriters. I know more about policies on any particular issue than my policy directors. And I'll tell you right now that I'm gonna think I'm a better political director than my political director." . . .*
>
> *Trump is hardly, by current standards, beyond the pale, much less that he is aberrant in U.S. presidential-campaign history. He is or is not as uncouth as Barack Obama, who has mocked the disabled, the wealthy, typical white people, the religious, and the purported clingers, and has compared opponents to Iranian theocrats and said that George W. Bush was "unpatriotic" — all as relish to wrecking America's health-care system, doubling the national debt, setting race relations back six decades, politicizing federal bureaucracies, ignoring federal law, and leaving the Middle East in shambles and our enemies on the ascendant.*
>
> *For those who point to Hillary Clinton as a more sober and judicious alternative, they might ask themselves whether the Trump financial shenanigans are on par with the quid pro quo Clinton Foundation scams, or whether the Trump companies are a bigger mess than Hillary's resets. True, a historical precedent could be set in the current campaign, but that would be if Hillary Clinton was the first presidential candidate indicted before the election, given that all her serial explanations about illegally using a private server to send and receive various classified information have only led to*

updated and further misleading backtracking, and will continue to do so until she is either charged or, for political reasons, exonerated.

In politics, like war, you go with the army you have.

~

What happens when the smartest man who has ever lived becomes president
March 17, 2016

The first of the Trump anti-Hillary ads and it's on foreign policy where a very large part of the battle for the presidency will be fought. After the last seven years and by then it will be eight, it will undoubtedly be time for a change, and Obama's former Secretary of State, the woman who oversaw the disaster in Libya and much else, will definitely not bring that change.

It's hard to imagine how bad Obama's foreign policy has been. Here in this article by Niall Ferguson we get some of it but hardly even here the full horror of its incompetence and arrogant stupidity. It's from *The Atlantic* and titled, 'Barack Obama's Revolution in Foreign Policy'.[145] The first para sets the scene:

> *It is a criticism I have heard from more than one person who has worked with President Obama: that he regards himself as the smartest person in the room—any room. Jeffrey Goldberg's fascinating article reveals that this is a considerable understatement. The president seems to think he is the smartest person in the world, perhaps ever.*

And after traipsing through Obama's deep thoughts on foreign policy, this is where we end.

> *If you think you are smarter than every foreign-policy expert in the room, any room, then it is tempting to make up your own grand strategy. That is what Obama has done, to an extent that even his critics underestimate. There is no "Obama doctrine"; rather, we see here a full-blown revolution in American foreign policy. And this revolution can be summed up as follows: The foes shall become friends, and the friends foes. . . .*

---

[145] *The Atlantic*, 13 March 2016.

If the arc of history is in fact bending toward Islamic extremism, sectarian conflict, networks of terrorism, and regional nuclear-arms races, then the 44th president will turn out to have been rather less smart than the foreign-policy establishment he so loftily disdains.

A lot of people will die as these forces work themselves out. Some new balance will eventually be established, but the likelihood that it will be anything like what the rest of us would like is very unlikely indeed.

~

V for Victory
March 17, 2016

I was going to give Donald a day off but came across this article from *The Daily Telegraph* on Drudge of all places, under the heading 'Trump Down Under'.[146] The same zombie Murdoch press that has brought us Malcolm as PM is using its resources to oppose Trump for President. I actually noticed the moment in the press conference yesterday when Trump held his two fingers up which was actually a gesture of no significance. But it did occur to me that if you were the sort of media organisation that liked to run anti-Trump stories, and of course if you were either in England or Australia since the gesture has no negative meaning in North America, then there it was. But then again, there it was when Churchill was doing the same during the war.

~

Commentators are insulated from the ramifications of failure
March 18, 2016

The Ruling Class Is King George III[147] which has as its sub-head, "The 2016 cycle has seen an utter collapse of the established order of things", wherein we find this very pertinent remark:

Politics is a business often insulated from the ramifications of failure. Like

---
[146] *The Daily Telegraph*, 18 March 2016.
[147] *The Federalist*, 10 March 2016.

> an ESPN commentator who is always wrong, the commentariat and the consultant class are not penalized for making mistakes with the frequency of people who pick stocks or games in Vegas. But the mistakes made this cycle are going to resonate because they reveal how distant the ruling class was from the people — that they might as well be separated by an ocean.
>
> If you are someone who lives in and among the elite, ask yourself if you know anyone legitimately supporting the two leading candidates for the Republican nomination — people who think Donald Trump is a good leader, or that Ted Cruz is a good man. If the answer is no, re-examine whether the knowledge you bring to this race is accurate, or skewed by the bubble that surrounds you, which kept suggesting all the way to the end that Jeb Bush, Scott Walker, or Marco Rubio could happen. Because they are not going to happen.

Of course, if you know me, you know someone who supports Trump. And I, as it happens, know one other who supports Trump. But we are very hard to find among the highly educated, I can tell you that. A Trump majority would occur in almost no media organisation in the world and on virtually no university campus, even restricting the ballot to those who teach. So if not us, then who is it, and why are we so cut off from what others think?

~

Only a Republican could be this stupid
March 18, 2016

There is a cartoon of Uncle Sam with his head in his hands with a thought bubble above his head to the left that says "President Trump" and another thought bubble above his head to the right that says President Clinton. The cartoon makes sense only if you really are in a dilemma about Trump v Clinton, which means you are a Republican who is too stupid to be allowed to vote. No Democrat would ever be in doubt, and Hillary is a liar, crook and dyed in the wool leftist of the most plundering kind. There is literally no facet of Trump v Clinton that ends up on the Hillary side of the ledger. Such Republicans are Democrats at heart, lacking any genuine desire for the preservation of our Western way of life. Worrying about the effect on international trade or the future viability of the Republican Party are such irrelevancies that it only irritates me to have to listen to it.

So let me spell it out. The one and only issue is open borders. This belief that anyone can migrate anywhere and it won't make any difference of any kind is such a stupidity that I have to say that when I hear it I can only think I am dealing with political morons who are incapable of learning any lessons from the fantastic array of social instruction to be seen at every turn.

Europe at this very moment is being invaded and only a minority of these invaders are Syrian refugees with nowhere else to go. The news we get is minimal. Every so often the media is forced to cover some part of it, such as "Cologne", or "Malmo" or "Charlie Hebdo", but as rapidly as it is possible to go back to other things, it is dropped and nothing more is said. Were it not for Drudge, I would feel I would not know a thing about what is going on. We have in no sense a free press, and the ridicule that Trump pours on the people who are covering him warms me. It is you, who cannot see through the media attack squads that get me down. No writer for any Murdoch paper in the world – and aside from *The Daily Mail*, his are the best there are – will ever say a positive word about Trump. There is this migrating evil in the world, and you cannot find it in the news you read. Trump is a phenomenon because he, for very particular reasons, does not depend on the media or outside money to get his message across.

The progressive internationalism of our present day is being driven by George Soros. What you will find is this, which was published only last December:

> *Human Events' readers, in an online poll, recently voted billionaire financier George Soros "the single most destructive leftist demagogue in the country."*

Here is the first on the list of ten, but go on to read the entire article. If you don't know any of this already, you should ask yourself why that is:

> *1. Gives billions to left-wing causes: Soros started the Open Society Institute in 1993 as a way to spread his wealth to progressive causes. Using Open Society as a conduit, Soros has given more than $7 billion to a who's who of left-wing groups. This partial list of recipients of Soros' money says it all: ACORN, Apollo Alliance, National Council of La Raza, Tides Foundation, Huffington Post, Southern Poverty Law Center, Soujourners, People for the American Way, Planned Parenthood, and the National Organization for Women.*

The American political system is driven by money and Soros is hardly the only one of his class and wealth who are driving this agenda. The graft and outright thievery of Hillary Clinton is no longer even hidden. She is a tool of the progressive internationalist cause. These people really do want to ruin your way of life, and it is not incidental. This is what they want to do. If you think they are well meaning socialists who want only the best for everyone, you are simply deluded. Billionaire socialists is not how to think of a working class movement. Our Western way of life – our "white privilege" – is being put to the torch and there is hardly a one amongst us who is willing to fight this one out.

But at least there is one, and he has support, and the way things are going there will soon be more. Whether there will be enough and whether it is even still possible to save ourselves, is yet to be determined. But if you cannot see what's going on, if you really cannot see what is going on, then you will just have to keep your heads in the sand.

And it is here that left and right meet. Let me finish with a quote from Murray Rothbard discussing Ludwig von Mises in a little booklet titled, 'The Clash of Group Interests'.[148] The "consideration" referred to is how individuals continue to examine only their short-term interests and fail to see the long-run as clearly as Mises does.

> *This consideration becomes still more poignant in the noble and surprising essay, "The Freedom to Move as an International Problem," newly translated from a 1935 newspaper in Vienna. It is surprising because it presents a remarkably sharp attack on the immigration barriers erected by the United States and the British Dominions. For Mises trenchantly identifies these barriers as creating a ruling class elite, albeit a large one, in which workers in a particular geographical area with a high standard of living, use the State to keep immigrants from lower-wage areas out, thereby freezing the latter into a permanently lower wage. Mises correctly adds that, contrary to the Marxian myth of the international solidarity of the proletariat, it is the unions in the high living standard countries who have lobbied for the immigration restrictions. Mises is hard-hitting on the privileges conferred by immigration barriers: 'The oft-referred-to 'miracle' of the high wages in the United States and Australia may be explained simply by the policy of trying to prevent a new immigration. For decades*

---

[148] mises.org, 15 June 1978.

people have not dared to discuss these things in Europe." Mises concludes his essay with an implicit justification of overcrowded Europe making war upon the restrictive countries: "This is a problem of the right of immigration into the largest and most productive lands.... Without the reestablishment of freedom of migration throughout the world, there can be no lasting peace."

World peace through open borders, and cheaper labour as well. If these ideas weren't so unbelievably dangerous you would want to laugh at how stupid this is. Soros and Mises, left and right united in trying to end the civilisation of the West.

~

Replying to a #NeverTrump jerk
March 19, 2016

Another of these self-important fools who shows up under the heading of 'Why I'm Backing #NeverTrump: A "Cuckservative" Speaks'.[149] From the comments section to the post:

> *Too stupid for words. The whole point of the primary season is to fight for your guy (Walker, Cruz and Fiorina for me) and then absolutely most important of all, back whoever comes out on top, or else you are handing it to the Alinsky-communist Imelda Marcos serial mega-criminal Hillary Clinton, and NOBODY CAN BE THAT FRICKING STUPID! I just want to say go to stinking Hell to every person who can't get over the ridiculous mountains they keep making out of Trump molehills.*

> *Every time he reacts to criticism by doing something ridiculous like calling his critic ugly I say fine with me, because I know that it isn't just narcissism, that he feels that exact same visceral protectiveness for the country. THAT is what his blow-ups about killing the families of terrorists is about, to which I say it is about damned time. We have had eight years of a president who absolutely hates this country and face another four years of a woman who shares the exact same Islamophilic Alinsky communism. Two presidents in a row who are literal stinking communists, both direct acolytes of the leading American communist of the 20th century, and Stephanie is worried about Trump's lack of refinement.*

---

[149] therightgeek.blogspot.com.au, 18 March 2016.

> *Sorry Stephanie, but your judgment is insane at the CRUDEST level, you and all the other "never Trumpers." Absolutely horrible. Destroyers. Vapid, ludicrous, and self-centered beyond belief. Your moral posturing will be offended. Too bad. How about the survival of the nation?*

We'll do everything to save the country except get our nails dirty. Truly beneath contempt. There are plenty of other comments just like this one at the link.

~

Is Trump Derangement Syndrome at an end?
March 21, 2016

Hope so. From Roger Simon:[150]

> *I was heartened to read on Fox News today: "Donald Trump will reportedly meet Monday in Washington with nearly two dozen influential Republicans, with the apparent hope of improving relations with the GOP establishment."*
>
> *His supporters should not panic. I predict this is not the great sell-out. The meeting was arranged by Senator Jeff Sessions, the man said to have the greatest influence on Trump and not one known for selling out. This could be the beginning... even if a tentative one... of the end of Trump Derangement Syndrome and some kind of reconciliation.*

I have to admit quite some dismay over the reaction to Trump. Style over substance seems to matter much too much for their and our good among the policy establishment. Therefore it is important that they consider this, also from Simon:

> *Will and others are suffering from such acute Trump Derangement Syndrome that they don't allow themselves to acknowledge the obvious — most of Trump's views, his current ones anyway, fall well within the conservative mainstream.*

Add to that the certainty that no one else even has a ghost of a chance to beat Hillary, it really has been a shambles.

---
[150] pjmedia.com, 20 March 2016.

Donald Trump speaks on Israel
March 22, 2016

I thought this video of Donald Trump speaking at AIPAC (the American Israel Public Affairs Committee), might be worth seeing on its own rather than as an update to my previous post on Trump Derangement Syndrome. Aside from this being a speech that puts the state of New York into play in November, it has clearly been worked on by others in his foreign policy team. It is both sophisticated and measured, but it is also from the heart. For a change, a conviction politician in the mould of Margaret Thatcher, but someone, also like her, who can get things done and is every inch a conservative. It's less than half an hour long, and here you will discover a Donald Trump you have not seen before.

UPDATE: From *The American Spectator*, which begins with the now pro forma declaration of a preference for Cruz: 'Republicans: Who are You?'.[151] And this is the choice. First on the Republican side:

> *The people who attend Trump rallies and vote for him generally are conservative — fiscally and culturally. They hate big government, they are highly patriotic and wave flags, they hate taxes, affirmative action, gun control, government debt, climate change deals that destroy American jobs, government waste, welfare, political correctness, trade deals they think give away the store, and illegal immigration. They are people who work for a living, are economically stressed out, and see what Obama has done to America economically and culturally and they don't like it at all. You'd be surprised how many blacks, veterans, soccer moms, and legal immigrants you see at a Trump rally.*

And then there is Hillary:

> *Now many in the party are making the absurd argument that even Hillary Clinton in the White House would be better than Trump.*

> *Huh? This is the Hillary Clinton that wants to raise tax rates to 50 percent or more, is in favor of abortion on demand with no exceptions, wants trillions of dollars of new spending and debt, would shut down America's oil and gas and coal production, will double down on Obamacare, and was the architect of the disastrous Obama foreign policy of leading from behind. Other than that, apparently, she's conservative enough.*

---

[151] *The American Spectator*, 21 March 2016.

These independent think-for-themselves types who call themselves conservative but would vote for Hillary give me the impression they have never thought anything not first endorsed by the ABC.

~

"It is not necessary to change. Survival is not mandatory"
March 22, 2016

It has been frightening to go through the usual blogs I consult to find unanimity – 100% unanimity – in their opposition to Donald Trump as President. I do find it upsetting, but I am used to it, having had the same experience with Margaret Thatcher in 1979 and Ronald Reagan in 1980. The same again in opposing Obama in 2008 and 2012, where I don't recall anyone I personally knew or regularly read going for McCain and Romney. I therefore went looking today at The Diplomad who has been pretty reliable up until now, but then again, so has everyone else, up until now. And this is his conclusion, found here:[152]

> *For now, I'll go with Donald Trump.*

Pretty good, and a standout for me, making me feel I can trust him when things are less clear cut than now. He has more explanation for his view, always worth listening to in the past, and apparently still is:

> *I had been sitting uncomfortably on the fence re the GOP candidates. After listening to the Romney speech and the other "establishment" types, and hearing the anchor pundits, the pundit anchors, and all the other assorted wise ones, I have jumped off the fence. I have landed in Trump's farm. He is not perfect, far from it. I might even change my mind, but for now I support Trump.*
>
> *I don't know if Trump will be terrible; I do know that what we have right now is horrible beyond words. I can't bear the thought of a Hillary presidency. I know, I know. I have seen the advice about letting the Dems have the White House, and the GOP will hold the Congress, and thus freeze Hillary in place. Don't buy it. We have seen what has happened*

---
[152] thediplomad.com, 3 March 2016.

> over the past few years when the Dems did not have the Congress; we have seen the enormous damage that a progressive President can do even without Congressional approval. In addition, we have seen that the GOP members of the Washington Cartel refuse to fight Obama on what counts. So, I don't want another Democratic White House.

That was on March 3rd and he has not recanted thus far. Most intriguing, almost all of the commenters have agreed with his decision, and one has even given me a real laugh:

> I am reminded of W. Edwards Deeming's famous quote: 'It is not necessary to change. Survival is not mandatory.'
>
> So the GOP establishment's much anticipated comeback strategy is to drag from the political grave reserved for failed presidential nominees the man who could not get out, or win, sufficient votes in 2012, to stage a hit on Trump, who is winning, and in the process drawing out new GOP voters, all when the DNC's turnout is collapsing.
>
> Seriously, what could possibly go wrong? The stupidity is breathtaking.

Beyond insanity.

~

What now?
March 23, 2016

We all know the news:

> EXPLOSIONS ROCK BRUSSELS AIRPORT, SUBWAY…
> 'Allahu Akbar'…
> RAIDS UNDERWAY ACROSS BELGIUM…
> 'Shocking' Unpreparedness…
> INTERIOR MINISTER: 'Never could have imagined something of this scale'…
> Brussels Ran Ad Mocking Notion of Islamic Violence 2 Months Ago…
> FLASHBACK: ISIS Says Paris 'Start of Storm'…
> MAG: Islamic State Overwhelming European Counterterrorism Forces…
> Geert Wilders: 'We Ain't Seen Nothin Yet'…
> Belgium beefs up security at nuke plants…

> *Aftermath footage shows terrified travelers cowering behind suitcases…*
> *Europe vows to defend democracy on 'black day'…*
> *American missionaries, military family among wounded…*
> *Attack narrowly missed two visiting U.S. Senators…*
> *Attacks Fuel Debate Over Migrants in Fractured Europe…*

The real questions are, what do they want and what do we do?

AND THE VIEWS OF DONALD TRUMP: From Piers Morgan and in *The Daily Mail*: 'When it comes to terror, isn't it time we started listening seriously to Trump?'[153]

> *Trump told me countries must tighten their borders in light of these terror attacks, especially to anyone related to an ISIS fighter in Syria.*
>
> *Is he so wrong?*
>
> *He told me he wants law-abiding Muslims to root out the extremists in their midst, expressing his bafflement and anger that someone like Abdeslam was able to hide for so long in the very part of Brussels he had previously lived.*
>
> *Is he so wrong?*
>
> *He told me America must make it far harder for illegal immigrants to enter the U.S. and thinks European countries should follow suit.*
>
> *Is he so wrong?*
>
> *He told me he believes there are now areas of many major European cities which have become poisonous breeding grounds for radicalized Islamic terror.*
>
> *Is he so wrong?*

Or we could just stand still and do nothing.

~

Do you think that just maybe he's on to something?
March 23, 2016

This was published on January 27 in *The New York Times*: 'Donald Trump Finds New City to Insult: Brussels'.[154] It opens:

---

[153] *Daily Mail*, 23 March 2016
[154] *The New York Times*, 27 January 2016.

He incensed Paris and London by saying that some of their neighborhoods were so overrun with radicals that the police were too scared to enter.

He raised Scottish tempers by threatening to pull the plug on his investments there, including his luxury golf courses, if British politicians barred him from entering Britain.

Now Donald J. Trump has upset the already beleaguered people of Belgium, calling its capital, Brussels, "a hellhole."

Asked by the Fox Business Network anchor Maria Bartiromo about the feasibility of his proposal to bar foreign Muslims from entering the United States, Mr. Trump argued that Belgium and France had been blighted by the failure of Muslims in these countries to integrate.

"There is something going on, Maria," he said. "Go to Brussels. Go to Paris. Go to different places. There is something going on and it's not good, where they want Shariah law, where they want this, where they want things that — you know, there has to be some assimilation. There is no assimilation. There is something bad going on."

Warming to his theme, he added that Brussels was in a particularly dire state. "You go to Brussels — I was in Brussels a long time ago, 20 years ago, so beautiful, everything is so beautiful — it's like living in a hellhole right now," Mr. Trump continued.

Feel free to read the entire article online.

~

You know, I cannot even begin to think of a title that can capture how surreal this is
March 26, 2016

The story comes with a title that exactly captures what an American president can now say in public: OBAMA: 'THERE'S LITTLE DIFFERENCE BETWEEN COMMUNISM AND CAPITALISM'.[155] And it is not just that the American president is a vacuous cypher, but that it has been evident from the beginning that everything he said today is what

---

[155] infowars.com, 25 March 2016.

he has always believed. That it will only be the usual suspects who are riled by these words that is the disaster. Since he can say them without much worry about capsizing his presidential boat, you now know a very great deal about the country that elected him, its education system, and possibly about why the American economy refuses to recover.

> *Obama responded to a question about nonprofit community organizations and the necessity of attracting funding from both the public and private sectors.*
>
> *"So often in the past there has been a division between left and right, between capitalists and communists or socialists, and especially in the Americas, that's been a big debate," Obama said.*
>
> *"Those are interesting intellectual arguments, but I think for your generation, you should be practical and just choose from what works. You don't have to worry about whether it really fits into socialist theory or capitalist theory. You should just decide what works," he added.*
>
> *Obama went on to praise Cuba's socialist system under dictator Raúl Castro, touting the country's free access to basic education and health care, although he acknowledged that Havana itself "looks like it did in the 1950s" because the economy is "not working".*

A phenomenon of idiocy. And it is not just the march through the institutions, but comes right down to the way we teach economics that he can be as ignorant as he is since it is an ignorance now shared with many. That the article merely states that Obama "has stoked controversy" shows even the writer of the story sees nothing much out of the ordinary. It's not even the feature story at Drudge where this was found.

~

None of my best friends are Trump supporters
March 29, 2016

And more's the pity, it's lonely out here. The following is an article along these lines of some interest: 'Some of my best friends are Trump supporters'.[156] The writer is Oleg Atbashian, a former denizen of the Soviet Union. It is

---

[156] *American Thinker*, 28 March 2016.

worth reading through, but I will focus on this bit on how writers in the media never seem to come across Trump supporters:

> *There's a big probability that Trump supporters are, in fact, all around them, even in their own families — and the reason why these writers don't know it, is their own snobbery. No one likes to be called stupid, his IQ questioned, or presumed to be an unthinking herd animal, and many simply don't have the time to stop and explain their reasons whenever a #Nevertrump activist feels like trashing Trump voters. Many simply choose to remain silent. . . .*
>
> *Trump has consistently polled better on anonymous online polls than on phone surveys because some of his supporters were unwilling to identify themselves publicly. In other words, public shaming didn't unwean Trump from his supporters but caused them to go underground.*
>
> *Doesn't this also describe how the majority of Americans have felt in recent decades, being constantly shamed into silence by the "progressive" media, education, and the cultural establishment? I know this too well, having worked in New York's "progressive" corporate environment. My co-workers would ask me about life in the USSR and I would tell them exactly what I thought about socialism and political correctness until I realized that most of them didn't like my answers and I was only hurting myself by speaking my mind. Some gave me frightened looks, others stopped talking with me. I might as well have told them that life in the USSR was similar to life in New York, where people had to learn to keep their mouths shut and to look over their shoulders before saying anything remotely political. So much for emigrating into a free country. It felt like history was about to repeat itself. Until now.*

Actually, nothing has changed. The sensational ganging up on Trump is incredible. I can now see he has only a minimal chance of winning in November, but for all that he has more chance than any other Republican. When you see every news media network, including the Murdoch empire and Fox, gunning for him, when you find virtually every "conservative" site from *National Review* to Powerline out to see him lose, when you see so many so-called conservatives say they would rather see Hillary win than Trump, when you see a virtual absence of positive comment anywhere, you do have to appreciate how deep the resentment is that drives his campaign. He might still win, and if he does he will owe no one anything, which will be the best thing about the administration he oversees.

The problem is that most people are too young to remember the world before it went insane

March 30, 2016

My thoughts on the photo story of Ivanka Trump, her husband and children in a normal mother, father, kids relationship,[157] on the day she came home with their third child. It is just like how it used to be. And then there is the picture of Donald Trump with his grandchildren having an Easter lunch. Many people can any longer relate to such a world.

~

Trump and his New York values

April 3, 2016

I don't know if it is permissible for anyone to declare someone else's view the most sensible because it happens to be the same as theirs, but this piece on Trump in *The Weekend Oz* by John O'Sullivan is the best I have seen: 'US election 2016: Donald Trump continues to defy the rules of politics-as-usual.'[158] As I see it, Trump is essentially a New Yorker with many of the attitudes and sensibilities of someone from New York. But he is also in his late sixties and has a residual set of values based on the way things were half a century ago. A liberal in the 1960s is someone whose values were laid down around the time JFK was president, which means he has approximately the same values that Ronald Reagan would have twenty years later. Over the span of those years, what was mainstream Democrat became mainstream Republican. Today, mainstream Democrat is Bernie Sanders and Barack Obama, while Hillary is held back by a residual, although minimal, grasp of the values of the early sixties. But here the issue is Trump who in many ways sees the world much the same way as I do, and I think in much the same way as O'Sullivan.

It is this that causes Trump to make those peculiar kinds of mistakes when he tries to walk away from the things he believes in and try to imitate what he thinks a Republican believes. My advice to him is just to do the

---

[157] *Daily Mail Australia*, 30 March 2016.
[158] *The Australian* 2 April 2016.

Kennedy thing and not try to pander to the religious right. They will never support him so long as Cruz is running, and in any case, it is those same fools who decided not to vote for Romney in 2012. The bigger game is in pulling Democrats across to the Republican side, not trying to shore up his near-certain constituency should he become the nominee. This, I think, is the same point O'Sullivan has tried to make.

> *Will Trump's suggestion this week that women who have had abortions should face legal penalties finally trip him up?*
>
> *This was a serious mistake on two levels. To pro-choice voters it looked like a barbaric threat to a constitutional right millions of American women have personally exercised. Echoed by the media, also mainly pro-choice, it will confirm the caricature of him as brutalist right-winger. To conservative voters and anti-abortion organisations, however, it revealed the very thin and outdated understanding that Trump has of the conservatism he now espouses. The anti-abortion movement long ago abandoned any thought of penalising women for having the procedure. Today they typically characterise such women as victims and direct almost all their criticisms at "abortion mills" that murder women through negligence as well as babies intentionally, or at organisations such as Planned Parenthood that provide abortion almost as a late stage method of birth control.*

Or then this:

> *On other issues as well, such as killing the families of terrorists, Trump expresses what he supposes to be hardline conservative opinions; but because he is late to the faith (and perhaps not very devout), he constantly gets it wrong, and expresses instead what liberals (like himself until recently) think conservatives believe in their dark hearts.*
>
> *Reporting that concentrated on this misunderstanding might weaken Trump with at least a segment of the Right. But most mainstream journalists have a view of conservatism only slightly less skewed than Trump's.*

What Trump doesn't get is that there are plenty of us on the right that, whatever our religious beliefs, hold other values as more important, with the preservation of our way of life high on that list. We are not worried that he won't get the exact nuance right about abortion nor about the way that terrorists should be dealt with through constitutional procedures. We don't need him to take the hardest most-Rambo line he can think of. For myself,

I am content to let him enter the Oval Office and in the company of the cabinet he chooses, work through what needs to be done. It is his instincts that I am looking for him to guide him as these issues arrive on his desk. Again I think O'Sullivan is exactly right about this.

> *Trump voters discovered their hero in the early debates not because he was an alpha male or a star of reality television — though these things helped — but because he expressed their own feelings and opinions on matters that both major parties sedulously avoided. . . .*
>
> *Trump discovered his voters and their issues almost as much as his voters discovered Trump. Once he had done that, however, reporters and sociologists noticed the existence of entire classes of voters whose interests government had largely ignored and whose angry discontents were fuelling an insurgent campaign that broke half the rules of polite electioneering. So angry were these voters, indeed, that they simply tuned out criticisms of Trump, however seemingly justified, as emerging from a failing, inactive, and remote establishment that despised them and therefore him.*

And then these same non-insightful journalists and political insiders also discovered something else.

> *As the primaries wore on, Trump proved to be winning votes at all levels of wealth and education, even if disproportionately at the lower end. And Tea Partiers were more concerned with fiscal solvency, expenditure control and constitutional limits on what government can do, whereas Trump supporters were enthusiasts for activist government that would get things done at home and abroad.*

It therefore comes down to what Trump can and cannot do if elected. But the one thing he most certainly could do by winning the election is deprive Hillary of the office herself, with this conclusion:

> *Trump could never inflict the same amount of damage on the Republican vision of America as Clinton. She would enjoy the support of a major party, the media, the judiciary, the bureaucracy, and all the great social and cultural institutions of America. She would be virtually unimpeachable as the first woman president.*

This really is the reality since it is all of the above who will do all they can to elect her, and without Trump her success is assured, at the 95% level.

None of the other 17 Republicans who have gone for the nomination has ever had the slightest chance of winning. The immense amount of money that is coming to Cruz and Kasich from among the largest Democrat donors is a sure sign they know who Hillary's most formidable opponent is. O'Sullivan ends with this:

> *Trump would have none of [Hillary's] advantages as president — not even the support of congressional Republicans. He would be unable to pass controversial parts of his program. His administration would become a byword for gridlock.*
>
> *The Road Runner would run out of steam and finish up wrapped entirely in red tape — not a cartoon threat but a cautionary tale.*

I would expect more, but first we have to see Trump win. Although O'Sullivan doesn't say so in words, he seems to have been saying it very clearly between the lines of his article, the best analysis of the election I have so far seen anywhere.

~

The writers and critics who prophesize with their pens
April 3, 2016

The fantastic amount of anti-Trump material pouring out across the media and throughout the whole of the left means they perfectly well understand the threat Trump poses to them. If they thought he was not the most serious threat to the Democrats among the Republicans, they would stay silent and let nature take its course. They are not silent and are doing all they can to stop him. At the beginning they thought of him as the easiest one to beat and brought him forward out of the pack. Now they have seen the error of their ways and are pushing as hard as they can in the other direction.

I have just gone through Lucianne and the headlines there. It was near on a quarter of the stories were anti-Trump from every media source you could name. They mean it – the writerly class, they understand that he needs to be stopped, and of course this writerly class consist of almost as many Republicans as Democrats.

Hillary Clinton and the rights of the unborn
April 4, 2016

Can you see why everyone was upset with this from Hillary Clinton?[159] More particularly, why did it upset so many of those on the left?

> *Democratic primary front-runner Hillary Clinton ran afoul of both the pro-life and pro-choice sides of the abortion debate Sunday when she said constitutional rights do not apply to an "unborn person" or "child." ...*
>
> *Mrs. Clinton also said "there is room for reasonable kinds of restrictions" on abortion during the third trimester of pregnancy.*

Here's the reason they were upset.

> *Describing the fetus as a "person" or "child" has long been anathema to the pro-choice movement, which argues the terms misleadingly imply a sense of humanity.*
>
> *In addition, the specific term "person" is a legal concept that includes rights and statuses that the law protects, including protection of a person's life under the laws against homicide. Pro-choice intellectuals have long said that even if an unborn child is a "life," it is not yet a "person."*

See the distinction? You may think this is sick and depraved, but what do you know? You have to be a constitutional scholar or an intellectual to understand these things.

Even an old pro like Hillary can't get it right even after all these years, although you may be sure this is nothing but a passing moment on her way to the White House. I only mention it as a reminder of the extent to which the media makes everything into a sensation when it wants to get you. But with those it supports you hardly hear a sound. I point this out just so you know which side you are on when you buy into American politics. Because if these eight months old "fetuses" are actually persons with constitutional rights – you know, actual real people – then perhaps some of you were just a tad harsh the other day in your judgements of what nameless others had been saying on this very issue. Not that he was necessarily right, but only that you are picking up your cues from George Soros and *The New York Times*.

---

[159] *The Washington Times*, 3 April 2016.

Lasched to the massed
April 8, 2016

The article starts with the obligatory anti-Trump statement but once you get past the opening the text is not anti-Trump at all. Christopher Lasch is one of my favourite writers of all time and the article is 'Donald Trump and the Ghost of Christopher Lasch'.[160] So get past the opening with its "Trump would be the end of the world as we know it" to read this:

> *In 'The Revolt of the Elites' Lasch foresaw the disconnect between the nation's political classes and the governed, as UCLA law professor Stephen Bainbridge has recently observed. America's elites have devoted so much energy to building their collective moral system that they expect ideological obedience. When Trumpists say strong families in the 1950s were a positive, the cognoscenti respond: "So what. It was a terrible time for minorities and gays."*

> *Trump's armies feel the sting of comfortable, upscale, post-industrial winners who can barely conceal their contempt for those they dismiss as Wal-Mart people. The disdain for yeoman America—which is overwhelmingly white— is visceral, longstanding, and profound.*

> *"Middle Americans, as they appear to the makers of educated opinion, are hopelessly shabby, unfashionable, and provincial, ill informed about changes in taste or intellectual trends, addicted to trashy novels of romance and adventure, and stupefied by prolonged exposure to television," Lasch wrote in 1995, not yesterday. "They are at once absurd and vaguely menacing."*

And why does this matter?

> *As Lasch anticipated, the nation's ruling classes style themselves to be citizens of the world, living in "a global bazaar" to be savored indiscriminately, "with no questions asked and no commitments required." From Pacific Palisades to Cambridge, far from the madding crowd, well-heeled transnational citizens of the world may hold assets in Singapore or the Cayman Islands. Their identities are post-national. Amid the affluence, obsequious Third World helpers work at minimum wage or off the books, doing the scut work and producing an exotic, multicultural vibe as a bonus.*

> *Abandoning the left's original intent to protect the common man, Lasch observed,*

---
[160] *The American Conservative*, 5 April 2016.

> *progressives chose instead to pursue diversity, secularism, and cultural revolution. Families, schools, and churches were left behind. For thought leaders, family values, mindless patriotism, religious fundamentalism, white racism, homophobia, and retrograde views of women stood in the way of progress.*

Progress should, of course, be written as "progress". And so how do those elites think, and remember this is Lasch who was writing this two decades ago:

> *For progressive elites, delicate moral confections and debatable ethical positions became acts of faith. "It is no longer necessary to argue with opponents on intellectual grounds or to enter into their point of view," Lasch pointed out. "It is enough to dismiss them as Eurocentric, racist, sexist, homophobic – in other words, as politically suspect." When these novel moral systems are challenged, Lasch added, progressives react with "venomous hatred," the toxic ill feeling that seems abundant in the 2016 election year.*

Go to the link and read it all right through to the end, which is not an attempt to dissuade anyone from voting for Trump.

> *A Trump victory of course is "impossible." It would require a massive, almost unimaginable white, yeoman flight from the Democratic Party. It is quite likely that we are even now experiencing Peak Trump. But "impossible" now stands in quotes.*

And my congratulations to the author, Gilbert Sewall, for putting this together in just such a way that it has been featured at Instapundit,[161] by Ed Driscoll who would have understood it perfectly, but also at Powerline which perhaps was uploaded by Steve Hayward, but I doubt any of the others. Our elites are ruining the world and the only thing that might save them and us is this revolt from below.

---

[161] pjmedia.com/instapundit, 7 April 2016.

Fields of dreams and hallucinations
April 10, 2016

I don't post this in any genuine political sense but really as a study in social psychology and mass delusion. I don't know if any of you have been paying attention to the assault charges on Donald Trump's campaign manager but to me this is possibly the most extraordinary part of the entire election so far, even going beyond Bernie Sanders eating up those Democrat voters and Hillary not being indicted by the FBI. This one is really for the ages.

It's like all those folk back then who looked through their telescopes and saw the canals on Mars. In this case, it is the battery inflicted on Michelle Fields by Donald Trump's campaign manager. Here is a description from the formerly reliable Jeff Jacoby in an anti-Trump article titled, 'Authoritarian in Chief':[162]

> *Authoritarian abuse of power in a Trump administration isn't just a theoretical possibility. Should the New York businessman win the presidency, it's a certainty. Trump's campaign, with its torrent of insults, threats of revenge, and undercurrent of political violence, is the first in American history to raise the prospect of a ruthless strongman in the White House, unencumbered by constitutional norms and democratic civilities.*
>
> *When Trump's campaign manager, Corey Lewandowski, was arrested last week on misdemeanor charges of battery against reporter Michelle Fields, the candidate's reaction was typical. Though Fields's account was never in doubt — it was corroborated at once by an eyewitness (Washington Post reporter Ben Terris), by an audio recording, and then by security-camera video footage —Trump offered no apology and didn't rebuke his staffer. Instead he went on the attack: He claimed that Fields had "made the story up," he went out of his way to praise Lewandowski, and he gleefully trashed the journalists covering him as "disgusting" and "horrible people." Trump even hinted that he might sue Fields.*

A campaign manager is not the candidate himself, and even the most abusive principal will fire subordinates if they cause trouble. But Trump did not and in fact told Lewandowski that under no circumstances was he to apologise or concede anything at all. So let me bring Gavin McInnes to

---

[162] jeffjacoby.com, 3 April 2016.

put the other side of the case in an article he titles, 'Michelle Fields Is Not Black and Blue'.[163]

> There is plenty of photographic and video evidence of the exchange, but it doesn't seem to affect people's perception of what happened. Once again, the more we are confronted with evidence that contradicts our beliefs, the more steadfast we are in those beliefs. The initial videos show a close-up of Fields touching Trump, and an aerial view was released by police this week that shows more details. What is irrefutable is that on March 8, after a press conference in Jupiter, Fla., Breitbart reporter Michelle Fields approached Donald Trump and was moved out of the way by Trump's campaign manager, Corey Lewandowski. There is audio of Fields acting like it was a big deal to The Washington Post's Ben Terris, but I was happy to get on with my day a few seconds after seeing the first video.

~

Voter judgment and Donald Trump
April 13, 2016

This is a post about political judgment,[164] or more to the point, the lack thereof. And it relates to Donald Trump versus Justin Trudeau and its previous PM, Stephen Harper:

> The fact that he steered the country safely through the market crash of 2008, signed lucrative international trade deals, kept taxes down, reduced the GST (Goods and Services Tax) and provided the country with a balanced budget plainly counted for nothing. His emendation of citizenship protocols in an effort to check the spread of culturally barbaric practices, chiefly associated with Islam, counted against him. At the end of the day, he was simply unlikeable, he was "Harperman," and he had to go.

Compared with Harper we have Trudeau:

> Trudeau has been in office for half a year, more than enough time to engineer the rapid deterioration of a once-prosperous and relatively secure nation. He has brought in 25,000 "Syrians" and is aiming for many

---

[163] takimag.com, 1 April 2016.
[164] pjmedia.com, 12 April 2016.

thousands more, all living off the public dole and no doubted salted with aspiring jihadists. He intends to build mosques (which he calls "religious centers") on military bases and is re-accrediting Muslim terror-affiliated organizations that Harper defunded. He inherited Harper's balanced budget and in just a few short months was busy at work racking up a $29.4 billion deficit. Not to worry, since Trudeau is on record saying that budgets balance themselves. Magic is afoot.

So the issue is now Trump or not Trump. The summation which is similar to my own:

Would any sane person choose a Trudeau-type figure over a Harper or a Trump to lead their country into a problematic future? The larger issue is whether any reasonable person should predicate his voting preference on personal liking or disliking. Trudeau is intellectually vapid, has the wrong instincts, and is unlearnable. But he is liked. As for Trump, I am not suggesting that he would be a better choice than Cruz may be or Rubio may have been, though I suspect he might. He still has much to learn about the intricacies and priorities of governing and about looking "presidential." What matters is that a candidate for political office is smart, has the right instincts, and is willing to learn. I believe Trump qualifies in these respects. Disliking him is beside the point.

Writing for The Federalist, Timm Amundson acknowledges that Trump can be rude, arrogant and reckless, and asks: "How can a principled, pragmatic, deliberate conservative be drawn to such a candidate?" And answers: "It is because I believe conservatism doesn't stand a chance in this country without first delivering a very heavy dose of populism," that is, "a platform built largely on the principle of economic nationalism… focus[ing] on three primary policy areas: trade, defense, and immigration." This is Trump's bailiwick.

So we are into an American election where all of the best educated are siding with candidates that will doom their country because they do not personally like Trump, or prefer a woman irrespective of any other considerations. But the #NeverTrump are the worst buffoons of all, but there you are since they may yet carry the day.

Writing in code
April 13, 2016

One of the great philologists used to argue that you could not read the ancient Greek writers without appreciating that it was more than their lives were worth to actually say what they meant. Now we are unlikely to boil you in oil, but still, you might lose your writing gig at *National Review* if you said what you really meant. Take Victor Davis Hanson, who begins and ends his column on 'White versus White America',[165] with the standard demand that we be spared a Donald Trump as President, but then says this in the middle:

> *Trump is not so much appealing to the ethnic prejudices of the white poor and working class, or playing on their perceived resentments of the Other. It's more that he, a crass member of the elite ("It takes one to know one"), is resonating with their deep dislike of the hypocrisies of the white elite, both Republican and Democratic. Middle-class whites should be outraged at the cruel and gross manner in which Trump insulted John McCain and Megyn Kelly, but they are not. Perhaps, if asked, they would prefer to have the latter pair's money and power if the price was an occasional little slapdown from Donald Trump. What they see as outrageous is not Trump's crude "Get out of here" to Spanish-language newscaster Jorge Ramos, but rather the multimillionaire dual-citizen Ramos predicating his con on a perpetual pool of non–English speakers, many of whom have broken federal immigration law in a way a citizen would not dare break the law on his tax return or DMV application. For an angry Arizonan, ridiculing "low energy" Jeb is not as crude as Jeb's own crude "act of love" description of illegal immigration. An act of love for exactly whom?*
>
> *What is the perceived white elite? Perhaps a Hillary Clinton raking in $300,000 per half hour at UCLA or shaking down Wall Street for $600,000, even as she pontificates on privilege and the dangers of racism (obviously embraced, in her view, by whites other than those of her class). Or a Chelsea Clinton deprecating the attraction of riches, as her Wall Street internships and marriage perpetuate the Clinton model of pay-for-play enrichment — all to be camouflaged by professions of progressive empathy. Or an elite media that snores when an ex-president of the United States jumps on the private plane of convicted child-assaulter Jeffrey Epstein for a trip to his fantasy island. Or a former anti-*

---

[165] *National Review*, 12 April 2016.

government "conservative" congressman who hangs around Washington and mysteriously becomes a multimillionaire leveraging his past government service. Our popular culture is one of Pajama Boy, Mattress Girl, and the whiny, nasal-toned young metrosexual with high-water pants above his ankles and horn-rimmed glasses who "analyzes" on cable news. Is it any wonder that millions sympathized with the heroism of Benghazi's middle-class defenders rather than with the contortions of the far better-educated, smoother, more sensitive, and wealthier Rhodes scholar Susan Rice, novelist Ben Rhodes, or former First Lady Hillary Clinton?

Whom do these sometimes incoherent Trump supporters likely despise? I would wager anyone who has never been sideswiped in a hit-and-run by an illegal-alien driver but lectures others on why "illegal alien" is a racist term; anyone who has lucrative government employment and whose job description does not exist in the poorer-paying private sector; any politician or his appendage who somehow became quite wealthy on a GS salary in Washington; anyone who makes more than $50 an hour and lectures others on why the country is going broke and must tighten its belt; anyone who sermonizes on free trade and knows few people who ever lost jobs through outsourcing; anyone who freely uses the word "white" in a way and context that he would never use "black" or "Latino"; or anyone who hires someone else to clean his house, watch his kids, and take care of his yard, and then lectures others on their illiberality.

Or to put it this way, whom do these sometimes very coherent Trump supporters likely despise? I'll leave it to you to work it out.

~

Corey Lewandowski will not be prosecuted
April 14, 2016

Showing Trump's virtues. Stood by his man.

A case study in media deceit
April 15, 2016

For the history of this bizarre Michelle Field-Correy Landowski attempt at a set up, you can read it on catallaxyfiles.com.[166] If you would like a longer, more extended version of these events, Stefan Molyneux is the one for you.

But really, this is the central issue: you cannot trust the media to tell you the truth. The story that would have been the final nailed down version would have been Fields' version of having been thrown to the ground by some thuggish Trump employee. It is only because the evidence has been so overwhelming showing she is a complete liar that his critics – and they were both Democrat and Republican – have reluctantly had to back down. Open and shut in this case. In the others, you are with certainty being manipulated and your views shaped by a media with a very left-of-centre perspective who are personally opposed to everything Donald Trump stands for: a strong America, with closed borders who will defend the interests of the West against all comers. He may not have the nuance of running for office exactly down pat, but he would be a formidable president in the sense that he could and would get things done.

~

You can see why they prefer Hillary to Trump
April 19, 2016

What's the problem? Sounds like a good return on investment.[167]

> *GIVE $300K TO CLINTON FOUNDATION, GET $13M BACK IN STATE DEPARTMENT GRANTS! Not a bad deal, at least for former Nobel Prize winner and long-time Clinton friend Muhammed Yunus. Government panels in Bangladesh and Norway accused him of extensive banking and charitable corruption but that didn't disqualify Yunus from receiving millions in U.S. tax dollars via loans, grants and contracts from Hillary Clinton's State Department, according to the Daily Caller News Foundation Investigative Group's Richard Pollock.*

---

[166] catallaxyfiles.com, 10 April 2016
[167] dailycaller.com, 17 April 2016

"The awards, totaling $13 million, were issued by the U.S. Agency for International Development, the development arm of the State Department, beginning when Clinton became secretary of state. Another $11 million in federal funds went to organizations allied with Yunus," Pollock reports.

Yunus "is a high-profile fixture at most of the Clinton Foundation's major gatherings. The foundation features him at 37 places on its website," according to Pollock, who also reports that when he asked for details about the $13 million, "USAID Spokesman Raphael Cook said the agency didn't have the 'manpower' to respond to questions about the transactions." The agency has nearly 4,000 employees.

~

Spring thaw – they're warming to Donald
April 21, 2016

The Great Negotiator is about to open his dialogue with the Republican national executive. 'Republican establishment warms to Trump after big New York win'.[168]

The New York real estate mogul's win Tuesday in his home state over rivals Ted Cruz and John Kasich was an important milestone for RNC members, who said it could put him on a pathway to acquire the 1,237 delegates needed to win the nomination outright without a contested convention.

"There are a fair number of RNC members who were discounting his chances of success when we met in January and now see that he's building a substantial lead and may in fact get to 1,237 before we get to the convention," said Steve Duprey, an RNC member from New Hampshire.

"The New York results were such an overwhelming win," Duprey said. "It's impressive. That's what I've heard people talking about."

RNC members said Trump could help improve the climate by taking steps to end the bad blood that has developed between him and the committee's leadership, including RNC Chairman Reince Priebus.

And why wouldn't he move towards them. The most important realignment in politics since The New Deal is there for the asking.

---
[168] ca.news.yahoo.com, 21 April 2016.

Delusional
April 24, 2016

Ignorant to an extent never seen before in a major world "leader", we have this from Obama today:

> *President Barack Obama boasted of his legacy during a town hall in Britain, asserting that he single-handedly saved the world during his presidency.*
>
> *"Saving the world economy from a Great Depression — that was pretty good," Obama bragged when asked by a student in London what he wanted his legacy to be.*
>
> *He recalled that when he visited London in 2009, the world economy was in a "freefall" because of irresponsible behavior of financial institutions around the world.*
>
> *"For us to be able to mobilize the world's community, to take rapid action, to stabilize the financial markets, and then in the United States to pass Wall Streets reforms that make it much less likely that a crisis like that can happen again, I'm proud of that," he said.*

What made the difference was the TARP that was put in place by his predecessor. A reminder since it is now so long ago even Obama seems to have forgotten:

> *The Troubled Asset Relief Program (TARP) is a program of the United States government to purchase assets and equity from financial institutions to strengthen its financial sector that was signed into law by U.S. President George W. Bush on October 3, 2008. It was a component of the government's measures in 2008 to address the subprime mortgage crisis.*

Obama's contribution was the stimulus that came immediately after, which has made America's recovery for all practical purposes non-existent, along with everyone else's. As if a law professor turned community organiser would have the slightest idea about how an economy works.

But if he doesn't even remember who put the TARP in place, it might be a consequence of his **choom-gang youth**, which from **other news also today**[169] we learn:

---

[169] breitbart.com, 23 April 2016.

Using marijuana earlier in life is linked to poorer psychological health, and that can contribute to more health problems down the road.

"It is well-established that if you begin using at an early age and use a lot then, there are significant negative outcomes particularly in terms of mental health..."

Earlier cannabis use is linked to cognitive problems. Hills said, "One 2012 study showed early, regular use of marijuana – the kind of level they describe in this study — led to an eight point decline in IQ over time."

If Obama really thinks he had much if any involvement in stabilizing international financial markets after the GFC, he must have been somewhere else at the time to be so unaware of what was going on.

~

Is this an anti-Trump cartoon?
April 25, 2016

This is apparently an anti-Trump cartoon but looks exactly like reality to me. It shows the GOP elephant looking over a cliff at the end of short path with a sign pointing towards "Hillary". And then there is another path leading at least somewhere that is marked with two arrowed signs that read "Cruz" and "Trump". The question is why the #NeverTrump people have the belief that going over the cliff with Hillary is preferable to keeping to the path with Donald. But they do. Here we have this: 'Charles Koch: 'It's possible' Clinton is preferable to a Republican for president'.[170]

Billionaire businessman Charles Koch said Sunday that "it's possible" another Clinton in the White House could be better than having a Republican president.

Koch, the CEO of Koch Industries, made the comment to ABC News' Jonathan Karl during an interview that aired on ABC's "This Week."

The comment came after Karl asked about Bill Clinton's presidency. Koch said Clinton was "in some ways" better than George W. Bush. "As far as the growth of government, the increase in spending, it was 2½ times under Bush than it was under Clinton," he said.

---

[170] politico.com, 23 April 2016.

Four years of Hillary does not sound like the answer to me, but since everyone is a political genius and sees more perfectly than anyone else into the nature of things, here we find one more answer among the many others.

~

Oh by the way, Trump won five more states today
April 27, 2016

I find the absence of focus on the US primary results even in the United States quite creepy, although what do I know about what's newsy? Up until now, there would be quite a story across the page about Trump wins. Near as I can see, there is practically nothing at all. You would almost think there was a wish across the media to take the momentum out of Trump's astonishing wins, to pull the wind from his sails.

It reminds me how *The Australian* decided that Turnbull should replace Abbott and from then on that was how the news and comment was bent. It has now been decided that the United States needs its own Malcolm Turnbull and Justin Trudeau, and that is how the news is being bent. Anyway, this is the best I could do, from USA Today:[171]

> *Donald Trump went five-for-five in sweeping a set of northeastern primaries Tuesday and declared himself the "presumptive" Republican nominee for president in the face of allied opposition from rivals Ted Cruz and John Kasich.*
>
> *"As far as I'm concerned, it's over," Trump said in claiming easy victories in Pennsylvania, Maryland, Connecticut, Rhode Island and Delaware. He said, "this is a far bigger win than we even expected — all five."*
>
> *Citing a large number of delegates and votes in the face of Republican establishment opposition, the maverick businessman said "the best way to beat the system" is to have evenings like this.*
>
> *Cruz and Kasich, who have formed a loose alliance to try to block Trump in some future contests, are hoping to pick up some delegates after Tuesday's primaries, but their totals will likely be minimal in the wake of Trump's landslide wins.*

Somebody is voting for him but it's apparently no longer big news.

---

[171] usatoday.com, 26 April 2016.

Trump and the realignment of the parties
April 29, 2016

Anyone who believes Hillary will defeat Trump must have zero faith in democratic processes. Hillary has never achieved a single political purpose in her entire life that did not benefit herself personally. She has no ideas and no track record. She is corrupt to an extent possibly unprecedented even in the American politicians-for-hire system of government. She should be going to jail, not running for president. Her one achievement occurred at birth (conception?) and since then she has added nothing of value to her résumé. It ought to make you sick to realise how close she is to accomplishing her goals. And if she does, the line that democracy is the worst form of government except for all the others may have to be amended. There are circumstances in which democracy clearly does not work, and the Hillary story is the case study.

We however have this: Democratic Strategist: Trump Will Beat Hillary Like 'A Baby Seal'.[172] He may not be right, but at least he has broken ranks to say what needs to be true:

> Democratic strategist Dave "Mudcat" Saunders believes Donald Trump will beat Hillary Clinton like a "baby seal," and that working class whites who haven't already left the Democratic Party for cultural reasons will do so now for economic ones.
>
> "I know a ton of Democrats — male, female, black and white — here [in southern Virginia] who are going to vote for Trump. It's all because of economic reasons. It's because of his populist message," Mudcat told The Daily Caller Wednesday.
>
> Saunders has experience working with Jim Webb, helping getting him elected to the U.S Senate in 2006 and advised his failed bid for the presidency in 2016. Saunders was also an advisor to John Edwards in his 2008 presidential bid. The Democrat strategist is renowned for connecting politicians to "Bubbas" — white, working class Southerners.
>
> "Working class whites in the South have already departed the Democratic Party for cultural reasons. Well the working class whites in the North are now deserting the Democrats because of economic reasons," Mudcat told The DC. He added, "this is the new age of economic populism, man. This

---
[172] dailycaller.com, 27 April 2016.

is about survival for a lot of people."

If it is down to survival and people will still vote against their interests, then there will be a new system coming and it won't be the one we have been used to in the past.

~

Which wall is it, by the way, that you want torn down?
April 29, 2016

There is something so perfect about this hand-made sign – "tear down the walls Trump is a racist, fascist, misogynistic, capitalist pig" – so exact, so preciously inane, so rhetorically empty yet jargon-filled that it deserves to be memorialised as almost the perfect caricature of the left. From the anti-Trump rally held in California[173] today, by illegal migrants protesting on behalf of their assumed right to illegally migrate into the United States. But whatever they know or don't know, however American they are or are not, they have the idiom down to its vacuous perfection.

At the other extreme, we find this from the pages of *The New York Times*. Trump and the Madness of Crowds.[174] It never seems to occur to the writer that each of the people who end up at a Trump rally has done so deliberately with conscious intention while on their own, at their home or wherever they were before setting out to hear a political leader. And it is not they who are the mob. Each is an individual in their own right coming to listen to a political speech. The question that dominates is why do people keep voting for him when – don't they know – he can never win the election in the fall?

> *Since last fall Republican voters have consistently told pollsters that they think Trump is the candidate most likely to win in November. So the party's voters are choosing electability — as they see it — over ideology; they're just in the grip of a strong delusion about Trump's actual chances against Hillary Clinton.*
>
> *The reason for this delusion might be the key unresolved question of Trump's strange ascent.*

---
[173] *Daily Mail Australia*, 29 April 2016.
[174] *New York Times*, 28 April 2016.

Nothing to do with policy. Nothing to do with stopping a rot that many had thought was unstoppable. Nothing to do with trying to save the United States in the form that these voters had once known. Not that at all. Trump is only popular because these voters think he is more likely to win than any other candidate. There may be a madness of crowds, but there is another version that besets political writers when they sit by themselves writing columns for other like-minded people to read.

~

What is needed for free institutions to work
April 30, 2016

John Stuart Mill once observed that democracy could work only among a unified homogeneous people. This ominous passage is from Chapter XVI of his Considerations on Representative Government:[175]

> *"Free institutions are next to impossible in a country made up of different nationalities. Among a people without fellow-feeling, especially if they read and speak different languages, the united public opinion, necessary to the working of representative government, cannot exist. The influences which form opinions and decide political acts are different in the different sections of the country. An altogether different set of leaders have the confidence of one part of the country and of another. The same books, newspapers, pamphlets, speeches, do not reach them. One section does not know what opinions, or what instigations, are circulating in another. [...] For the preceding reasons, it is in general a necessary condition of free institutions that the boundaries of governments should coincide in the main with those of nationalities." (Mill [1861] 1991: 291-294).*

There is nothing there we do not see at every turn across the world today. What a dark future there must be if he was actually right. Even if you're not partial to his economics, he is the man who wrote *On Liberty*.

On this note, we bring news from the election in the United States.

VIDEO: Trump Forced To Hop Fence After Protesters Form Human Chain,

---

[175] Mill, John Stuart. [1861] 1991. *Considerations on Representative Government*, In J. Gray (ed.) *On Liberty and Other Essays*. Oxford: Oxford University Press, 203-467

Block Entrance To San Fran Hotel…
'It Felt Like I Was Crossing The Border'…
Rioters rage outside Trump rally in SO CAL…
Smash police car, hurl rocks at motorists…
Hundreds waving Mexican flags…
Cops outnumbered…
Video…
'He's gonna build a wall in our land'…
'Everybody is scared right now because they know change coming'…
Rush to naturalize immigrant voters before election…

Where in the world is Mill shown not to be right. The Declaration of the Rights of Man – not the rights of a Frenchman or an Englishman – will be the death of our civilisation, which we may be witnessing before our eyes.

~

Listen Brooks, aren't Donald's trousers creased well enough for you?

May 1, 2016

There are some people whose views you never forget, and for whom one statement becomes the one thing everyone remembers because it is so grotesque. This is from an article from *The New Republic* dated August 31, 2009. It is about David Brooks, who *The New York Times* chooses to call its columnist from the right:[176]

> *In the spring of 2005, New York Times columnist David Brooks arrived at then-Senator Barack Obama's office for a chat. Brooks, a conservative writer who joined the Times in 2003 from The Weekly Standard, had never met Obama before. But, as they chewed over the finer points of Edmund Burke, it didn't take long for the two men to click. "I don't want to sound like I'm bragging," Brooks recently told me, "but usually when I talk to senators, while they may know a policy area better than me, they generally don't know political philosophy better than me. I got the sense he knew both better than me."*
>
> *That first encounter is still vivid in Brooks's mind. "I remember distinctly an image of—we were sitting on his couches, and I was looking at his pant leg and*

---

[176] *The New Republic*, 31 August 2009.

> his perfectly creased pant," Brooks says, "and I'm thinking, a) he's going to be president and b) he'll be a very good president." In the fall of 2006, two days after Obama's The Audacity of Hope hit bookstores, Brooks published a glowing Times column. The headline was "Run, Barack, Run."

Now there's a man with acute political judgement, someone you can turn to if you want to see past the superficial and get to the heart of the matter. "His perfectly creased pant" is now often quoted as the most perfect example of stupid in a political analyst in the United States, and there is a lot of stupid to compete. But he won it hands down. And now, showing just how unerring his judgement is, he is back with this: another article that says vote Hillary in that ever reliable more in sorrow than in anger column criticising Trump. To catch the flavour, here are the first two paras:

> Donald Trump now looks set to be the Republican presidential nominee. So for those of us appalled by this prospect — what are we supposed to do?

> Well, not what the leaders of the Republican Party are doing. They're going down meekly and hoping for a quiet convention. They seem blithely unaware that this is a Joe McCarthy moment. People will be judged by where they stood at this time. Those who walked with Trump will be tainted forever after for the degradation of standards and the general election slaughter.

This from someone who endorsed Obama and has never rescinded a word of it. It will be the brain dead such as Brooks who may yet get Hillary over the line, but to call Brooks a "conservative" is worse than repulsive and disgusting, it is merely to realise he is a journalist, the modern synonym for liar. There will be not a voter in the United States influenced by a word he says but there are plenty around who think it. But what's amazing is that he still has the nerve to say anything at all.

BTW does anyone know who the owner of *The New York Times* happens to be?

AND THIS JUST IN: Here's a story that won't surprise a soul: Poll: Not a Single White House Reporter Is a Republican.[177]

> Not a single member of the White House press corps is a registered Republican, according to survey results recently published by Politico.

---

[177] freebeacon.com, 29 April 2016

Those results are buried in a story this week on President Barack Obama's relationship with the press. An infographic posted in the story reveals that not a single one of the 72 members of the White House press corps surveyed by the Virginia-based trade publication identifies with the GOP.

And the more you think about it the more astonishing the bias becomes. It's therefore no surprise to find that "eighty-six percent said they expect Clinton to win" which is the outcome they intend to bring about if at all possible.

~

Trump is also helping us work out which commentators should be ignored from now on and into the farthest future

May 2, 2016

Conservative is not defined as idiots who prefer a socialist of the opposite party in government than a person closer to their own perspective representing their own party if not every conservative box is ticked. This is George Will – quoted at Powerline[178] – demonstrating that he is long past his use-by date:

> *Were [Trump] to be nominated, conservatives would have two tasks. One would be to help him lose 50 states — condign punishment for his comprehensive disdain for conservative essentials, including the manners and grace that should lubricate the nation's civic life. Second, conservatives can try to save from the anti-Trump undertow as many senators, representatives, governors and state legislators as possible.*

This man is a certifiable loony and to think he has been seen as a respected commentator for two generations. These are the same people who prefer Labor to the Libs if the more conservative party is led by someone on the left. Here is a reply to what Will has written from the Powerline comments section in relation to Trump. Something similar could be written about Australia. You know, like how perfection is the

---

[178] powerlineblog.com, 1 May 2016.

enemy of the good.

> *George Will is a prissy little girl in a bow-tie. He is the future of nothing. His views on Trump, like those of the worthless National Review, are foolish, exaggerated and wrong. The certitude folks express here about Trump losing 50 states. Jeez. Is that wishful thinking, or do you all have dead people whispering in your ears? I think it is just as likely Trump wins in a landslide.*
>
> *I get the negatives on Trump. Who can miss them? He wears them like a billboard on his orange head. But stop dismissing Trump supporters or rather, voters who might vote for Trump over Hillary as idiots and uninformed imbeciles. That simply isn't true, certainly not in all cases.*
>
> *I tire too of the conservative purity test. Reagan granted amnesty to illegals, got Marines killed in Beirut because at the time he was as ignorant of the middle east as Obama is today; Nixon invented the EPA; Romney was never a conservative; George W. Bush? One of America's worst presidents. I get that he's a nice guy. He's also a Christian proselytizer, who looked in Putin's eyes, and saw his soul (Putin gave it up long ago), found democracy in the beards of tribal crazies, got us into two wars he managed to lose, passed a prescription drug benefit for old white people that still costs billions. Did I mention that he spent money like a sailor in a whorehouse?*
>
> *Conservatives? Really? Conservatives have done NOTHING in almost 60 years to curb the growth of government. Trump is no damn white knight. But right now America is run by a big-eared ignorant ass, who gets his advice from people of color Marxist ideologues he met in Chicago or college, and twenty-something pinheads who never worked outside of government.*
>
> *On his worst day, Trump would be better than them. Try looking at it this way. Cruz thinks the system works, that he can fix it. You want idiocy? There it is. The system can't be changed. It will roll along, getting bigger and bigger and more inept until it caves in.*
>
> *Trump may even be the only man in the race who understands this. And he will in no way, no matter what he does, be worse that pompous self-absorbed ass Americans put two times into the white house.*

He will be the Republican nominee
May 4, 2016

'This one is over, folks': Donald Trump delivers 'crushing blow' with huge Indiana victory.[179] Wherein we find:

> *W/ all 57 delegates, Trump would get to 1,055 – 182 from nomination.*
> *Path:*
>   *WV: +25*
>   *OR: +12*
>   *WA: +22*
>   *NJ: +51*
>   *NM: +12   =just needs 60 from CA*

Meanwhile, on the Democrat side, 100% of the vote went to socialists. WITH THIS FURTHER NEWS: CRUZ WITHDRAWS.

~

Do American "conservatives" even know what a conservative is?
May 5, 2016

Let me therefore tell you what a conservative is: someone who wishes to preserve the best things from our past even while accepting the necessity of change. Going further, it is to learn from our own past about how to negotiate the future.

The question for the day is whether the following is or is not a "conservative" policy: "'They're destroying Europe – I'm not going to let that happen to the United States' Trump doubles down on non-citizen Muslim ban.'[180]

> *On the Muslim ban, which is likely Trump's most controversial position, he's not budging.*
> *'I don't care if it hurts me,' he told hosts Joe Scarborough and Mika Brzezinski. 'I'm doing the right thing.'*
> *'I've been guided by common sense, by what's right,' he continued.*

---

[179] twitchy.com, 3 May 2016.
[180] *Daily Mail Australia*, 5 May 2016.

'We have to be careful. We're allowing thousands of people to come into our country,' he said. 'Thousands and thousands of people being placed all over the country that, frankly, nobody knows who they are.'

'We don't know what we're doing,' he added.

He may be wrong about what he's doing, but the policy is the very essence of conservative.

~

And so it begins
May 5, 2016

The relentlessly anti-Trump media "analysis", even here in Australia with virtually no one voting in the US election. The Murdoch Press is anti-Trump to the furthest extent it can go, and this is the supposed right-side of the media. Today's screed is by Caroline Overington, the Associate Editor in Sydney, who has written the first of what will no doubt be many similarly hysterical pieces by many others. Her column is titled, 'US Election 2016: Donald Trump is rising on a wave of anger'. She writes:

As absurd as that idea once seemed, Donald Trump is the last man standing, and therefore — bar the most extraordinary revolt — he's the Republican candidate for president.

They have only themselves to blame, of course. The Republicans, I mean. They've had eight years to get their gear together, and this is what they've come up with.

A guy who got rich by putting up buildings shaped like special-edition Zippo lighters.

Such depth! Such analysis! You can feel the lifetime of study that has gone into this. And etc etc etc *ad nauseam*. Here, however, are the 16 top comments – I went all the way down to Number 16 because I liked it so much. And I left out not a single one. Quite a different perspective.

1) Overington's insulting remarks and Greg Sheridan's equally condescending piece today in some measure explain why Americans are lining up in droves to vote for Trump. Paid political commentators and their taxpayer-supported informants in Congress and the bureaucracy make up the establishment elites that detest the people who put them in office, pay their inflated salaries and keep journalists in jobs.

The members of this arrogant class believe they have a monopoly of knowledge to which their inferiors in the world of business, commerce and the professions, cannot hope to aspire, hence the spurious claim that Trump voters are uneducated and ignorant. It is anathema to them that ordinary people have the audacity to reject the candidate chosen for them by their superiors and vote instead for someone outside that narrow and insular elite group.

2) I cant wait for Trump to win, and then proceed to actually make a positive difference. Methinks journalist are frightened stiff he will succeed and make them irrelevant in policy direction and outcomes. If there is one grain of uniformity among journalists its that they think they know better and are better than the average joe/jill citizen. Time to kick the media to the curb

3) Bring it on. I have no idea what sort of a president he will make but I REALLY want to see the leftist backlash when he gets in. It'll be the most entertaining thing we've seen in years!

4) The elites are desperate now. Overington is an intellectual wet lettuce.

5) It is articles like this that ensure Trump will be President. The media sneer and belittle him yet at the same time reveal what is actually wrong with society…that is the Media think only their opinion count and the voters are too stupid. By the way, Obama sure didn't go to War – but he has stood by and allowed millions to die in Syria and create the worst humanitarian crisis since World War 2 – and yet you think this makes him great!!! Oh the humanity.

6) Oh, the lefties are getting so scared. Including the writer of this blog! The anxiety of the ABC interviewers is palpable, one could taste it. Go for it Donald. Stick it up the PC self-righteous bike riding, tofu sucking, sandal wearing idiots!

7) The more the chatterers complain, the more I like Trump. Anything is preferable to more of the same.

8) Not only hopelessly jaundiced as a piece of political journalism, is it possible that the chatterati have not yet realised it is quite precisely articles like these

that have been fuelling the Trump phenomena? Are they seriously so clueless?

9) How does a piece like this end up in a quality paper like The Australian?

10) The writer is obviously looking for a job with the ABC and will produce this article in the job application.

11) If Socialists like you hate Trump he would have my vote. If only we had him here.

12) Keep up the sneering, the condescension and the mockery, Caroline. It only makes him stronger, and his supporters more resolute.

13) "Who ran because he thought it might be a good advertisement for his new casino." Shallow and untrue. Trump set out to make a full, frontal attack on the political elites, both sides, and he's succeeded. He also awakened the nation. The man, if elected a president, will morph into a statesman like person. He's too intelligent and competent to not know that.

Remember, too, that when Ben Carsons endorsed him and was asked about all the ugly things he'd said about Trump, Carsons replied, "Oh, that's just politics," or words to that effect. Apply the same thinking to Trump's outbursts.

14) You journalists just cannot stand it that people do not think as you tell them to.

15) "Obama (who, for the record, has endured not one scandal involving his marriage or his kids, nor embarked upon a single unnecessary war.)" that's right, he just did NOTHING.

16) We should build a hall of journalism, wallpapered with all the articles saying Trump can't win, leading to a feature about the election of the 45th President of the USA. It will be a tourist attraction, and a reminder to future generations that the job of journalists is to report the news, not make it up.

If this keeps up, *The Australian* will either have to stop allowing comments or find some other way to rebalance the opinion in a more correct direction.

Trump and economic policy
May 5, 2016

Most business people don't have the ability to convert their understanding of the corporate world into a coherent set of policies that will work across the economy and particularly on the supply side. They know what might work for them, but not necessarily across the board. I hadn't even known Trump had even begun to develop a coherent approach to economic recovery, and it certainly does look to me as if he has had some very clued-in assistance in putting it together. It is in part outlined here: 'Beyond All the Bluster Trump's Economic Plan Focuses on Growth, Jobs'.[181] This is the sort of thing that will work:

- slash the corporate tax rate to 15%, down from the current 40%, the highest rate in the industrialized world
- a one-time 10% repatriation tax on profits American companies made overseas and kept there to avoid the 40% rate
- allow companies to write off the purchases the year they're made, rather than over several years, as current law requires
- the lower 15% rate business rate would also apply to small businesses that usually get taxed at individual income tax rates
- his "make America rich" plan targets impoverished cities like Baltimore with incentives for companies to move there
- convert the current State Department program that brings about 100,000 young foreigners into America to work in restaurants, camps, and seaside resorts under J-1 visas into a jobs bank for American inner city youth.

Meanwhile Hillary:

> Compare Donald Trump's blueprint with Secretary Clinton's nightmare scenario: Higher taxes, more tax complexity, and an avalanche of new regulations. Over-regulation has depressed growth for the last fifteen years. The Obama administration suffocated business with 81,000

---

[181] nysun.com, 5 May 2016.

> *pages of new regulations in 2015 alone. Hillary Clinton is pushing for even more – with controls on hiring, pay, bonuses and overtime to promote "fairer growth." Translation: gender and racial preferences, plus meddling in how much you get paid.*
>
> *Remember President Obama's statement, "You didn't build that." Well, Mrs. Clinton assumes "you don't own that." Government will run your business. Mrs. Clinton wants companies to stop maximizing quarterly earnings for shareholders – what she derides as "quarterly capitalism." She wants "farsighted investments," as defined by government, of course. Companies that can get out of the U.S. will rush for the exits. She's even promising an end to "the boom and bust cycles on Wall Street." As plausible as ending rainy days.*

Infantile versions of fairness seldom mix well with sound economic policy. Trump has nevertheless put together a package that will work, although the cuts to spending and the scaling back of programs will also at some stage have to be included as well. But what we find above is very good, and about time.

And for what it's worth, the article was written by Elizabeth "Betsy" McCaughey, who was Lieutenant Governor of New York from 1995 to 1998, during the first term of Governor George Pataki.

FURTHER REPORTS: It's Reuters reporting on what CNBC is reporting, which is remarkable in itself: 'Trump wants to help U.S. businesses by lifting slew of regulations: CNBC'.[182]

> *U.S. Republican presidential candidate Donald Trump said on Thursday that if elected he would scrap a slew of federal regulations that he said are even more of a burden on American business owners than high taxes, and would try to refinance longer-term U.S. debt.*

Not much detail in the story but you may be sure these are the kinds of things he means to do and will know which regulations ought to go.

---

[182] ca.news.yahoo.com, 6 May 2016.

My absolute favourite blog comment of all time
May 6, 2016

Mitchell Porter #2021329, posted on May 5, 2016 at 10:37 pm (Edit)

I want to show some respect to Steve Kates for outsmarting basically the entire Australian commentariat and seeing that Trump's candidacy made sense. It naturally makes me wonder what else he is right about – maybe Say's Law?

~

As unknown to the world of politics as anyone I have ever seen
May 6, 2016

Here is one example of Trump dishonesty from a post titled 'Donald Trump Lies'.[183]

> *I once received a tip that Trump and Richard Nixon had had a lengthy meeting in Trump's office. Trump said he knew nothing about it. I ran the story, not only because I had an excellent source, but also because a Nixon aide confirmed it.*

Got it? Trump denied to some journalist that he had been meeting with the President of the United States when in fact he really had been, and this is classified as a lie. My take: Trump doesn't even care if other people know he met with the President, and second, he can keep a secret. Third, he seems to have been dealing at a very high political level for quite a long time. Trump is as unknown to the world of politics as anyone I have ever seen.

Meanwhile, back in the world of Republican politics we have Paul Ryan. Does he not have even the most basic irony-detection device?

> *House Speaker Paul Ryan is refusing to support Donald Trump as the Republican nominee for president, insisting Thursday that the businessman must do more to unify the GOP.*

And just what is the bit that Ryan is doing towards achieving this unity? You might well ask since no answer is at all obvious to me.

---

[183] pjmedia.com, 2 May 2016.

The Obama White House counted on the ignorance and stupidity of the media
May 7, 2016

This is how the foreign-policy media is described by the would-be novelist who manages American foreign policy: "They literally know nothing." You don't know about this? Maybe it's for the best if you want to continue to sleep peacefully through the night. Just read the rest below and think how much greater the depth and professionalism of a Trump White House will be. This may be the single most astounding revelation about the abysmal Obama administration to have surfaced, although no doubt more will be revealed as the years go by.

As with almost everything else of significance, if you haven't been following this story, it's only because it's almost impossible to find in your local press. But it does start at *The New York Times* and is about someone named Ben Rhodes: 'The Aspiring Novelist Who Became Obama's Foreign-Policy Guru'.[184] So begin with this from the story:

> *The Boy Wonder of the Obama White House is now 38. . . .*
>
> *As the deputy national security adviser for strategic communications, Rhodes writes the president's speeches, plans his trips abroad and runs communications strategy across the White House, tasks that, taken individually, give little sense of the importance of his role. He is, according to the consensus of the two dozen current and former White House insiders I talked to, the single most influential voice shaping American foreign policy aside from Potus himself.*

And this is a bit more on who he is and what he does:

> *According to Denis McDonough, Obama's chief of staff, who is known for captaining a tight ship, "I see it throughout the day in person," he says, adding that he is sure that in addition to the two to three hours that Rhodes might spend with Obama daily, the two men communicate remotely throughout the day via email and phone calls. Rhodes strategized and ran the successful Iran-deal messaging campaign, helped negotiate the opening of American relations with Cuba after a hiatus of more than 50 years and*

---

[184] *The New York Times Magazine*, 5 May 2016.

> has been a co-writer of all of Obama's major foreign-policy speeches. "Every day he does 12 jobs, and he does them better than the other people who have those jobs," Terry Szuplat, the longest-tenured member of the National Security Council speechwriting corps, told me. On the largest and smallest questions alike, the voice in which America speaks to the world is that of Ben Rhodes.

And here, just a bit more, to get the full flavour of what we are dealing with, that is, an absolute policy cypher who knows nothing about foreign policy but knows a lot about how to craft a media campaign to make the policy acceptable to the ignorant and gullible:

> *Like Obama, Rhodes is a storyteller who uses a writer's tools to advance an agenda that is packaged as politics but is often quite personal. He is adept at constructing overarching plotlines with heroes and villains, their conflicts and motivations supported by flurries of carefully chosen adjectives, quotations and leaks from named and unnamed senior officials. He is the master shaper and retailer of Obama's foreign-policy narratives, at a time when the killer wave of social media has washed away the sand castles of the traditional press. His ability to navigate and shape this new environment makes him a more effective and powerful extension of the president's will than any number of policy advisers or diplomats or spies. His lack of conventional real-world experience of the kind that normally precedes responsibility for the fate of nations — like military or diplomatic service, or even a master's degree in international relations, rather than creative writing — is still startling.*

So we proceed through the article to find this first mention of his contempt for the media, which also comes with a kind of implied contempt for Obama himself:

> *When Rhodes joined the Obama campaign in 2007, he arguably knew more about the Iraq war than the candidate himself, or any of his advisers. He had also developed a healthy contempt for the American foreign-policy establishment, including editors and reporters at The New York Times, The Washington Post, The New Yorker and elsewhere, who at first applauded the Iraq war and then sought to pin all the blame on Bush and his merry band of neocons when it quickly turned sour. If anything, that anger has grown fiercer during Rhodes's time in the White House. He referred to the American foreign-policy establishment as the Blob. According to Rhodes, the*

Blob includes Hillary Clinton, Robert Gates and other Iraq-war promoters from both parties who now whine incessantly about the collapse of the American security order in Europe and the Middle East.

But what has made this profile so infamous is this passage with its direct quotes:

Rhodes singled out a key example to me one day, laced with the brutal contempt that is a hallmark of his private utterances. "All these newspapers used to have foreign bureaus," he said. "Now they don't. They call us to explain to them what's happening in Moscow and Cairo. Most of the outlets are reporting on world events from Washington. The average reporter we talk to is 27 years old, and their only reporting experience consists of being around political campaigns. That's a sea change. They literally know nothing."

We ought to be terrified and sickened but we're not because we find it so hard to believe that this is the way the US is governed. But it is. Sound policy criticism, no doubt on every aspect of the Obama administrations, is messaged to death which happens because the media is ignorant and incompetent. Once you know that, and combine it with Obama's far-far-to-the-left beliefs, much of what you see around you falls into place.

You should, by the way, read the whole article linked to above. This is the world of virtual reality we are all living in.

~

Trump endorsing Netanyahu in 2013 Israeli election
May 7, 2016

More of the story in the *Jerusalem Post*.[185]

The man who organized the video endorsement and the interview was 30-year-old British-born public relations phenom Jonny Daniels, who runs the Holocaust commemoration organization From The Depths and is arguably the Israeli closest to Trump. . . .

"It is very good news for Israel that he will be the Republican candidate for

---
[185] *The Jerusalem Post*, 7 May 2016.

president, because we really do have a good friend in Donald Trump," Daniels said. *"I'm not sure people realize who he is beyond his media persona. He is a politician playing politics, and there are certain things you do and say for votes, and if it's inflammatory so be it. Netanyahu and Obama have also reached out to their voter base, and that's what Trump has been doing."*

Meanwhile, the editor of the *Weekly Standard*, supposedly a friend of Israel, is trying to organise a different candidate from the right. These are the friends of Hillary and therefore the deepest most implacable enemies of Israel, not to mention the United States: 'Mitt Romney met privately with William Kristol, who is leading the effort to draft an independent candidate'.[186] If you want to know why Republicans are beyond useless, this is hard to beat:

> *Thursday, both Kristol and Romney attended an awards gala for American Friends of The Hebrew University, an area group that supports the Jerusalem-based school.*
>
> *At the dinner, when asked in front of the attendees about possibly running as an independent this year, Romney said he was not interested.*
>
> *"No, I'm certainly going to be hoping that we find someone who I have my confidence in who becomes nominee. I don't intend on supporting either of the major-party candidates at this point," Romney said, according to the Washington Examiner.*
>
> *But, Romney added, "I am dismayed at where we are now, I wish we had better choices, and I keep hoping that somehow things will get better, and I just don't see an easy answer from where we are."*

Thursday, that is AFTER Trump had locked the nomination process up. Whose side are these people on, because it does not appear to be on the same side as those who support the long-term survival of the Israeli state.

---

[186] *The Washington Post*, 6 May 2016.

The single most important story of the Obama years
May 7, 2016

This is the single most important story in the last eight years. It involves the utterly absurd and bizarre way in which American foreign policy is made, and the absence to an infinite degree of the media as a check on government. It explains better than anything I have read why the Western world is finished and done. If you are not on top of this story, you have no serious conception about how deranged the world in which you live actually is.

I have discussed it already – **The Obama White House counted on the ignorance and stupidity of the media** – but my impression from the lack of interest and the comments is that no one thinks of this as anything very much at all and I don't just mean here but everywhere. Perhaps there is a weariness in dealing with Obama and his lying that everyone just says, so what else is new? For me, however, this is one of the most clarifying stories I have ever read since what it says is that there is literally nothing that a party of the left can do that will cause outrage. Literally nothing at all. And the blame here cannot be landed on the left, but on the right, who has no idea how to fight and so far as the party administrations on the right are concerned, are of zero use at all. If anyone can read this and then worry about Donald Trump, they are too hopelessly gone. We will deserve what we get if the one lifeline we are finally thrown is rejected. All of the following are different takes on this same story.

Richard Fernandez: The Men Who Would Be King

Thomas Ricks: A stunning profile of Ben Rhodes, the asshole who is the president's foreign policy guru

John Podhoretz: White House admits it played us for fools to sell Iran deal

Ace of Spades: Obama's Foreign Policy (Disaster) Czar Ben Rhodes: Reporters In DC Know Absolutely Nothing. It's Embarrassingly Easy to Spin Them, Since They Have Zero Knowledge Base

Lee Smith: Obama's Foreign Policy Guru Boasts of How the Administration Lied to Sell the Iran Deal

The Daily Mail: White House BRAGS about how it tricked reporters into cheerleading for Obama's Iran nuclear deal by creating a media 'echo chamber'

Alex Griswold: Obama Advisor Openly Brags About Lying to Public, Media Yawns

Claudia Rosette: Meet the Flimflam Man Behind Obama's Foreign Policy 'Narrative'

Eli Lake: Obama's Foreign Policy Guru Is the 'Blob' He Hates

David Gerstman:Error! Hyperlink reference not valid.

David Rutz: Seven Takeaways from the NY Times Profile of Failed Novelist Ben Rhodes

Paul Fahri: Obama official says he pushed a 'narrative' to media to sell the Iran nuclear deal

Scott Johnson: The runt of Rhodes

Clarice Feldman: An Epiphany on the Road to Tehran

Jed Babbin: The Eight-Year Amateur Hour

New York Daily News: Obama's Iran scam: The President hard sale of the nuclear deal with the mullahs was chock full of spin and half-truths

Fred Flietz: Ben Rhodes: The Sycophantic Political Operative Shaping Obama's Foreign Policy

Nicole Duran: Obama blasts Trump: 'This is not entertainment' or a 'reality show'

Ed Driscoll: BEN RHODES SAYS OTHERWISE. Obama hammers Trump: Presidential Race 'not a reality show'

Aaron Klein: 7 Shocking Revelations in NY Times' Profile of Obama's Foreign Policy Guru

Aaron Klein: NY Times: White House Used 'Often Misleading Or False' Narrative To Sell Iran Deal To 'Clueless' Reporters

Allahpundit: Ben Rhodes's brother, the day after Benghazi: The government thinks this could be a coordinated attack, not a video protest

John Podhoretz: "Meet the Press" panel doesn't discuss Obama @ morningmoneyben House gloating about scamming America on Iran and insulting WH reporters

Aaron McLean: Ben Rhodes, Liar

Lee Smith: The Ben Rhodes Blow-up

Daniel Drezner: My extremely lukewarm take on Ben Rhodes

Carlos Lozada: Why the Ben Rhodes profile in the New York Times Magazine is just gross

Clifford May: Obama's 'boy wonder'

Scott Johnson: The Goldberg Variations

Patrick L. Smith: Did the New York Times just accidentally tell the truth about the Obama administration?

John R. Schindler: As Boyish Ben Rhodes Drops Truth Bombs, Obama's Media Mask Crumbles

The Diplomad: On the Iran Deal: Guess What?

Michael Totten: Washington's Idiotic Echo Chamber

The Observer: Deception on—Not Just in—Iran

What I cannot fathom is why this is not the single most debated issue on the conservative right side of politics. There are thirty-five stories that I have collected to go with my own which are listed in the order in which they were found. Everyone sees how sensationally incredible this is, but no matter how much tinder there is, it is obviously not possible to generate genuine heat about any issue since it will never enter in any way into the mainstream media and therefore into popular consciousness. This is the world we are in. And this is the problem we are facing on the right if we cannot find a means to break through and have a scandal of such dimension recognised for what it is. You really do have to appreciate that Rhodes could say without any concern that he, a failed novelist, is the single most important influence on Obama's foreign policy and have it confirmed by others in the White House. And I regret to say that even those among us who read these blogs don't see this as the absolute beyond the pale scandal it is because they didn't read it on a front page or see it repeated on the news for three nights in a row.

Living in a virtual reality policy bubble
May 9, 2016

How do you account for this: 'Obama report card: Approval up, economy down?'[187] In fact, Obama's approval rating remains well up into his eighth year in office in spite of the wreckage not just to the economy, but to the American health care system, the refugee crisis across the Middle East and throughout Europe, the open borders on the American south (and increasingly its north), continuous reductions in living standards, worsening racial relations, and an all-round deterioration in every aspect of American life. You account for it by understanding that the average American knows less about America than you do, and lives in a media bubble almost as tight as the bubble that once surrounded the Soviet Union.

Which is why this[188] remains the single most important story of the Obama years because it explains everything else that would otherwise be inexplicable:

> *In the "New York Times Sunday Magazine', David Samuels details how Ben Rhodes, a script writer, author of the Beloit Journal fiction piece titled "The Goldfish Smiles, You Smile Back," and brother of CBS president David Rhodes, a man with zero foreign policy experience, shaped and promoted the president's foreign policy narratives. Samuels observes: "His lack of conventional real-world experience of the kind that normally precedes responsibility for the fate of nations — like military or diplomatic service, or even a master's degree in international relations, rather than creative writing — is still startling." (In this respect, of course, he matches the president's foreign policy background: None.) The article details how these two shaped and spun make-believe about the facts and their policies and with the aid of a supine press and a number of think tanks and social media outlets helped propagate the false narratives these two wove out of their fantasies.*

This story happens to be about foreign policy. But it is just as true about every aspect of policy undertaken by Obama. The media, along with a relative handful of "think tanks" and social media outlets, has been able to stop dead in its tracks serious discussion about every aspect of policy. The deliberate warping of reality that surrounds every voter is not just the

---
[187] *The Washington Examiner,* 7 May 2016.
[188] *American Thinker,* 8 May 2016.

accidental result of politics as usual. It is the specifically designed outcome of the Obama White House.

In an article published in *Quadrant* in 2013, I wrote about the virtually identical Obama technique in winning the election he ought never to have won in 2012: 'The New Politics of Data-Driven Elections'.[189] This was the central point although there were many ancillary issues raised as well.

> *The media everywhere have generally been supporters of the Left. But whether because of the limited availability of alternative sources of information or because of an even more decided shift to the Left, the flow of information to the community is now so entirely biased that straightforward reporting of the views of a mainstream party of the Right can hardly find its way into the national conversation. In many respects during the election, media reports and analysis consisted of Democratic Party talking points. For the Republican Party, as for all parties of the Right, it is as if all games are away games with the media providing the crowd noise. A goal by the home team comes with cheers and general all-round satisfaction; a goal by the other side is met with polite applause or even silence. A foul behind play by a player on the team from the Left is taken as part of the rough and tumble of the game; a much lesser offence committed by the Right-of-centre away team brings down the hostility of the crowd—that is, the mass condemnation of the media.*
>
> *And it is not that the media are in some ordinary sense corrupt and corrupted. They are not influenced to take positions against their own beliefs. It is, instead, that these are the views of the mainstream media. They call it as they see it, but they see it with eyes far to the Left. It is not possible to succeed in the media unless one sees the issues in this way. The hiring practices of mainstream media organisations (the MSM) are designed in a kind of apostolic succession of like-minded individuals of the Left in major positions of influence.*

These same techniques have become Obama's standard means of governance. The following para from the Samuels article, with its direct quotes, ought to be the single most damning statement ever written about the media. But even though it is being discussed across the right side of politics in the United States, it is an absolute non-story where it counts,

---

[189] *Quadrant Online*, 1 January 2013.

in the conscious understanding among Americans of how deeply they are being manipulated at every turn.

> Rhodes singled out a key example to me one day, laced with the brutal contempt that is a hallmark of his private utterances. "All these newspapers used to have foreign bureaus," he said. "Now they don't. They call us to explain to them what's happening in Moscow and Cairo. Most of the outlets are reporting on world events from Washington. The average reporter we talk to is 27 years old, and their only reporting experience consists of being around political campaigns. That's a sea change. They literally know nothing."

Rhodes can say it in print, spitting in the eye not just of every Democrat opponent but also into the eyes of the reporters he describes, because after more than seven years in the White House he knows you and they don't count. Conservative opinions are of no consequence since whatever influence we might think we have in writing blog posts and specialist articles read by like-minded people, they are utterly irrelevant given the forces that are ranged against us. If Obama can permit Iran to build nuclear weapons in plain sight of everyone without bringing the world down on his head, what is it you think he cannot do by using the same techniques across every other area of government policy?

~

Paul Johnson on Donald Trump
May 9, 2016

This is Paul Johnson writing at *Forbes* discussing Donald Trump: 'When Excess Is A Virtue'.[190] It is full on with no suggestion of ironic intent or a claimed superiority to the cretins of the left. He takes them for what they are, dangerous and deluded, who are ruining the world in which we live. Nothing funny about what they say or do. This is what he wrote:

> THE MENTAL INFECTION known as "political correctness" is one of the most dangerous intellectual afflictions ever to attack mankind. The fact that we began by laughing at it—and to some extent, still do—doesn't diminish its venom one bit.

---

[190] *Forbes*, April 19, 2016

PC has an enormous appeal to the semieducated, one reason that it's struck roots among overseas students at minor colleges. But it also appeals to pseudo-intellectuals everywhere, since it evokes the strong streak of cowardice notable among those wielding academic authority nowadays. Any empty-headed student with a powerful voice can claim someone (never specified) will be "hurt" by a hitherto harmless term, object or activity and be reasonably assured that the dons and professors in charge will show a white feather and do as the student demands. Thus, there isn't a university campus on either side of the Atlantic that's not in danger of censorship. The brutal young don't even need to impose it themselves; their trembling elders will do it for them.

The insidious thing about PC is that it wasn't—and isn't—the creation of anyone in particular. It's usually the anonymous work of such Kafkaesque figures as civil servants, municipal librarians, post office sorters and employees at similar levels. It penetrates the interstices of society, especially those where the hierarchies of privilege and property are growing. To a great extent PC is the revenge of the resentful underdog.

Nowhere has PC been more triumphant than in the U.S. This is remarkable, because America has traditionally been the home of vigorous, outspoken, raw and raucous speech. From the early 17th century, when the clerical discipline the Pilgrim Fathers sought to impose broke down and those who had things to say struck out westward or southward for the freedom to say them, America has been a land of unrestricted comment on anything—until recently. Now the U.S. has been inundated with PC inquisitors, and PC poison is spreading worldwide in the Anglo zone.

For these reasons it's good news that Donald Trump is doing so well in the American political primaries. He is vulgar, abusive, nasty, rude, boorish and outrageous. He is also saying what he thinks and, more important, teaching Americans how to think for themselves again.

No one could be a bigger contrast to the spineless , pusillanimous and underdeserving Barack Obama, who has never done a thing for himself and is entirely the creation of reverse discrimination. The fact that he was elected President—not once, but twice—shows how deep-set the rot is and how far along the road to national impotence the country has traveled.

Under Obama the U.S.—by far the richest and most productive nation on earth—has been outsmarted, outmaneuvered and made to appear a second-

class power by Vladimir Putin's Russia. America has presented itself as a victim of political and economic Alzheimer's disease, a case of national debility and geopolitical collapse.

TIME FOR A SCARE

None of the Republican candidates trailing Trump has the character to reverse this deplorable declension. The Democratic nomination seems likely to go to the relic of the Clinton era, herself a patiently assembled model of political correctness, who is carefully instructing America's most powerful pressure groups in what they want to hear and whose strongest card is the simplistic notion that the U.S. has never had a woman President and ought to have one now, merit being a secondary consideration.

For Johnson, what many see as Trump's largest failings are his greatest strengths.

This was picked up at Tim Blair. It is the supposed right-wing conservative, P.J. O'Rourke quoted at *National Review*:[191]

I am endorsing Hillary. The second worst thing that could happen to this country. But she's way behind in second place, you know? She's wrong about absolutely everything — but she's wrong within normal parameters!

Vacuous and empty. We have been watching the normal parameters in action over the last eight years. If more of the same is what he has in mind, he really hasn't worked out why there have been millions streaming towards Trump who seem to have a series of problems they wish to see dealt with, problems that the likes of O'Rourke find invisible and for which they have no useful advice to offer.

~

And there are still people who prefer her to Trump
May 10, 2016

You know where Hillary Clinton's real expertise lies: in UFOs,[192] and this is according to her biggest fans at *The New York Times*. If you don't think she's a nutter, then you should read the full article at the link, but this will

---

[191] *National Review*, 8 May 2016
[192] *The New York Times*, 10 May 2016.

give you a taste.

> *Known for her grasp of policy, Mrs. Clinton has spoken at length in her presidential campaign on topics ranging from Alzheimer's research to military tensions in the South China Sea. But it is her unusual knowledge about extraterrestrials that has struck a small but committed cohort of voters.*
>
> *Mrs. Clinton has vowed that barring any threats to national security, she would open up government files on the subject, a shift from President Obama, who typically dismisses the topic as a joke. Her position has elated U.F.O. enthusiasts, who have declared Mrs. Clinton the first "E.T. candidate." ...*
>
> *In a radio interview last month, she said, "I want to open the files as much as we can." Asked if she believed in U.F.O.s, Mrs. Clinton said, "I don't know. I want to see what the information shows." But, she added, "There's enough stories out there that I don't think everybody is just sitting in their kitchen making them up."*

This woman is a moonbat, fully disassociated from reality. Is it possible that there is intelligent life in the universe? Sure. Is it possible that we have been visited by creatures from outer space? Maybe but very very unlikely. Is this the sort of thing that should preoccupy the mind of a president? Even crazier than her are the people who would make her president.

~

Rhodes to ruin
May 11, 2016

The deal with Iran was a sell out. The Iranians got everything they wanted and the United States got nothing in return. If there is a single obstacle to Iran developing nuclear weapons whenever they please, no one has yet identified what that obstacle is. But of more recent interest has been the contemptuous arrogance of Obama's spirit double on foreign affairs, Ben Rhodes, who provided an interview to *The New York Times*[193] that has been commented on endlessly across the net. But as the most infamous passage from that interview, reprinted below, would explain, these criticisms have not yet surfaced within the media in general.

---
[193] *The New York Times Magazine*, 5 May 2016.

> Rhodes singled out a key example to me one day, laced with the brutal contempt that is a hallmark of his private utterances. "All these newspapers used to have foreign bureaus," he said. "Now they don't. They call us to explain to them what's happening in Moscow and Cairo. Most of the outlets are reporting on world events from Washington. The average reporter we talk to is 27 years old, and their only reporting experience consists of being around political campaigns. That's a sea change. They literally know nothing."

Why would these bumpkins mention that the source of all their stories has called them clueless and ignorant? But now Rhodes has returned fire, and given how little he cares about what anyone else thinks as the Middle East blows up, he dismisses everything that has been said[194] in a tepid statement that is designed to be read in four minutes. This is his evidence that all is well:

> Today, Iran verifiably cannot obtain a nuclear weapon. That, more than anything I or anyone else can say, makes the case for the Iran deal.

If it were true, then he's right but it is very early days yet. If it is a lie, like just about everything else that has been said by Obama, then he has sabotaged American interests in the Middle East, although that is by no means the only measure of failure since there are so many others to go with this one. And there's that word "verifiably" that seems a qualifier of some significance. But the story about Rhodes himself, to the extent it was ever a scandal, has now fully disappeared. That is the one thing that is verifiable and shows again not only how insignificant the media is as an obstacle to Obama doing whatever he can get away with, but how insignificant the critics of the right to anything whatsoever.

Lee Smith has just touched on this very point: 'The Ben Rhodes Blow-up'.[195]

> The echo chamber is mad—but not at Ben Rhodes for what he said. They're mad at Samuels for getting the story they didn't—or didn't even see was there, and they're mad at him for what he reported. The Washington Post has published three different pieces on Samuels, none favorable, including one by the editor of the book section. The Post is mad of course because the Samuels piece publicly shamed the paper—after all, its main brief is to cover

---

[194] medium.com, 8 May 2016.
[195] *The Weekly Standard*, 10 May 2016.

the local industry—the workings of the government of the United States. And yet as the article makes plain, Post reporters and especially columnists got spun and conned about the Iran deal. But much worse than that is that the Post got scooped on the story explaining how gullible they are. Scooped by the New York Times, in their own backyard on the biggest foreign policy story of the past four years! That's embarrassing.

A world run by the emptiest shirts with the shallowest minds submerged within the sleaziest ideologies. Possibly ever thus, but what remains the most important part of the story is that it remains a non-story for virtually the whole of the world who know nothing about any of this at all. That ignorance does not include the governments of Iran or Russia, but what difference does that make to getting elected in the United States, the country with the least informed electorate across the developed world.

~

Democrat voters are fools according to Obama's White House team
May 11, 2016

It's getting to be a bit of a habit among these Obama people, first Ben Rhodes and now this: Charlie Rose and President's Speechwriters Laugh About ObamaCare Lie. They just play their own voters for fools, and rightly so:

> *CHARLIE ROSE: My point is do you have equal impact on serious speeches? Because it's about style, use of language, etcetera?*
>
> *JON LOVETT, FORMER OBAMA SPEECH WRITER: I really like, I was very — the joke speeches is the most fun part of this. But the things I'm the most proud of were the most serious speeches, I think. Health care, economic speeches.*
>
> *JON FAVREAU, FORMER OBAMA SPEECH WRITER: Lovett wrote the line about "If you like your insurance, you can keep it."*
>
> *LOVETT: How dare you!*
>
> *[laughter]*

LOVETT: And you know what? It's still true! No.

So let me remind you what Obama's foreign policy "expert" said about how dimwitted the journalists he deals with are and how easily it is to get them to report the party line to get voters to swallow industrial strength idiocy:

> *"The average reporter we talk to is 27 years old, and their only reporting experience consists of being around political campaigns. That's a sea change. They literally know nothing."*

Their voters are poorly informed but the saddest part is that these Obama advisors, although a bit more polished, are as dumb as the voters they deceived, since all they tried to do was convince them of the ridiculous things they believe themselves.

~

Trump is right and Ryan is duplicitous and dangerous

May 12, 2016

This is going to be a bruising election season for me. Here in Australia you can see my deeply hostile attitude to voting Labor to punish the Libs[196] for replacing Tony Abbott with Malcolm Turnbull. I find voting Labor at any time, but particularly now, both self-destructive and absurd. Other than in some revenge fantasy, it achieves nothing but harm. The Libs already deeply regret the change but there is nothing to be done now. We just have to get the Coalition back and then dispose of Malcolm later. If the only way we count is to allow the Labor Party to return to government, then count me out. I cannot stand Malcolm, and have been on the record for a very long time opposing him and everything he stands for – just go to the link to see my history. But at least he is constrained by his party room which still has Tony Abbott plus the other 42 amongst them, not to mention the Nationals who are the Coalition partners. It is a lot more than will ever constrain Labor.

And now this from *Quadrant Online*, which seems to be as anti-Trump as

---
[196] *Quadrant Online*, 27 April 2016.

the Murdoch press. This is an election for the soul of Western civilisation, and there is only one good side and that side has for all practical purposes decided who will be its presidential candidate, and in my view the right person ended up as the candidate. If that hopeless loser Paul Ryan, worst VP candidate I have ever seen – charmless and unpersuasive in all he did – and who as Speaker of the House handed Obama everything he had sought on a plate – if he now wants to play funny buggers about Trump as the Republican candidate, then he needs to have every bit of authority he has in the party taken from him. His antics have set up someone to contest his House seat among the Republicans, and there is this as well: Poll: Nearly half of GOP voters disapprove of Ryan.[197] The real way to read the data is that more Republicans disapprove of him as Speaker than approve.

> *Only 40 percent of GOP voters are happy with Ryan's stint as speaker so far, while 44 percent disapprove. Those numbers worsen among all voters, with just 30 percent approval and 48 percent disapproval.*

But now that Trump has won the primaries and will be the candidate unless some kind of suicidal death wish overtakes the Republicans (which is not impossible) Ryan's job is to unite the party around its chosen candidate. That is not just a suggestion – it is his job. That is what his function requires. Anything else weakens the Republicans going into the next election, and Trump's anger at such disgusting disloyalty is righteous. Ryan is playing a Judas role. Which brings me back to *Quadrant Online*.

QoL, for reasons known only to itself, has decided that the best person to cover the US election is someone by name of Michael Warren Davis who describes himself as "an assistant editor at *Quadrant* and poetry editor for the *Quarterly Review*". He is an American studying in Sydney. And this is what he has to say about Trump v Ryan:[198]

> *I have exactly zero sympathy for those who now turn around and tell Paul Ryan, Jeb Bush, the National Review writers et al. that they must be paid-up, loyal, dutifully and unquestioning members to the Trump Movement. That's complete tosh. Either you believe it is the duty of all to oppose corrupt and wrong-headed authority – which is, basically, what the American Revolution was all about – or you don't. There's no in-between.*

---

[197] thehill.com, 11 May 2016.
[198] *Quadrant Online*, 12 May 2016.

You, Michael Warren Davis, can do as you like, but you are not the Republican Speaker of the House. Trump has every right to run Ryan over with a steamroller if he is going to play the coy maiden in withholding his support. Trump is trying to win the presidency on behalf of the Republicans and create as much tailwind as possible to carry others along with him. By now I imagine Ryan has little influence on the outcome of the American election, but whatever influence he does have should be directed towards electing Trump. Because otherwise, it is being directed towards Hillary. Understanding this is the equivalent of understanding iambic pentameter in Shakespeare. That is, it is understood by everyone except the most dull-witted, bone headed and stupid.

AND NEWS JUST TO HAND: 'Trump-Ryan Meetings Begin With Nominee in No Mood for Compromise'.[199] And here's the point:

> *"Mr. Trump doesn't need to do anything," said Representative Duncan Hunter, the California Republican who co-chairs Trump's U.S. House Leadership Committee. "As Republicans in the House, we got used to the idea that our speaker was the de facto leader of the party. We didn't have somebody to represent our party against President Obama's administration. But that's over now — it's Trump, whether people like it or not."* ...
>
> *Some of Ryan's fellow Republicans, however, won't have much patience for a long, drawn-out reconciliation. Even two of his own top lieutenants have already publicly backed the New York billionaire — McCarthy of California and Scalise of Louisiana.*
>
> *"I don't think Trump necessarily needs Paul Ryan to get elected president — he hadn't needed him so far," said Representative Lynn Westmoreland of Georgia, who is among those who argue it is time for all Republicans need to get behind Trump.*

And this at the end of the story is as revealing as it is surprising:

> *In public, Trump has so far been mostly respectful toward Ryan. During a Trump campaign rally in March in Ryan's hometown of Janesville, Wisconsin, the billionaire asked for his supporters' thoughts on their local congressman.*
>
> *"How do you like Paul Ryan? Do you like him?" Trump asked the packed*

---

[199] bloomberg.com/politics, 12 May, 2016.

conference room. The capacity crowd of about 1,000 people erupted in loud boos. "Wow," Trump said, surprised. "I was told to be nice to Paul Ryan."

Shame they didn't tell Ryan the same about being nice to Trump.

~

Newt Gingrich discussing Donald Trump
May 12, 2016

This is interesting. 'Donald Trump Is Considering Newt Gingrich for Vice Presidential Role'.[200] And the following may give some idea why that is. I do note there is dispute about whether Gingrich really did say all that, but the points are well taken irrespective of the source.

> *Donald Trump is a genuine phenomenon. He may or may not become the Republican nominee for president. He may or may not win the presidency even if he becomes the nominee. Yet it is clear that he is a phenomenon and that any history of the 2016 presidential race will have to spend a good bit of time analyzing Trump and his impact.*
>
> *From the time he announced on June 16, Trump has dominated social and mainstream media. He dominates the conversation despite the lack of paid advertising. Trump says outrageous things and his supporters shrug it off. At every turn, his poll numbers continue to rise.*
>
> *As a step toward understanding this amazing performance, I spent part of the Christmas break reading his first bestseller, 'The Art of the Deal'. Written in 1987, this book is a classic among American business books and has influenced a generation of entrepreneurs. Trump wrote 'The Art of the Deal' when he was 41 years old and having a successful run. The book's popularity contributed to Time Magazine's decision to feature Donald Trump on its cover in January 1989.*
>
> *The portrait that emerges from this easy-to-read and remarkably interesting book is of an aggressive, ambitious person who is constantly pushing, constantly learning, and always seeking the next challenge. Reporters and analysts who are trying to understand Trump would be well served by slowing down and reading this nearly three-decade-old bestseller.*

---

[200] bloomberg.com, 12 May 2016.

They would discover that Donald Trump has developed a remarkable set of rules and principles that allow him to make decisions with incredible speed. Trump knows a lot, but what is amazing is how rapidly he figures out what he doesn't know.

My favorite story is of the Wollman Skating Rink in New York's Central Park. The Wollman Rink was a heavily used public skating rink which had fallen into disrepair in 1980. New York City tried for six years to fix it, spent $13 million, and the rink still was not ready to open. In June of 1986 Trump, who could see the rink from his apartment, finally got tired of the embarrassment and offered to fix the rink at his own expense. At first the city turned him down because its bureaucracy did not want to be embarrassed by someone fixing something they couldn't fix. Trump kept pushing and finally out of embarrassment the city gave in.

The key part of the story is Trump's reaction to being put in charge. He promptly recognized that he didn't know anything about fixing a skating rink. He asked himself who built a lot of skating rinks. "Canadians!" he concluded. He found the best Canadian ice skating rink construction company. When the Canadians flew in to assess the situation, they were amazed at how bad the city had been at solving the problem. They assured Trump that this was an easy job. Trump fixed the six year embarrassment two months ahead of schedule and nearly $800,000 under-budget. (The city did end up paying for the work, and Trump donated the profits to charity.)

After reading this chapter you begin to think that maybe Donald Trump really could build a wall along our southern border for a lot less than our current government estimates.

'The Art of the Deal' is filled with stories like this — stories of common sense stories of calculated risk taking, and stories of innovation and marketing. Anyone who would like to better understand Donald Trump would be helped by reading this remarkable book.

Another is his pledges and I have no way of knowing if he will make good on all of them but I do agree with all of them. Trump is the only candidate that is serious about building The Wall"! Two other important pledges Trump has made that no other candidate of either party has matched! First, deportation of millions of illegals that are demanding and costing American taxpayers billions of dollars and second, closing 34 Muslim training camps throughout our country! I WOULD LIKE TRUMP OR

ANY OTHER CANDIDATES PLEDGE TO REINSTATE ANY AND ALL MILITARY OFFICERS DISCHARGED BECAUSE THEY DISAGREED WITH OBAMA OR HIS POLICIES!!

Here is another that kind of wraps up my feelings about Trump. Raccoon's in your basement! An interesting analogy.

You've been on vacation for two weeks, you come home, and your basement is infested with raccoon's. Hundreds of rabid, messy, mean raccoon's have overtaken your basement. You want them gone immediately so you hire a guy. A pro. You don't care if the guy smells, you need those raccoon's gone pronto and he's the guy to do it! You don't care if the guy swears, you don't care if he's an alcoholic, you don't care how many times he's been married, you don't care if he voted for Obama, you don't care if he has plumber's crack...you simply want those raccoon's gone!

You want your problem fixed! He's the guy. He's the best. Period. That's why we need Trump. Yes, he's a bit of an ass. Yes, he's an egomaniac, but you don't care.

The country is a mess because politicians suck, the Republican Party is two-faced & gutless, illegal's are everywhere. You want it all fixed! You don't care that Trump is crude, you don't care that he insults people, you don't care that he had been friendly with Hillary, you don't care that he has changed positions, you don't care that he's been married 3 times, you don't care that he fights with Megyn Kelly and Rosie O'Donnell, you don't care that he doesn't know the name of some Muslin terrorist ... this country is weak, bankrupt, our enemies are making fun of us, we are being invaded by illegal's, we are becoming a nation of victims where every Tom, Ricardo and Hamad is a special interest group with special rights to a point where we don't even recognize the country we were born and raised in.

"AND WE JUST WANT IT FIXED" and Trump is the only guy who seems to understand what the people want.

You're sick of politicians, sick of the Democratic Party, Republican Party, and sick of illegal's. You just want this thing fixed. Trump may not be a saint, but doesn't have any lobbyist money influencing him, he doesn't have political correctness restraining him, all you know is that he has been very successful, a good negotiator, he has built a lot of things, and he's also not a politician, so he's not a cowardly politician. And he says he'll fix it. You don't care if the guy has bad hair. You just want those raccoon's gone. Out of your house!

This one is more about why we don't want Hillary. I think this sums it up well!

Donald Trump and Hillary Clinton are in a bar. Donald leans over, and with a smile on his face, says,
"The media are really tearing you apart for That Scandal."
Hillary: "You mean my lying about Benghazi?"
Trump: "No, the other one."
Hillary: "You mean the massive voter fraud?"
Trump: "No, the other one."
Hillary: "You mean the military not getting their votes counted?"
Trump: "No, the other one."
Hillary: "Using my secret private server with classified material to Hide my Activities?"
Trump: "No, the other one."
Hillary: "The NSA monitoring our phone calls, emails and everything Else?"
Trump: "No, the other one."
Hillary: "Using the Clinton Foundation as a cover for tax evasion, hiring cronies, and taking bribes from foreign countries?
Trump: "No, the other one."
Hillary: "You mean the drones being operated in our own country without The Benefit of the law?"
Trump: "No, the other one."
Hillary: "Giving 123 Technologies $300 Million, and right afterward it Declared Bankruptcy and was sold to the Chinese?"
Trump: "No, the other one."
Hillary: "You mean arming the Muslim Brotherhood and hiring them in the White House?"
Trump: "No, the other one."
Hillary: "Whitewater, Watergate committee, Vince Foster, commodity Deals?"
Trump: "No the other one:"
Hillary: "The IRS targeting conservatives?"
Trump: "No the other one:"
Hillary: "Turning Libya into chaos?"

Trump: "No the other one:"
Hillary: "Trashing Mubarak, one of our few Muslim friends?"
Trump: "No the other one:"
Hillary: "Turning our backs on Israel?"
Trump: "No the other one:"
Hillary: "The joke Iran Nuke deal?"
Trump: "No the other one:"
Hillary: "Leaving Iraq in chaos?"
Trump: "No, the other one."
Hillary: "The DOJ spying on the press?"
Trump: "No, the other one."
Hillary: "You mean HHS Secretary Sibelius shaking down health insurance Executives?"
Trump: "No, the other one."
Hillary: "Giving our cronies in SOLYNDRA $500 MILLION DOLLARS and 3 Months Later they declared bankruptcy and then the Chinese bought it?"
Trump: "No, the other one."
Hillary: "The NSA monitoring citizens'?"
Trump: "No, the other one."
Hillary: "The State Department interfering with an Inspector General Investigation on departmental sexual misconduct?"
Trump: "No, the other one."
Hillary: "Me, The IRS, Clapper and Holder all lying to Congress?"
Trump: "No, the other one."
Hillary: "Threats to all of Bill's former mistresses to keep them quiet"
Trump: "No, the other one."
Hillary: "You means taking the $145,000,000.00 from Putin for the Uranium Bribe?"
Trump : " No the other one ."
Hillary: "I give up! ... Oh wait, I think I've got it! When I stole the White House furniture, silverware and China when Bill left Office?"
Trump: "THAT'S IT! I almost forgot about that one".
****

Everything above is true. Yet she still gets the Democratic votes. Could there be that many stupid people in this country? Does anyone understand this? If not, I think we're doomed!

Hirsi Ali discussing Donald Trump
May 13, 2016

We went to see Ayaan Hirsi Ali tonight. And the only reason I asked a question was because my sciatica meant I couldn't sit for too long so got up and stood in the queue among those with something to ask. And when my turn came, my question was this:

What advice would you give a President Donald Trump?

That was not a gotcha question. She is worried about Muslim immigration. Trump is worried about Muslim immigration. So it seemed natural to ask her what advice she would give him. This is what happened next, as I reprint the text from the note I wrote on my iPhone to a friend on the train ride home.

She went all outraged about how awful he is and gets palpitations thinking of him with his finger on the bomb. And about what a misogynist he is. So I repeated my question about what advice she would give. Same answer. She was more filled with anger at Trump than at jihad! So discouraging.

The title of her presentations, as you can see, was "Dilemmas for Liberal Society: Security & Jihad in a World of Mass Migration". Only a percentage of us even see the issue as genuine, yet as she said right at the start, it is "the challenge of our time". I was asking what advice she might have for the next president. As my wife said after, perhaps I should have asked what advice she would give Hillary since even the mention of Trump put her completely off her stride. I will dwell on this for a while because it spoilt my night. To quote Kant once again: if you would will the end you must will the means. I find the ends she has in mind quite obscure after all this, but how she would achieve whatever ends she intends is now completely opaque.

REPLY TO COMMENTS: Not that at this stage will anyone be reading this post who hasn't already, and particular those who have linked to the post from Instapundit and Five Feet of Fury. (Truly extraordinary, by the way, what a link from Instapundit does for a small blog's traffic.) But I didn't say Hirsi Ali had directly stated that she was filled with greater anger at Trump than at jihadists. What I said was that the only time she showed deep anger during the evening was when I asked what she would say to a President Trump, which she point blank refused to answer, but instead showed genuine passion at the very idea of Trump as president and would not go to the question asked. My wife describes the moment as Hirsi Ali preferring to show her deep dislike of Trump rather than to share with the audience what advice she would give him if he became president. No one has to wish him to be president to recognise that if he were elected, he would be the one making many of the decisions that matter. And the fact is that I still don't know what advice she would have for an incoming president, whoever it might be. And I also would like to point out that none of this is a criticism of her personally, but as a concern I often have of people who know what they like and don't like but cannot turn their views into a coherent plan of action, including not just what to do but who they will get to do it.

Idiots led by idiots
May 13, 2016

As I've said before, this remains the single most important story of the Obama years.[201] It highlights the incompetent ignorance of the Obama administration which is matched by the ignorant incompetence of the American media. This is by John Schindler: 'As Boyish Ben Rhodes Drops Truth Bombs, Obama's Media Mask Crumbles'.[202]

> *Across the country, wherever people gather to talk national security, the hot topic for days now has been the New York Times Magazine's big interview with Ben Rhodes, President Obama's foreign policy guru-cum-salesman. Especially inside the Beltway, Mr. Rhodes' pointed comments about his work—particularly his admissions about manipulation of the media to sell Mr. Obama's nuclear deal with Iran—have caused a stir that's unlikely to die down soon.*

It is not just a scandal as in routine errors of misjudgement. It exposes everything that Obama has done in foreign policy as not just hollow and empty but as positively endangering the survival of the West. Australia's national security – the entire national security of the West – is dependent on the United States so when you see it run by far-left ideological zombies with zero background knowledge or historical understanding in any of the matters they are dealing with, it ought to terrify you. There is no one in charge who wishes to protect our interests. There is no one guarding us as we sleep. We are being sold down the river. That to my knowledge this has not been raised anywhere in Australia truly reminds me of what a sleeply hollow we are. So how was Obama able to get away with it? How could American foreign policy be left in the hands of a 38 year old failed novelist with absolute zero background in international relations? Back to Mr Schindler:

> *Mr. Rhodes made it plain that the reporters he deals with every day—that's the essence of his job—are idiots.*
>
> *"They literally know nothing," he explained. "The average reporter we talk to is 27 years old, and their only reporting experience consists of being around*

---

[201] catallaxyfiles.com, 8 May 2016.
[202] observer.com, 12 May 2016.

political campaigns." It's difficult to deny the truth of that statement, and any journalist who's being honest won't try. With the decline of foreign bureaus, a distressing number of those reporting on national security and foreign affairs are pretty much as Mr. Rhodes described them.

Idiots led by idiots. It is the same as the Jonathan Gruber story about how Obamacare was sold on a continuous series of outright lies[203] that were never exposed by the media. Obama's election and re-election occurred in exactly the same way. Everyone who paid any attention at all had from the beginning understood that Obama was allowing the Iranians to secure nuclear weapons[204] that will have devastating consequences in the years to come. And it has been a media cover up, because the media is 90% left-wing trolls.

The American economy, turning to my own expertise, is being managed at about the same level of competence, with the same level of media attention, as foreign policy. We are flying blind and if nothing is done to change direction, we will eventually crash into the side of the mountain.

~

Waiting for a miracle is not a plan
May 15, 2016

My obscure and personal blog is in the midst of experiencing the largest number of hits in its history. My post on Ayaan Hirsi Ali has made its way out beyond these precincts[205] so we will have our fifteen minutes of notoriety and then fade back into the pack. It did even occur to me as I wrote that earlier post that this was something I should leave alone since Hirsi Ali is a brave woman with a crucially important message. I remain disappointed that she cannot see in Donald Trump a vehicle for some kind of reversal if it is not entirely too late. And that is why I ended up writing what I did.

There is no one else anywhere to be found who might be able to take a stand and reverse this tide. There are a thousand things wrong with

---
[203] thediplomad.com, 14 November 2014.
[204] thediplomad.com, 7 May 2016.
[205] pjmedia.com, 14 May 2016.

Trump but whatever they are, they are mere flea bites compared with the things that are wrong with Hillary and Obama. I therefore remain astounded at the way so many of the people I know dismiss Trump because of various personal characteristics of his, and ignore, or set to the side, his potential to do a quite large amount of good in spite of all the negatives he may come with.

If you are the sort of person who thinks the nation states of the West need to be preserved, there is no one else who is anywhere near being in a position to achieve this end than Trump. I am therefore not for the first time reminded of this very old story which seems to get to the heart of the issue.

> *There once was a flood and everyone had reached safety except for one man.*
>
> *He climbed to the top of his house where the water was getting dangerously deep when a rescue helicopter came by and hovered above him and let down a rope, but the man waved it away shouting, "I don't need saving! My Lord will come"*
>
> *Reluctantly, the helicopter left.*
>
> *The water continued to rise and a boat came to him but, once again, the man shouted, "No! Go away! the Lord will come and save me!" and so the boat, too, went off.*
>
> *Finally, a raft came by and invited him to climb aboard, but the man was deeply religious and said, "It's all right! The Lord will save me!"*
>
> *The rain continued to pour, the water continued to rise and the man drowned.*
>
> *At the gates of heaven, the man met St. Peter. Confused, he asked, "Peter, I have lived the life of a faithful man – why did you not rescue me?"*
>
> *"For pity sake!" St. Peter replied. "We sent you a helicopter, a boat and finally a raft! What else did you expect us to do?"*

Donald Trump, it seems to me, is that raft.

Spinning make-believe about the facts
May 15, 2016

I still find this the single most important story of the Obama years[206] and what I find ultra remarkable is how little controversy it has led to. But it's not for want of trying. If you go to the link, you will see the thirty-six individual sets of commentaries that I have come across since the original interview with Ben Rhodes was published. In Australia, so far I have come across not a single comment except for the ones I have written myself. To which I now add another, published at *Quadrant Online*.[207] I won't even quote myself, but one of the people I discuss in the article. If you don't find this terrifying about our collective futures and the defence of the West, I don't know what would.

> *In the New York Times Sunday Magazine, David Samuels details how Ben Rhodes, a script writer, author of the Beloit Journal fiction piece titled "The Goldfish Smiles, You Smile Back," and brother of CBS president David Rhodes, a man with zero foreign policy experience, shaped and promoted the president's foreign policy narratives.*
>
> *Samuels observes: "His lack of conventional real-world experience of the kind that normally precedes responsibility for the fate of nations — like military or diplomatic service, or even a master's degree in international relations, rather than creative writing — is still startling." (In this respect, of course, he matches the president's foreign policy background: None.)*
>
> *The article details how these two shaped and spun make-believe about the facts and their policies and with the aid of a supine press and a number of think tanks and social media outlets helped propagate the false narratives these two wove out of their fantasies.*

It may be recalled that Jonathan Gruber did the same in relation to the changes made to the American health care system, as discussed here: 'Obamacare Architect: Yeah, We Lied to The "Stupid" American People to Get It Passed'.[208] And I have watched an economic policy as badly constructed as has ever been inflicted on an ignorant population. Which

---

[206] catallaxyfiles.com, 8 May, 2016.
[207] *Quadrant Online*, 15 May, 2016.
[208] townhall.com, 10 November 2014.

leads me to my own conclusion in the *Quadrant* article:

> *If Obama can permit Iran to build nuclear weapons in plain sight without bringing the world down on his head, what is it you think he cannot do by using the same techniques across every other area of government policy?*

You know that if any of this were done by a Republican, the explosions would be loud and never ending which is why such actions are almost never done by parties of the right.

The consequence of a supine media is an American health care system in a shambles, the economy in permanent stagnation and the Middle East in chaos, with an Iranian nuclear capability now just a matter of time.

UPDATE: There are some who understand the evil that these clowns have caused, and no people are more concerned than the Israelis. It is Obama's fundamental anti-semitism, disguised as anti-Zionism, that has driven his policy. Which brings us to the latest development: 'ISRAELI LEADER: IRAN MOCKS WWII HOLOCAUST, PREPARES ANOTHER'.[209] This is the altered face of the Middle East Obama has created. Such hollow lies when this outcome has been Obama's almost certain policy intent.

> *Israeli Prime Minister Benjamin Netanyahu lashed out at Iran Sunday for staging a Holocaust-themed cartoon contest that mocked the Nazi genocide of 6 million Jews during World War II and said the Islamic Republic was busy planning for another one. . . .*
>
> *State Department spokesman Mark Toner, traveling with Secretary of State John Kerry in Saudi Arabia, said the United States was concerned the contest could "be used as a platform for Holocaust denial and revisionism and egregiously anti-Semitic speech, as it has in the past."*
>
> *"Such offensive speech should be condemned by the authorities and civil society leaders rather than encouraged. We denounce any Holocaust denial and trivialization as inflammatory and abhorrent. It is insulting to the memory of the millions of people who died in the Holocaust," Toner said.*

It is disgusting that the State Department merely sees this about denying historical events no one doubts occurred. It is not words and opinion that matter here, but the future battle lines in the Middle East. With the media comprised of compliant idiots, you will find no truth about anything of

---

[209] foxnews.com, 15 May 2016.

significance by reading the American press. Facilitating another Holocaust has been Obama's aim from the start. Since we know they never tell the truth, their words mean nothing. It is the reality on the ground that matters, which absolutely everyone in the Middle East perfectly well understands. No one who wished to forestall an Iranian attack on Israel could have acted in the way Obama has done.

~

He can't go soon enough
May 16, 2016

As I wrote the title I thought there are a lot of people I would say that about, but in this case it's Barack Obama. I wish him a long and frustrated retirement as he watches Donald Trump reverse everything he set in place. Which brings to mind two stories from today.

First there's this: 'Obama goes after Trump in Rutgers commencement address and slams building 'walls,' isolationism, and 'conspiracy theories' – and even defends the 'rigged' political system'.[210] It is only because he is a narcissistic loon that he thinks anyone still pays attention to what he says, in the sense that what he says actually changes anyone's mind about anything. He is regularly the stupidest man in any room he enters, and is almost certainly always the least informed. He can talk through a teleprompter, but off the cuff he is famously incapable of stringing two coherent words together. It is unimaginable how smart this pathological dishonest dumbbell thinks he is to be quoted as saying this:

> *'In politics and in life, ignorance is not a virtue,' Obama said. 'It's not cool to not know what you're talking about. That's not keeping it real or telling it like it is. That's not challenging political correctness. That's just not knowing what you're talking about.'*

> *'When our leaders express a disdain for facts. When they're not held accountable for repeating falsehoods and just making stuff up, and actual experts are dismissed as elitists, then we've got a problem,' Obama said.*

At least he's right that we have got a problem. It's just that he doesn't

---
[210] *Daily Mail Australia,* 16 May 2016.

know what that problem is.

So to the second story: 'Donald Trump insists Britain would NOT be at the back of the queue for a trade deal if he wins the White House'.[211] Here we have a head to head comparison between Obama and Trump. Obama blunders his way across the world, and in this case offending large sections of the British public, buying in where he has no business to be. Trump just says that this is a decision for the UK to make and whatever they decide the US will do what it can to accommodate.

> *Donald Trump today insisted Brexit would not put Britain at the 'back of the queue' to secure a US trade deal should he become president.*
>
> *The presumptive Republican nominee said it would make no difference to him whether Britain decides to stay with the European Union or chooses to leave next month.*
>
> *The remarks struck a markedly different tone to incumbent president Barack Obama who issued a stark warning about the prospects for a trade deal for Britain on a visit last month.*
>
> *Mr Obama triggered outrage from Out campaigners who warned foreign leaders should not be intervening on Britain's referendum.*

He will be gone in less than a year, but the damage he has left behind will go forward into the deepest future.

~

One more "conservative" to scratch off my list
May 17, 2016

There are so many people who have discredited themselves in my eyes as representatives of the right, and conservatism in particular, that by the time this election season is over, there will be virtually no one left I trust.

Now it is Daniel Hannan who has entered the fray. He takes the pose of an above-it-all intellectual, too pure to endorse the far from perfect Donald Trump. He has published a brief note on 'The real reason Donald Trump

---

[211] *Daily Mail Australia*, 15 May 2016

is unfit to be president'.[212] And here is the reason:

> *The real disqualification, from a conservative point of view, is Trump's refusal to recognize that he is aspiring to an office bigger than he is.*

Well la dee dah. Now aren't we being precious. In fact, it is worse than that. He is off with the pixies in thinking that there is some kind of fastidious approach in which politics ends can be accomplished without strength of character and a hardline approach to getting one's own way rather than another being allowed to get their way. If Hannan weren't so famous as a torch bearer for the right, you could ignore him. In fact, from now on I will feel he can be safely ignored.

In the meantime let me repeat his various arguments, which amount to absolutely nothing at all. I might add, that I also don't think he is right about a single thing he says. And for such a short article the number of false analogies is astonishing. A comparison of any of these with the likes of Hillary shows a blindness that is quite remarkable.

> *"He is a narcissistic, thin-skinned bully, a serial liar, a man who shows not the slightest respect for the office to which he aspires."*

> *"Next to his moral unsuitability, the fact that he is bad news for conservatives seems almost trivial. It's not his big-government protectionism that ought to bar him from high office. It's not even the way in which he will undo decades of progress and taint the Republicans once again with xenophobia."*

> *"This isn't about Hillary. It's about defending the republic from a candidate who is hostile to its foundational values."*

> *"Donald Trump is inimical to the core Republican values of personal freedom, limited government, enterprise and a patriotic foreign policy."*

> *"I say only one thing with absolute certainty: Don't vote for an unfit candidate simply because you dislike another unfit candidate. Doing so makes you complicit. It means endorsing one of two amoral, power-hungry people who would very probably ignore their oath of office."*

> *"As Vaclav Havel used to say in Czechoslovakia, living under a Communist regime doesn't mean that you have to legitimize it. A citizen can still retain his or her integrity by refusing to vote for the approved list, refusing to display party posters, refusing to repeat official slogans. And integrity matters.*

---

[212] *The Washington Examiner*, 16 May 2016.

> *Indeed, at present, it's pretty much all that American conservatives have left. For the love of God, cousins, don't throw it away."*

Conservatives understand that perfection is not found in human affairs and one must work with the tools one has at hand. Hannan is one more pompous fool whose lack of judgement explains why he has failed to rise among the British Conservative Party. How is this for a rounded full-on idiocy?

> *"Is Trump any worse than Hillary?" isn't just setting the bar absurdly low; it's also the wrong question. The right question is, "Is Donald Trump fit to be president?" And the answer must surely be, "No."*

Look, stupid. The only question is which one of these two you prefer to the other. It is infuriating to read such stuff. I guess I will have to wait another 25 years for Trump to have become the perfect representation of conservative thought, which will finally occur, as it has with Reagan today, when there is someone else trying to disturb the establishment of the time that is yet to be, and the usual suspects are lamenting there is no one like Donald Trump around any more.

~

Why Democrat are guaranteed to be corrupt and sleazy
May 17, 2016

From *The New York Times*, in a story with the title, 'Little Is Off Limits as Donald Trump Plans Attacks on Hillary Clinton's Character'.[213]

> *Donald J. Trump plans to throw Bill Clinton's infidelities in Hillary Clinton's face on live television during the presidential debates this fall, questioning whether she enabled his behavior and sought to discredit the women involved.*
>
> *Mr. Trump will try to hold her accountable for security lapses at the American consulate in Benghazi, Libya, and for the death of Ambassador J. Christopher Stevens there.*
>
> *And he intends to portray Mrs. Clinton as fundamentally corrupt, invoking*

---
[213] *The New York Times*, 16 May 2016.

everything from her cattle futures trades in the late 1970s to the federal investigation into her email practices as secretary of state.

These are all true. The question is why he is the only one who would use these stories? That is what is wrong with American politics and its media. If telling the truth about Democrats in relation to character issues that matter is considered unfair, the election of Democrats of bad character is guaranteed.

~

A case study of a Trump supporter who works for the Murdoch press
May 17, 2016

If you work for Murdoch, them's the rules. You cannot support Donald Trump for president. So let us see how Tim Blair gets around it.[214]

A number of friends and many readers are fans of Donald Trump. That's OK. I understand his appeal, even if he's a fraud. Although it's true that he does sometimes make the right calls.

Donald Trump on Friday picked a prominent climate change skeptic to help him craft his energy policy and pushed back against renewed calls that he release his income tax returns — saying his tax rate is "none of your business."

But for Melbourne-based artist and writer Aubrey Perry, support for Trump is an absolute deal-breaker. This applies even when Trump's supporters are her parents.

I'd known for a while that my mum was open to the idea of Trump as her candidate. My dad has been a Trump supporter from the beginning. But I've lived in Australia for the past seven years. They live in the US. We text and Facebook with each other, but we don't discuss politics.

And I don't use Twitter much. But, wow. My mum does. I recently checked her Twitter page for the first time in a while and was shocked…

I was shocked.

I told her so. Publicly. Finally. I wrote back, "Your Twitter feed makes

---
[214] *The Daily Telegraph,* 17 May 2016.

> me disappointed and embarrassed of you as a person, a supposed critical thinker, and my mother. Shocked."
>
> Here's her mother's Twitter page. It isn't shocking at all. It's just the opinions of someone who happens to be very enthusiastic about a certain presidential candidate. Yet this has led Aubrey to denounce her family as racists and to "sever all ties with my parents as long as they promote these ideologies of hate and xenophobia".
>
> A reminder to Aubrey, who is evidently a Clinton backer: Hillary attended Trump's wedding. Shocked!
>
> But do go to her mother's twitter page and you will find a quite nicely put and succinct summary of why sensible people support Trump and abominate Hillary.

~

An even more than usually repulsive and disgusting anti-Trump "conservative"

May 17, 2016

This time it is Bill Kristol who has a strategy of his own to stop Trump, explained here.[215]

> Their plan is to run a candidate who could win three states and enough votes in the electoral college to deny both parties the needed majority. This would throw the election into the House of Representatives, which would then elect a candidate the Kristol group found acceptable. The fact that this would nullify the largest vote ever registered for a Republican primary candidate, the fact that it would jeopardize the Republican majorities in both the House and Senate, and more than likely make Hillary Clinton president, apparently doesn't faze Kristol and company at all.

And why should Trump be stopped. These are hardly the kind of specifics that amount to any kind of charge at all:

> Their chief justification for opposing Trump is that he is not a "constitutional conservative" and in fact is "without principles" and therefore dangerous.

---

[215] breitbart.com, 15 May, 2016.

> *The evidence offered is that he has supported Democrats in the past and changed his positions on important issues.*
>
> *A second charge against Trump is that his character is so bad (worse than Hillary's or Bill's?) that no right-thinking Republican could regard him as White House worthy.*
>
> *In addition to alleging that Trump is lacking in principles and character, Kristol claims that the Republican candidate is a crackpot conspiracy theorist, a disqualifying trait. Kristol's evidence is a remark Trump made on the eve of the Indiana primary suggesting that Ted Cruz's father might have something to hide about his alleged acquaintance with Kennedy assassin Lee Harvey Oswald.*

The article is by David Horowitz and the title is "Bill Kristol: Republican Spoiler, Renegade Jew". I might have had some qualms about the title, but Horowitz explains himself in a way I am completely sympathetic with.

> *All these dishonesties and flim-flam excuses pale by comparison with the consequences Kristol and his "Never Trump" cohorts are willing to risk by splitting the Republican vote. Obama has provided America's mortal enemy, Iran, with a path to nuclear weapons, $150 billion dollars, and the freedom to develop intercontinental ballistic missiles to deliver the lethal payloads. Trump has promised to abandon the Iran deal, while Hillary Clinton and all but a handful of Democrats have supported this treachery from start to finish. Kristol is now one of their allies.*
>
> *I am a Jew who has never been to Israel and has never been a Zionist in the sense of believing that Jews can rid themselves of Jew hatred by having their own nation state. But half of world Jewry now lives in Israel, and the enemies whom Obama and Hillary have empowered — Iran, the Muslim Brotherhood, Hezbollah, ISIS, and Hamas — have openly sworn to exterminate the Jews. I am also an American (and an American first), whose country is threatened with destruction by the same enemies. To weaken the only party that stands between the Jews and their annihilation, and between America and the forces intent on destroying her, is a political miscalculation so great and a betrayal so profound as to not be easily forgiven.*

Utterly beyond the pale and all comprehension. Kristol is siding with the greatest carriers of evil in our time, and a bleak centuries-long future for the entire human race will be the result of their success. The arrogant, smug brainlessness of those who would risk the election of Hillary where there is no other viable candidate beyond Donald Trump makes these people vile and despicable. And that goes for *Commentary* who has published this article by Jonathan Tobin criticising Horowitz titled, 'Breitbart's 'Renegade Jew' Disgrace'.[216] And beyond that, it extends to Powerline, who has made Tobin's article one of its "picks". Unforgivable and worthless.

REACTIONS TO THE HOROWITZ ARTICLE: Just because they state the obvious does not make it nonetheless true: 'Renegade Conservative Site BREITBART's Sin–Not Anti-Semitism, But Pro-Trumpism'.[217]

AND NOW TO ADD TO THE REST: Found here:[218]

> David Horowitz incidentally has been a great friend to me over the years. I have known him since I was 15 years old when I once worked for Alan Dershowitz. He is now a Trump delegate and I know he will have Trump's ear on the issues that matter regarding world peace.

Wow. If ever there were a killer argument to vote for The Donald, that is it.

~

A little test you can try at home
May 18, 2016

Scott Adams – that' right, Dilbert's Scott Adams – on About those policy details.[219] It is Trump's policy details he had in mind, but the issue is no doubt universal in democracies if the argument is actually valid:

> Here's a little test you can try at home. In your mind, divide your friends and coworkers into two groups. One group understands a lot about making business decisions and one group has no business experience. Ask each of them individually this question:
>
> How much detail should Trump provide on his policies?

---

[216] commentarymagazine.com, 16 May 2016.
[217] vdare.com, 16 May 2016.
[218] gotnews.com, 16 May 2016.
[219] blog.dilbert.com, 11 May 2016.

A. *Lots of detail so we know exactly what he plans to do.*

B. *We only need the big picture now because the details will be negotiated later, and the environment will change by then. Also, presidents have access to better advice and information than candidates.*

I predict that your most experienced friends and coworkers will choose B. Let me know in the comments how it goes.

By the time I got to it, there were 3651 comments.

~

The Murdoch-Trump alliance
May 19, 2016

I might start being able to read *The Oz* again: 'Why Rupert Murdoch Decided to Back Donald Trump'.[220] It is dearly to be wished. From which:

> *The Murdoch-Trump alliance is the result of at least two private meetings between the billionaires this spring as well as phone calls from Trump's son-in-law, Jared Kushner. Murdoch's view, according to those who've spoken with him, is that Trump is a winner whom the "elites" failed to take seriously. "He doesn't like people to be snobs and treat Trump like a clown," one person explained. Murdoch's outlook is also informed by his take on the winnowed GOP field. When it came down to the final three candidates, Murdoch simply saw Trump as the best option. "He never liked Cruz," the source explained. Kasich made a personal pitch to Murdoch that he could win on a second ballot at the convention, but failed to persuade. In March, Murdoch tweeted that the GOP would "be mad not to unify" behind Trump.*

And hopefully after our election, he can have another look at Turnbull, assuming the Libs win, of course. I look forward to Niki Savva's next book on *The Subtle Genius and Hidden Strengths of Tony Abbott*. But first the Coalition has to win.

---

[220] nymag.com, 17 May 2016.

America's anti-American foreign policy
May 19, 2016

This is one of the most insightful articles on American politics I have come across in quite a while. The title is "Anti-Americanism is the Foreign Policy of Fools", but it's his sub-title that more closely explains the text: 'Anti-Americanism is the only foreign policy that the American Left needs'.[221] The point is that the left has no foreign policy other than to oppose Republicans. It is simply a vehicle for domestic political advantage. The actual outcomes across the world are of no consequence other than in terms of whether or not it allows Democrats to win elections. But what makes this policy so profoundly striking is that at the centre of the political views of the left, and what gives it whatever consistency it has, is a deep and unabiding anti-Americanism. The article begins with an observation on Ben Rhodes, who by now should need no introduction.

> *Ben Rhodes knows next to nothing about foreign policy. He has no idea whether Iran will get nukes and couldn't care less whether it's moderate or not. He's a failed fiction writer whose goal is "radically reorienting American policy in the Middle East in order to make the prospect of American involvement in the region's future wars a lot less likely". . . .*
>
> *Rhodes sneers at the reporters whom he manipulated as knowing nothing. And he's right. But he also doesn't know anything. The condition is typical of an American left which has no foreign policy. It only has an anti-American domestic policy which it projects internationally without regard to its relevance.*

What has brought Rhodes to prominence is his involvement in selling Obama's capitulation to Iran.

> *The Iran deal had to happen to defeat "neo-conservatives", the "war lobby" and whatever other leftist boogeyman was lurking around the premises. The men and women doing the defeating, like Rhodes, had zero interest in what was actually happening in Iran or what its leaders might do with nuclear weapons. They would tell any lie to help sell the deal because they were fighting a domestic battle of narratives. Iran wasn't a real place. It was a fictional counter in a domestic ideological battle.*

---
[221] frontpagemag.com, 13 May 2016.

He provides another example from the previous Democrat administration:

> *Bill Clinton had no foreign policy. Like Obama, he viewed foreign policy in terms of his domestic conflicts with Republicans. He tried to engage diplomatically while retreating militarily. His botched intervention in Yugoslavia had strong similarities to Obama's disastrous intervention in Libya.*

The argument is that American foreign policy is, so far as the Democrats are concerned, merely domestic policy. The consistent theme is opposition to traditional American values which means opposition to the Judeo-Christian tradition.

> *Anti-Americanism, like most prejudices, is a license for ignorance. By embracing a prejudice against their own country, Democrats have lost any skill at foreign policy that they once had. Instead of learning anything about the world, they resort to the easy answer of turning away from the confusing problems of other countries to blame them all on us. Anti-Americanism is the only foreign policy that they need.*

Until now, the Democrats could maintain this position without actually damaging America itself although the damage elsewhere has been immense. That is no longer so. Either the policy will have to go or America will. It will be impossible for both to exist long term.

~

Do Donald Trump and Andrew Bolt not have exactly the same position on migration?
May 20, 2016

My wife and I have just watched the segment on Bolt with Niall Ferguson and then Rowan Dean where the issue of multiculturalism and immigration was at the centre of the conversation. The way I would construct what was said is this:

- there is this problem associated with migration where some people are entering the country who do not wish to become part of the majority culture

- this has now created social tensions causing people to look for political solutions
- the result has been this terrible situation where "populists" like Donald Trump are now able to get political traction.

My question then is this: In what way is Donald Trump not attempting to solve the very problem Andrew Bolt and the others have raised? They can give it any name they please, but when you get right down to it, the issue is how do we ensure that those allowed to migrate into Australia will become Australians, or in the US case, Americans.

So I will repeat what I have said before, following Kant: if you would will the end, you must will the means. Commentators, historians and magazine editors are not political leaders, and their skills are not in devising political programs. Are not Trump's ends their ends? If not, what is it exactly that they do want? And if they more or less do share Trump's ends, do they not see that he is onto something in the approach he is taking? Or if they support the ends but not the means, how would they go about achieving these ends?

It just does seem to me that they do support the ends that Trump is promoting, but for some reason find themselves unwilling to endorse either the means or the man.

~

Anti-Trump Republicans are the worst kind of fools
May 21, 2016

Whether he knows it yet or not, Paul Miringoff at Powerline will vote for Donald Trump. There are nerves to settle and plenty of time to do it. But in his quite informative column discussing his uncertainties[222] he brings two other columnists into it who are both deeply anti. You really do have to think these people ought to have their keyboards taken away from them for their own safety. The first is Michael Gerson:

> *Gerson contends that Trump is unfit to be president:*
>
> *It is not enough for GOP partisans to assert Trump's superiority to Clinton*

---

[222] powerlineblog.com, 20 May 2016.

on this issue or that. They must justify that Trump has the experience, knowledge, temperament, judgment and character to be president of the United States.

Gerson argues that Trump fails this test because of his positions on illegal immigration and Muslim entry into the U.S., and because a New York Times piece showed Trump to be a "cave-man" when it comes to women.

The second article is by Robert Kagan:

He argues that Trump will bring fascism to America. . . . Kagan has announced that he supports Hillary (some attribute this decision to an affinity with the Democrat on foreign policy issues).

It's not just an over-heated brain. The man is a moron with pretensions to insight. My wife gets mad at me for not explaining myself when I kick such stupidity out the door without discussion. But there are morons everywhere and you cannot parse their idiocies to the end of time.

Paul, you gotta stop reading these guys and worrying about their opinions. Steve Hayward is trying to explain things to you on your own blogsite: 'THE ENDLESS ENIGMA OF DONALD TRUMP'.[223] This is where things are heading, and you should be heading there along with everyone else: 'New Poll: Republicans Are Increasingly Positive About Donald Trump'.[224]

~

They think we're fools
May 23, 2016

Gavin McInnes has done something quite extraordinary and it turns out that having done what he's done, the result is even more extraordinary than you might ever have imagined it would be. He has gone and interviewed Jesse Hughes, lead singer of Eagles of Death Metal, the group playing at the Bataclan in Paris on the night it was stormed by Islamists and where almost 100 members of the audience were killed. The piece is titled 'Surrendering to Death[225] where his point is that we are unprepared for what is being

---

[223] powerlineblog.com, 20 May 2016.
[224] hannity.com, 20 May 2016.
[225] takimag.com, 14 May 2016

inflicted on us and are doing nothing to toughen up. I begin towards the start of the interview but there is much more there:

- Do you think political correctness is killing our natural instincts and making us vulnerable?

Definitely. There were two girls who were involved. They were at the venue and vanished before the shooting, and these women were in traditional Muslim garb. They knew people wouldn't check them because of the way they were dressed. They got caught a few days later.

- The fear of offending Muslims is a terrorist's greatest weapon.

"When the cops went in after the attack, they shut down, what, 450 mosques? They found recruitment material in every single one of them." Look at the guys who bombed Brussels. They were wearing black gloves on one hand. Their luggage was too heavy to lift, but they didn't want anyone helping them with it. Nobody brought any of this up until after the bombs went off.

- We'd rather die than be called a bigot.

How is a faith being associated with racism? Just take out the word "Islam" and replace it with "communism." It's an ideology. The same way the Rosenbergs could sell nuclear secrets from within America is the same way Muslim terrorists can attack us from within. It's okay to be discerning when it comes to Muslims in this day and age.

Where is this push coming from? Is it all our fault?

Of course not. When you're at a soccer game in Europe and you see the words "United Arab Emirates," you know there is a lot of Arab money floating around and influencing the dialogue. The conversation is constantly being steered away from scrutiny. They think we're fools.

- Political correctness kills.

Davey [bassist Dave Catching] was in the middle of the stage and when the lights went on, he saw shit he'd never seen before in his life, awful stuff. It has no parallel. It's not just death. It's the most unsuspecting, innocent victims you can imagine—people who are gripped in terror and can't move as a result of it.

- It's like a metaphor for all of Western civilization.

I watched about seven people die. A couple of them were three feet from the barrier. They could have fallen backwards and been alive but they were too scared to even turn around. I remember a woman just standing with her hands up in a surrender pose. The terrorist finally saw her and all she did was go, "No no no." She surrendered to death in front of my very eyes. I was yelling at her, "HEY!" and I don't think she could hear me. She was so terrified, I think she'd already given up.

It's not long but whether it is or not, it is filled with a kind of detail about the modern non-defence of the West that should be thought about. They are out to kill us and take our countries from us – including your very own country, the one you are living in right now. They want to take your country and make it their country. That's exactly what they want and this is the kind of article that reminds you why they may well end up doing what they have set out to do.

~

Just how corrupt is she?
May 25, 2016

I'm used to Australian commentary on the American election to be one-sided and Democrat, but the AFR piece this morning – 'These times call for a serious president, not a childish one like Donald Trump'[226] – reaches a new low in stupidity and ignorance. You would at least think that after eight years of Obama, he might be just a touch reticent about his own judgment in such things, but instead he writes about the difference between outsiders entering the race when Obama did in comparison to now when it is Trump:

> In 2008, the challenger was The One. In 2016, it's The Donald. Then, the themes of the day were hope and change. Now, the themes are anger and retreat.

If he can still write "The One" without feeling the irony and disappointment, then this is one commentator who can with the greatest safety be ignored. I wonder why he thinks all this is taking place after eight years of Obama:

---

[226] *Australian Financial Review*, 25 May 2016.

> Every day, the liberal international order that has existed for 70 years seems less liberal, less international and less orderly. The United States has inched back from the world and challengers have stepped into it. The West is drooping. The historic project to unite the European continent seems shaky. The Middle East is a bloody mess. There are more refugees, asylum seekers and displaced people than at any time since the end of the Second World War.

So his solution: more of the same. So let us have a look at who will be president if it is not Donald Trump. This is from Instapundit:[227]

> CLINTON FOUNDATION GOT $100 MILLION FROM "BLOOD MINERALS" FIRM: *Then-Secretary of State Hillary Clinton unaccountably delayed implementation in 2009 of a congressionally mandated certification process designed to bar human rights abuses by mining companies in Africa.*
>
> *The Daily Caller News Foundation Investigative Group's Richard Pollock found a hundred million reasons for Clinton's dallying. Two years before, the Clinton Foundation got a $100 million pledge from the Vancouver, Canada-based Lundin Group.*
>
> *Lundin is one of the giants of the global mining industry, with huge operations in the Congo, Sudan and Ethiopia. Those operations were repeatedly condemned by human rights groups claiming native populations were being forced to flee their homelands and even being killed because they stood in the way of Lundin projects.*
>
> *"'Blood minerals' are related to 'blood diamonds,' which are allegedly mined in war zones or sold as commodities to help finance political insurgencies or despotic warlords," according to Pollock. Lundin has a long history of "cutting deals with warlords, Marxist rebels, military strongmen and dictatorships" in war-torn Africa.*
>
> *The least surprising aspect of this story? Spokesmen for the Clinton Foundation and Lundin refused to comment.*

Not the Nine O'Clock News, or the news anywhere. And this is one that comes to our attention. How many others just like it are there? And that wasn't even what I thought was the worst of it. So let me add this from the Daily Caller link:

---

[227] pjmedia.com/instapundit, 24 May 2016.

It wasn't the first time Clinton consorted with mining moguls. In the waning hours of his presidency in 2001, Clinton pardoned Glencore International mining and oil magnate Marc Rich after his wife, Denise, made generous donations to the Democratic Party, Hillary Clinton's Senate campaign and his Clinton Library.

Clinton's pardon erased a 65-count indictment against Rich for trading with Iran against the oil embargo. Rich did the Iranian oil sales while Americans were held captive in the country by the Mullahs.

Just how deep and far does it go? Which really does make this article more than odd which is 'A Response to My Conservative #NeverTrump Friends'[228] on why he won't vote for Hillary. Why is such an article even necessary? How can anyone who is even remotely Republican think of voting for her?

Here, then, are nine reasons (there are more) why a conservative should prefer a Trump presidency to a Democrat presidency:

- *Prevent a left-wing Supreme Court.*
- *Increase the defense budget.*
- *Repeal, or at least modify, the Dodd-Frank act.*
- *Prevent Washington, D.C. from becoming a state and giving the Democrats another two permanent senators.*
- *Repeal Obamacare.*
- *Curtail illegal immigration, a goal that doesn't necessarily have anything to do with xenophobia or nativism (just look at Western Europe).*
- *Reduce job-killing regulations on large and small businesses.*
- *Lower the corporate income tax and bring back hundreds of billions of offshore dollars to the United States.*
- *Continue fracking, which the left, in its science-rejecting hysteria, opposes.*

For these reasons, I, unlike my friends, could not live with my conscience if I voted to help the America-destroying left win the presidency in any way.

---

[228] jewishworldreview.com, 24 May 2016.

> *I just don't understand how anyone who understands the threat the left and the Democrats pose on America will refuse to vote for the only person who can stop them.*

It is hard to understand, almost as hard as to understand why people on the left also want to vote for Hillary.

~

Practical politics and political opinion
May 26, 2016

It is a fact that both Charles Murray and Jonah Goldberg have left me frigidly cold in almost everything they have written. I stopped reading both years ago and am not surprised to find that Goldberg had invented the #NeverTrump tag. Now Murray has lined up in the same way.[229] And here in a single sentence he captures everything that is wrong with #NeverTrump:

> *While I am already on record with my sympathy for the grievances that energize many of Trump's supporters, I am thinking about writing a book that is even more explicitly sympathetic with those grievances.*

He has sympathy for such grievances and what does he intend to do: write a book. For some of us – me included – that is the best we can do. But for some of us, but not the #NeverTrump bozos, we are grateful that ever so often someone comes along who can turn our concerns into a practical political outcome. That Donald Trump is somewhat more risky than some others because he has never actually held office so has no record in dealing with political situations is a valid concern. But after that, you just have to look at what he says he wants to do, which are congruent with what he has said all his adult life. Meanwhile Murray writes:

> *In my view, Donald Trump is unfit to be president in ways that apply to no other candidate of the two major political parties throughout American history.*

So therefore Hillary. Let us therefore go to the specifics as outlined:

> *But it's worse than that. It's not that Trump makes strategic decisions about*

---
[229] *National Review*, 25 May 2016.

what useful untruths he will tell on any given day — it looks as if he just makes up stuff as he goes along. Many of his off-the-cuff fictions are substantively unimportant: He says Rex Ryan won championships when he coached the New York Jets, when he didn't.

You know, that being the first example of an untruth that came to mind portrays such a trivial mind that he ought to be embarrassed to the final degree by even bringing it up. But let them all reveal themselves and let their names be recorded. The list of political commentators we can forever ignore just keeps getting longer.

~

Let 'em worry
May 26, 2016

From *The Japan Times*: 'Trump sends shivers down spines of nations trying to solidify global warming pact'.[230] Here I agree there is reason to worry, or there is reason to worry if you think global warming isn't the greatest con job in human history, which it is. Future generations are going to look back at us in amazement. Meantime:

The talks in Germany to flesh out December's historic global climate deal are probably not at the top of Donald Trump's agenda this week.

But the diplomats from 196 nations huddled in Bonn are keenly aware of the fact that the "The Donald" is now within spitting distance of the White House — and it is making a lot of them nervous.

It is not hard to see why.

The last Republican standing in the U.S. presidential race has described climate change as a hoax perpetrated by China to gain competitive advantage in manufacturing over the US, an eccentric theory even among climate skeptics.

More recently, he said he was "not a big fan" of the Paris Agreement, the fruit of two decades of stop-and-go (but mostly stop) wrangling between rich and developing nations.

---

[230] *The Japan Times*, 26 May 2016.

> "I will be renegotiating those agreements, at a minimum," Trump told Reuters in an exclusive interview last week, betraying an unfamiliarity with the U.N.'s consensus-based process.
>
> "And at a maximum I may do something else."

Go for the max, I say, aim for the absolute full wreckage. So one more round from the report, just to cheer us up:

> The prospect of a Trump presidency precisely at the moment when nations are inching toward ratification of the delicately balanced deal sends shivers down the spines of negotiators here.
>
> When asked what worried him most at this stage, Seyni Nafo, climate ambassador for Mali and president of the Africa Group, snapped: "Trump winning the election."

Ah, the global begging bowl will be taken away, or at least this one.

~

He's over the top
May 27, 2016

There is a picture which comes with this: 'To Celebrate Winning 1,237, Trump Eats McDonald's, Has Diet Coke'.[231] Been there myself. I've often said the worst thing about my children growing up is that I no longer have an excuse to go to McDonald's. It is still an incongruous picture which must have some intended meaning but one that eludes me for the moment.

In the news today: Trump reaches 1237.[232] And so now he begins to say what he really thinks:

> Trump, whose support from North Dakota national convention delegates put him over the top for securing the party's nomination earlier in the day, told the crowd he'd eliminate regulation he says is killing the fossil fuel industry as well as be favorable to additional pipeline projects and exports of American oil.
>
> Thunderous applause greeted Trump's declaration that in his administration

---

[231] PJMedia.com, 26 May 2016.
[232] bismarcktribune.com, 26 May 2016.

there'd be an "America-first energy plan."

"We will accomplish a complete American energy independence," Trump said. "We're going to turn everything around. We are going to make it right."

~

The Dunning-Kruger effect meets the Kates effect
May 28, 2016

Honestly, what can one do with a story like this: 'Obama: World Leaders 'Rattled' by Trump's 'Ignorance' and 'Cavalier Attitude'.'[233] The following, please note, is in quotation marks and the person quoted is Obama!

> *They're rattled by him — and for good reason — because a lot of the proposals that he's made display either ignorance of world affairs, or a cavalier attitude, or an interest in getting tweets and headlines instead of actually thinking through what it is that is required to keep America safe and secure and prosperous, and what's required to keep the world on an even keel.*

I found this quote at Instaundit[234] where I also discovered the 'Dunning–Kruger effect' which is new to me as a named psychological syndrome but very straightforward as a frequent picture of reality.

> *The Dunning–Kruger effect is a cognitive bias in which relatively unskilled persons suffer illusory superiority, mistakenly assessing their ability to be much higher than it really is. Dunning and Kruger attributed this bias to a metacognitive inability of the unskilled to recognize their own ineptitude and evaluate their own ability accurately.*

Someone must also make a study of the related effect – call it the Kates effect – which I describe as follows. We are here discussing a syndrome that often affects the media and academics studying in the social sciences and humanities:

> *The Kates effect is cognitive bias in which relatively unskilled persons are believed to have superior abilities, where the minimal abilities they do have are mistakenly assessed to be much higher than they really are. Kates attributes*

---

[233] pjmedia.com, 26 May 2016.
[234] pjmedia.com/instapundit, 27 May 2016.

> this bias to a metacognitive inability of the similarly unskilled to recognize ineptitude in others because of a deep desire to escape reality and live in a fantasy world of their own construction.

Obama is delusional but he really is the president. The more remarkable form of insanity – the Kates effect discussed above – is found among those who feed these delusions with affirmations that permit those delusions to persist, sometimes for as long as eight years.

~

Why Republicans will vote for Trump (and Democrats too)
May 29, 2016

From Victor Davis Hanson[235], the topic headings are listed below but read the lot:

> *First, Trump stays in the news not just by taking extreme positions, but also by taking extreme positions on issues that are already extreme.*
>
> *A second reason why many conservatives will vote for Trump is that they, like everyone else, are cynical about what candidates say and what they, as presidents, actually do. . . .*
>
> *Third, we have become so inured to the outrageous, that many conservatives are not quite sure whether Trump is just a more in-your-face version of current politicians or if he truly is an outlier in his vulgarity.*
>
> *Fourth, most Republicans do not quite buy the #NeverTrump argument that Trump is running to the left of Hillary Clinton. [Does anyone?]*
>
> *Finally, Republicans might embrace a democratic fatalism—or the opinion, in other words, that "if that's what the people want, that's what the people get."*

Of course, the real reason is that Trump is offering to do what voters want their government to do and no one else is.

---

[235] hoover.org, 24 May 2016.

Going after our deadliest enemy
May 29, 2016

Two stories via Instapundit focusing on the media as the black-hearted true source of our political troubles. First: 'ACE OF SPADES: Why I Hate The Media, A Continuing Series'.[236] And if you go to AoS there is this conclusion about the media and its talking heads:

> *Who the fuck do these ghastly grinning pancake-makeup smeared brain-damaged communications majors think they fucking are?*
>
> *A society that worships carnival-barkers appearing on idiot boxes is a society that is already brain-dead and which should be euthanized out of simple mercy.*
>
> *Fuck them all to hell.*

Second: 'PAST PERFORMANCE IS NO GUARANTEE OF FUTURE RESULTS'[237] where we find among quite a bit of other criticisms:

> *By rejecting the authority of the press to judge him, Trump has debilitated if not destroyed the power of the interview, befuddling a press corps that still believes it can bring him down with one more gotcha, one more "Pinocchio", one more "Pants On Fire" from the fact-checkers. Trump is laughing at them now.*

They still have enormous power which they won't give up without a fight. But at least their flank has been turned, and who knows, others may yet learn from Trump's example.

~

It is a smear tactic, you buffoons
May 30, 2016

"Some opponents have likened Donald J. Trump to Adolf Hitler and Benito Mussolini; *supporters call that a smear tactic.*"

The one essay I did at university from which I learned the most and have

---

[236] pjmedia.com/instapundit, 28 May 2016.
[237] pjmedia.com/instapundit, 28 May 2016.

often thought about was titled, "Fascist Criticisms of Liberalism". And what I learned was that fascism was a form of totalitarian ideology that was essentially tied to an authoritarian leader-principle and whose economic principles were basically socialist. Central planning was at the heart of its economic methodology. It was the nation that counted and not the individual. Hitler alone among the pre-War fascists, married the ideology to racism, but none of this was found in the ideologies of Mussolini, Franco or Salazar. You can tell a fascist state by its use of police power to suppress dissent. Fascism remains as alive today as a living reality – see Cuba and Castro – but the word itself has transmogrified into a term of abuse used by socialists to criticise everyone else. The reality, however, is that fascism is a Soviet-type Marxist socialism without its international dimension. Any ideology can be at its centre as long as it claims to be absolute truth from which no deviations are permitted.

The above quoted text is from *The New York Times* in an article titled, 'Rise of Donald Trump Tracks Growing Debate Over Global Fascism'.[238] Here's the definition they use:

Fascism, generally defined as a governmental system that asserts complete power and emphasizes aggressive nationalism and often racism.

Let's see which of the following would characterise the US if Donald Trump were elected:

- an ideology to which every member of the community must subscribe
- a police state in which opponents of the regime are in peril of their lives and are often imprisoned
- a centrally planned economy
- suppression of dissent
- a state run media

Not one of these is even remotely possible if Donald Trump were elected president. The article is worth a read since it represents just how far the modern media has fallen. The plain reality is that they cannot criticise Trump on the specifics of what he has in mind since even to state Trump's

---

[238] *The New York Times*, 28 May 2016.

aims would only add to his support. So it is just ignorant name calling by people who have no idea what they are talking about but manage to have their views printed in what was once one of the prestige newspapers of the world.

Calling Trump a fascist is ignorance attempting to deceive the willingly ignorant. If they don't know that calling Trump a fascist is slander without content then why would you read such a newspaper ever again, other than to remind you of what great dangers our civilisation must now face in dealing with the actual fascists in our midst.

~

Common sense about Trump and conservatism
May 31, 2016

This is a very accurate article about a truly vexing question. It is by John O'Sullivan and surprisingly in *National Review*: 'Conservatives in Crisis — American 2016 Edition'.[239] And if you doubt my own belief that I am a conservative, here is some evidence you can read that I wrote just this year – The Indispensable Roger Scruton.[240] This time, however, it is O'Sullivan saying what needs to be said, which begins by noting how many different varieties of conservatism there are.

> *So give me a break! Stop yattering on about the death of Republicanism or the terminal crisis of conservatism. They're not even in the intensive-care unit. This is not their finest hour, perhaps, but they will survive.*
>
> *But what will they survive as? Both Trump admirers (broadly defined) and Trump detractors (ditto) see Republican and conservative establishments reeling before a hostile takeover by an invasion of populist Vikings and Visigoths who have come from nowhere under the banners of "No Entitlement Reform" and "America First" nationalism. Peggy Noonan celebrates this; Jonah Goldberg will resist it just short of in perpetuity. But the main truth here is that this invasion doesn't come from outside. It is an invasion mainly of people who have been in the ranks of conservatism all along.*

---

[239] *National Review*, 27 May 2016.
[240] *Quadrant Online*, 5 March 2016.

> *It is understandable if most commentators haven't fully grasped this, because the invasion is led by Donald Trump, who does come from outside both movement and party and who, as Camille Paglia noted in a very different context, makes a very fetching Viking ("bedecked with the phallic tongue of a violet Celtic floral tie . . . looking like a triumphant dragon on the thrusting prow of a long boat"—wow!). But the more we look at who votes for The Donald, the more they look like people who have voted Republican in the past. As Michael Brendan Dougherty, echoed by Ross Douthat, points out, they may belong disproportionately to the working and lower-middle classes, but they also belong to the Republican-voting sectors of those classes. (They were voting in GOP primaries, after all.) And if common observation counts for anything, it is the lower social end of the Republican electorate where conservative views are most often to be found (though less on finance, say, than on crime.)*

It is a long but excellent article, worth every minute of your time. My only caveat is that I do think of Trump as conservative in a similar mould to myself.

~

There at the start
June 1, 2016

The news story below is how I remember it as well. It was the time when the Democrats' dearest wish was that Trump become the nominee. So this is how it began.

> *LAS VEGAS – Political junkies and skeptics are still scratching their heads, wondering "How did this happen? How did Donald Trump take over the Republican Party?"*
>
> *It may come as a surprise, but Trump's luck began last July in Las Vegas. In the summer of 2015, Trump's fledgling campaign was in trouble. After his unrehearsed remarks about Mexicans, his relationship with NBC ended, Macy's failed to renew his contract, and Univision released unrelenting attacks on the Trump campaign. Poll numbers suffered in response, reflecting a campaign headed for certain demise.*
>
> *Amid the chaos of campaigning that summer, Trump agreed to appear*

before several thousand wealthy investors and concerned citizens at a conference called FreedomFest, billed as, "the world's largest gathering of free minds." He spoke to a standing room only audience Saturday, July 11. Yes, it was 7-11 in Vegas. And it was Trump's lucky day. His appearance attracted major media coverage including CNN, Fox News, ABC, NBC, MSNBC and the Daily Mail, among others. Trump's poll numbers rose sharply right after his appearance at FreedomFest and he dominated the Primaries thereafter.

And if you would like to recall the moment, I live blogged his speech and Q&A. It is dated July 12 since the blog is Australian and it was already the next day where the blog was posted. What Trump said includes everything that has since made him the Republican nominee, including "Make America Great Again". A fantastic speech as well.

~

Trump dealing with the media
June 1, 2016

Almost an hour long but very entertaining as well as enlightening, reported here: 'Trump taunts media to its face'.[241] This may have been the most dramatic moment as the largest part of the press conference was devoted to replying to the media about whether or not he had raised money for veterans.

He called out Tom Llamas, a journalist with ABC News.

"I could have asked all these groups to come here and I didn't want to do that. I'm not looking for credit. But what I don't want is, when I raise millions of dollars, have people say, like this sleazy guy right over here from ABC," Trump said, pointing to Llamas. "He's a sleaze in my book. You're a sleaze because you know the facts and you know the facts well."

To establish the facts, he therefore read out the individual cheques that had been distributed to Veterans Organisations which totalled so far $5.6 million. A reminder of just how much the media can be trusted to report those facts. He also seemed to have recognised that he will not win

---
[241] politico.com, 31 May 2016.

California in the election:

> *In his opening remarks, he wished LeBron James and the Cleveland Cavaliers good luck in the NBA finals.*

He is thus still hoping to win Ohio who are playing Oakland.

~

More of what else you don't know
June 2, 2016

This story is bizarre because it is bizarre, but also because you cannot find this written in any of the mainstream media: 'Stunning Hidden Agendas Exposed – Trump University Lawsuit Brought By Firm Who Paid $675,000 To Bill and Hillary Clinton….'[242] And if you find that bizarre, then what about this about the judge:

> *Donald Trump has accused Judge Gonzalo Curiel as having a bias, a specific agenda bias, to the benefit of the plaintiffs in the case; and it appears he is correct.*
>
> *Judge Curiel, an activist for illegal immigration, even went as far as to work on behalf of San Diego La Raza activists to select illegal aliens for scholarships.*

Go to the article and see it for yourself.

> *UPDATE: Never to be found in the mainstream press, but now at least posted at Drudge: Judge Presiding Over Trump University Case Is Member Of La Raza Lawyers Group.*[243]
>
> *United States District Court Judge Gonzalo Curiel, the man presiding over the class-action lawsuit against Trump University, is a member of the La Raza Lawyers of San Diego and oversaw the gift of a law school scholarship to an illegal alien.*
>
> *In his 2011 judicial questionnaire to become a federal judge, Curiel revealed his history with La Raza. GotNews.com originally reported this Tuesday,*

---

[242] theconservativetreehouse.com, 31 May 2016.
[243] dailycaller.com, 1 June 2016.

and The Daily Caller has independently verified.

Curiel lists "La Raza Lawyers of San Diego" as a legal association he has been a part of in the questionnaire. Curiel's office at the United States District Court for the Southern District of California confirmed to TheDC the judge's membership in the group.

Curiel reveals more ties to the group in his questionnaire. He has spoken at two receptions held by La Raza Lawyers of San Diego, the most recent being in 2011. Last year, the group also held a reception for Curiel. The description of the event says, "This year we are proud to be honoring Judge Gonzalo Curiel at our reception and recognizing him for his leadership and support to the community and to our Association!"

That won't, of course, stop Hillary, the Democrats and the media from pushing the case as an example of something. And this fact doesn't, of course, mean that there isn't something questionable here, although it raises many, many doubts that there is. And there would not have been anyone on the Republican side with some skeleton, either real or manufactured, that could not have been produced. It remains the case with Donald Trump, however, that at least he will fight it out on the ethical end and will not be cowed into retreat.

~

Nazis thought they were nice people too
June 3, 2016

There is a photo of a woman trying to go to a Trump rally spattered with eggs, with the twitter comment:

"Woman who supports Trump surrounded by protestors, who taunt her, then throw eggs and bottles at her."

The tweet comes via Instapundit[244] where we find this in the comments:

F—k Godwin's Law-
I hate nazis.
That is what they are. Wondering how many of them are paid by a guy

---

[244] pjmedia.com/instapundit, 2 June 2016.

who worked for the nazis.

BTW do you know who he means by the "guy who worked for the nazis"? A genuine possibility. More of the story from *The Guardian*: 'Protesters attack Trump supporters, as Trump calls for Clinton to 'go to jail'.'[245]

> *Inside the rally, the presumptive Republican nominee for president responded to a fiery speech earlier in the day by his main rival, Hillary Clinton, in which she lambasted him as "temperamentally unfit" to be president and castigated his "thin skin".*
>
> *Trump struck out at Clinton, attacking her on her email controversy, saying: "I will say this: Hillary Clinton has to go to jail."*

It really is the White House or the Big House.

~

Does Obama have anything to do with the American election this year?
June 5, 2016

This is not a particular good article, but the point it makes is a serious one: '3 Reasons We've Forgotten Obama in the 2016 Race — and Why We Shouldn't.'[246]

> *[Let me] illustrate a particular media trend — a blindness to the powerful impact of over seven years of a disastrous presidency. How does Obama get off the hook for all this? Why do we not see the 2016 election for what it rightly is, a referendum on his failed presidency? Here are three key reasons, from the least effective to the most.*

The real reason is that virtually the whole of the media support the Democrats and can barely push the keys to say a word of criticism of Obama. This will be the problem from here to November. Whether Trump can withstand what he will need to deal with over the coming months is the question, along with how much help will he get from the RNC along with how much he will ask for. As noted here, 'The media have reached a

---

[245] *The Guardian*, 2 June 2016.
[246] pjmedia.com 3 June 2016.

turning point in covering Donald Trump. He may not survive it'.²⁴⁷ It's the *Washington Post*, so they will do all they can to make sure that he doesn't survive it, but we are certainly about to find out.

~

Facts be damned
June 5, 2016

Obama said the economy is great, thanks to him, and Trump therefore tweeted the above sets of data which the Washington Post then fact checked. The result: 'WashPost's Bump 'Fact-Checks' Trump's Retweeted Obama Economy Charts: Facts Win, 9-0.'²⁴⁸

> *Readers can rest assured that despite [The Washington Post's] pitiful efforts, the chart-containing tweet which Trump retweeted still stands tall. Trump struck out the Obama-supporting side on nine pitches, er, charts. Bump doesn't even have a clue that this is objectively the case.*
>
> *The charts in the retweet are based purely on facts. Each clearly indicates in*

---
²⁴⁷ *The Washington Post*, 3 June 2016.
²⁴⁸ newsbusters.org, 4 June 2016

its red-shaded area what has happened during Barack Obama's presidency, Each shows that the trends presented have gotten worse under Obama.

You would actually think these journalists would prefer to see the economy run well than have a Democrat in the White House. In fact, they just don't care. They will continue to lie and mislead to protect the Obama legacy, such as it is, and to get Hillary elected in spite of everything. It is all politics all of the time, and facts be damned.

~

Chapter One: The Vase
June 6, 2016

'Secret Service agent to release tell-all book about the Clinton White House and the culture that 'sickened' him.'[249] The main points:

- *Gary Byrne says he was posted outside Bill Clinton's Oval Office in 1990s*
- *Was one of the agents who testified to a grand jury about Monica Lewisnky [sic]*
- *Complained about her behavior and 'out of hours' access to the West Wing*
- *Releasing book so voters understand the 'real' Clinton before the election*
- *Reports say his expose is causing deep concern in the White House*
- *The release of the book comes a month before the Democratic convention*
- *Secret Service agents have openly discussed protecting Hillary in the past*
- *Investigative journalist Ron Kessler said agents detested Hillary*

My guess is that if the book is being published there's nothing in it that will disturb Hillary. I've heard every story before and it has not made any difference. Character may be destiny, but policy sense is what we are looking for in a president, which this discusses not at all. If Obama can get away with his book being written by Bill Ayers, this will make less noise than a tree falling in the forest.

---

[249] *Daily Mail Australia*, 7 June 2016.

Jake Tapper asked if he thought it was a conflict of interest

June 6, 2016

This is the bit from this story – 'Sanders hits Clinton Foundation over foreign donations'[250] – that has to make you ponder just how corrupt the American media is:

> *Democratic presidential hopeful Bernie Sanders criticized the Clinton Foundation for accepting donations from foreign governments in an interview aired Sunday, calling it a conflict of interest.*
>
> *"Do I have a problem when a sitting secretary of State and a foundation run by her husband collects many, many dollars from foreign governments — governments which are dictatorships?*
>
> *"Yeah, I do have a problem with that. Yeah, I do," Sanders said on CNN's "State of the Union."*
>
> *When host Jake Tapper asked if he thought it was a conflict of interest, Sanders said, "I do."*

Look Jake, you wouldn't want to jump to any conclusions, would you?

~

The elites do not even notice what the working class sees at every turn

June 6, 2016

This is Victor Davis Hanson explaining why there are people who favour Trump for President (including him): 'Class, Trump, and the Election'.[251]

> *Donald Trump seems to have offended almost every possible identity group. But the New York billionaire still also seems to appeal to the working classes (in part no doubt precisely because he has offended so many special-interest factions; in part because he was seen in the primaries as an outsider using his own money; in part because he seems a crude man of action who dislikes*

---

[250] thehill.com, 5 June 2016
[251] victorhanson.com, 31 May 2016.

> *most of those of whom Middle America is tired). At this point, his best hope in November, to the extent such a hope exists, rests on turning 2016 into a referendum on class and a collective national interest that transcends race and gender — and on emphasizing the sad fact that America works now mostly for an elite, best epitomized by Clinton, Inc.*

That's how it starts. Read the rest.

~

Justice American style
June 7, 2016

That the American justice system is corrupt to its very roots has been obvious to anyone who has followed Mark Steyn's "trial of the century". Steyn has just provided an update on where things are.[252]

> *On the vast placid frozen lake stretching unbroken beyond the horizon that is the Mann vs Steyn case there has been a small development. As our more elderly readers may recall, four years ago, before Barack Obama's re-election, climate mullah Michael E Mann sued me and various other parties for mocking his global warm-mongering in general and pooh-pooh-ing his "hockey stick" in particular.*

> *That was in the year 2012. Notwithstanding that it's the most consequential free-speech case in half-a-century (as the ACLU, NBC, The Washington Post, The Chicago Tribune et al recognized in their amicus brief), in the DC courts it just sits there, with no discovery and no trial date. . . .*

> *This sclerotic court system can't expedite nuttin'. The case has now been stalled for two years in an interlocutory appeal. If you don't know what an "interlocutory appeal" is, consider yourself lucky. If you do know, you'll be thrilled to learn that one of the questions at the heart of this interlocutory appeal is whether, under the relevant DC law, the interlocutory appeal is even interlocutorily appealable at all. Fascinating! Adding to the fun, as I noted in my recent testimony to the US Senate, one of the judges hearing the interlocutory appeal, Vanessa Ruiz, takes up to three years to issue an opinion. . . .*

---

[252] steynonline.com, 1 June 2016.

My legal chums at Popehat and the Volokh Conspiracy seem to think that, when I gripe about the dysfunctional DC courts, I'm somehow showing disrespect for the justice system. Au contraire, it's because of my profound respect for justice that I would like this bizarre perversion thereof to return itself to the community of functioning Common Law jurisdictions. (While we're at it, this judge in the Trump University case seems all too typical.)

Ah yes, the Trump case. Trump is determined to show every piece of dirty linen that makes the US fit only for the very wealthy and the dirt poor. Middle class and bourgeois is a definite mistake in modern America. 'Alberto R. Gonzales: Trump has a right to ask if Judge Gonzalo Curiel is fair.'[253]

But there may be other factors to consider in determining whether Trump's concerns about getting an impartial trial are reasonable. Curiel is, reportedly, a member of a group called La Raza Lawyers of San Diego. Trump's aides, meanwhile, have indicated that they believe Curiel is a member of the National Council of La Raza, a vocal advocacy organization that has vigorously condemned Trump and his views on immigration. The two groups are unaffiliated, and Curiel is not a member of NCLR. But Trump may be concerned that the lawyers' association or its members represent or support the other advocacy organization.

Coupled with that question is the fact that in 2014, when he certified the class-action lawsuit against Trump, Curiel appointed the Robbins Geller law firm to represent plaintiffs. Robbins Geller has paid $675,000 in speaking fees since 2009 to Trump's likely opponent, Hillary Clinton, and to her husband, former president Bill Clinton. Curiel appointed the firm in the case before Trump entered the presidential race, but again, it might not be unreasonable for a defendant in Trump's position to wonder who Curiel favors in the presidential election.

These circumstances, while not necessarily conclusive, at least raise a legitimate question to be considered. Regardless of the way Trump has gone about raising his concerns over whether he's getting a fair trial, none of us should dismiss those concerns out of hand without carefully examining how a defendant in his position might perceive them — and we certainly should not dismiss them for partisan political reasons.

And that's from *The Washington Post*. Here's someone more likely to see

---

[253] *Washington Post*, 4 June 2016.

Trump's point: 'Never "dumb" to shine the spotlight on activist judges'.[254]

> *"Lou Dobbs of Fox Business News, in a recent interview with Gingrich, read from a list of ethnic organizations in which Judge Curiel holds membership. All are activist Spanish-heritage groups. Dobbs also pointed out a possible conflict of interest in the case. One of the attorneys in the law firm appointed by Curiel to represent the plaintiffs has contributed money to Hillary Clinton's 2016 run for President. (American Spectator)*
>
> *"When Lou Dobbs made the case that Trump could have reason for concern, given the judge's associations and conflicts of interest, Gingrich brushed him off responding that Trump's spotlighting of Curiel's heritage "in a negative way" was "dumb."*
>
> *"First, pointing out a judge's heritage when that heritage probably leads to bias, especially against Trump because of Trump's commitment to build a wall on the Mexican border, would seem neither negative nor dumb. Second, Trump's concern that this judge is an activist, as are so many ethnic legal professionals, is not racist. It's not at all unreasonable to think that Curiel wants to officiate this particular lawsuit, as a strike at Donald Trump, the wall-builder."*

When you remember that the fall guy after Benghazi was a movie producer who was sent to jail[255] for a year, you might think of the American justice system in a far less benign way.

~

The media don't even pretend any more
June 8, 2016

You don't often find an honest reporter in the US, but here we have finally found one. She honestly explains how the media must distort the news every day in ensuring that Trump loses. Here is the full posting by John Hinderaker: 'Wapo Columnist: Let's Gang Up on Trump.'[256]

> *The Washington Post's media columnist, Margaret Sullivan, who is also a former Public Editor of the New York Times, has an idea that she claims is*

---
[254] canadafreepress.com, 6 June 2016.
[255] *Washington Times*, 13 May 2013.
[256] powerlineblog.com, 6 June 2016.

novel, but may sound familiar to Republicans: news outlets should coordinate their efforts to defeat Donald Trump! It really is an extraordinary column:

> Media outlets have given the likely Republican presidential nominee something like $2 billion worth of free exposure and, in many cases, let him get away with blatant falsehoods — even about something as basic as whether he did or didn't support the U.S. invasion of Iraq.
>
> Maybe I missed it, but I don't recall liberal columnists objecting to Trump's free publicity during the primary season, when it helped him defeat Republicans who would have been stronger general election candidates.
>
> Fairness is of utmost importance, no doubt, whether the reporting is on Trump, Hillary Clinton or Bernie Sanders. But what, exactly, does it mean in campaign coverage? It should mean keeping an open mind, not bringing preconceived ideas to one's reporting, and listening seriously to candidates' explanations.
>
> It should never mean false equivalency, where equal time and emphasis are given to candidates or dissembling is allowed to go unchallenged....
>
> News outlets ought to rethink the purpose of their campaign coverage. It's not to be equally nice to all candidates. It's to provide Americans with the hard information they need to decide who is fit to lead the country.

In other words, the job of a reporter is to help win the election for Hillary Clinton. It isn't long before this conclusion becomes explicit:

> There have been encouraging moments: CNN's Jake Tapper pushing Trump hard for clarity on an endorsement from former Ku Klux Klan leader David Duke. Fox's Megyn Kelly (before she went all fan-girl) asking a searing question about Trump's treatment of women in a Republican debate. The Times's investigation into Trump's hiring of foreign workers at his Florida club, Mar-a-Lago. The Post's reporters pushing so hard for answers on Twitter about claimed charitable contributions to veterans that Trump found it necessary to hold a news conference.

> *We need much more of this in every medium. Every day, in every news cycle.*

Every day, every news cycle, in every medium: beat up on Trump!

> *Rather than promoting the same treatment for each candidate, how about this: rigorous and sustained truth-telling in the public's interest. Citizens deserve some fairness, too.*

Don't treat Trump the same way you would treat a Democrat!

> *It's time for tough follow-up questions, time for TV news to pick up on some of the hard-hitting reporting being done elsewhere, and maybe — radical notion alert! — it's even time for news organizations to get together and prepare to defend themselves.*

So news organizations should form a cabal to smear Donald Trump. But, hey, it's self-defense!

> *That won't come naturally to these highly competitive outfits, but given the assault on press rights that surely would come with a Trump presidency, strength in numbers is a far better idea than providing even-handed, nonconfrontational coverage.*

What is the "assault on press rights" that "surely" would accompany a Trump presidency? It's hard to say. Maybe she is referring to Trump's desire to liberalize defamation law, or maybe she imagines there is a press right not to be contradicted. In any event, it's not every day you see a journalist come out openly against "even-handed coverage," while advocating ganging up on a disfavored politician, i.e., "strength in numbers." We always knew that this is how liberals think, but it is unusual to see one of them put it in writing.

~

Attack is the best form of defence
June 8, 2016

Donald Trump is not of the opinion that absorbing punishment is a useful way to show one's strength. He is, in fact, the first person in politics on my side of the fence who thinks attack is the best form of defence. The business with Trump University is almost a perfect example of how he goes about his business. The case has existed for quite some time, but the minute it was raised, he slammed the judge overseeing the case as hopelessly biased against him, the evidence being that he was a member of *La Raza*, a race-based group supporting illegal migration into the United States.

Hillary wants to argue that Trump represents a War on Women. Back he comes with an attack on Bill's serially abusive relationships with women, for which Hillary has been the enabler.

And then there was the story of how Trump's campaign manager had thrown reporter Michelle Fields to the ground that was reported as unvarnished truth across the media, even when the videos, they had not known existed, showed none of it was true. Trump just stared them down and would not give an inch. Admirable qualities I would say in a president who you want to be looking after your interests.

In every way, Trump has shown an amazing willingness to counter punch, to refuse to accept even minimally the premises of his opponents. He may yet lose the election because of the array of forces ranged against him – including many supposedly on his own side – but he is more likely than any of the other Republicans to win. And he is changing the debate. And here is how he is changing the debate and will be putting Hillary on the back foot: 'TRUMP Announces MAJOR SPEECH on Clinton Corruption and Scandal Next Week.'[257]

> *The Clintons have turned the politics of personal enrichment into an art form for themselves. . . .*
>
> *Hillary Clinton turned the State Department into a private hedge fund.*

All true, but no one else has said it. Attack, attack, and then attack some more. If he loses, it won't be because the facts weren't out there. As he asks, I wonder whether the press will be there to cover next week's speech.

---

[257] thegatewaypundit.com, 7 June 2016.

Will the Republicans nominate Trump?
June 9, 2016

Donald Trump is the Stephen Curry of Republican politics.

> *Hillary Clinton Received 1.5 Million FEWER Votes in 2016 than in 2008 — Democrats Down 7 Million Votes*
> *Trump Shatters Republican Primary Vote Record by 1.4 Million...*
> *Historic 13M Vote Blowout...*
> *Beats Own Campaign Prediction, Reaching 1,536 Delegates...*

Too bad they're not playing basketball but politics. This is close to the vibe I see everywhere across Republican websites. From Ace of Spades: "So, Who Is the GOP Going to Install as Its Nominee Instead of Trump?" First he says this:

> *Let me explain my entire political raison d'etre:*
> *BEAT HILLARY CLINTON.*
> *That's it. That's the ballgame.*

But then he says this about the leadership of the Republican Party:

> *I happen to think the White Upper Middle Professional Class is silly and overproud — the status conscious bourgeoisie who are a bit too fashionable and frivolous in their political passions.*
>
> *They're just not good in a fight. They back down too quickly from the left's threat of reducing their social status.*
>
> *Yet the fact is, you can't win an election without them. This group, which isn't only white, but is Super White, is a core group of any GOP coalition. Including the losing ones, even.*

He thinks they won't allow Trump to be the nominee. Trump's task was not just to win the votes but to make himself acceptable to the white upper middle class leaders of the party.

> *I do think the GOP is actually gearing up to do something drastic in three weeks.*
>
> *I think all the shrieking you're seeing right now is part of the battlespace preparation to prepare for that moment.*

> *To justify it, to defend it. To show: "We had no other choice."*
>
> *To say, "We tried working with him. You saw how hard we tried working for him! But he's just impossible. He's an animal, and we can't do anything to educate him."*
>
> *The question I'm asking myself isn't whether they'll do this (if Trump keeps sinking in the polls, and stinking up the reputation of the Upper Middle Class Professionals that make up the high ranks of the party, they will), but who they'll replace him with.*
>
> *The word is Paul Ryan. He denies that. He denies a lot of things.*
>
> *I think he's a sneaky little rat who would be flattered by it, and flattered by it, he'd leap at it.*
>
> *I'd go berserk if they tried that, personally. I think a lot of people would. He's already a proven electoral loser — he got beaten by the Imbecile Joe Biden in a debate, for god's sake — but they may try it anyway.*

And so we shall see. There are many who are walking away. A random sample from today:

> *Trump/La Raza Judge Row Blows Lid On GOP Establishment Plan: Sabotage His Campaign, Wait For 2020*
>
> *Uh Oh: Scott Walker Now Backing Away from Pledge to Support Republican Nominee*
>
> *GOP Tool Hugh Hewitt TURNS On BFF Trump, DEMANDS GOP Tell Him To QUIT Campaign!!*

You get the idea. Meanwhile, Ann Coulter is not really surprised in spite of what the headline might make you think: Stunning New Development!!! Media Calls Trump Racist.[258]

> *The effrontery of this double standard is so blinding, that the only way liberals can bluff their way through it is with indignation. DO I HEAR YOU RIGHT? ARE YOU SAYING A JUDGE'S ETHNICITY COULD INFLUENCE HIS DECISIONS? (Please, please, please don't bring up everything we've said about white judges and juries for the past four decades.)*

---

[258] anncoulter.com, 6 August 2016.

They're betting they can intimidate Republicans — and boy, are they right!

The entire Republican Brain Trust has joined the media in their denunciations of Trump for his crazy idea that anyone other than white men can be biased. That's right, Wolf, I don't have any common sense. Would it help if the GOP donated to Hillary?

~

Trump replies – Man Up
June 9, 2016

They're not used to fighting to win. From The New York Times: 'Donald Trump's Advice to Panicked Republicans: Man Up'.[259]

Donald J. Trump has some advice for panicked Republicans in Washington who are melting down over his most incendiary statements: Man up.

"Politicians are so politically correct anymore, they can't breathe," Mr. Trump said in an interview Tuesday afternoon as fellow Republicans forcefully protested his ethnically charged criticism of a federal judge overseeing a lawsuit against the defunct Trump University.

"The people are tired of this political correctness when things are said that are totally fine," he said during an interlude in a day of exceptional stress in the Trump campaign. "It is out of control. It is gridlock with their mouths."

Even as he chastised Washington's political class for a lack of backbone, Mr. Trump exhibited modest signs later on Tuesday that he was getting the message that some remarks—such as questioning the fairness of Judge Gonzalo P. Curiel because of his Mexican heritage—crossed a line.

While he did not apologize, he issued a statement that his comments on Judge Curiel had been "misconstrued." In a final Republican primary night victory speech, he struck a more conventional tone—at least for him— giving a more disciplined address using the teleprompter he has mocked while promising to make the Republican Party proud in the general election campaign.

But anyone thinking that Mr. Trump is going to suddenly adopt a more

---

[259] *New York Times*, 10 June 2016.

cautious, strategic approach yearned for by election-conscious congressional Republicans is likely to be disappointed. He wrinkled his nose in disgust at the mere mention of the word "pivot," though he conceded he wants to get on to broader discussion of the economy.

In his view, it is clear that his way has worked and the establishment's has failed. After all, he vanquished every senator, governor or former governor who challenged him for the party's nomination.

"I disagree with a lot of things I've watched in politics over the years, that's why I'm running," Mr. Trump said over a meatball lunch he barely touched in the restaurant of Trump Tower. "And that may make me less popular with politicians. But I have to be honest. I didn't get there by doing it the way a lot of these people do it."

Back in Washington, congressional Republicans were in a fever, with Speaker Paul D. Ryan, a reluctant Trump convert to begin with, calling Mr. Trump's comments about the judge "the textbook definition" of racism. Senator Mitch McConnell, the Kentucky Republican and majority leader, denounced Mr. Trump's crusade against Judge Curiel as stupid and urged him to apologize. Senator Mark Kirk of Illinois withdrew his endorsement, and others were pondering it.

Mr. Trump, arms crossed tightly across his chest during lunch, was aggrieved and considered some of the Republican pushback inappropriate and unhelpful — though he did not want to address specific critics. He insisted that he is anything but a racist and, with his usual rebuttal by the numbers, stressed that voters have rewarded his outspokenness with a record haul of primary votes while Washington is held in dismal regard.

"People want people to represent them who are going to stick up for what they believe in," Mr. Trump said. "Politicians have been very weak and very ineffective over the last quite long period of time."

Mr. Trump is also unhappy with the media, and noted that he is nearing the ability to reach 20 million people by himself through his personal Twitter, Facebook and Instagram accounts, providing an alternative way to reach the public, even if it's largely a one-way conversation.

His is a campaign like no other, conducted out of a luxury office tower in Manhattan named for its most prominent occupant, the presumptive nominee himself. A few floors below his personal office with a Trumpian view of

Central Park is unfinished space being leased to his campaign team, a relatively skeleton crew of 80 or so running a national campaign.

He is flabbergasted by critiques that he is woefully undermanned compared to the hundreds working for Mrs. Clinton, many just over in Brooklyn.

"To me, that is smart," Mr. Trump said about his lean team, though he says he will soon increase his work force.

As the primary season came to an odd close with him under Republican fire in the nation's capital — an unheard-of spectacle in the last half century of presidential politics — Mr. Trump took some time to huddle with his campaign team. His daughter Ivanka, a trusted adviser, was close at hand, as was his campaign manager, Corey Lewandowski, his press secretary, Hope Hicks, and his special counsel, Michael Cohen.

As he headed to the Trump Grill for lunch, tourists and workers hailed him, congratulated him and urged him on as they lined up to take photos with their phones.

He posed with some women and looked back at a reporter to point at the women and boasted "Hispanics!" Afterward, he bragged: "They say 'We love you, Mr. Trump. We're from Mexico.'"

After he was seated, the Secret Service erected a temporary partition to shield him from other guests.

UPDATE: You cannot, of course, trust the American media on a single thing. According to this, 'NYT Frames Donald Trump's Advice To Pearl Clutching DC Politicians As "Man Up"…',[260] he didn't say "Man Up". Not that I would be upset if he had, but here's the story:

Priceless. The only problem for the New York Times is, Trump never said: "Man Up".

A recent Times article, which was transparently structured to present candidate Trump with gender references, outlines Donald Trump's opinion of the weak-kneed professional political class. His position is essentially the same as Senator Jeff Sessions, get over it.

---

[260] theconservativetreehouse.com, 8 June 2016.

The usual news round of a Friday night in the US
June 10, 2016

You know. Walk in the house. Scan the net. Usual things.

> *HILLARY HUMILIATION: BILL BRAGGED ABOUT SLEEPING WITH 2,000 WOMEN!*
>
> *U.S. Taxpayers Are Funding Iran's Military Expansion*
>
> *U.S. Pilots Confirm: Obama Admin Blocks 75 Percent of Islamic State Strikes: 'We can't get clearance even when we have a clear target in front of us'*
>
> *Bill, White House staff lived in fear of Hillary: Ex-Secret Service officer*
>
> *How Ayatollah Khomeini suckered Jimmy Carter*
>
> *Emails in Clinton Probe Dealt With Planned Drone Strikes*

Followed, of course, by this.

> *Paul Ryan under fire for Trump remarks…*
>
> *Wants Him To Lose So He Can Run In 4 Years?*

My very thought about Chris Christie in 2012. These GOPe types make you sick with fury. As Glenn Reynolds asks: 'The Democrats' ability to goad the GOP into forming a circular firing squad is a major strength of theirs. Why does the GOP play along?'[261]

~

Party not for sale for the moment
June 12, 2016

I wonder if billionaires really do have their finger on the pulse of the electorate. This really is a strange, strange story: 'Furious GOP donors stew over Trump: At an exclusive Park City retreat, some of the Republican Party's top financiers lashed out at their nominee'.[262] How likely is it that their interests coincide with the interests of most Americans?

---

[261] pjmedia.com/instapundit, 10 June 2016.
[262] politico.com, 11 June 2016.

> On Friday afternoon, at an exclusive Republican donor retreat here hosted by Mitt Romney, frustration boiled over. During an off-the-record question-and-answer session with House Speaker Paul Ryan, Meg Whitman, the billionaire Hewlett Packard chief executive officer, confronted the speaker over his endorsement of Trump. Whitman, a major GOP giver who ran for California governor in 2010, compared Trump to historical demagogues like Adolf Hitler and Benito Mussolini and wanted to know how the speaker could get behind him.
>
> At another discussion session during the day, which featured top Romney alumni Stuart Stevens and Matt Rhoades, Ana Navarro, a Republican contributor and ubiquitous cable news personality, called Trump a "racist" and a "vulgarian and a pig who has made disgusting comments about women for years." (Neither Whitman nor Navarro would comment.)
>
> Even Ryan, who has endorsed Trump despite criticizing his behavior, joked during his presentation on Friday that in a recent conversation with magician David Copperfield, he said that he wished he could make himself disappear.
>
> The incidents, which were relayed by three sources who were present — one of whom described them as "shocking" — illustrates the intense anger coursing through the GOP donor community. Far from letting go of their white-knuckled opposition to Trump, they're stewing in it. . . .
>
> Some are convinced the situation is growing increasingly bleak. In an interview here, Spencer Zwick, Romney's former finance chair and one of the most prominent fundraisers in Republican politics, said that some of Romney's donors would stay on the sidelines — and that others would even give to his Democratic opponent.

Just what it is that Trump would do or wouldn't do that upsets them – or why it would or should upset them – is hard to work out from the article. Values voters they are not. These are unlikely to be small-government types, opposed to a crony capitalist relationship between business and government. Getting money out of politics is an imperative in a Republican system far more than in a Parliamentary democracy, but it should be done everywhere it can. And it shows why this needs to be done in ways that you would think those with the money to spend ought to do their best to keep quiet.

The political calculus of creating poverty-stricken dependent slaves
June 12, 2016

Turn 'em into poverty-stricken dependent slaves and you will get their votes forever. Or what is known apparently as 'The Curley Effect'.[263] Apparently, Obama is a past master.

> *The Curley effect (named after its prototype, James Michael Curley, a four-time mayor of Boston in the first half of the 20th century) is a political strategy of "increasing the relative size of one's political base through distortionary, wealth-reducing policies." Translation: A politician or a political party can achieve long-term dominance by tipping the balance of votes in their direction through the implementation of policies that strangle and stifle economic growth. Counterintuitively, making a city poorer leads to political success for the engineers of that impoverishment.*

It may only have been discovered by accident, but you do have to think this may well explain many things that are otherwise not all that clear. But it also requires a population that are happy to become poverty-stricken dependent slaves which does in many ways explain a good deal of otherwise inexplicable parts of policy, like the mass migration of millions of unskilled non-workers that is now found supported by every party of the left.

~

The open society and its enemies
June 13, 2016

The round-up of events from Ed Driscoll at Instapundit:[264]

> *AFTER ORLANDO TERRORIST ATTACK, USUAL SUSPECTS SPOUT USUAL NARRATIVE:*
>
> Tom Brokaw: 'In this County,' 'Everything Seems to Get Settled by a Gun.'
>
> ABC Blames Orlando Terror on Election Rhetoric and Guns in America

---

[263] *Forbes*, 31 May 2012.
[264] pjmedia.com/instapundit, 12 June 2016.

> *AP Calls Orlando Terrorist Massacre 'Just the Latest Mass Shooting'*
>
> *Media Matters: "The NRA made anti-LGBT attacks during their annual meeting just weeks ago."*
>
> *Yahoo: "Bernie Sanders Just Nailed the Real Culprit Behind the Mass Shooting in Orlando…Sanders explained to Chuck Todd on NBC's Meet the Press Sunday, the real culprit, according to Sanders, is gun control — or more precisely, lack thereof."*
>
> *Kansas City Star Editorial Writer Yael T. Abouhalkah: "Dear God: Today I am so sickened by the evilness of the NRA and gun industry. May their leaders be plunged into ever-lasting hell. Amen."*
>
> *Jeffrey Goldberg: "Obama cautious on motive of shooter because caution is required until the investigation advances."*

UPDATE: Transcript of Obama's boilerplate speech on the incident.[265]

Related: 'Trump Blasts Obama For Not Mentioning "Radical Islamic" Terrorism As ISIS Claims Responsibility.'[266]

The rest of the links above can be opened at Instapundit if you really need to read them. Plus there's this: 'Trump takes credit for 'being right on radical Islamic terrorism'.'[267] They make it sound like he's at fault:

> *Donald Trump wasted little time seeking political advantage in the massacre at a Florida nightclub, taking credit for "being right on radical Islamic terrorism" in the wake of the worst mass shooting in American history.*
>
> *The suspect in the attack, identified by authorities as a U.S. citizen of Afghan descent named Omar Saddiqui Mateen, killed 50 people and injured another 53 during a rampage through a gay dance club in Orlando. He died in a gunfight with SWAT officers after initially firing shots into the club and later taking hostages.*
>
> *"Appreciate the congrats for being right on radical Islamic terrorism, I don't want congrats, I want toughness & vigilance. We must be smart!" the presumptive Republican presidential nominee tweeted.*

---

[265] slate.com, 12 June 2016
[266] zerohedge.com, 12 June 2016.
[267] politico.com, 12 June 2016

Trump followed up that tweet with a statement expressing "My deepest sympathy and support goes out to the victims, the wounded, and their families."

But he also attacked President Barack Obama, whom he said "disgracefully refused to even say the words 'Radical Islam'" during his comments on Sunday afternoon. "For that reason alone, he should step down.

~

Camel News Network
June 13, 2016

This was from Carol in the comments on Facing reality.[268]

In the reaction to this tragedy on some American blogs, I saw more than one comment, in relation to spin about this story on the Fox news channel, that some wealthy Saudi Arabian mogul had recently bought a large share in News Corp. Could this possibly be true? I didn't see exactly when beyond recent, but, if true, it would be interesting to know, because it might have a bearing on The Australian coming across as more leftish of late?

Remember about the last capitalist selling the rope that will be used to hang him. Read on. This is what I have since found out. Just read through this story, 'Saudis Influencing Fox News'[269] and then this one, 'Fox News Channel unbalanced by Saudi influence',[270] both by Diana West, because it is certain to be the only time you will see this mentioned ever again.

And then make your plans accordingly.

---

[268] catallaxyfiles.com, 13 June 2016.
[269] clarionproject.org
[270] nhregister.com, 2 August 2010.

The progressive hierarchy of identity groups
June 14, 2016

The question is why did this take so long: 'I'm a Gay Activist, and After Orlando, I Have Switched My Vote to Trump'.[271] It's an interesting post with many different facets even given how short it is.

> *I also now realize, with brutal clarity, that in the progressive hierarchy of identity groups, Muslims are above gays. Every pundit and politician — and that includes President Obama and Hillary Clinton and half the talking heads on TV — who today have said "We don't know what the shooter's motivation could possibly be!" have revealed to me their true priorities: appeasing Muslims is more important than defending the lives of gay people. Every progressive who runs interference for Islamic murderers is complicit in those murders, and I can no longer be a part of that team.*
>
> *I'm just sick of it. Sick of the hypocrisy. Sick of the pandering. Sick of the deception.*
>
> *And you know what makes me angrier still? The fact that I have to hide my identity and remain anonymous in writing this essay. If I outed myself as a Trump supporter, I would be harassed and doxxed and shunned by everyone I know and by the Twitter lynch mobs which up until yesterday I myself led.*

Everyone is just part of an identity group to the left where everything depends on how many votes and how much money there is in supporting you.

~

And what do we want?
June 14, 2016

As Ed Driscoll says,[272] it's comforting to know that America's newsrooms and television studios are flooded with experts who know ISIS better than ISIS itself.[273] At least Donald Trump seems to know what I want: "It's absolute war!' Trump demands tougher domestic surveillance of mosques

---
[271] pjmedia.com, 12 June 2016.
[272] pjmedia.com/instapundit, 13 June 2016.
[273] pjmedia.com/instapundit, 11 December 2015.

as he says Hillary Clinton is 'almost like a maniac' for avoiding mention of Islamic terrorism in the wake of Orlando massacre.'[274]

And in regard to fighting with one arm behind our back, this was sent out this morning by Freedomfest, where I heard Trump speak last year: Facebook Censures FreedomFest…the message Facebook wouldn't let us post. The posting begins:

Dear FreedomFest friends and attendees,

First We Mourn

Like all Americans, FreedomFest is mourning the horrifying loss that took place in Orlando Sunday morning. Our next thought is on the minds of all Americans too: What can we do to stop this terrorism?

Dr. Tawfik Hamid will offer an answer and a solution in his talk at FreedomFest, "How Radical Islam Works, Why It Should Terrify Us, and How to Defeat it."

Dr. Hamid is particularly equipped to address this topic. He is an Islamic thinker and reformer and a one-time Islamic extremist from Egypt. He was a member of a radical Islamic organization in Egypt with Dr. Ayman Al-Zawaherri (who later became the first in command of Al-Qaeda). More than 30 years ago he started a reformation within Islam.

We attempted to share this same information on Facebook on Sunday, but Facebook censured the post. That's right, Facebook would not allow us to post this information. We assume that it is because it was filled with "trigger words" that Facebook would not allow. We've never had this happen before. It's a strange feeling to press "Publish" only to see Facebook ignore it and do absolutely nothing.

We will only work this out if we have a free debate with all sides all in discussing all of the issues. You may be sure Islamists have no problem saying anything they want to each other, even on Facebook.

---

[274]   *Daily Mail Australia*, 13 June 2016.

Trump on the growing threat of terrorism inside our borders
June 14, 2016

"If we don't get tough and we don't get smart and fast, we are not going to have our country any more."

~

Whatever you do, don't do anything
June 15, 2016

The article by Michael Totten is titled, 'Banning Guns and Muslims Isn't the Answer to Orlando'.[275] And this is what he concludes:

> *So what's the answer? The answer is that The Answer doesn't exist.*

So therefore don't try anything, except more war in the Middle East which has worked so well. On the other hand, we could follow someone's advice given to Mark Steyn:[276]

> *"I listen to people say 'oh, we're now going to have to have metal detectors in night clubs, security in nightclubs.' Ok, so what happens next? They blow up a bakery, they blow up a little pastry shop, so then you're gonna have to have metal detectors to get into the pastry shop?*
>
> *"Instead of having all these individual perimeters around every Dunkin Donuts franchise or every gas station, or every J.C. Penny, why not have just one big perimeter around the country?" Steyn concluded. "We could call it a border! And we could have, like, a border security!"*

Well, at least it is an answer.

---

[275] worldaffairsjournal.org, 13 June 2016.
[276] www.steynonline.com, 13 June 2016.

Good ideas need even better organisation
June 16, 2016

Running a presidential campaign is not an amateur hour. One of the things that Trump offered, or it seemed to me, was that he could work through others. This is a very big worry to me: 'Trump's relationship with RNC sours'.[277]

> *"I don't think we are going to take a lot of political advice from Priebus," a campaign official said. "From my perspective, we should not be relying on the RNC for much, because I'm not sure they are fully supportive yet," the campaign official said, adding "but we hope and expect to soon be on the exact same page."*

> *The fraught dynamic is a potentially serious liability for an insurgent campaign that has proudly eschewed political infrastructure and is dwarfed by Democratic presidential candidate Hillary Clinton's operation, which is expected to raise $1.5 billion or more. And the situation is equally problematic for the Republican Party, which typically relies on its presidential candidate to help boost down-ballot candidates, enhance voter data and raise money.*

There are a million snares that are out to derail this campaign. Either Trump gets everyone on board he can or he will be sunk by September. Meanwhile, the media distortion grows by the hour and will become immense over time, with this recent example by Ann Coulter[278] the sort of thing that can only be expected.

> *Now you see why reporters aren't quoting Trump and have to hope you won't read the speech for yourself.*

Of course the ratio will be 100-1 of those who read reports versus those who read the speech. I just hope he is up for the discipline of the campaign because that is what it will need from this moment on in. And yet, as Victor Davis Hanson explains, the US will sink without this change in direction: 'Same Old, Same Old Horror – The Orlando massacre brings up familiar lessons that we never quite learn'.[279]

> *The inability of Barack Obama and the latest incarnation of Hillary*

---

[277] politico.com, 15 June 2016.
[278] vdare.com, 15 June 2016.
[279] city-journal.org, 13 June 2016.

> Clinton to utter "radical Islam" or "Islamic terrorism" in connection with Muslims' murderous killing sprees again is exposed as an utterly bankrupt, deadly, and callous politically correct platitude. Mateen did not learn to hate homosexuals from the American government, popular American culture, or our schools, but rather from radical and likely ISIS-driven Islamic indoctrination. From Iran to Saudi Arabia, the treatment of gays is reprehensible—but largely exempt from Western censure, on the tired theory that in the confused pantheon of -isms and -ologies, multiculturalism trumps human rights.
>
> Finally, the Left will blame guns, not ideology, for the mass murder, forgetting that disarmed soldiers who could not shoot back were slaughtered by Major Hasan, that the Tsarnaev brothers preferred home-cooked explosives to blow up innocents in Boston, that the Oklahoma and UC Merced Islamists did their beheading or stabbing with a knife, and that Mateen likely followed strict gun-registration laws in obtaining his weapons.

Who but Trump would deal with it? No one, and that is the catastrophe that stands before us.

~

The nightmare world they are helping to create
June 19, 2016

You really do wonder how out of the picture our media and elites are if they are in any way surprised by this:[280]

> Gay and lesbian people should be put to death or otherwise punished under sharia, according to two imams who share leadership positions with Shady Alsuleiman, the controversial sheik invited to a Ramadan dinner at Kirribilli House by Malcolm Turnbull.
>
> The Australian National Imams Council, of which Sheik Alsuleiman is president, has at least three executive members who believe the only punishment for homosexuality is the death penalty, according to Islamic law.

This is a 1400-year old legal code that is brought with imams wherever they go. There is no changing their minds or arguing another point of view.

---

[280] *The Australian*, 18 June 2016.

As for you, you either believe in freedom of religion – and that is their religion – and you believe in freedom of speech – and their right to say what they believe – or you don't. It's all very well to have these abstract principles but they don't always work in concrete situations. They rightly take us for fools, but if you have some plan to stop their religion and their philosophy becoming dominant in the West over the next century, you had better put your plan into operation soon, because it is already nearly too late if it isn't too late already.

It is the hatred of Christianity by our atheist left that is the largest part of our undoing. Half our society is blind, ignorant and insane. But at least it is mostly the younger half who will have to live most of their lives in the nightmare world they are helping to create.

~

How the media frames its stories
June 19, 2016

Strangely accurate.

MEDIA NARRATIVE CHART
for reporting violent crime

ATTACKER	VICTIM	NARRATIVE
Non-white shooter	White	Gun control
White shooter	Non-white	Racism, flags
Non-white	Non-white	Run story about the Kardashians instead
Police officer	Non-white	Police brutality
Non-white shooter	Police officer	Reaction to brutality
Male	Female	Sexism
Female	Male	Reaction to sexism
Female shooter	Female	Gun control
Female	Fraternity	Ban fraternities
Non-Muslim	Muslim	Islamophobia
Muslim	Non-Muslim	Reaction to Islamophobia
Muslim	Muslim	Kardashians
Atheist shooter	Christian	Gun control
Terrorist	Artist	Need for censorship
Terrorist	Christian	The Crusades
Israeli	Terrorist	Ban Israel
Terrorist	Israelis	Ban Israel
Terrorist	Any Jew	Ban Israel

created by: Jon Gabriel, Ricochet.com

Do you really believe you live in a free society?

June 20, 2016

From Drudge today. First this:

> LYNCH: *Transcript Of Orlando 911 Calls Will Have References To 'Islamic Terrorism' Removed...*
> *Heavily edited...*

And then there's this:

> *Gay Voters Say 'Dangerous' to Come Out for Trump...*
> *Physical Violence...*
> FLASHBACK: *Trump Defends Gays from Clintons in 2000...*
> APPLE *won't aid Republican convention...*

~

Donald Trump full Hillary speech

June 23, 2016

Donald Trump gives a speech attacking Hillary Clinton, responding to her "I'm with her" slogan but saying that he himself is "with you, the American people." I wouldn't think you had to say a thing it is all so self-evident, but here he is saying what needs to be said.

~

Donald Trump's statement on Brexit

June 25, 2016

This is DONALD J. TRUMP STATEMENT REGARDING BRITISH REFERENDUM ON E.U. MEMBERSHIP:[281]

> The people of the United Kingdom have exercised the sacred right of all free peoples. They have declared their independence from the European Union and have voted to reassert control over their own politics, borders and economy. A Trump Administration pledges to strengthen our ties

---

[281] www.donaldjtrump.com, 24 June 2016.

> *with a free and independent Britain, deepening our bonds in commerce, culture and mutual defense. The whole world is more peaceful and stable when our two countries – and our two peoples – are united together, as they will be under a Trump Administration.*
>
> *Come November, the American people will have the chance to re-declare their independence. Americans will have a chance to vote for trade, immigration and foreign policies that put our citizens first. They will have the chance to reject today's rule by the global elite, and to embrace real change that delivers a government of, by and for the people. I hope America is watching, it will soon be time to believe in America again.*

For the contrasting response from Barack Obama, who had supported Remain, you can read it online.[282] In April, Hillary had supported Remain[283] as well:

> *Hillary Clinton believes that transatlantic cooperation is essential, and that cooperation is strongest when Europe is united. She has always valued a strong United Kingdom in a strong EU. And she values a strong British voice in the EU.*

And from the BBC, 'Five reasons Brexit could signal Trump winning the White House'.[284] It begins:

> *The two most surprising political phenomena of this year have been the rise of Donald Trump and the success of the Leave Europe camp in Britain's referendum on Brexit.*
>
> *Few pundits saw either coming (and full disclosure, I include myself here, particularly on Trump) – but we should have and now would be a good chance to make up for past oversight by looking at how the two are linked.*

---

[282] rollcall.com, 24 June 2016.
[283] breitbart.com, 23 June 2016.
[284] BBC News, 20 June 2016.

If you like Brexit but not Donald Trump then it is you who are confused
June 26, 2016

The round-up:

> Shadow over Hillary...
> 'Open revolt against encrusted establishment'...
> Could a Brexit sentiment sweep Trump into office?

~

Trade occurs when your goods are cheaper than theirs and their goods are simultaneously cheaper than yours
June 27, 2016

GWB's Secretary of the Treasury has endorsed Hillary Clinton for President.[285] Mostly known for falling to his knees in front of Nancy Pelosi to beg her to pass his bailout. A globalist clown and clueless in the way only a merchant banker can be. But it is this in particular that I wish to bring to your attention.

> Paulson insists that "it's wrong to tell the American people" that we achieve economic success by "walling ourselves off from the remaining 7 billion people and the markets they represent".

This is the mentality that has caused modern economics to descend to the economic stupidities of the Mercantilists. A favourable balance of trade, and the import of gold, was the aim of every government. The aim was to sell and bring in gold. The value of the rest of the world's economy to Paulson, and I suppose quite a few others, is that they will buy what you produce. I suppose it is true that you can only buy from others if you first sell. But that is not the point he is making. It is the selling that is the benefit. Exporting is what they think makes you wealthy.

So let me point out that the reason to export is to import what you cannot produce as cheaply as others. It is not done to create jobs, which

---
[285] breitbart.com, 25 June 2016.

will be created in any case. And it is not done to build up foreign exchange, which is economically useless unless it is spent.

Because the fact is that unless they buy from you they cannot sell to you. If the people you trade with are as crazy as Paulson, they will break their necks to sell and trade will go on without anyone having to do a thing. Without deliberately raising tariffs and other forms of protection, I wonder how it is even possible to wall off the US economy, or any economy, from everyone else. If your goods are cheaper than theirs, and their goods are simultaneously cheaper than yours – which is the paradox of trade how both can happen at the same time – trade will just go on without anyone else having to do a thing.

You might actually go into the link to see just how hopelessly out of it the people at the top of our economic tree are.

~

Who will save us from the experts?
June 29, 2016

There are two articles paired at Instapundit that really do capture the Brexit moment. The first is 'It's Time for the Elites to Rise Up Against the Ignorant Masses'[286] which is exactly what the article is about and is offered without the slightest sense of irony or humility. Here is the para that captures it all:

> *The Republican Party, already rife with science-deniers and economic reality-deniers, has thrown itself into the embrace of a man who fabricates realities that ignorant people like to inhabit.*

These are the experts: global warmists and Keynesians! Who would trust such expertise? Reading the comments at Instapundit[287] shows the level of distrust with such people. Here are a couple:

> *It's funny how they keep harping on Nigel Farage supposedly lying to the British voters in order to win their votes. The nerve of such people! Why, progressives and neofeudalists would never dare do such a thing!*

---
[286] foreignpolicy.com, 28 June 2016.
[287] pjmedia.com/instapundit, 28 June 2016.

> Ted Kennedy, on the 1965 immigration: "The bill will not flood our cities with immigrants. It will not upset the ethnic mix of our society. It will not relax the standards of admission. It will not cause American workers to lose their jobs."

> Ted Kennedy, on the 1986 amnesty: "This amnesty will give citizenship to only 1.1 to 1.3 million illegal aliens. We will secure the borders henceforth. We will never again bring forward another amnesty bill like this."

> Yet suddenly Leftists are insisting on truth in advertising laws for politicians. If they want to roll back every left-wing lie of the last six decades they can gladly have a redo on Thursday's vote.

And then there's this:

> Homogeneous societies are happier. They have much higher social trust and a good deal more willingness and less resentment in looking after their have-nots. Multi cultural societies rob people of a true sense of belonging. The lions share of what is good in life has nothing to do with money and economics. A nation is more than just a souless shopping mall packed with culturally atomized individuals. The elites are indifferent to the cultural destruction they have wrought in their blindered pursuit of a few more pieces of silver and a lot more centralized control. Globalization is a disaster of epic proportions. It can only end in tyranny.

All right. One more:

> I *do* believe in reason, expertise, and the lessons of history. However, the "elite" are more wedded to their delusions and power than any of the above. Fer crissake, the people who claim to be "believers" in evolution are now pushing the idea that "male" and "female" are entirely learned! Their learning the "lessons of history" is to ignore the lesson of WWII — when lunatics promise to kill you *BELIEVE THEM*!

> And expertise? At what? Fraud, extortion, ginning up hatred? Keeping their hands clean of the violence they incite? At laundering money for their elections through an "education" system that leaves those most in need of an education barely literate and trained to hate?

OK. Another, they are so addictive.

> "Science deniers"? Which party thinks "male" and "female" are learned traits and surgically alterable? Which clings to a prediction of ever-rising

temperatures despite more than a decade of no change? Which clings to a demonization of CO_2 when there simply isn't any more energy CO_2 can "trap"?

There is expertise in how to fix a broken sewer pipe. There is similarly expertise in how to take out an appendix. But expert opinion on social, political and economic issues? I'm afraid that wherever self-interest plays a hand in the decisions of experts, their reliability is not to be trusted. Which is why a democratic process, where the rulers must seek the endorsement of the ruled, remains the only way a modern society should be run.

~

Hillary no charges, unsurprisingly
July 6, 2016

Almost no one I know that I talk to about it has any idea what the issues are. So why should you be surprised that no prosecution will follow. Here is the story at *The Daily Mail*, since you won't find it covered in much detail in the American media: 'Clinton cleared on email scandal by FBI – despite sending and receiving top-secret information on a server which was 'possibly' hacked by America's enemies.'[288] The word "possibly" in quotes means it's not theirs but the Department of "Justice".

The reality is that every email sent and received by Hillary was illegally kept on a private server which also meant, firstly, that every email she sent and received was monitored by every foreign agency across the world and secondly, that much of what she wrote is unavailable for others within the American political system to review, should they actually wish to. Naturally Donald Trump has criticised. I imagine most others will say hardly a word. Whatever else, the story has already blown over even before it became a story.

Meanwhile, on Instapundit, 'The IRS Scandal, Day 1153'.[289] The US political system is corrupt to its very core, but the complicity between the

---

[288] *Daily Mail Australia*, 6 July 2016.
[289] cnbc.com, 5 July 2016.

Democrats and the media will ensure no issue is ever allowed to blow up about anything that harms its party of choice. Again from Instapundit, the media are Democrat Operatives with Bylines.

BTW the story at Instapundit is titled, The fix was in all along[290] which is, of course, true but hardly pictures the gravity of the story. From the comments:

> 1) *The most mendacious paragraph of the whole statement: "In looking back at our investigations into mishandling or removal of classified information, we cannot find a case that would support bringing criminal charges on these facts. All the cases prosecuted involved some combination of: clearly intentional and willful mishandling of classified information; or vast quantities of materials exposed in such a way as to support an inference of intentional misconduct; or indications of disloyalty to the United States; or efforts to obstruct justice. We do not see those things here."*
>
> *She set up the server explicitly in a premeditated attempt to obstruct justice, in order to at a minimum, deny Freedom of Information requests. I would say this outcome is unbelievable, but I have realized since November 2012 there is no organization of government not utterly corrupted by this President and his cabal. USA RIP.*
>
> *2) This goes beyond, far beyond, Prosecutorial Discretion ... We're deep into "Parador" country here. We no longer have a Criminal Justice System, but a System of Justice of Criminals!*
>
> *3) The worst national security breach in the history of the US doesn't warrant anything more than a shoulder shrug from the DOJ.*
>
> *Disgusting. If she were a Republican they'd be literally calling for her head on a pike.*

Not much heat in the response, only resignation about that is how things are.

AND LET ME JUST ADD THIS: This is taken from Lucianne where it was picked up from Gateway Pundit[291] so it is from the more respectable side of the conservative blog world. The article is titled, 'Coincidence? UN Official "Accidentally" Crushes Throat and Dies Before Testifying

---

[290] taxprof.typepad.com/taxprof_blog, 5 July 2016.
[291] pjmedia.com/instapundit, 5 July 2016.

Against Hillary Clinton'.²⁹² Well, in fact, the story goes back to Zero Hedge²⁹³ where the article begins:

> *Call it conspiracy theory, coincidence or just bad luck, but any time someone is in a position to bring down Hillary Clinton by testifying they wind up dead. In fact, there's a long history of Clinton-related body counts, with scores of people dying under mysterious circumstances.*

I do not think any of it is true, but I do find it interesting that it is being said and repeated outside the *National Enquirer*.

FURTHER VIDEO UPDATE: This is Donald Trump in his own more direct version of the contrast between what Comey said and what Hillary said. Trump's video, which can be seen online,²⁹⁴ has already had more than five million hits.

~

Politics discussed – from Trump to Rand Paul
July 16, 2016

I am at Freedomfest again, listening to the Libertarian candidate for President, Gary Johnson. Former Governor of New Mexico whose Vice President would be the former Governor of Massachusetts. Warmish applause, and if he can't do better here, he will not do well anywhere else. What can you do with someone who has just said the biggest international threat in the world is North Korea.

More to the point was "Trump Pro and Con: The YUGE Debate". Wayne Allan Root and Dan Mangru versus Jeffery Tucker and Matt Welch. A year ago Trump was himself here whose favourite son was Rand Paul. Today, a full room who had no patience for any of the anti-Trump people. The issues that came up as questions:

Hillary
Supreme Court
Islam

---

²⁹² www.thegatewaypundit.com, 2 July 2016.
²⁹³ zerohedge.com, 4 July 2016.
²⁹⁴ theamericanmirror.com, 5 July 2016.

immigration
pseudo-free trade

The vote by applause at the end was 90% Trump. The booing and catcalls from the audience for Tucker and Welch was amazing. Tucker literally tried to win the argument by declaring Trump is a fascist, about as empty an argument as I could imagine, but he had no other. His colleague began by stating that Hillary was unfit to be president, but then discussed Trump's threats to Bezos and *The Washington Post*.

What has been astonishing is that in the six days I have been in the US I have not seen or heard a single pro-Trump story in the media.

Brent Bozell

This is now Brent Brozell discussing the media and the election. Trump, he says, understands what no Republican has understood re the media – you attack me, I attack you. The new approach by the national press has been not just to lie by statement but now there has been bias by omission. You all know about Benghazi, the IRS, the emails here, but in the media, it is deliberate misrepresentation.

Not one "investigative" reporter in seven and a half years has looked at Barack Obama. We are in the middle of the greatest communication technological innovation, with the social media now connecting 80% of the world. In 2012, Obama spent most of his money on social media. It is this that the right will have to do to overcome the left-media.

Rand Paul

And now Rand Paul. Starts with Brexit – he not only thinks they should have left, he thinks they should never have joined. Talks about the EU Regulated Man from *Brexit the Movie*. Regs are like being surrounded by invisible barbed wire. US predicament is not much different.

The presidency is a thousand-fold more powerful than Congress. No one wishes to pull it back. But the lesson from history is that power corrupts. Need to surround the power of government with invisible barbed wire.

Brings up the surveillance state. FBI wants judgeless-warrants. Needed 60 votes to pass and got to 58 on the Senate floor. And then there was twenty minutes to find another two. Ultimately failed but close.

The question remains, how can we have a constitutional republic. The question he now has is, "are we doomed"? The majority can now plunder the minority. We can continue but will only work if most Americans still have hope in the American dream. Will only survive if the majority continue to believe in the capacity in self-advancement. People must believe they can be personally successful.

I look at immigrants as assets. Must offer migrants and children of migrants the promise of success. Individuals must believe they can succeed. We should leave their tax money with individuals. If we don't voters will be seeking wealth by voting.

Conclude: it is harder to sell our message. But that is what has to happen.

In answer to a question on Trump v Clinton, very weak support, based on no more than his promise at the debates to support the eventual nominee.

~

Focusing on the small stuff
July 20, 2016

Reading the puppet columnists at *The Australian* – you know the ones, for example, who went after Tony Abbott on orders from their boss – is a trial that too often starts the day on the wrong foot. Here we have Greg Sheridan going after Melania Trump's speech writer for cribbing a passage from Michelle Obama. At least it wasn't the passage where Michelle had said she was for the first time proud to be an American. So as we decide the fate of Western civilisation, this is what Sheridan writes: 'US Republican race: Donald Trump circus adds plagiarism to act.'[295] From which:

> There were the rowdy demonstrations from anti-Trump Republicans, the powerful theme of Make America Safe Again, a stage entry from The Donald himself straight out of World Championship Wrestling, former New York mayor Rudy Giuliani doing his version of "I'm Mad as Hell and I'm Not Gunna Take It Anymore", and Melania Trump plagiarising

---
[295] *The Australian*, 20 July 2016.

> her cliches from Michelle Obama. I didn't know that anyone would bother to plagiarise cliches. After all, they're cliches, right?

Given that Sheridan is repeating the identical meme from the left-media in the US, you can see how useless his analysis is going to be for the rest of the American presidential election. Nothing on Guiliani, for example.

~

Trump Derangement Syndrome
July 21, 2016

Apparently Melania told her speech writer that she admired Michelle Obama, the speech writer took a couple of passages from Michelle's speech and put it in Melania's and Donald Trump has refused to sack the speech writer. That this absolute nothing has become anything, has become the frenzied talking point it has is a reminder of how corrupt the media has become. It is also something of a sign of how little there really is to criticise Trump about that won't resonate with most American voters.

> Trump embraced the swirling attention.
>
> "Good news is Melania's speech got more publicity than any in the history of politics especially if you believe that all press is good press!" Trump said on Twitter.

What a maelstrom of contending views surround a presidential candidate. How anyone can keep a calm weather eye in the midst of it I'll never know but Donald is more likely to do it than anyone.

~

"I'm a Christian, a conservative and a Republican in that order"
July 21, 2016

You won't find it anywhere else. American cornpone at its finest. Mike Pence accepts the nomination for Vice President. As he says, "conservative principles work every time you put them into practice". And he does mention border protection. Not with full conviction but it is there.

Trump acceptance speech
July 22, 2016

I haven't had the time to listen but will get to it tonight. You can watch it on Youtube. His opponents will be the Democrats, of course, but also this: 'ROUND UP: MEDIA MOCKING OF REPUBLICANS INTENSIFIES…'.[296] But whatever happens between now and then, it will be the head-to-head debates between Trump and Clinton that will settle the issue. But let me just link to this, an article by Peter Wales[297] at *Quadrant Online*, which captures what ought to be known. Here is a quote, but it far from the most important.

> *Finally, "He's not a conservative!" Yes, he is. There is not a single Trump policy position that does not fit under the very wide umbrella of freedom-loving, free-market conservatism. It is certainly possible to disagree about some aspect of social policy, or trade, for example. But any position taken in these discussions is a long way from large government socialism. At best, #nevertrump can claim that Trump's opinions now are not what they were twenty years ago. No intelligent person's opinions are what they were twenty years ago. Values clarify as one gets older. Practical experience and knowledge of the world is gained. The world changes, problems and issues change, and ways of dealing with them change. There would be much more reason for concern if Trump's opinions had not changed with changing times.*

That there is virtually no public support for Trump across Australia is a sad fact because if not Trump, then Hillary.

~

Political fools and the American election
July 23, 2016

The problems with Trump has never been in doubt. He is a property developer without a well-developed expertise in many of the political issues of our time. He has a bombastic personality and little relevant historical knowledge (although he is miles ahead of Obama). But having watched him over the past year, there is no doubt that unlike anyone else in the

---

[296] newsbusters.org, 6 January 2017.
[297] *Quadrant Online*, 21 July 2016.

American political establishment, he understands what the issues are and what needs to be fixed. If it turns out he won't be able to achieve what he says, I will be disappointed, but not sorry that he was my choice since there was no one else on the Republican side who offered to do what he has said he will try to do. And now that we are down to him and Hillary, the choice of Hillary is to choose evil and the almost immediate decay and destruction of the American Republic. Four supreme court picks and an open border naturalisation policy will mean no Republican ever becomes president again. Out past 2020, the nature of the US becomes almost unimaginable.

But Trump has genuine strengths, of which a will to have his own way is going to be extremely useful. He has also run a large organisation, so is in a similar situation to army commanders who have become president. He is not going to be as bad as Woodrow Wilson who was merely an academic and who had run nothing in his life other than a university (OK – he was governor of NJ for about a year before running for president).

You look at that story above. These are the forces that have been let loose because of Obama and Hillary. According to *The Daily Mail*, 'Grinning Obama JOKES during statement on Munich carnage as he shifts gears to say he'll miss daughter Malia when she leaves the nest for college.'[298] There are fools everywhere, and there may be just enough of them in the US to make Hillary president. But they are the same kind of fools who made Obama president for the last eight years so there are plenty of them about.

~

Clinton Cash – the movie
July 26, 2016

Breitbart has released the movie[299] so that anyone can now download. Fantastically corrupt and in the open as well. Meanwhile in Philadelphia, the Democrats are in chaos:

> BOOING DURING INVOCATION...
> FLOOR BATTLE...

---

[298] *Daily Mail Australia*, 23 July 2016.
[299] breitbart.com, 25 July 2016.

BERNIE TEXTS: PLEASE DON'T PROTEST IN ARENA!
Dems confiscating pro-Sanders signs…
Arrests and heat injuries…
Jeers for Pelosi at California Breakfast…
Wasserman booed off stage, escorted out by security…
LEFT EATS ITSELF…
4 brutal poll numbers greet Clinton at convention…

Yet the media and the American establishment will make her president if they can. You know all of the above only because it cannot be hidden from view. But to those who wish to see her president, none of it matters even the smallest amount. A week from now it will disappear from the news while they go on and on about Melania's plagiarism.

~

Is it possible for her to lose?
July 27, 2016

There is no level of corruption that seems to matter. There is nothing she can do that will turn the media against her. 'Hillary Clinton makes history as first female presidential nominee – but is met with fury by Bernie Sanders supporters who walk out of Democratic convention.'[300]

> *Hillary Clinton became the first woman to earn a major party's presidential nomination on Tuesday evening as Democratic delegates officially gave her the votes she needed to win the election.*
>
> *'History,' was what she tweeted with a photo of herself on stage at a rally.*
>
> *Bernie Sanders made a surprise appearance and moved to have Clinton named the nominee by acclamation after she had more than enough votes to win.*
>
> *He joined his home state of Vermont, which passed the first time around in the roll call vote, for the history-making moment.*
>
> *'I move that all votes, all votes cast by delegates be reflected in the official record, and I move that Hillary Clinton be selected as the nominee of the Democratic Party for president of the United States,' he said.*
>
> *The gesture was to be a signal of unity and reconciliation during the fractured*

---
[300] *Daily Mail Australia*, 27 July 2016.

Democratic Convention.

His delegates, on the hand, were not so moved to accept the result of the vote. A group of them walked out in protest after Clinton officially won the nomination.

Not that it will stop this steamroller, but Julian Assange: 'A lot more material' coming on US elections.[301] I wonder if he will include material on Trump this time.

~

"I watched her partner with President Obama to restore our country's reputation around the world"
July 27, 2016

This is from Hot Air's Live Blog[302] of the second day of the Democrat National Convention.

> *9:58pm Ex-Secretary of State Madeleine Albright for Bill Clinton: "We need a leader with the experience and judgment to keep America safe…When Hillary served as Secretary of State I watched her partner with President Obama to restore our country's reputation around the world. She fought terrorism. She stopped the spread of nuclear weapons…Smart power in every corner of the world…*
>
> *"She knows that safeguarding freedom and security is not like hosting a TV reality show. It is a complex, round-the-clock job that demands not only a steady hand and a cool hand but also a big heart."*

Every word is untrue. Everyone knows it's untrue, as well. Yet we have a former Clinton Secretary of State saying what she pleases with no fear of contradiction anywhere, except out here where it doesn't matter. I won't even bother with 'You should elect her because the greatest country on Earth has always been about tomorrow': Bill Clinton gets romantic about 'best friend' Hillary and blasts Trump in lengthy, unedited speech.[303] It's as if the past has no existence and from which nothing can be learned.

---

[301] edition.cnn.com, 27 July 2016
[302] hotair.com/archives, 26 July 2016.
[303] *Daily Mail Australia*, 27 July 2016.

Hillary's America – it's closer than you think
July 28, 2016

At Rotten Tomatoes Hillary's America[304] is 5% among the critics and 82% among the audience. Here is the only positive review listed.[305] It begins:

> *Hillary's America: The Secret History of the Democratic Party is a searing, powerful and persuasive exposé on the Democratic Party and Hillary Clinton. Just like in America: Imagine the World Without Her, director Dinesh D'Souza re-examines American history and highlights the facts that should make you horrified and alarmed if you're a critically-thinking individual. Yes, you might find yourself in denial at first, but denial is a crucial and natural step in the process of coming to terms with a harsh truth. D'Souza includes some re-enactments and archival footage which help to enliven the film so that it's not just a bunch of talking heads. The fact that D'Souza remains calm and collected, unlike Michael Moore, throughout the film, is a testament to his strengths as a documentarian and investigator. Did you know that it was actually the Democratic Party [that] was racist [during] the Civil War? Or that the "hood" or "ghettos" are essentially the modern versions of plantations? In other words, the Democratic Party is still just as racist now as it was back in the Civil War, but Democrats, will, of course, deny their racism. Did you know that the KKK originated from the Democratic Party and its members were Democrats themselves? Or how about that Planned Parenthood is mostly found in areas where minorities can be found is a form of eugenics started by Margaret Sanger, the founder of Planned Parenthood? Hillary Clinton just so happens to consider Margaret Sanger to be a role model. D'Souza explains something that you ought to know about Hillary: her mentor was writer Saul Alinksy who began scamming people early on in his college days by ripping off his school's cafeteria while convincing others to take part in the scams as well. That scam serves as a microcosm of what Hillary Clinton plans to do in our country.*

And on it goes. The 95% who hate this film are Democrat Operatives with Bylines, and these are merely film critics. The political commentators are worse. Whether we end up seeing it in Australia, it is worth noting that Box Office: Dinesh D'Souza's 'Hillary's America' Becomes Top Grossing Doc of 2016.[306] Fighting the left is a continuous ongoing uphill battle.

---

[304] rottentomatoes.com
[305] nycmovieguru.com, 15 July 2016.
[306] hollywoodreporter.com, 27 July 2016.

Trump fires back
July 29, 2016

Just follow Trump's twitter feed. Devastating criticisms of Hillary at every turn.[307] Her supporters must have protective shields of the toughest steel and as impervious to logic and reality as a March hare.

~

Niallist rhetoric
July 31, 2016

It is one thing to recognise that no political vehicle is perfect, it is quite another to reject someone who goes most of the way with you because he doesn't have everything you want. Donald Trump has no political history, no past set of political judgements to assess him against, and there is no certainty how he will act in any particular set of circumstances. But I don't worry about renegotiating trade arrangements, I am not worried that he will start some war by accident and it never crosses my mind that me will renege on his stated aim to close the American border and restrict immigration. He is also more likely than anyone to take on the most dangerous issue of our time which is the jihadist rampage across the West.

Meanwhile, we have Niall Ferguson in a particularly vacuous article titled, 'Paranoid Republidents for Trump'.[308] You would think that given his previous concerns about immigration, he might at least lean towards Trump for President. If he believes any of what he has written here, he is instead among the shallowest of our current commentators on Trump's run for the president who has no idea how to achieve anything he says he wishes to see achieved. He is, by the way, Mr Aayan Hirsi Ali and this is what he has to say:

> *Trump's acceptance speech was a ghastly masterclass in what Richard Hofstadter more than 50 years ago called "The paranoid style in American politics." As Hofstadter summarized it, the paranoid view was that "the old American virtues have already been eaten away by cosmopolitans and intellectuals; the old competitive capitalism has been gradually undermined*

---

[307] twitter.com/realDonaldTrump
[308] *Boston Globe*, 25 July 2016.

by socialistic and communistic schemers; [and] the old national security and independence have been destroyed by treasonous plots."

The paranoid worldview verged on the religious: "The paranoid spokesman sees the fate of conspiracy in apocalyptic terms ... He is always manning the barricades of civilization ... Like religious millennialists, he expresses the anxiety of those who are living through the last days." Yet even as he denounces the corrupt, cosmopolitan elite, the political paranoiac is implicitly expressing a kind of attraction. He hates intellectuals, yet he provides extensive footnotes.

This — including the footnotes, 282 of which the Trump campaign supplied on Friday — is about all you need to know about Trump's acceptance speech. It was all here, beginning with the conspiracy theory. "America is a nation of believers, dreamers, and strivers," yelled Trump, "that is being led by a group of censors, critics, and cynics ... No longer can we rely on those elites in media, and politics, who will say anything to keep a rigged system in place."

"Big business, elite media, and major donors" were backing Hillary Clinton, Trump declared, "because they have total control over everything she does. She is their puppet, and they pull the strings." As a result, "corruption has reached a level like never before."

For me, adjusting for the typical rhetorical flourishes that are the basics of political discourse, there is nothing there that seems exaggerated. But if you cannot see how dangerous a Clinton presidency would be, even if you think of her as the lesser of two evils, then your ability to make sound political judgements is running on empty.

Found at Five Feet of Fury which even has a link to me.[309]

---

[309] lawofmarkets.com, 13 May 2016.

100 days to go
July 31, 2016

How dangerous would Hillary be as president. This dangerous:[310]

> "In my first 100 days, we will work with both parties to pass the biggest investment in new, good paying jobs since World War II. Jobs in manufacturing, clean energy, technology and innovation, small business, and infrastructure."

If this kind of cross between Keynes and Alinsky[311] doesn't worry you, you don't know when to be worried. And that is the least of my concerns about what a third Clinton presidency will include.

For another take, you can try Roger Simon on 'America's First Major Socialist Party Debuts in Philadelphia'.[312] Guess which party that is.

Meanwhile, Trump may have his nose ahead in the polls but he will have to win by a lot to overcome the vote early, vote often approach taken by the residents of local cemeteries.

~

Obama paid $400 million ransom to Iran
August 3, 2016

How could this be even remotely true? 'U.S. Sent Cash to Iran as Americans Were Freed: Obama administration insists there was no quid pro quo'.[313]

> The Obama administration secretly organized an airlift of $400 million worth of cash to Iran that coincided with the January release of four Americans detained in Tehran, according to U.S. and European officials and congressional staff briefed on the operation afterward.
>
> Wooden pallets stacked with euros, Swiss francs and other currencies were flown into Iran on an unmarked cargo plane, according to these officials. The U.S. procured the money from the central banks of the

---

[310] *Los Angelas Times*, 28 July 2016.
[311] frontpagemag.com, 29 July 2016.
[312] pjmedia.com, 29 July 2016.
[313] *The Wall Street Journal*, 3 August 2016.

Netherlands and Switzerland, they said.

The money represented the first installment of a $1.7 billion settlement the Obama administration reached with Iran to resolve a decades-old dispute over a failed arms deal signed just before the 1979 fall of Iran's last monarch, Shah Mohammad Reza Pahlavi.

The settlement, which resolved claims before an international tribunal in The Hague, also coincided with the formal implementation that same weekend of the landmark nuclear agreement reached between Tehran, the U.S. and other global powers the summer before.

"With the nuclear deal done, prisoners released, the time was right to resolve this dispute as well," President Barack Obama said at the White House on Jan. 17—without disclosing the $400 million cash payment.

It's not just that they lie to you but that the media never says a word of complaint but just swallows it whole and repeats back whatever a Democrat administration chooses to say.

THE DAILY MAIL VERSION: You won't get it properly reported in the usual media, but there is still the UK's Daily Mail: US delivered $400m in CASH stashed inside wooden pallets to Iran on same day as American hostages were freed but the Obama administration DENIES it paid a ransom.[314] Of course they deny it; they always lie.

~

Trump pro and con at Freedomfest
August 5, 2016

You can find me sitting in the front row in the youtube video. And I have to say that for myself, the two speakers opposed to Trump as President provided such empty arguments that it was offensive. The audience was overwhelmingly pro-Trump by the way.

---

[314] *Daily Mail Australia*, 3 August 2016.

Pathetic and disgusting
August 5, 2016

Compare and contrast:

> *Obama on Iran payment: 'We do not pay ransom'.*[315]

> *Freed Iranian Hostage: Iranians Told Me They Were Waiting For Another Plane To Arrive Before Letting Us Go.*[316]

I wonder who is telling the truth.

> *On Thursday's broadcast of the Fox Business Network's "The Intelligence Report with Trish Regan," Saeed Abedini, one of the four hostages released from Iran back in January, stated that on the night he was freed, his captors told him they were waiting on another plane to arrive before letting him go.*

> *Abedini said, "I just remember the night that we'd been in a[n] airport, just take hours and hours there. And I asked one of the…police that was with us, that, why are you not letting us to go to the…plane? And he told me we are waiting for another plane, and if that plane take off, then we're going to let you go."*

> *He added, "[T]hey told us you're going to be there for 20 minutes. But it took like hours and hours. We slept at the airport, and when I asked them why you don't let us go, because the plane was there, pilot was there, everyone was ready that we leave the country, they said we are waiting for another plane, and until that plane doesn't come, we never let you go."*

> *Abedini was then asked, "Were they effectively waiting for the money to come in before they then let you take off?" He answered, "Yeah. They didn't talk about money. They just told us about the — they told me about the plane. … So, the reason that they said you're here in the airport is — was just because we are waiting for another plane."*

> *Abedini was also asked if he believed a ransom was paid, to which he stated he was grateful for his freedom, but there are others still left behind in Iran.*

AND A BIT MORE ON OBAMA'S CHOSEN SUCCESSOR: From a quite compelling article by Daryl McCann at *Quadrant Online*: 'The Audacity

---

[315] edition.cnn.com, 5 August 2016.
[316] breitbart.com, 4 August 2016.

of Crooked Hillary'.³¹⁷ From which, but you owe it to yourself to read the whole thing:

> *The corrupt cabal that currently rules — and betrays — America and the entire West is not going anywhere. Hillary Clinton magnanimously invited the supporters of Sanders to put aside their acrimony and get with the strength. Bernie, who had always been too gentlemanly — or should we say too PC? — to confront Clinton on the meaning of the private server and the deleted 30,000 emails, now meekly submitted. Hillary Clinton has not participated in a proper news conference for over nine months and yet over and over again, during the televised Democratic debates, Bernie Sanders passed up the opportunity to address the record of the woman in the spotlight immediately adjacent to him. His faint-heartedness, we could conclude, amounts to a form of complicity.*

~

Any lie will do
August 6, 2016

This is picked up from John Hinderaker at Powerline: 'ON IRAN, ISRAELIS SAY: OBAMA IS WRONG'.³¹⁸ This has large implications and will add to the tensions between the US and Israel, but sometimes clarity is more important:

> *Israel is rejecting remarks by President Barack Obama contending it no longer opposes the nuclear deal that world powers struck with Iran in 2015.*
>
> *Prime Minister Benjamin Netanyahu said on Friday that "Israel's view on the Iran deal remains unchanged."*
>
> *Israel's Defense Ministry reportedly compared the deal to the 1938 Munich Pact ahead of World War II, which Britain and France signed with Germany and which averted war at the time but effectively gave then-Czechoslovakia to the Nazis.*

The final point made in the post is the right one: "We have entered a bizarro world in which facts seemingly make no difference. Any lie will do,

---
³¹⁷ *Quadrant Online*, 5 August 2016.
³¹⁸ powerlineblog.com, 5 August 2016.

as far as the Obama administration and Hillary Clinton are concerned." How Israel, or the rest of us for that matter, are going to survive this period of history is now anyone's guess.

~

He may really be the great negotiator he says he is
August 6, 2016

Think of how nicely the ducks are falling into line:

> WE ARE FAMILY: *Trump endorses House Speaker Paul Ryan…*
> *Expresses support for McCain and Ayotte…*
> *Escalates attacks on HRC…*
> *Plans biggest tax cuts since Reagan…*

I still think it will be the debates that settle the issue, one way or the other. But if the Republicans can now all start supporting each other, there is no telling how well this could go. Trump's Facebook ad, by the way, has had more than two million hits in less than 24 hours.[319]

The largest issue remains the phenomenal dishonesty and bias of the American media. An important example here: 'Pat Caddell on 'Cooked' Reuters Poll: 'Never in My Life Have I Seen a News Organization Do Something So Dishonest'.'[320] There is nothing in any mainstream news report you can trust but if the media can do it, they will get Hillary over the line.

~

A free press and an informed public
August 8, 2016

Talking American politics with anyone who does not look at various right-of-centre blogs is a depressing experience. The picture from this blog: SHOCK PHOTO: Multiple staffers help unstable Hillary up stairs[321]

---

[319] theconservativetreehouse.com, 6 August 2016.
[320] breitbart.com, 1 August 2016.
[321] theamericanmirror.com, 7 August 2016.

was found on Drudge which carries the story further.

And then there's this: 'Clinton discussed executed Iranian scientist on email.'³²²

> Hillary Clinton recklessly discussed, in emails hosted on her private server, an Iranian nuclear scientist who was executed by Iran for treason, Sen. Tom Cotton, R-Ark., said Sunday.

How many other policy disasters have followed from every foreign government having immediate access to everything Hillary illegally wrote as Secretary of State on her private email accounts. Ah well. What you don't know can't hurt you, I suppose. Or at least not right away.

~

In the American election, which side do you suppose The Australian takes?
August 8, 2016

See if you can guess. *The Australian* has a supplement on the American Election.³²³ Not all that neutral, as you can see by clicking the link. [The link has been replaced by an update published on election day!] But in case you cannot be bothered, here is what you see right after the intro:

> President Obama said Republican nominee Donald Trump is "unfit" to be president and questioned why top GOP lawmakers continued to endorse Trump for the White House while denouncing his actions.

The Oz also went for Turnbull which shows you how out to lunch these people are. The power of self-deception within the media class is extraordinary. They pass off their shallow and subjective valuations as deeply considered objective truths. This from *The New York Times* is almost beyond parody: 'Trump Is Testing the Norms of Objectivity in Journalism'.³²⁴ That the media fail this test in every single election is neither here nor there. That they believe they are objective is the true idiocy. Let me quote:

---

³²² washingtonexaminer.com, 7 August 2016.
³²³ media.theaustralian.com.au/multimedia
³²⁴ *The New York Times*, 7 June 2016.

> If you're a working journalist and you believe that Donald J. Trump is a demagogue playing to the nation's worst racist and nationalistic tendencies, that he cozies up to anti-American dictators and that he would be dangerous with control of the United States nuclear codes, how the heck are you supposed to cover him?
>
> Because if you believe all of those things, you have to throw out the textbook American journalism has been using for the better part of the past half-century, if not longer, and approach it in a way you've never approached anything in your career. If you view a Trump presidency as something that's potentially dangerous, then your reporting is going to reflect that. You would move closer than you've ever been to being oppositional. That's uncomfortable and uncharted territory for every mainstream, nonopinion journalist I've ever known, and by normal standards, untenable.

Uncharted territory!!! What a bunch of self-deluded bozos these media people are.

~

Hillary's health
August 9, 2016

As worrying as this video is (www.youtube.com watch?v=OqbDBRWb63) it seems to understate the urgency of the problem which ought to terrify anyone who thinks there is anything to it.

~

Unfit to be president in many ways – here's one more
August 10, 2016

Donald Trump suggests that political pressure could be applied to a President Clinton on the selection of supreme court justices in relation to the 2nd amendment and every unhinged journalist goes off the deep end accusing him of advocating violence. The story: 'Trump: Maybe 'Second

Amendment People' Could Stop Clinton From Picking Judges."[325]

> *Trump said at a rally in Wilmington, North Carolina, on Tuesday that if Clinton gets to pick federal judges as president, there is nothing that can be done to protect the right to bear arms.*
>
> *But then he adds without elaboration that maybe supporters of the Second Amendment could figure out a way. . . .*

Like, say, through the Senate rejecting a nominee, maybe. Anyway, here he is:

> *Trump himself seemed unaware of the controversy in an interview shortly after the rally, but he repeated that his point was that Second Amendment advocates are a powerful lobby. Former Mayor Rudolph Giuliani also came to Trump's defense.*
>
> *"I think you are talking about — I'm not sure because I haven't' heard this question — but I think you're talking about the power of people that are in favor of the Second Amendment, and they have tremendous political power," he said.*
>
> *When asked about Democrats' statements equating the remark to condoning violence, Trump said: Oh no, no. This is political power."*
>
> *Giuliani added, "I mean, this is the Clinton trick book that you fall for all the time."*
>
> *Trump senior communications adviser Jason Miller told CBS News' Major Garrett the accusations the GOP nominee was calling for violence are "completely ridiculous."*
>
> *"Donald Trump was obviously talking about American voters who are passionate about their Second Amendment rights and advocating they use that power at the ballot box," Miller told CBS News. "The Clinton campaign is desperate and is obviously throwing all sorts of outrageous charges. I am surprised so many reporters are falling hook-line-and-sinker for what is obviously a ridiculous charge."*

I'm not surprised, of course, but who can be so disciplined in everything they say so that nothing cannot be twisted to make it seem anything you like.

---

[325] newyork.cbslocal.com, 9 August 2016.

Then there is this story which, as always, shows up in The *Daily Mail* and thus will have virtually no impact in the United States: 'Child rape victim comes forward for the first time in 40 years to call Hillary Clinton a 'liar' who defended her rapist by smearing her, blocking evidence and callously laughing that she knew he was guilty'.[326] The story is an old one but not the statement of the 12-year old victim of a rapist who was defended by Hillary Clinton. The victim is now 54.

- *'Hillary Clinton is not for women and children,' says Kathy Shelton, 54, who was 12 years old when she was raped by Thomas Alfred Taylor in Arkansas*

- *Clinton was the rapist's defense lawyer, pleading him down to 'unlawful fondling of a minor'*

- *The 41-year-old drifter served less than a year in prison*

- *The plea came after Clinton was able to block the admission of forensic evidence that linked her client to the crime*

- *Shelton says she's furious that Clinton has been portraying herself as a lifelong advocate of women and girls on the campaign trail*

- *Clinton accused Shelton of 'seeking out older men' in the case and demanded that she undergo a grueling court-ordered psychiatric examination*

- *The presidential candidate later laughed while discussing aspects of the case in a recently-unearthed audiotaped interview from the 1980s*

~

The killer instinct
August 11, 2016

Let's go to what he is reported to have said: Trump: Maybe 'Second Amendment People' Could Stop Clinton From Picking Judges.[327]

> *Trump said at a rally in Wilmington, North Carolina, on Tuesday that if Clinton gets to pick federal judges as president, there is nothing that can be*

---

[326] *Daily Mail Australia*, 10 August 2016.
[327] newyork.cbslocal.com, 9 august 2016.

> *done to protect the right to bear arms.*
>
> *But then he adds without elaboration that maybe supporters of the Second Amendment could figure out a way. . . .*

My first reaction on hearing that he had said this was to think that it was the first time I had heard him utter a defeatist word, hypothesising that Hillary might win in November. But then I have watched the reaction across the media, and even among the supposed conservative media, accepting the left-media's interpretation of what Trump had said, that he had been advocating some kind of violence against Hillary. There are political morons everywhere, I'm afraid, but the left-media must be amazed at how stupid the conservative side of politics is. I will go to the logic of what Trump is supposed to have said, which is that:

- *if Hillary is elected*
- *and she gets to choose the next Supreme Court justices*
- *and she chooses nominees who are opposed to the second amendment*
- *then, what?*

It ought to be obvious that if she is already president, her death would have no effect on who is chosen for the Supreme Court. Suppose she nominates Judges X and Y and then another blood clot to the brain carries her off. The same nominees will go forward under President Kaine.

The thing that makes Trump so different from all of the other Republicans is that he is not gun shy of a serious fight. He must be no little dismayed and quite a lot disgusted by the Republican first eleven who are weak beyond measure and who have no fight in them. The way the story continues is how it looked to me even as I read his words:

> *Trump himself seemed unaware of the controversy in an interview shortly after the rally, but he repeated that his point was that Second Amendment advocates are a powerful lobby. Former Mayor Rudolph Giuliani also came to Trump's defense.*
>
> *"I think you are talking about — I'm not sure because I haven't' heard this question — but I think you're talking about the power of people that are in favor of the Second Amendment, and they have tremendous political power," he said.*

> When asked about Democrats' statements equating the remark to condoning violence, Trump said: Oh no, no. This is political power."
>
> Giuliani added, "I mean, this is the Clinton trick book that you fall for all the time."
>
> Trump senior communications adviser Jason Miller told CBS News' Major Garrett the accusations the GOP nominee was calling for violence are "completely ridiculous."
>
> "Donald Trump was obviously talking about American voters who are passionate about their Second Amendment rights and advocating they use that power at the ballot box," Miller told CBS News. "The Clinton campaign is desperate and is obviously throwing all sorts of outrageous charges. I am surprised so many reporters are falling hook-line-and-sinker for what is obviously a ridiculous charge."

I'm not surprised, of course, and I would be surprised if he really were surprised. The media are Trump's most relentless enemies.

What I like about Trump is that he brings a gun to a knife fight. He does not back down. He's new at this political game, but what he is not new at is fighting to win. You want to win yourself, you want to get your policies up even with the gale force media winds in front. It disgusts me to see how weak his support is. Here it is, you dummkopfs. We are down to the last two, and if it's not Trump then its Hillary. Don't tell me about all of your concerns with this and that. If you are not all in for Trump, then do me a favour and just shut up.

~

Hope and change
August 12, 2016

There is a chart that shows that the major American television networks spend four time as much airtime on Trump controversies than on Hillary's scandals. This is gale force media bias that anyone voting for Trump has to take into account as they look into their own political souls.

I don't know if others have worked it out yet but if Trump doesn't become president then Hillary does. It also does seem to me that there are far too many independent minds who are locked into the left-media narrative and seem to repeat almost verbatim the things they find in *The New York Times*, handily repeated for them by *The Oz* and Fairfax Press. And what does get me is that with Hillary you will get nothing you say you want – not a single thing – other than a continuation of the Obama years which Hillary's stint as Secretary of State has well and truly prepared her for.

You like open borders, she's your woman. You like unrestricted immigration, then you know who to vote for. Want spending even more undisciplined than now, then that's the way to go. Want the sleaziest and most corrupt administration in history – one guaranteed to be sold to the highest bidder – then just keep plugging Hillary.

Trump is unusual, truly never been tested with high office. OK, but why is it an advantage that Hillary has been, when everything she has done, to the extent that she has done anything at all, has turned to ashes? A candidate without a single accomplishment to her name, other than name recognition. The funny thing is that Trump really does offer Hope and Change. He may not deliver, but he might. I know what he wants to do and my wish is that he is actually able to do it.

I thought Romney was the last hope for the West, and maybe he was. But there is now Donald Trump. (1) He is not Hillary. (2) He knows something about balancing a set of books. (3) He might even be able to close the American border. (4) He loves America and the American way of life – that is, our way of life.

You don't see it so you don't see it. But let me tell you, if you don't see it, you have nothing to tell me about who to vote for in the American presidential election in November.

And there is plenty of stupid going around
August 13, 2016

"Irony is wasted on the stupid." -- Oscar Wilde

You know, no one thinks that Obama and Hillary really did set up ISIS. Saying so is kind of a metaphor for geopolitical incompetence of the most extraordinary kind. If they had not blundered as they had across the Middle East, and in particular in Iraq and Libya, ISIS would never have formed, or if formed, would never have reached the kind of extension it now has. The above sentiment therefore comes with this one:

Sarcasm

Because beating the crap out of people is illegal

The problem is, if you are among those who are irony-free, you won't see the point. And while there is some satisfaction in laughing at you, the reality is that when stupid reaches the highest levels of political decision making, there is nothing really to laugh about.

~

Will talking sense work?
August 17, 2016

This is Donald Trump talking directly to America's black communities:[328]

> Republican Donald Trump made his most direct appeal yet Tuesday for black voters in the presidential race, pushing forward an agenda to restore law and order and revitalize inner-city neighborhoods that he said suffer from years of misguided Democratic policies.
>
> In a speech delivered not far from Milwaukee neighborhoods rocked by anti-police riots, Mr. Trump laid the blame for urban despair and conflict between police and minorities at the feet of Democratic nominee Hillary Clinton.
>
> "I am running to offer you a much better future," Mr. Trump said in a

---
[328] *The Washington Times*, 16 August 2016.

speech in West Bend, Wisconsin. "Crime and violence is an attack on the poor and it will never be accepted in a Trump administration."

He said the policies holding back minority neighborhoods were part of the "rigged system" led by Mrs. Clinton, who he said pandered to black voters but didn't really care about their suffering.

"The political class that Mrs. Clinton has been a part of for 30 years has abandoned the people of this county. They only care about themselves," he said. "I am going to give the people their voice back."

And there's more at the link. There is also no doubt he means it. What has disappeared into history is that the entire Ku Klux Klan was Democrat. This really does look like America's last chance, but it's a genuine one.

Meanwhile, there is only +/-2% in it. And Hillary is not a well woman.

~

Why do people believe what reporters say?
August 21, 2016

Here is Ann Coulter discussing the distortions and lies of the journalistic profession in a column titled, 'How the media work'.[329] It is, as always, an interesting column that gets to the point, but this is I think particularly true. She is discussing the reporting that surrounds Donald Trump, but she could mean anyone on the right who actually gets political traction. The actual example she gives is about herself, but the general principle is the point.

Even sensible people can't think straight in the middle of one of these [media] hate campaigns.

It can be very difficult for people to overcome whatever meaning the press superimposes on what someone has said, no matter how psychotic. Throw in incessant repetition and uniform agreement among the pundits (Hillary cheerleaders versus Never Trumpers), and completely deranged interpretations become historical facts.

We treat media corruption and its cultural Marxism like bad weather,

---

[329] anncoulter.com, 17 August 2016.

as just the way things are. But the vile misrepresentation of the world they are reporting on is one of the most important of the entrenched problems we face. The Western world – our way of life – is in mortal danger because the media wilfully distort the world they describe. It is not that they do not know any better. They know exactly what they are doing, which is unmistakeable given what they consistently leave out and what they do say about what they decide to discuss. There is nothing haphazard or accidental about it. Here is Donald Trump discussing the problem[330] as part of a more comprehensive speech he gave last week. What makes Trump so unique is that he will raise this at all. Who else does? Not another politician I have ever seen. And every word of the following is unarguably true.

> *The establishment media doesn't cover what really matters in this country, or what's really going on in people's lives. They will take words of mine out of context and spend a week obsessing over every single syllable, and then pretend to discover some hidden meaning in what I said.*
>
> *Just imagine for a second if the media spent this energy holding the politicians accountable who got innocent Americans like Kate Steinle killed – she was gunned down by an illegal immigrant who had been deported five times.*
>
> *Just imagine if the media spent this much time investigating the poverty and joblessness in our inner cities.*
>
> *Just think about how much different things would be if the media in this country sent their cameras to our border, or to our closing factories, or to our failing schools. Or if the media focused on what dark secrets must be hidden in the 33,000 emails Hillary Clinton deleted.*
>
> *Instead, every story is told from the perspective of the insiders. It's the narrative of the people who rigged the system, never the voice of the people it's been rigged against.*

And here is one more article that discusses this same problem where the sub-head reads: Honest Reporting Died Long Ago.[331] Yet even if you know it, how many are capable of suspending judgement on things they see in the press? And just to pile a bit more on, there is now also this from *The New York Post*: 'American journalism is collapsing before our eyes'.[332] On the off

---

[330] thehill.com, 18 August 2016.
[331] observer.com, 18 August 2016.
[332] *New York Post*, 21 August 2016.

chance you need a bit more reminding, there is then this, although I'm not sure I quite agree with the first sentence:

> *The shameful display of naked partisanship by the elite media is unlike anything seen in modern America.*
>
> *The largest broadcast networks — CBS, NBC and ABC — and major newspapers like The New York Times and Washington Post have jettisoned all pretense of fair play. Their fierce determination to keep Trump out of the Oval Office has no precedent.*
>
> *Indeed, no foreign enemy, no terror group, no native criminal gang, suffers the daily beating that Trump does. The mad mullahs of Iran, who call America the Great Satan and vow to wipe Israel off the map, are treated gently by comparison.*
>
> *By torching its remaining credibility in service of Clinton, the mainstream media's reputations will likely never recover, nor will the standards. No future producer, editor, reporter or anchor can be expected to meet a test of fairness when that standard has been trashed in such willful and blatant fashion.*

It's not simply that they do it that is the worry, but that they are so ignorant that in acting this way they believe they are doing good.

~

In praise of a tasteless, publicity seeking, coarse, billionaire, reality TV star
August 23, 2016

There has always been one trouble for me with the books Ann Coulter writes. No sooner do I start one than I have reached the last page. No one, and I do mean no one, writes like her. And while there may have been, now and then, something she has written I didn't quite agree with, nothing of that kind comes to mind at the moment. Her latest is '*In Trump We Trust: E Pluribus Awesome!*'[333] from which you can find an online excerpt on brietbart.[334] This section of the book, I'm afraid, truly made me laugh. Go to the link but I will put up the premise she begins with and then you can see what she does.

---

[333] Ann Coulter, *In Trump We Trust: E Pluribus Awesome*, 2016.
[334] breitbart.com, 22 August 2016.

> *If we were in the laboratory, designing the perfect presidential candidate, it's unlikely we would have produced a tasteless, publicity-seeking, coarse, billionaire, reality TV star.*
>
> *Ha! Look at how wrong we were. It turns out, that is exactly what we needed.*

Now go and read it all, and if you still want to vote for Hillary after that, then do your worst you sour misbegotten fool. I'll let you know what I thought of the whole book when I finally have had it in my hands plus the one additional day I will need to read it.

~

Trump goes to Mexico
September 1, 2016

If, by now, you do not see Donald Trump as someone who might actually achieve many of the things that you who might pretend to be on the right side of politics want, then you might as well own up to being an open-borders socialist at heart. If this isn't "presidential" – as in agenda setting and developing policies to achieve your ends – then I don't know what is.

> *MEXICO CITY: TRUMP LAYS OUT FIVE SHARED GOALS…*
> *PROMOTES RIGHT TO BUILD WALL…*
> *MEX PREZ: 'OPEN AND CONSTRUCTIVE' CONVERSATION…*
> *Willing to Deal on NAFTA…*
> *Hillary Hits Donald Hard…*
> *YORK: Big gamble…*
> *RAMOS GOES LOCO…*
> *WASH POST LEAD THURSDAY: Some Mexicans angry at their own president for meeting…*

In politics – in life – you don't get everything you want. But it doesn't come much closer than this. For our time, he may be the Winston Churchill of the West. And there is no one else who could possibly do what needs to be done. He may not succeed, but at least he wants to and seems to have the skills and savvy to do it.

Murdoch is open borders and closed to Trump
September 4, 2016

An old story but not yet reported on or confirmed till now: 'Rupert Murdoch instructed Fox News to take down Donald Trump'.[335] The link takes you to a quote from an article in *NY Mag*.

> *Murdoch was not a fan of Trump's and especially did not like his stance on immigration. (The antipathy was mutual: "Murdoch's been very bad to me," Trump told me in March.) A few days before the first GOP debate on Fox in August 2015, Murdoch called Ailes at home. "This has gone on long enough," Murdoch said, according to a person briefed on the conversation.*
>
> *Murdoch told Ailes he wanted Fox's debate moderators — Kelly, Bret Baier, and Chris Wallace — to hammer Trump on a variety of issues. Ailes, understanding the GOP electorate better than most at that point, likely thought it was a bad idea. "Donald Trump is going to be the Republican nominee," Ailes told a colleague around this time. But he didn't fight Murdoch on the debate directive.*
>
> *On the night of August 6, in front of 24 million people, the Fox moderators peppered Trump with harder-hitting questions. But it was Kelly's question regarding Trump's history of crude comments about women that created a media sensation. He seemed personally wounded by her suggestion that this spoke to a temperament that might not be suited for the presidency. "I've been very nice to you, though I could probably maybe not be based on the way you have treated me," he said pointedly.*

~

Ending the insanity
September 7, 2016

> *This is insane. This is the mark of a party, a society, a country, a people, a civilization that wants to die. Trump, alone among candidates for high office in this or in the last seven (at least) cycles, has stood up to say: I want to live. I want my party to live. I want my country to live. I want my people to live. I want to end the insanity.*

From The Flight 93 Election.[336] Needs to be read in full.

---

[335] theconservativetreehouse.com, 3 September 2016.
[336] claremont.org, 5 September 2016.

A "basket of deplorables"
September 11, 2016

I know you shouldn't raise such issues about someone as ill as Hillary obviously is, but this business about Trump's support base[337] is quite extraordinary.

> She claimed that half of Trump's supporters nationally—millions of people—were a "basket of deplorables" who were "irredeemable" and "racist, sexist, homophobic, xenophobic, Islamophobic."

Hillary and the truth are almost total strangers, but this story[338] is from John Hinderaker at Powerline. It's worth reading it all, but this is his conclusion:

> The real Hillary is a small, unoriginal, not very talented woman who was fortunate enough (in some respects) to marry Bill Clinton. Pretty much everything else is a lie.

You might also be interested in knowing that she had failed the DC bar exam[339] and was only eventually able to become a lawyer by passing the exam in Arkansas. What is truly deplorable is that this is a story you may not have come across in the normal course of events.

~

Voters left in dark
September 12, 2016

CLINTON 'FAINTS' AS SHE IS RUSHED OUT OF 9/11 MEMORIAL…
SECRET SERVICE ATYPICAL PROTOCOL…
'OVERHEATED'…
VIDEO…
STRUGGLES TO WALK…
Knees buckle, loses shoe…
WASH POST: HEALTH NOW AN ISSUE…

---

[337] breitbart.com, 10 September 2016.
[338] powerlineblog.com, 10 September 2016.
[339] snopes.com, 29 August 2016.

DRUDGE *Vindicated...*
Medical History Now Under Microscope...
She embraces child — despite 'pneumonia'...
Press left in dark...[340]
No probe into flaring hypothyroidism/Hashimoto's...
FLASHBACK 2012: CLINTON FALLS BOARDING PLANE...
The Roughest Week...

It's the "press left in dark" which really is the joke. Everyone knows that Hillary is a very sick woman and is in no condition to be the President of the United States. This is the media supporting Hillary to the bitter end. You cannot trust the media, but if they can, as unfit in so many ways as she is for the presidency, they will see her win. This is the death of democracy, and the media are the surest symptom of its collapse in the US. They have covered for Obama for the past eight years and will do the same for Hillary if they can. Democracy depends on an informed electorate. The American media is no longer a free press, although with the internet the flow of information is no longer as controllable as it once was.

~

This irreversible decision
September 13, 2016

The quiet that surrounds Obama's mismanagement of every aspect of American society may have reached a moment of resistance in a rare agreement between Republicans and Democrats. You may not even know the internet is in need of saving, but this a story that is worth pondering, not just for what it says about the issue itself, but about the governance of the United States when in the hands of Democrats. The story from *The Wall Street Journal*: 'Congress Can Save the Internet'[341] which comes with the sub-heading, "The White House will end U.S. oversight at month's end, unless lawmakers step in." We are used to the freedom of the internet but that is not a future given.

---

[340] nbcnews.com, 11 September 2016.
[341] *The Wall Street Journal*, 11 September 2016.

President Obama wants this to be the last month of an open, uncensored internet guaranteed by the U.S. government. His plan to end American stewardship would hand new power to authoritarian governments offended by the internet as we know it. . . .

"This irreversible decision could result in a less transparent and accountable internet governance regime or provide an opportunity for an enhanced role for authoritarian nation-states."...

The broader point is that the internet ain't broke and doesn't need fixing. Icann's stakeholders—developers, engineers, network operators and entrepreneurs—are free to operate an open internet because U.S. protection prevents Moscow, Beijing, Tehran and other authoritarian regimes from meddling. The Obama administration may not be comfortable with American exceptionalism, but the internet fosters free speech and innovation because it was built in the image of the U.S.

Obama will do as much damage as he can before he is finally on his way. If you are interested in freedom of speech, you have to be interested in this.

~

A political scandal of the highest order
September 13, 2016

Is this not one of the most obscene scandals in American political history? If they knew she had these mental conditions, problems that make her unfit to take on the role of the president, why would anyone concerned about the future of the United States cover it up?

> *PAPER: HILLARY MYSTERY 'NURSE'...*
> *ON-SITE NEUROLOGICAL TEST?*
> *Clinton Admits She Has Passed Out 'A Few Times'...*
> *Can't Remember...*
> *Campaign Avoided ER To Conceal Details of Medical Treatment...*[342]
> *FLASHBACK: FAINTS DURING SPEECH...*
> *FLASHBACK: HEAD FIRST BOARDING PLANE...*
> *FLASHBACK: SCARY COUGHING FIT AT BENGHAZI HEARING...*

---

[342] *The New York Post,* 12 September 2016.

FLASHBACK: SURGERY TO REPAIR ELBOW
FRACTURED IN STATE DEPT FALL…
Allies grow angry over secrecy…
MORE DOCTORS SOUND ALARM…
Three blood clots, a concussion, deep vein thrombosis…
DEMS READY FOR KAINE…

Most people seem to treat this as just what you would expect as part of politics, but I cannot believe it is. There are other Democrats who can serve as president. Why risk having someone elected who cannot fulfil the duties of office? If they actually knew she was this unwell, and it is certain they did, she should have been made to withdraw long before now. Someone needs to explain why this has been allowed to continue to within two months of the election.

~

If Hillary wins
September 14, 2016

I originally linked to the post on *The Flight 93 Election* which is a post you really ought to read. The writer, who goes under the pseudonym Publius Decius Mus, has now written a follow-up which is even better since because of the wide circulation of the original, has attracted an immense amount of criticism. This he titles, Restatement on Flight 93[343] where he picks up the various criticisms of the first article and replies to them one by one in ascending order of importance. This is where the article leads, but all of it should be read:

> *If Hillary wins, there will still be a country, in the sense of a geographic territory with a people, a government, and various institutions. Things will mostly look the same, just as—outwardly—Rome changed little on the ascension of Augustus. It will not be tyranny or Caesarism—not yet. But it will represent, in my view, an irreversible triumph for the administrative state. Consider that no president has been denied reelection since 1992. If we can't beat the Democrats now, what makes anyone think we could in 2020, when they will have all the advantages of incumbency plus four more*

---
[343] claremont.org, 13 September 2016.

> years of demographic change in their favor? And if we can't win in 2016 or 2020, what reason is there to hope for 2024? Will the electorate be more Republican? More conservative? Will constitutional norms be stronger?
>
> The country will go on, but it will not be a constitutional republic. It will be a blue state on a national scale. Only one party will really matter. A Republican may win now and again—once in a generation, perhaps—but only a neutered one who has "updated" all his positions so as to be more in tune with the new electorate. I.e., who has done exactly what the Left has for years been concern-trolling us to do: move left and become more like them. Yet another irony: the "conservatives" who object to Trump as too liberal are working to guarantee that only a Republican far more liberal than Trump could ever win the presidency again.

It is a depressing article but what do you know that makes what he describes seem anything other than the most likely outcome we face?

~

'LES DEPLORABLES!'
September 17, 2016

Via Drudge "LES DEPLORABLES!' Trump floors cheering Miami crowd as he enters to Broadway anthem and speaks in front of giant 'Les Mis' video screen art."[344]

Whatever you may think about his policies, he is a marketing genius.

~

Why would anyone support Hillary?
September 17, 2016

There is a cartoon that shows two doctors propping Hillary up, each holding her by one of her arms with the caption, "We Support Hillary Clinton". And there's a story to go with the picture: '*Hillary's Enthusiasm Gap Could Cost Her the Election*'.[345]

---

[344] *Daily Mail Australia,* 18 September 2016.
[345] breitbart.com, 16 September 2016.

In the never never
September 21, 2016

Victor Davis Hanson, writing in the #NeverTrump *National Review*, puts his own point of view in an article titled, 'Never NeverTrump'.[346] Note the double negative. Here's the point, but it is worth reading end to end:

> *In sum, if Trump's D-11 bulldozer blade did not exist, it would have to be invented. He is Obama's nemesis, Hillary's worst nightmare, and a vampire's mirror of the Republican establishment. Before November's election, his next outburst or reinvention will once again sorely embarrass his supporters, but perhaps not to the degree that Clinton's erudite callousness should repel her own.*
>
> *In farming, I learned there is no good harvest, only each year one that's 51 percent preferable to the alternative, which in 2016 is a likely 16-year Obama-Clinton hailstorm.*
>
> *It may be discomforting for some conservatives to vote for the Republican party's duly nominated candidate, but as this Manichean two-person race ends, it is now becoming suicidal not to.*

I don't think he could be more clear.

~

Is Obama the biggest jerk ever to be president?
September 21, 2016

If he isn't the dumbest, least informed, least capable president in history, he must come close. Reading almost anything he says or does is a trial on the nerves. How do others take it? A sample from today:

> *Obama at U.N.: A walled-off nation 'imprisons itself'*
> *At United Nations, Globalist Obama Condemns 'Crude Populism' Sweeping the Planet*
> *Obama won't acknowledge terrorism — and it's great news for Trump*
> *Days after attacks, Obama pitches more refugees*
> *Obama led the world downward into chaos*

---

[346] *The National Review*, 20 September 2016.

88 senators press Obama to uphold US policy to veto one-sided UN resolutions

White House: ISIS Doesn't Represent Islam In Fight Against West

Armed forces chiefs confirm sense of Obama distrust

Obama Admin 'Laundered' U.S. Cash to Iran Via N.Y. Fed, Euro Banks

It's hard to work out whether his ignorance is more significant than his lack of intelligence, or whether it is the other way round. But whichever it is, he cannot be gone soon enough. In '08 I thought anyone but Hillary, so this was the answer and I learned my lesson. Although not much better, she would have been better. That he is still the apple in the eye of the media is all you need to know about the American media, which is as ignorant and unintelligent as Obama.

I HAVE RECEIVED THE FOLLOWING COMMENT ON THIS POST: Source unknown, but entirely apt:

> *"The danger to America is not Barack Obama, but a citizenry capable of entrusting a man like him with the presidency. It will be far easier to limit and undo the follies of an Obama presidency than to restore the necessary common sense and good judgment to a depraved electorate willing to have such a man for their president. The problem is much deeper and far more serious than Mr. Obama, who is a mere symptom of what ails America. Blaming the prince of the fools should not blind anyone to the vast confederacy of fools that made him their prince. The republic can survive a Barack Obama, who is, after all, merely a fool. It is less likely to survive a multitude of fools, such as those who made him their president."*

~

One of the many many many things she doesn't understand

September 22, 2016

I often ask the same question, but with the names reversed: 'Clinton asks why she isn't beating Trump by 50 points'.[347] "Fierce", by the way, is apparently the new word for "stupid".

> *Hillary Clinton gave voice Wednesday to a question on the minds of many*

---

[347] *The Washington Post*, 21 September 2016.

of her fiercest advocates in her race against the controversy-prone Donald Trump: Why isn't she way, way ahead?

The Democratic nominee raised the issue here during an address via video conference to a gathering in Las Vegas of the Laborers' International Union of North America.

The former secretary of state ticked off her pro-union positions, including investing in infrastructure, raising the minimum wage and supporting collective bargaining.

"Having said all this, 'Why aren't I 50 points ahead?' you might ask?" Clinton said. "Well, the choice for working families has never been clearer. I need your help to get Donald Trump's record out to everybody. Nobody should be fooled."

"Nobody should be fooled"! That's my wish as well, but with the media the way it is, not much hope of that.

~

The nightmare scenario
September 22, 2016

Two articles of the highest importance on the same theme.

The first is Yellen helps Clinton dodge a bullet[348] which comes with the sub-head: "Federal Reserve policymakers keep their key interest rate steady, putting the central bank on the sidelines until after Election Day." The first sentence of the article is merely about politics. The economics is about what lies in wait. But first that opening sentence:

Scratch one big economic worry off the list for Hillary Clinton.

The worry being scratched off is that interest rates will be raised before the election. Trump knows what a problem this would be for the Democrats better than anyone. Yellen knows exactly what Trump knows, but lies like the rest of her leftist tribe:

Fed Chair Janet Yellen also strongly rejected claims lobbed at her by GOP

---
[348] politico.com, 21 September 2016.

> *presidential nominee Donald Trump that she is keeping rates artificially low to boost stock prices and aid Democrats.*
>
> *"I can say emphatically that partisan politics plays no role in our decisions about the appropriate stance of monetary policy," Yellen said at a news conference after the Fed announced its decision. "We do not discuss politics at our meetings and we do not take politics into account in our decisions..."*
>
> *"The Federal Reserve is not politically compromised," she said. "I can't recall any meeting that I have ever attended where politics has been a matter of discussion. I think the public if they had been watching our meeting on TV today would have felt that we had a rich, deep, serious, intellectual debate about the risks and the forecasts for the economy."*

Since she cannot say otherwise, that was the pre-fab answer. But they of course do think politically 100% of the time, and know full well what will happen when rates start to rise, or even if they hinted that they would rise. It will happen immediately if it's Trump, more slowly if it's Hillary, but up they will go. As noted at the end of the article:

> *The decision [to leave rates where they are] should be a bit of a boost for Clinton, more because it avoids a nightmare scenario than does much to strengthen the economy.*

"Nightmare scenario"? What could they possibly mean?

There is then this second article dealing with the same issues: 'Yellen rejects Trump charges that Fed plays politics'.[349] Shorter and again outlines Trump's complaints in the company of Yellen's untruths. But it ends with this:

> *By statute, the Fed is an independent body intended to be shielded from political pressure and whose operations are not funded by the US Congress.*
>
> *But Fed governors are nominated by the White House and approved by the Senate.*

You can see the cynicism in the article but there is even more in the comments to the story. I will just list one, which is like most of the others, and which follows more or less my own sentiments about all of it:

> *Her denial proves the point. Yellen is a marxist who does Obama's bidding.*

---

[349] yahoo.com/news, 22 September 2016.

If Trump wins in November this fool will raise interest rates in December. Bet the farm on it.

For all that, the sad fact is that the only way our economies can ever get on track is for rates to rise. It will be a rough ride, but without the redirection of savings in productive directions, there is no chance of a recovery either short term or long.

~

Where have all the Flowers gone?
September 25, 2016

Gone to the first debate,[350] that's where. Jennifer Flowers, that is. American politics is in a class of its own.

~

Trump meets with Netanyahu
September 26, 2016

---
[350] *The Washington Post*, 24 September 2016.

This communique is found at Powerline under the heading, 'Bibi calls on Trump and Clinton'.[351]

> Donald J. Trump met privately today with Prime Minister Netanyahu for over an hour at Mr. Trump's residence in Trump Tower. The two have known each other for many years and had the opportunity to discuss many topics important to both countries.
>
> Mr. Trump and the Prime Minister discussed the special relationship between America and Israel and the unbreakable bond between the two countries. The topics of military assistance, security and regional stability were addressed. Mr. Trump agreed that the military assistance provided to Israel and missile defense cooperation with Israel are an excellent investment for America. Mr. Trump said that under a Trump administration, there will be extraordinary strategic, technological, military and intelligence cooperation between the two countries. Mr. Trump recognized Israel as a vital partner of the United States in the global war against radical Islamic terrorism.
>
> They discussed at length the nuclear deal with Iran, the battle against ISIS and many other regional security concerns.
>
> Mr. Trump and Prime Minister Netanyahu discussed at length Israel's successful experience with a security fence that helped secure its borders. They discussed Israel's burgeoning hi-tech and biotech economy and how it has made stunning advances improving and saving lives around the world. In particular, Mr. Trump noted Israel's emergence as a world leader in cyber defense and security and its cooperation with the United States in this regard.
>
> Mr. Trump recognized that Israel and its citizens have suffered far too long on the front lines of Islamic terrorism. He agreed with Prime Minister Netanyahu that the Israeli people want a just and lasting peace with their neighbors, but that peace will only come when the Palestinians renounce hatred and violence and accept Israel as a Jewish State.
>
> Finally, Mr. Trump acknowledged that Jerusalem has been the eternal capital of the Jewish People for over 3000 years, and that the United States, under a Trump administration, will finally accept the long-standing Congressional mandate to recognize Jerusalem as the undivided capital of the State of Israel.
>
> The meeting concluded with both leaders promising the highest level of

---

[351] powerlineblog.com, 26 September 2016.

mutual support and cooperation should Mr. Trump have the honor and privilege of being elected President of the United States.

For Clinton's summary of the discussion you can read it online.[352]

~

The first debate
September 27, 2016

I cannot deny that I was disappointed at the end of the debate. Trump ought to have put her away with so many issues opened up for which there are answers aplenty. He went after her in the first half and drove her to the edge of the field but then let her back.

So let me think about this a bit more. First, the totally one-sided "moderating" really is irritating. The issues that will matter looking forward for the next four years do not include where Obama was really born or what Donald Trump shows on his tax form. These are not policy matters and do not much matter. What counts are the things that were not touched, such as Benghazi, her public email server which has allowed every foreign intelligence agency to read every email she sent, the open border that is not being sealed off and would not be by Clinton, her inveterate lying on everything, large and small. These were not brought into the mix by the moderator.

Second, I think Trump is conscious of the Romney experience. Romney won the first debate and then didn't win the election. If there is anything that Trump has shown, it is that he gets his timing right. I thought he let her off the hook in a number of places which he ought to have driven a Panzer division through, but didn't. I don't know if it was deliberate, but on purpose or not, he will be back for the second and third events. What did Hillary learn from this? Nothing that I think can help her, while Trump learned a lot.

Third, the Trump I saw was not the Trump I believe he can be. The Trump others saw for the first time was, however, someone who does not scare the horses and had as presidential a look about him as one could wish.

---

[352] www.scoopnest.com/user/ZekeJMiller

That Trump has won every one of the online polls asking who won the debate says something about the common expectation which he more than seems to have filled.

Fourth, Hillary's desire to raise taxes on "the rich" and increase the minimum wage are massive disasters that would ruin the working lives of many, especially those at the bottom. Trump, on the other hand, wants to lower taxes and remove regulations on business. Hillary panders to the ignorant while Trump has a more sophisticated view of how a capitalist system works. It is not a zero-sum game in the way it is discussed by Clinton. Adding to that, his aim to re-negotiate the various trade deals, and have others contribute to the cost of their defence by the United States. These are the kinds of changes that really can make the American economy succeed. Nothing that Hillary says or has ever done, makes you think she has much of an idea how things work, other than via various forms of patronage and corruption.

In all, I wish it had been more of a win for Trump. But on this very day the electoral college for the first time rolled in his favour. He has till the start of November to build on what he has achieved, and there is no reason to think he cannot do what needs to be done. And there is always the possibility that the people who are voting understand that they are not selecting a debating team but who will lead their nation for the next four years during one of the most perilous times in its history.

~

My take on the debate
September 28, 2016

You can see my own views of the debate at *Quadrant Online*[353] [a reprint of the previous post above] which in many ways is similar to Trump's.[354]

> *Donald Trump said on "Fox & Friends" this morning that last night's presidential debate went well, despite the fact that he was asked much tougher questions than Hillary Clinton . . . .*

---

[353] *Quadrant Online*, 28 September 2016.
[354] insider.foxnews.com, 27 September 2016.

> Trump pointed out that moderator Lester Holt pressed him on his tax returns, the President Obama birther scandal and his stance on the Iraq War.
>
> He said that Clinton, on the other hand, was not asked about her email scandal, the Clinton Foundation or the Benghazi terror attack.
>
> Trump said that even though it was obvious that Holt leaned "more than a little" to the left, he was satisfied with the message he got out to the American people, particularly his policies on illegal immigration, law and order, and trade.
>
> "Those are basically the three things we're going to have to get out. And I got them out early and strong," Trump said. "And a lot of people think the poll numbers are going to go up because of that."

And his poll numbers are going up with virtually every poll that is run untouched by human hands – that is, every poll not run through the media and their polling organisations – show Trump having won last night.[355] In the end, as I point out at *Quadrant*, American is not electing a debating team, it is electing the person who must lead them through the next four years which may be among the most perilous in American history. Who knows what is happening, but I will end with this from a comments thread at Lucianne:

> There is a truly unscientific poll going on wherever 7-11 is found…they have a sale on hot beverages in their new "thermal" extra large cups with either "Republican", "Democrat" or a "rant" design. On the east end of Long Island (of all places) there is a shortage of Republican cups and it's attributable to brisk sales, not someone hiding the pubbie cups. The discount to buy these cups is significant (around 33 cents with tax) but the demonrat cups aren't selling according to a friend who's an owner.
>
> Granted it's unscientific but in the past when they've done this you don't see the pubbie cups selling out.
>
> This election has a feel like the one in '72 where no one "voted" for Nixon yet he won 49 States over McG.

The media are all-in for Hillary and it is up hill for Trump in every way, but we shall see in November, and before that we will have two more debates.

---

[355] *Daily Mail Australia*, 27 September 2016.

What would a journalist know about anything?
September 29, 2016

This from today's Cut & Paste:[356]

> But at The Sydney Morning Herald, veteran Canberra hand Tony Wright suggested The Donald had enjoyed some familiarity with lines of Peruvian marching powder:
>
> Donald Trump made a fool of himself so many times it wasn't worth counting. He told half-truths and plucked lies out of the air ("I opposed the invasion of Iraq"). He blurted streams of incomprehensible free association. He raved, interrupted and sniffled like a coke addict.

As it happens, I didn't then and don't now oppose the war in Iraq. It has turned out disastrous, but who could have expected an incompetent foreign policy dunce like Obama would become the American President (who, for the record, is equally incompetent on domestic policy).

Trump did oppose the War in Iraq, but not the War in Afghanistan, which means he took the same position as Obama but I would not expect any "journalist" to know this since few of them seem to want to know facts that are contrary to what they prefer to believe. My guess, though, is that if Trump had been president since 2008 he would not have done everything he could to undermine the stability in the Middle East that had finally been created. ISIS belongs to Obama and Hillary. Hillary is the last person in the world anyone should ask to fix up the mess she is largely responsible for.

~

Cheating at the debate
October 1, 2016

There are issues large and small that do make you wonder. This is among the small, but is neither irrelevant nor insignificant: 'Presidential Debate Commission Admits Trump's Mic Was Messed Up'.[357] Trump said it on

---

[356] *The Australian*, 29 September 2016.
[357] dailycaller.com, 30 September 2016.

the day but now it is confirmed.

But then there is the larger ones the most extraordinary one being the removal of Hillary's notes from her podium by someone who then immediately crosses paths with the moderator after exchanging knowing looks. At Google, it is practically gone, although there were a few versions of this available a few days ago in a more extended form. I only found the one which followed on from a much more brief version. It shows a man with grey hair and glasses taking something from Hillary's podium and then looking over at the moderator before they briefly cross paths in the middle of the stage, but then goes on with much much more.

Why would you doubt for a second that if they could cheat they would cheat? And why would you doubt that the media would be in on it to the hilt?

~

Hillary's remake of The Sting
October 3, 2016

Thought of this comparison last night with the video showing her tapping her nose during the debate which may (or may not have been) a signal to the moderator. It is surprising that more has not been made of the possibility that Hillary was in cahoots with the moderator[358] although I can see that this is not the time for a distraction of this kind. The lessons of the first debate have no doubt been absorbed. Remembering *The Sting* may require you to be of a certain age. A fantastic film if you haven't seen it with a surprising degree of relevance in the present election.

---

[358] lawofmarkets.com, 1 October 2016.

The VP's debate
October 6, 2016

The most interesting part about the Vice Presidential debate was that there was not a dime's worth of difference between the arguments put by Mike Pence and the views of Donald Trump. The difference is entirely in presentation along with the various self-imposed constraints that Pence has learned through many years of experience. He knows how to phrase what he says and knows how to craft the arguments just so. But so far as what they amount to, they are exactly the same as Trump's.

Kaine on the other hand was a much worse version of Hillary. She was more polished and understood her position and how to present it to the back teeth. I found Kaine irritating and shallow to a startling degree. I have always recognised that anecdote is the replacement for analysis when you are dealing with people unused to complex ideas. But if underneath anything he said there actually was a complex idea of any sort, I missed it.

Pence described how a Trump administration would deal with national defence, illegal immigration, economic revival and racial tensions. He defended removing illegals along with stop and frisk policing. What possibly surprised me most about Kaine was the extent to which he repeated Trump's policy proposals over and again, I imagine under the assumption that just to hear what Trump wishes to do is automatically to be in opposition. That's what comes from locking oneself onto the media sounding board where no other ideas seem to come through. My suspicion, however, is that for those who like what Trump has to offer, it is exactly what he proposes that is what they like. Kaine did no more than reinforce in the minds of Trump's supporters why they are voting as they are.

Who knows if any of the more difficult parts can be done? But there is little doubt that most Americans want a stronger military, defeat of ISIS, border security, a revival of the economy, a tax system that promotes economic growth and a more cohesive community.

And then there were the two personalities on display. Kaine had no presence or substance. Pence seemed a deeper thinker who has had his ideas forged in the fires of debate among those who disagree with many of the things he says. As a conservative, even in a party of the right, he would be a lonely presence. It was a positive pleasure to listen to him.

Trump-Pence are not just running mates, but might hopefully even be thought of as a succession plan. I think this election remains a toss-up. But if Trump should manage to win in November, and Pence remains a typical example of the kinds of personnel that Trump chooses for the various slots in his administration, there is reason – perhaps only dimly – but there is reason to hope for improvement, and not just a minor relief but even long term.

Only Trump makes this at all possible. Pence, however, provides evidence how it might even be done.

~

VP debate post mortem at Quadrant Online
October 6, 2016

I have a post at *Quadrant Online* dealing with yesterday's VP debate under the fantastic heading (not mine): Razing Kaine[359] [a reprint of the above post]. It was obviously Kaine's intent to win the interruption derby which he clearly did, but not in any way that prevented Pence from stating just what he had in mind. How much it matters I do not know, but Pence came across as thoughtful and considered while Kaine was a more than usually superficial emissary from the left. My final para:

> *Trump-Pence might amount to more than running-mates — they might be a succession plan. I think this election remains a toss-up. But if Trump should win next month and Pence is typical of the personnel he chooses to fill the slots in his administration, there is reason to hope. Only Trump can make this at all possible. Pence provides the evidence of how it might even be done.*

No doubt I am getting ahead of myself since the first obstacle is for Trump to be elected. The notion that anyone can remain uninfluenced by the continuous media storm created around Trump is a self-delusion. But if

---

[359] *Quadrant Online*, 6 October 2016.

Trump has remained competitive in this environment in spite of it all, you have to know there are a lot of people in the United States who really are enraged by what is going on around them but which they have no ability to prevent.

~

Conservative fools
October 6, 2016

Far too many on the supposedly conservative right are utter fools. Working class Americans see the problem, but these people are too high minded to understand even the basics. They are Democrats in every respect: 'Dozens of former GOP lawmakers announce opposition to Trump'.[360] Think of this in relation to their never having said anything like it about Obama:

> *"Given the enormous power of the office, every candidate for president must be judged rigorously in assessing whether he or she has the competence, intelligence, knowledge, understanding, empathy, judgment, and temperament necessary to keep America on a safe and steady course," the letter continues. "Donald Trump fails on each of those measures, and he has proven himself manifestly unqualified to be president."*

The list of those who have signed on are a bunch of nobodies, but they are trying their best to wreck what little chance there is to save an America that will remain worth saving. And then there is this from Paul Mirengoff at Powerline reflecting on the VP debate.[361]

> *We also saw the real Mike Pence. In my view, he is the only one of the four candidates who, ideology aside, wouldn't be an embarrassment in high office.*

In one sentence two statements that basically say that Hillary will be all right since the Republicans aren't providing the right kind of a choice. Trump would be "an embarrassment" if elected. But even Pence is OK only so far as embarrassment goes, but to accept Pence you also have to shift that ideology aside. Once ideology comes into it, Pence is no good either.

---

[360] thehill.com, 6 October 2016
[361] ibid.

He goes off on an even more stupid tangent in his next post: 'ESCAPISM ANYONE? A LOOK AT 2020'.[362] Here he lightly considers what to do in 2020 when and if Hillary wins. By then, he says:

> To a considerable extent, GOP voters may be willing to overlook both ideological and genuineness concerns in the name of nominating someone who can defeat Hillary Clinton or whichever leftist the Democrats nominate.

But that is for 2020. Right now he's fine with bagging the only person in the entire universe who can prevent Hillary Clinton from becoming President since Trump is the Republican nominee and we have three weeks to go.

There are many many like that, but these are the examples I have come across just now. There are many many of these everywhere you turn and the may end up carrying a very heavy responsibility on the morning of November 9th.

A COUPLE OF ADD-ONS: To continue with the same theme: Donald Trump Makes History With Zero Major Newspaper Endorsements.[363]

> So far Trump has gotten no general election endorsements, a stunning development considering even Libertarian presidential candidate Gary Johnson, known best for his head-scratching "Aleppo moment," has scored a few.

There is more to it than pure choice since the costs of not supporting Trump for many of these papers are far less than going out on a limb. But if you see the election in the way some of us do, then this is nothing but a round-up of despair. And do look at this: 'Ann Coulter: This Election Will Determine the Survival of Western Civilization'.[364]

You don't think so. Vote Hillary and find out.

---

[362] powerlineblog.com, 5 October 2016.
[363] sfgate.com, 6 October 2016.
[364] realclearpolitics.com, 6 October 2016.

Staging reality
October 8, 2016

There is a video at the link which you should examine closely to better understand the world in which you live: 'Hillary Caught Using Child Actor At Pennsylvania Town Hall'.[365] The first paragraphs:

> At a Hillary Clinton town hall yesterday in Haverford, Pennsylvania, a 15 year old girl was supposedly "chosen at random" to ask a question of the former Secretary of State. But, the well-scripted performance raised some suspicion with a YouTuber named Spanglevision who decided to dig a little deeper. And, wouldn't you know it, the "random" participant was none other than child actor, Brennan Leach, whose father just happens to be Pennsylvania democratic State Senator Daylin Leach. Oh, and in case it wasn't obvious, Daylin supports Hillary for president…shocking.
>
> And this is the question she asked:
>
> "Hi Madam Secretary. I'm Brennan and I'm 15 years old. At my school, body image is a really big issue for girls my age. I see with my own eyes the damage Donald Trump does when he talks about women and how they look. As the first female president how would you undo some of that damage and help girls understand that they're so much more than just what they look like?"

This story has been picked up at Instapundint under the heading: 'HILLARY CAUGHT USING CHILD ACTRESS AT PENNSYLVANIA TOWN HALL'.[366] And as part of that post, there is this incredible footage from the movie, *Wag the Dog* that replicates as part of a film what you have just seen as an actual reality.

The problem may be that I am unable to be as cynical as I need to be about the way things really are to comprehend in full the dishonesty that seems to be found in every part of the public world that I would like to think I know something about.

But really, the question that ought to be asked is why is this even an issue in an American presidential election?

---

[365] zerohedge.com/news, 5 October 2016.
[366] pjmedia.com/instapundit, 7 October 2016.

The American election and the fate of the West
October 8, 2016

What you would have hoped the American election would be based on: determining who can best handle these kinds of issues. All are from Drudge right now:

> *ISIS to send 'serial killers' to the West in bloody new terror tactic…*
>
> *Debt Under Obama Up $9,000,000,000,000…*
>
> *SEPTEMBER JOBS: +156,000…*
> *Unemployment rate climbs to 5%…*
> *94,184,000 NOT In Labor Force…*
>
> *Russia Nuke Surge…*
> *Russian Military considers return to Cuba, Vietnam…*
>
> *Experts said Arctic sea ice would melt entirely by Sept '16…*
> *They were wrong…*
>
> *G20: Populist political foes of globalization pose serious risk…*
>
> *Hacked emails show excerpts of paid Hillary speeches…*
> *She Dreams Of 'Open Trade and Open Borders'…*
> *2,000 Messages From Podesta Exposed…*
> *Campaign Coordinating With Soros Organization…*
>
> *Study: Non-Citizens Voting In Virginia By The Thousands…*

What the election will actually be based on. All these are also from Drudge right now:

> *HOT MIC: TRUMP ON THE PROWL*
> *HILLARY SHOCKED BY SEX TALK!*
> *OCTOBER SPOOK: GHOSTS OF BILL'S PAST…*
> *MORE CLINTON 'RAPIST' SIGNS, PROTESTS…*
> *RACE TURNS CATTY!*
> *Gennifer Flowers: Bill Clinton Told Me 'Hillary Had Eaten More Pussy Than He Had'…*

What's that old proverb: if you want to make God laugh, tell Him your plans.

TRUMP'S APOLOGY: This is from Scott Johnson at Powerline.[367]

I've never said I'm a perfect person, nor pretended to be someone that I'm not. I've said and done things I regret, and the words released today on this more than a decade-old video are one of them. Anyone who knows me knows these words don't reflect who I am. I said it, I was wrong and I apologize.

I have traveled the country talking about change for America, but my travels have also changed me. I've spent time with grieving mothers who've lost their children, laid-off workers whose jobs have gone to other countries, and people from all walks of life who just want a better future. I have gotten to know the great people of our country and I've been humbled by the faith they've placed in me. I pledge to be a better man tomorrow, and will never, ever let you down.

Let's be honest, we're living in the real world. This is nothing more than a distraction from the important issues we're facing today.

We are losing our jobs, we are less safe than we were eight years ago and Washington is totally broken. Hillary Clinton and her kind have run our country into the ground. I've said some foolish things, but there's a big difference between the words and actions of other people. Bill Clinton has actually abused women, and Hillary has bullied, attacked, shamed and intimidated his victims. We will discuss this more in the coming days. See you at the debate on Sunday.

~

Sunshine conservatives
October 9, 2016

"These are the times that try men's souls: The summer soldier and the sunshine patriot will, in this crisis, shrink from the service of their country; but he that stands it now, deserves the love and thanks of man and woman."

This has been a fearfully clarifying election. There are people who declare themselves on the right side of politics, who are in truth sham defenders of freedom and our way of life, and who will be forever shunned by those of us who stood for saving the American Republic and the Western world at this moment of great peril.

---

[367] powerlineblog.com, 8 October 2016.

The American election will determine the fate of the West. An America with open borders, unprepared, unwilling and unable to defend our freedoms from predators of every kind, from Islamic terrorists, from economic vandals, from those who masquerade their profound ignorance as concern for the environment, it is from these we must defend ourselves against or our way of life will be lost. It is now we must take our stand or see it go forever. The American Republic as it has been since 1776 will disappear. We will live to see our own fall of Rome.

Sunshine conservatives: those who pretend to represent freedom, individual rights and personal responsibility, but who refuse to stand with the only person who could make a difference. They are people whom history will recognise as the enemies of freedom, who refused to stand for the right when the moment arrived. It is Donald Trump alone, the most improbable candidate in American political history, who provides even this sliver of hope. He is elected or Hillary is. There is no other possible outcome.

The mounting hostility among those supposedly on his own side is a disgrace. The array of enemies who have been uncovered from within what is nominally his own side of politics has demonstrated better than anything else might have, that the Republican Party as it has become is a rotting curse on everything it is supposed to represent.

Those who stand with Hillary in this dark hour will have revealed they cannot be trusted and their counsel is without value. They are enemies of freedom. If you support Hillary Clinton in this election, nothing you write and say will from this time forward be worth the slightest attention. Your judgements will have been revealed as eternally worthless.

Donald Trump has not yet lost this election. If anything, this latest attempt to distract voters from the genuine issues which confront us may finally have focused the election on what actually matters. No one defends Trump's words, or his attitude to women, least of all Donald Trump. This was his own assessment.

> *Let's be honest, we're living in the real world. This is nothing more than a distraction from the important issues we're facing today.*
>
> *We are losing our jobs, we are less safe than we were eight years ago and Washington is totally broken. Hillary Clinton and her kind have run our country into the ground. I've said some foolish things, but there's a big*

difference between the words and actions of other people. Bill Clinton has actually abused women, and Hillary has bullied, attacked, shamed and intimidated his victims. We will discuss this more in the coming days.

The American election is not about who has lived the most blameless life. It is about who can best protect our collective interests. Trump has been from the very beginning the only person running in this election who has understood the nature of the times in which we live and the actions that must be taken. You are either a sunshine conservative, or are instead prepared to fight this to the very end which means supporting Donald Trump for president.

~

My take on the second debate
October 10, 2016

We know who doesn't want Trump to win. Hillary for one, along with the Democrats in general, the 47% who have probably grown to around 55% by now, to which, strangely, you can add many if not most of the wealthiest financial institutions across the world. There is then the media, and not just the journalists and reporters but the owners who are all-in for Hillary. And there's a large proportion of the Republican Party which must include the #NeverTrumps who are the supposedly right-side conservative writers, bloggers and columnists, but who are part of the political establishment with no obvious allegiance to small government and the preservation of the American Republic. And, of course, there are the dead citizens and non-dead non-citizens who will also be lining up to vote her in, along with those who vote early and often. Not to mention those who will vote for her because she is a woman irrespective of any other considerations whatsoever.

Formidable. Almost impossible odds. And the fact is that even after a flawless presentation against his Obama-clone opponent, in which he took Hillary apart in every phase of the debate in spite of every effort by the laughably "impartial" moderators, the bad news is that Donald Trump remains no better than 50-50 to win. But that is also the good news. He has not yet lost and might yet win.

And why that is so is because he represents the last chance for the United States to save itself, and approximately 51% of the voting American public know it.

The supposed killer issue was a 2005 tape made of Trump discussing in crude terms his approach to women. And possibly in anyone else's hands, this would have been the death blow that it may even still turn out to be. But for Hillary Clinton, married to a genuine sexual predator, this is an issue that can only be used carefully since the blow-back is so enormous. Whatever Trump has done is as nothing in comparison with what Bill Clinton has done, who was protected by Hillary in quieting the many and various "bimbo eruptions" (her term). I regret to have to deal with this, but since you'd have to have been born before 1980 to have an active memory of any of it. I will deal with only one, the story of Paula Jones, and I will include it only at the end.

I find all this repulsive, and the Paula Jones story which is summarised below is the least disturbing among the stories that surfaced at the time, and it is plenty disturbing since it was only one instance of what must have been more common at the time. But what is more repulsive is listening to others go on about Trump, as if Clinton were not orders of magnitude worse. But what is actually significant is that bringing that tape to light has enraged Donald Trump so that we ended up with the single most devastating, one-sided debate in American political history, since with Bill's past in everyone's mind, Hillary could not truly exploit the tape to the full extent. Trump's was a cold anger, but it was devastating.

Donald Trump had two tasks before him. The first was to demonstrate Hillary's immense hypocrisy in even bringing the tape into the conversation. Trump said that his misdeeds were words but Bill Clinton's involved deeds. Whatever Hillary might say about Trump, applied with immensely more force to her husband.

The second task was to insist that all of the above was a distraction from the real issues a presidential election should be about. He then forced Hillary to deal with policy issues and on each of these, the substance of the argument was entirely with Trump. There was not an issue that at the end of the debate one could say Trump had not shown a better understanding of the complexities, and that the policies he intended to put in place were not superior. This, in particular, I found quite remarkable. It is Trump speaking.

> "These are radical islamic terrorists and she won't even mention the word, and nor will President Obama. He won't use the term 'radical Islamic terrorism'. Now, to solve a problem, you have to be able to state what the problem is or at least say the name. She won't say the name and President Obama won't say the name. But the name is there. It's radical Islamic terror."

And just as Trump had said, she would not use those words. But irrespective of the words one chooses, there was no denying, as Trump repeatedly pointed out, that Hillary was deeply complicit in creating the problem we now face in ISIS, and Trump made that point very well. In discussing the Middle East, and the "stupidity" of our military strategy, what may have been the most remarkable part of the debate was Trump disagreeing point blank with his running mate, Mike Pence, over the use of the American military in Syria. Pence thought America should. Trump's reply: "He and I haven't spoken and we don't agree." Not only did he show decisive leadership, it was an answer that ought to quieten at least some of those who worry about Trump leading the US into war. It was also the right answer politically, since the controversy that has occurred since has been over the disagreement with Pence, not whether Trump had the better answer.

What must, of course, be included is this, which is for the ages:

> *Hillary: You know, it's just awfully good that someone with the temperament of Donald Trump is not in charge of the law in our country.*
>
> *Trump: Because you'd be in jail.*

What he said is that he'd appoint a special prosecutor to look into the many scandals that have surrounded her time in politics, not least the email server she illegally used during her time as Secretary of State. There is much more that could be said, but at the end, what matters is that Trump is back. The obstacles are formidable, but at least it is possible. And there is still the third debate to come.

A BRIEF OUTLINE OF THE PAULA JONES SAGA

Let me quote from Paula Jones's written deposition[368] and then the events that led to Bill Clinton resigning his licence to practise law. First the Paula Jones deposition:

13. We talked for a few minutes. Mr. Clinton asked me about my job. He told me that Dave Harrington (who at that time was in charge of the AIDC) was his "good friend."

14. Mr. Clinton then unexpectedly reached over to me, took my hand, and pulled me toward him, so that our bodies were close to each other. I removed my hand from his and retreated several feet.

15. Mr. Clinton approached me again, saying "I love the way your hair flows down your back" and "I love your curves." While saying these things, Mr. Clinton put his hand on my leg and started sliding his hand toward my pelvic area. I did not consent to him doing this. He also bent down to kiss me on the neck, but I would not let him do so.

16. I exclaimed, "What are you doing?" and escaped from Mr. Clinton's reach by walking away from him. I was extremely upset and confused and I did not know what to do. I tried to distract Mr. Clinton by asking him about his wife and her activities, and I sat down at the end of the sofa nearest the door. Mr. Clinton then walked over to the sofa, lowered his trousers and underwear, exposed his penis (which was erect) and told me to "kiss it."

17. I was horrified by this. I jumped up from the couch and told Mr. Clinton that I had to go, saying something to the effect that I had to get back to the registration desk. Mr. Clinton, while fondling his penis, said: "Well, I don't want to make you do anything you don't want to do." Mr. Clinton then stood up, pulled up his pants and said: "If you get in trouble for leaving work, have Dave call me immediately and I'll take care of it." As I left the room, Mr. Clinton detained me momentarily, looked sternly at me and said: "You are smart. Let's keep this between ourselves."

Was he guilty? He has, of course, never owned up to a thing, but the eventual result was that Bill Clinton was disbarred from practising law in the State of Arkansas. The details are at Wikipedia: Clinton v. Jones. The outcome:

---

[368] *The Washington Post*, 13 March 1998.

The Arkansas Supreme Court suspended Clinton's Arkansas law license in April 2000. On January 19, 2001, Clinton agreed to a five-year suspension and a $25,000 fine in order to avoid disbarment and to end the investigation of Independent Counsel Robert Ray (Starr's successor). On October 1, 2001, Clinton's U.S. Supreme Court law license was suspended, with 40 days to contest his disbarment. On November 9, 2001, the last day for Clinton to contest the disbarment, he opted to resign from the Supreme Court Bar, surrendering his license, rather than facing penalties related to disbarment.

~

Summer soldiers and fair weather friends
October 11, 2016

I am now not one, but two posts behind at *Quadrant Online*. This is from today[369] which begins:

> We know who doesn't want Trump to win. Hillary for one, along with the Democrats in general, the 47% who have probably grown to around 55% by now, to which, strangely, you can add many if not most of the wealthiest financial institutions across the world. There is then the media, and not just the journalists and reporters but the owners who are all-in for Hillary. And there's a large proportion of the Republican Party which must include the #NeverTrumps who are the supposedly right-side conservative writers, bloggers and columnists, but who are part of the political establishment with no obvious allegiance to small government and the preservation of the American Republic. And, of course, there are the dead citizens and non-dead non-citizens who will also be lining up to vote her in, along with those who vote early and often. Not to mention those who will vote for her because she is a woman irrespective of any other considerations whatsoever.

And then there was my post yesterday which discusses what I call "sunshine conservatives".[370] It is a take on Tom Paine's opening lines in his 1776 *Common Sense* which was one of the sparks for the American Revolution:

---

[369] *Quadrant Online*, 11 October 2016.
[370] *Quadrant Online*, 10 October 2016.

"THESE are the times that try men's souls. The summer soldier and the sunshine patriot will, in this crisis, shrink from the service of their country; but he that stands by it now, deserves the love and thanks of man and woman.

Sunshine conservatives are those windbags who are forever wringing their hands about the problems we face but will nevertheless support Hillary in this crisis because Donald Trump lacks perfection. To them nothing is owed but contempt.

~

Welcome home, Mark, all is forgiven
October 12, 2016

This is just to let you know Mark Steyn is back. His new post is dated October 9 and titled, 'As I Was Saying….'[371] And what is it he's saying? This is from his post.

> *P*ssygate? Sorry, I decline to play by Washington Post rules. Every GOP nominee is a sexist pig: last time round, it was poor blameless Mitt with his "binders full of women" and his long track record of giving cancer to laid-off workers' wives. The fact that this particular nominee for once actually is a vainglorious sexist is not even interesting in a media stopped-clock kind of way – because Trump has more or less been advertising the fact on the Howard Stern show for a quarter-century. So the story is chiefly of note as a near parodic example of the ludicrously lop-sided standards applied to Democrats and Republicans: I mean, the alternative to a Trump victory is the restoration to the White House of a credibly accused rapist and serial abuser, accompanied by the woman who has gleefully trashed his victims for 40 years. This race would be very different if Juanita Broaddrick and "You might want to put some ice on that" had received a thousandth of the media coverage given to Alicia Machado and "Miss Piggy".*

And to get down to brass tacks, Mark has left off where he was when he went:

> *Meanwhile, there's a gazillion-and-one emails piled up demanding to know*

---

[371] steynonline.com, 9 October 2016.

what I make of Trump vs Hillary in the final stretch. My view of Hillary hasn't changed in decades (she's the stinkingly corrupt enabler of a depraved sexual monster) and my view of Trump hasn't changed since I wrote about him a couple of weeks after he entered the race.

You can read what he said then, but even if he says his view hasn't changed, if you ask me, what he believed then he believes now to the power of ten.

~

Please share immediately
October 12, 2016

Normal political ad, right? Well then, read this: 'YouTube Hides and SLAPS WARNING on New Trump Ad About Hillary's Health'.[372] Then go to the video at Youtube itself (www.youtube.com/watch?v=WTylz2WToXw) and there you really will see just those words when the video has finished:

> "This video is unlisted. Be considerate and think twice before sharing."

They don't care what you think because they feel they have the 51% locked up. And if she wins, it will only get worse.

MURDOCH PRESS ADDITION: Another article, this time Janet Albrechtsen showing the same judgement she used in supporting Turnbull for PM: 'Hillary Clinton versus Donald Trump II was a debased freak show'.[373] The top comments do, however, remain a source of solace since common sense still prevails somewhere. Here is the first one. You can go to the link to read the others:

> You are absolutely correct Janet. The disenchantment with 'the establishment' or sneering political class will still be there, if not swell to anger. You can feel it now. Here in Australia too.
>
> But all this talk of seeking to understand us 'deplorables' (I'm a professional female and post grad qualified) smacks of patronizing condescension. Are we to be 'fixed' through more of the same? More spin, more dishonesty,

---

[372] thegatewaypundit.com, 11 October 2016.
[373] *The Australian*, 12 October 2016.

what the left like to call communications and the rest of us recognise as PC propaganda. Of course 'they' know what's best for 'us'.

You know, I put myself in that "bucket" not because I necessarily support Trump but can appreciate his disruptive role. In the bigger context we have something of a social rebellion underway. This wave of disenchantment hasn't peaked yet.

The media is part of the problem. They have played an active role in the US election, more so than Putin, I would argue — if indeed he even is behind the hacking but wasn't it good to know the truth about Clinton thanks to her own emails?

The utter hypocrisy of the predominantly left media has been something to witness. Trump is fair game but not the equally repugnant Clinton. Such one sidedness can only propel the momentum of this social uprising.

You're right however in picking that the self satisfied smugness of those who mistakenly think they're superior beings will endure, for now.

I was thinking along the lines of sanctimonious swill as I read Janet, but "self satisfied smugness" will do just as well.

~

Read this now while there is still time
October 13, 2016

This is the incredible Introduction to a book by Paul Hellyer written in 1999. Hellyer had been a Liberal Party cabinet minister from the days before I left Canada when the Liberal Party was the party of business. The title is Stop Think, *and given its message could have been written this morning on behalf of Donald Trump. It is the most accurate and prescient writing I have ever come across on anything. It may only just explain what now cannot be stopped, but there is still the possibility that Trump will win. This will help you understand how essential it is that he does. And to repeat, this was written in 1999.*

We seem to be hell bent toward a world without borders. Someone has decided to eradicate the nation state as an effective political entity and to rob it of much of its power by moving back to the corporatism of the medieval society; this is not forward-looking but a wish to move back to the pre-democratic era. Decisions that have been the prerogative of national governments are being transferred to outsiders including the World Trade Organization, the International Monetary Fund, the World Bank and transnational corporations.

Apart from the dubious merit of such a massive transfer of power is the undeniable fact that it is being done without the advice or consent of the people whose lives are being affected. They, whoever they may be, are re-engineering the world without asking for our opinions and without giving us the opportunity to express them in any tangible way through the ballot box.

To add insult to injury, globalization is being pushed down our throats without the courtesy of any vision of what the world will look like when the revolutions has run its course. Who will be in charge? To whom will they be accountable? How will changes be effected? What recourse will there be for the people who believe they have been seriously disadvantaged in the process?

A skeptic might conclude that there are no satisfactory answers to these questions because globalization is, in reality, a smoke-screen for the biggest power grab in history. The wealthiest, most powerful, people in the world have become impatient with democracy which sets standards of conduct and taxes wealth to provide services for the common good. To paraphrase, their battle hymn is Arthur Christopher Benson's immortal line, "God who made us mighty, make us mightier yet."

This can be achieved by shackling the nation states; by taking away their right to determine the conditions upon which direct foreign investment is welcome; by insisting that they must admit goods produced under the most despicable of circumstances; by requiring that their land and assets be "for sale" to foreigners; and that their central banks be immune to political control.

The aim of the game is a world where nation states are powerless to protect their citizens from external shocks and developments; where governments are mere pawns in the hands of international banks, supranational corporations and world bureaucracies accountable to no one. To an extent considered inconceivable to many, the globalized world would be a world dominated by power and greed.

No one would deny that there are benefits to international action. Treaties to ban the use of land mines and a World Court to try persons accused of crimes against humanity may be steps in the right direction. Similarly there can be benefits to liberalized and freer trade, but only if it does not undermine the viability of national economies and if the rules include acceptable safeguards and standards in areas such as labor and environmental protection.

Those standards do not yet exist, and the transnational corporations sponsoring globalization are determined that they never will exist, except on a purely voluntary and consequently ineffective basis. No mandatory restrictions on their freedom of action are on the negotiating table.

If liberalized trade may ultimately bring about some positive results the same cannot be said about globalized financial services and unrestricted capital flows. They are a recipe for international instability and chaos and there is no existing or potential financial watchdog that can prevent it. The principal beneficiaries of such a system are the parasitical currency traders and short-term money lenders who, like vampires, live by sucking the lifeblood from one target of convenience after another.

Yet this kind of system has been the object of the negotiations for a Multilateral Treaty on Investment under the OECD, the proposed Free Trade agreement for the Americas, the Article IV Amendments being pushed by the International Monetary Fund and other venues. They lead to a dead end that is difficult, almost impossible to reverse. Still, the trend must be reversed!

The claim that globalization is the road to nirvana for a desperate world is false. It is the road that will lead inevitably to another financial meltdown, the impoverishment of millions of innocent people and the death of democracy in any meaningful sense. This book is dedicated to alternatives that would lead to a world of greater justice and opportunity for all.

It is not intended to be anti-American because, in truth, it is not. Yet it is impossible to write about globalization, and the imposition of a neo-classical economic system with a track record of failure, without holding the coach accountable for a game plan resulting in injuries to most of the players.

Throwing Hillary into the briar patch
October 13, 2016

Oh, please don't throw me into the briar patch, cries Hillary, please no more of these terrible rape accusations about Bill, our former president and my loving husband. Oh please, let us not sidetrack ourselves, she pleads. Let us instead look at the real issues and not these minor matters, although the ones that apply to Donald Trump really are serious and should disqualify him from ever being president.

The latest from *The New York Times*: 'As protesters accuse her husband of rape, Clinton blasts Trump's 'scorched earth' tactics'.[374] Ouch, ouch, this is killing me, she says.

Here's the thing. Whatever else you might think, if Americans weren't disgusted enough about Bill Clinton when he was president to ensure he was removed from office, it will not prevent his wife from winning this time round. It is only to the advantage of the Democrats the dwelling on Bill as a rapist. My beliefs on that have been reinforced in steel by this latest supposed sexualised video of Obama[375] from 2008. But here is the key sentence:

> *The video, originally shot by CNN cameras, emerged Tuesday on Twitter, where it spread quickly.*

CNN is known as the Clinton News Network for good reason. This would only have found its way into the world if it works for Hillary. There are no new votes based on how depraved Bill is or how Hillary had done all she could to cover it up. It may all be true, but so what? The election will be won or lost on the issues. This diversion will see Hillary president. A return to the issues that matter is the only thing that might still make Trump president.

And in case you don't know about B'rer Rabbit and the briar patch, you can read the story here.[376]

---

[374] *The Washington Post*, 12 October 2016.
[375] news.grabien.com, 12 October 2016.
[376] americanfolklore.net/folklor

Another sunshine conservative
October 13, 2016

Andrew Bolt has a column behind the Murdoch paywall on 'Buffoon Trump is just the symptom'.[377] Here's what you can get at the link:

> THE question now isn't whether Donald Trump is just a moron or an outright menace who could blow up the world.
>
> The question is why a braggart, buffoon, liar, narcissist and sexist with almost no political principles came so close to becoming president of the world's greatest power.

Meanwhile, the top fifteen comments.

> 1) Hillary Clinton takes tens of millions of dollars in donations from the rich Sunni Arab States and wants to increase islamic immigration to the USA by around 550% even when she acknowledges in leaked emails that security cannot be guaranteed and there are large very large problems with integration... she also wants this unfettered Islamic migration for the rest of the world ... She also believes in open borders for the USA and in economic and governmental Globalization... basically a world government along the lines of the EU... Frankly I really don't care how crass Donald is.
>
> 2) The reason is because he is the ONLY person prepared to confront the mind numbing political correctness that is turning our society into a herd of dull obedient sheep.
>
> 3) Donald maybe crass but Hilary is evil.
>
> 4) I thought it was only the left that threw insults (according to Bolt). Just shows Bolt is no different from the rest. Use personal abuse when you can't argue the facts. Bolt is entitled to his view but he is just another talking head who has become a legend in his own lunch box. I have followed his stuff since he started his blog and although I have disagreed with him on quite a few issues that he got on his hobby-horse with,
>
> But this, and his many, anti-Trump rants is the end for me. I stuck with the Liberals for 50 years and look what that has done. I am out of here and to hell with the Republicans, Democrats, Liberals and Socialists.
>
> 5) I see you have taken the same bus as the anti-Trump air pirates. Trump did this, trump did that, ad nauseum. Nothing about the avalanche of

---

[377] heraldsun.com.au/blogs/andrew-bolt, 13 October 2016.

material against Clinton, enough in fact to put her in jail if she wasn't running for Presidency, unlike Trump who said some nasty words but did nothing illegal. Oh well let the establishment get their next puppet. The Americans must love the status quo, which in effect means the slippery decline into chaos and destruction. Don't get me wrong I don't like either candidate but under Trump at least the US has a chance no matter how small to slow down the decline. With Clinton there is no chance – in fact she will accelerate it. Hmmm. Perhaps that's why we should hope for Clinton to become President – to get it over and done with ASAP.

6) Andrew if you jump on the bandwagon with left in condemning writing off Trump …be careful your popularity doesn't go in the same directions as Turnbull's Libs…A huge number of people both here and in the States still are right behind him.

7) So you're happy to see hillary stack the supreme Court and have it attack free speech and gun ownership?

8) You know why Andrew, because the people are sick and tired of all this PC BS the media is running. We know when the United Nations comes out and says "don't vote for Donald" that is exactly what we will do.

9) Same reason Hansen is back, Farage in the UK, Le Pen in France, Wilders in the Netherlands, Golden Dawn in Greece, AFD in Germany, Establishment politicians stopped listening years ago but now they are actually going out of their way to provoke us with identity politics, eco twaddle, micro managing, abject failures and immoral trough gobbling parasites in every layer of govt.

10) You haven't gone all leftie on us have you Andrew? I heard your PC rubbish on 2GB last night. I get the feeling you're playing for a TV contract and neglecting your other paid gigs. I've worked with CEOs that speak just the way Trump did….10 years ago! I've heard women being just as forthright and crude about blokes. Why should Trump be barred from seeking election just because of words he uttered 10 years ago? Let the voters decide. Wasn't that what you were championing once?

11) The media destroyed Tony Abbott, now it's Trump's turn.

12) The world will be a lot safer place with Trump as President then it would be with Clinton as leader.

13) No politician is prepared to say what Donald Trump says when he explains the dirty details the politicians and the establishment renters use to keep themselves in power at the expense of the ordinary folk. And the

people are listening.

Donald Trump knows too much for his own good. I wouldn't be surprised if one morning the headlines read he has had an "accident".

The whole Ruling System stinks like a dead snake. I don't care if he said "naughty" words privately about a beautiful woman – he didn't turn around and rape her! Every red blooded man has said or thought these things.

He has given the people hope and they have become a Movement. He is a listener. As President, he will be very careful to get all facts first from the operators on the ground and advisers like Pence, Giuliano, Sessions and dozens more good people around him who have the American people at heart.

14) Even Clinton's Democrat leader Obama doesn't trust her. Obama said she will say anything and deliver nothing!

15) looks like Bolt has been bought. he is now investing his families future in the new world order, obviously been given a ticket for the bus to the shelter. Hope you have a plan B Mr Bolt because if your dream outcome doesn't eventuate you will be held to account, like all Elites (@ French History 101) if you do get your outcome it wont matter as the world war Clinton will start will finish the known world. lost respect for you, now a bona fide "Aussy Journo" who writes what they're told to.

~

Unequivocally equivocal oppositional support for Donald
October 14, 2016

That's setting them straight:[378]

It is with a heavy heart that I condemn the actions of GOP presidential nominee Donald J. Trump, and I encourage you to vote for him on November 8.

As the allegations of sexual assault pile up, my conscience will not allow me to support the man I plan to vote for. No woman should ever live in fear of someone like Donald Trump, who is going to Make America Great Again.

---

[378] dailycaller.com, 13 October 2016.

Four more years with a Democrat in the White House could mean the destruction of our great nation, and it can only be prevented by electing the man I repudiate in the strongest possible terms.

Donald Trump is a disgrace to the Republican Party and to the United States of America, and I hope you'll join me in supporting him on Election Day!

What more is there to say?

~

Another take on sunshine conservatives
October 15, 2016

This one by Publius Decius Mus titled, 'It's Clear That Conservatism, Inc. Wants Trump To Lose'.[379] To be read in full, but I found this summary quite accurate:

> *It's now abundantly clear that most of Conservatism, Inc. wants Trump to lose and is giddy at the prospect. They're dancing not just on his political grave (prematurely, and perhaps mistakenly) but on the supposed despondency of the rest of us over Trump's presumed impending loss.*
>
> *Let's be clear what this really boils down to, in a functional sense. It means: "We're thrilled that Trump is going to lose. And if that necessarily means a Hillary win, well, we're fine with that, with the certainty that the country will keep moving left. We have no problem with another four or eight years of strip-mining the heartland with 'free trade' and giveaways to high-tech and high finance. We have no substantive objection to granting de facto or de jure amnesty to 12 million or more illegal aliens. We will present no serious opposition to allowing 1-2 million young Muslim men into the country. And when Hillary goes pedal-to-the-floor on the entire Prog-left agenda—socially, culturally, and economically—that's OK too. We're happy about this because it will be just desserts for all you deplorable trogs who didn't listen to us but instead supported Trump against our orders. We're content to hand the country to a woman and an agenda we've outwardly spent our whole careers opposing just so you can eat crow."*

---

[379] amgreatness.com, 12 October 2016.

And when Hillary wins which these idiots have been pushing for, what will be the result, for them:

> *The time is coming when you will no longer be so useful, which points to my second expectation. I believe the Left, as it increasingly feels its oats, will openly discard the pretense that it need face any opposition. It's already started. This will rise to a crescendo during the 2020 election, which the Left will of course win, after which it will be open-season on remaining "conservative" dissent. Audits. Investigations. Prosecutions. Regulatory dictates. Media leaks. Denunciations from the bully pulpit. SJW witch-hunts. The whole panoply of persecution tools now at their disposal, plus some they've yet to deploy or invent.*

It's not over till it's over, and it's not over. As for sunshine conservatism, that however is over and out.

~

Come writers and critics who prophesize with your pen
October 15, 2016

People who write for a living ought to get out a bit more. This is from Andrew Bolt who clarifies what he was saying last week in his post on Buffoon Trump is just the symptom. He has now written a follow-up on Trump vs the elites.[380] Here's the point, which I agree with:

> *The elites are destroying the man, Donald Trump.*
>
> *But they will play with fire if they ignore his message and Trump, with nothing left to lose, is now shouting it out loud. Here is its essence, in his speech on Thursday:*
>
> *Our movement is about replacing a failed and corrupt — now, when I say 'corrupt,' I'm talking about totally corrupt — political establishment, with a new government controlled by you, the American people. There is nothing the political establishment will not do — no lie that they won't tell, to hold their prestige and power at your expense. And that's what's been happening.*

---

[380] heraldsun.com.au/blogs/andrew-bolt, 15 October 2016.

They will play with fire if Donald Trump is not elected president in November, full stop! He is irreplaceable. No one else can do what he might just possibly be able to. No one.

I spent 24 years as the Chief Economist for the Chamber of Commerce and I met no end of people just like him. If you want to run a business of any size, his is the personality type that is an absolute necessity if you are to succeed. Trump is in the construction business, for heaven's sake. Ever seen the unions from the construction industry? Ever tried to get something built on time and within budget? When you look at Trump, you are looking at possibly the only kind of personality type that works at that level. I admired these people endlessly but I couldn't do what they did. I used to be involved with union negotiations on the very periphery and these are not for the faint-hearted. And the one characteristic these business people had in common was the ability to lean hard strong wilfully and with no let up into people who would wreck their businesses if they could.

But what most of these people did not have was a clue how the economic system worked. That was my job, to explain to governments, the public service, the public, and sometimes even to them, what was necessary to make a market economy work. Very few of the people I dealt with had much of an idea about the economic and political system that surrounds us, the one that makes us the most prosperous people in history.

What makes Donald Trump different is that he does understand the politics and the economics. I only remember a single person I dealt with on my Economics Committee who was anywhere near his equal and he was gold. What you have in Donald Trump is someone – however "buffoonish" you might think him to be – who by force of personality will be able to achieve ends no one else before him would have been able to do, and in an international and domestic environment which has seldom been as explosive as the one we face right now. Who would you prefer to negotiate with the Russians, or the Syrians, or Iran – Donald or Hillary? Who do you think will genuinely wipe out ISIS? It's not even a contest.

Alpha males and females are a breed apart. They are rare but are the natural leaders of any society (like Margaret Thatcher). Donald Trump is on our side in every issue of the moment, and what you must hope for with all your heart is that he wins the election in November. I will not listen to such idiocies about his personal eccentricities and personality flaws when the stakes are as high as they are. The sunshine conservatives who would hesitate for a fraction of a second in making Donald Trump the American president are not on our side.

A bit of advice from our most recent Nobel Laureate in Literature which I hope will make others think about things and what's at stake:

> *"Come writers and critics*
> *Who prophesize with your pen*
> *And keep your eyes wide*
> *The chance won't come again*
> *And don't speak too soon*
> *For the wheel's still in spin*
> *And there's no tellin' who*
> *That it's namin'*
> *For the loser now*
> *Will be later to win*
> *For the times they are a-changin'.*

~

Our rendezvous with oblivion
October 17, 2016

That anyone thinks of Hillary Clinton as presidential is the genuinely most astonishing outcome of the American election. She can only be viable if the problems that beset the United States are invisible to the majority of the people who will be voting. She offers no solutions to any existing problems, she has failed to deal with every major political issue she has ever faced, and she has no policies that would in any way address any of the issues that are confronting the United States and the Western world.

Victor Davis Hanson has written another piece trying to alert others to the catastrophic future that lies right before us if Hillary is elected.[381] I am now astonished at the meme that has developed about how awful the two candidates are, as if one is as bad as the other. That is a Democrat

---

[381] hoover.org, 13 October 2016.

talking point that is aimed at those who might vote Republican. Why bother? Trump is just as bad as her, so what's the difference? Might as well vote for Hillary.

All I can say is that if you don't know what difference it will make, you are about as dumb as any of the people described by Hanson, who are our predecessors from the past. His article is titled, 'America's civilizational paralysis'. Here's the analogy – this is us:

> Given the hardship and sacrifice that would have been required to change the late Byzantine mindset, most residents of Constantinople plodded on to their rendezvous with oblivion in 1453.

It is, to mix metaphors, step by step until we are over the waterfall. He is filled with a kind of weariness about our collective attitudes that will be our doom.

> Under the Obama administration, the old postwar order led by the security guarantees of the United States abruptly ended—the vacuum filled by ascendant regional (and often nuclear) hegemons. Russia is expanding control, or at least influence, over the old Soviet republics and Eastern Europe. China carves out a new version of the old Japanese Greater East Asia Co-Prosperity Sphere at the expense of the democracies in Taiwan, Japan, South Korea, the Philippines, and Australia. Iran is on the path to be the nuclear adjudicator of the Persian Gulf's oil depot. Radical Islamic terrorism has made the Middle East a wasteland.
>
> America's "lead from behind" abdication is variously explained by financial weakness, anti-imperial politics, or simply exhaustion. But the result is not so ambiguous: to restore deterrence as it existed before 2009 could be in the short-term as hazardous and costly as the long-term consequences of appeasement are fatal.
>
> What would once have been seen as radical neglect of our existential problems is now the normal way of getting by one more day. What destroys civilizations are not, as popularly advertised, plagues, global warming, or hostile tribes on the horizon, as much as self-indulgence, self-delusion— and, finally, abject paralysis.

But here is David Gelernter with the now typical Republican, pass the smelling salts and vote for Trump. How pathetic this is:

> I'll vote for Mr. Trump—grimly. But there is no alternative, no shadow of a responsible alternative.
>
> Mr. Trump's candidacy is a message from the voters. He is the empty gin bottle they have chosen to toss through the window.

Are there no positive reasons to vote for Trump? Is there nothing in his policies or ambitions that overlap with the kinds of things you want? He mentions Trump's stand on open borders and migration as if it's just a fluke that he was the only candidate who wishes to do something. So in the end, this is what he writes:

> There is only one way to take part in protecting this nation from Hillary Clinton, and that is to vote for Donald Trump. A vote for anyone else or for no one might be an honest, admirable gesture in principle, but we don't need conscientious objectors in this war for the country's international standing and hence for the safety of the world and the American way of life. It's too bad one has to vote for Mr. Trump. It will be an unhappy moment at best. Some people will feel dirty, or pained, or outright disgraced.
>
> But when all is said and done, it's no big deal of a sacrifice for your country. I can think of bigger ones.

It's better than saying it will make no difference, but only by a bit.

~

"A lying, deceiving, manipulative, self-absorbed criminal without a shred of personal virtue"
October 18, 2016

A sort of amusing post where a group of students struggle to find a single accomplishment that would qualify Hillary for president.[382] That's a neutral way to put what is the actual point found here on The Clinton Record[383] which is a series of disasters of such gigantic proportions that you have to wonder about the sanity of those who support her. You can

---
[382] www.campusreform.org, 16 October 2016.
[383] frontpagemag.com, 14 October 2016.

read through the article to refresh your memory but these are the headings that are in themselves almost all you need to know. As you can imagine, a long article.

> *Clinton's Private Email Server & the Espionage Act*
> *The Clinton Foundation Scandals*
> *Clinton's Support for the Iran Nuclear Deal*
> *Clinton Helps Russia Gain Control of 20% of All U.S. Uranium*
> *The Benghazi Debacle, and Clinton's Role in Arming Jihadists in Libya and Syria*
> *The Radical Islamist Affiliations of Clinton's Closest Aide*
> *The Deadly Consequences of Clinton's Absurd Fictions About Islam & Terrorism*
> *Clinton's Role in the Rise of ISIS and the Stratospheric Growth of Worldwide Terrorism*
> *Clinton's Role in Squandering America's Victory in the Iraq War*
> *Clinton's Horrible Judgment Regarding Another Terrorist Enemy*
> *Clinton's Empty Talk Regarding Russia and China*
> *Clinton's Reprehensible Treatment of Israel*
> *Clinton Turns Libya into a Terrorist Hell Hole*
> *Clinton's Plan to Import 65,000 Syrian Refugees into the U.S. As Quickly As Possible*
> *Immigration: Clinton Explicitly Favors Amnesty, Sanctuary Cities, and "Open Borders"*
> *Clinton's Opposition to Gun Rights*
> *Clinton's Plans to Expand Obamacare into a Government-Run, Single-Payer System*
> *Rejecting School Vouchers for Poor Minority Children in Failing Urban Schools*
> *"Criminal Justice Reform": Going Soft on Crime, and Filling America's Graveyards*
> *Fighting Voter ID Laws As "Racist" Schemes to Disenfranchise Minorities*
> *Clinton's Affiliation with Al Sharpton & Black Lives Matter*
> *Clinton's View of the Supreme Court and Its Purpose*
> *Clinton Supports Partial-Birth Abortion*
> *Clinton's Personal Persecution of a Young Rape Victim*

The conclusion:

> *In the final analysis, Hillary Clinton is a woman with a mindset that is*

totalitarian in every respect. To make matters worse, she is a lying, deceiving, manipulative, self-absorbed criminal without a shred of personal virtue. Truly it can be said that never before in American history has anyone so unfit and so undeserving, run for president. Never.

And all this before we get to her misjudgements about markets and the economy. We are back to mediaeval forms of governance with a baronial class and the rest of us a peasantry who had better learn to mind our betters.

~

Injured innocence
October 18, 2016

From *The Washington Post*: 'The press always got booed at Trump rallies. But now the aggression is menacing'.[384]

> *Donald Trump's rallies have never been the friendliest places for reporters. But lately, as Trump has come under increasing fire, an unwelcoming atmosphere for the press has turned into outright hostility.*
>
> *Reporters who cover Trump on the campaign trail say his supporters have become more surly and abusive in the past week, egged on by a candidate who has made demonizing journalists part of his stump speech.*
>
> *Trump's traveling press contingent of about 20 has been met with boos, shouts and obscenities as it entered — as a single group — the venues where Trump has spoken this week. One reporter who is part of the traveling group described it as "a mob mentality," particularly at larger rally sites.*
>
> *"We've been on the receiving end of that throughout the election, so we've largely become numb to it," he said. "But in the last few days it's just been so much louder, so much angrier. The people who are shouting look at us like we're their immediate enemies, not as like ... primarily late-20-to-early-30-somethings there to do a job."*

And if the job happens to be to do everything they can to see Hillary elected, that is no one else's business but their own. The story is that the crowd boos and shouts at the press. But if the media becomes a player, this

---

[384] *The Washington Post*, 14 October 2016.

is not exactly unexpected? So far as the story goes, not so much as a tomato has made its way towards any of them.

~

Does it matter that she wants open borders and will pack the Supreme Court?
October 19, 2016

Obviously to Hillary's advantage pushing actual issues off stage.

There are some who think this is the final tipping point for the United States and whatever might have been once referred to as Western Civilisation.

Meanwhile, this is where the defence of the West now rests. The latest from Drudge:

> MYSTERY SWIRLS AROUND ASSANGE'S STATUS AT ECUADOREAN EMBASSY…
>
> Kerry Demanded Internet Cut?
>
> 17,150 Podesta emails, and counting!
>
> Zuckerberg Sought to Coordinate on 'Political Operations'…
>
> WIKILEAKS: Hillary Wants Obamacare to 'Unravel'…
>
> SHE 'CANNOT WALK AROUND'…
>
> 4 Million Ineligible and Dead Voters on Voting Rolls…
>
> Voter Fraud USA…
>
> O'KEEFE: Dems Explain How to Commit Fraud…
>
> Rigging Elections for 50 Years…
>
> They Incite Violence at Trump Rallies…
>
> Pay homeless to cause disruptions…
>
> Activist who bragged about starting Chicago riot was on Hillary payroll…
>
> RASMUSSEN: CLINTON +1
>
> LA TIMES: TRUMP +2

Final debate tomorrow noon our time.

A balanced look at Hillary and Trump
October 19, 2016

Something you should definitely read: 'The Unequally Terrible Election'.[385] It begins:

> *There seems to be a meme wandering about.*
>
> *"Both candidates are equally terrible!" it goes.*
>
> *Lotta entries there, huh?*
>
> *"Both Candidates are equally terrible!" bleats the anguished cry.*
>
> *Oh yeah?*
>
> *Really?*
>
> *Let's just examine that carefully for a moment, shall we? Hrmm.*

You are encouraged to read this one right through, and if you go to the link you will read it through. But let me first provide a sample of what you will find.

> *One Candidate is an unindicted career political criminal with a verifiable record of political and personal corruption and illicit activity stretching back more than a decade before her ascendance to her first major political position by virtue of marriage of convenience to an even more charismatic and electable political criminal.*
>
> *The other Candidate is a multi-decades long figure who's been in the world wide media and public scrutiny for longer than some hostile media figures have been out of diapers about whom the worst that has been dug up and exposed is that he's filed for bankruptcy a couple of times and that he once said "pussy" in a taped conversation. Oh, and he has tiny, vulgar hands, too. So there.*

Now go read it all.

---

[385] dailypundit.com, 17 October 2016.

And she can square the circle using her perpetual motion machine
October 19, 2016

Here's someone who gets it: 'Clinton's Pledge on Debt Emerges as a Risible Claim, In Light of Her Platform'.[386]

> The economic triad of rule of law, property rights, and sound money — which counter the nemeses of cronyism, interventionism, and redistribution — regained currency in the 1980s as supply-side economics and became indelibly known as the miracle of Reaganomics (and, in Britain, as Thatcherism).
>
> Partisanship stand in your way? Dispel it through its nineteenth-century nomenclature, "the law of markets," that reached its explicatory apogee in political economists J.B. Say and J.S. Mill. Exchange means exchange was its ethos and the inexhaustibility of demand its engine; rebutting with finality and prescience the latter-day Keynesian fallacy of demand deficiency, which served only as cover for political intrigue and aggrandizement under the guise of eliminating poverty.
>
> Economic growth is the route to eliminating deficits and debt, the route to employment and prosperity (and immigration reform). Any other path is the wrong one and, unlike Hillary Clinton's pledge not to grow the debt, no laughing matter.

There are many forms of insanity but political forms are the worst and largely incurable. If you are able to believe that she really can lower taxes, increase benefits, create more jobs and raise living standards all at the same time, then you are as politically deluded as it is possible to be.

~

Post mortem on the third debate
October 20, 2016

The issue of issues in the third debate is Trump's refusal to pre-commit himself to accepting the results of the election as tallied on the day. He has, in effect, stated that an election result would not be acceptable if there is serious evidence of voter and electoral fraud. I wish he hadn't said it since it

---

[386] nysun.com, 18 October 2016.

will diminish his outstanding performance on the rest. But what do I know about politics at that level, since what it will do is put the spotlight on the way in which the deceased vote early and often, how voting machines are hacked and the multiple voting that is rife across the American system. And for all my misgivings, he is the one that has taken the Trump train to the edge of the White House, so we shall see what happens now.

I have often thought about this issue, in particular in relation to the 2012 election: 'In 59 Philadelphia voting divisions, Mitt Romney got zero votes'.[387] Not one person voted for Romney, not even by accident, not even by pulling the wrong lever, not even my mis-reading the ballot paper! Not one? To quote:

> *The unanimous support for Obama in these Philadelphia neighborhoods – clustered in almost exclusively black sections of West and North Philadelphia – fertilizes fears of fraud, despite little hard evidence.*
>
> *Upon hearing the numbers, Steve Miskin, a spokesman for Republicans in the Pennsylvania House of Representatives, brought up his party's voter-identification initiative – which was held off for this election – and said, "We believe we need to continue ensuring the integrity of the ballot."*
>
> *The absence of a voter-ID law, however, would not stop anyone from voting for a Republican candidate.*

Which is exactly the point. The polls showed a super-majority voting for Obama, but the polls also showed the score at 94-6. Six percent is not zero percent. And then there's this:

A video was put up just the other day, 'Rigging the Election – Video II: Mass Voter Fraud' you can see this here: (www.youtube.com/watch?v=hDc8PVCvfKs), and comes with this caption:

> *In the second video of James O'Keefe's new explosive series on the DNC and Hillary Clinton campaign, Democratic party operatives tell us how to successfully commit voter fraud on a massive scale. Scott Foval, who has since been fired, admits that the Democrats have been rigging elections for fifty years.*

This is an issue of immense importance in a democracy. Legitimacy is bestowed only if the system is fair and perceived to be fair. Trump is in the

---

[387] philly.com, 12 November 2012.

middle of a battle he thinks, and I think, is for the future of America and the West. What he said is that he is not going to give the outcome his prior approval before he has actually seen what has happened on the day.

And I do have to say that I was surprised that he didn't bring up Al Gore and the disputed election in 2012 [actually 2000]. It would no doubt have crossed his mind, so you have to think Trump had sifted this through on the spot and didn't wish to change the focus to sixteen years ago. He wants this election, this year, run clean. And since this is his greatest vulnerability – an election stolen by those with a proven track record of electoral theft – he wants to keep the pressure on as best he can.

Politics is ultimately what works. Does it cost him votes to focus on voter fraud in this way? No doubt. But will it also gain him votes if he can contain the fraud? Yes again. The question really comes down to how it will play out.

Given the rest of the debate was overwhelmingly in his favour, a clear winner on each of the issues for someone like me who is seeking a stronger US both internationally and at home, he is the only candidate worth considering. Hillary, if elected, will trash America, leaving the 2020 election of no genuine interest since, by then, the US will be even farther on its way towards becoming a third world economy. Hillary's idiotic, but thoroughly focus-tested statement, that "we are going to go where the money is", that is, she is going to raid corporations and the wealthy for as much as she can shake them down for, is to guarantee a continuation of, if not an actual deterioration from the descending living standards that are now entrenched and becoming worse. The wealthier will get wealthier and the bottom 60-70% will find things getting worse by the year.

As for foreign policy, the election as president of the architect of what we see in Libya, Syria, Iran and Iraq ought to terrify anyone who thinks about the future. She has never shown good judgement, so why should she start now. Trump again described American policy as "stupid". It must have resonated with many across his constituency when he said it during the second debate. And stupid is really only the mildest term he might have chosen.

Not to mention open borders. Hillary's patent lie that when she was talking about open borders in her secret speech in Brazil she meant electricity is also such irritating stupidity that it is a wonder anyone can even pretend to believe a word. But what is more of a wonder is that those who support her are not personally terrified about open borders and what it will do to their country and their own individual way of life. Nothing stands still, but the changes that her presidency would bring will have the equivalent effect on just about everything that Obamacare has had on the health system. With Hillary it is all downhill from here. At least with Trump there remains hope. Not necessarily a lot, but at least some.

~

The morning after the debate last night
October 21, 2016

When at the end of the debate the question came up about whether the candidates would accept the election result, I said to myself that well, here is an exercise in the obvious. Of course you say that you will accept the result. And then Donald didn't. And therefore we have either seen one of the largest political mistakes in history, or an act of such genius that it raises Trump to among the greatest candidates ever to run for president. And on thinking it over, I am now almost convinced that the question may even have been suggested to the moderator by Trump himself, precisely so that he could give the answer he gave. All this is by way of an introduction to my take on the third debate which you can find at *Quadrant Online* under the heading, 'Lies and Loathing 3.0' [a reprint of the previous post].[388] From which:

> *This is an issue of immense importance in a democracy. Legitimacy is bestowed only if the system is fair and perceived to be fair. Trump is in the middle of a battle he thinks, and I think, is for the future of America and the West. What he said is that he is not going to give the outcome his prior approval before he has actually seen what has happened on the day.*
>
> *And I do have to say that I was surprised that he didn't bring up Al Gore and the disputed election in 2012 [actually 2000]. It would no doubt have crossed his mind, so you have to think Trump had sifted this on the spot and didn't wish to change the focus to sixteen years ago. He wants this election,*

---
[388] *Quadrant Online*, 20 October 2016.

> this year, run clean. And since this is his greatest vulnerability – an election stolen by those with a proven track record of electoral theft – he wants to keep the pressure on as best he can.
>
> *Politics is ultimately what works. Does it cost him votes to focus on voter fraud in this way? No doubt. But will it also gain him votes if he can contain the fraud? Yes again. The question really comes down to how it will play out.*

Trump has put voter fraud on the map, which is discussed further at the link, and is now, in fact, being discussed across America. That has got to work for the Republicans.

Also discussed at *QoL* is the way in which Trump massively defeated Clinton on the issues, showing far greater depth and understanding on every topic raised. And I will finish with another quote from the article which is what I think all of this really comes down to.

> *Nothing stands still, but the changes that her presidency would bring will have the equivalent effect on just about everything that Obamacare has had on the health system. With Hillary it is all downhill from here. At least with Trump there remains hope. Not necessarily a lot, but at least some.*

Three weeks from now and we shall see.

~

Why isn't everyone on "the right" desperate to see Hillary lose?

October 22, 2016

This is from Mark Steyn: Laws are for the Little People.[389]

> *Like everything else the Clintons touch, Comey's FBI is hopelessly corrupted – and certainly more corrupt than J Edgar Hoover's FBI, at least in the sense that Hoover was independent enough not to get rolled. The revelations of what happened reveal Comey to be a hack and a squish: he offered immunity to Hillary's aides not to facilitate his investigation but to obstruct any further investigation; he allowed witnesses to Hillary's crimes to serve as her "lawyers"; and he physically destroyed the evidence – that is, the laptops.*

---

[389] steynonline.com, 19 October 2016.

A 6' 8" gummi worm would be more of a straight arrow.

Now come the latest revelations. Powerline's John Hinderaker writes:

In the first page, an unidentified FBI employee says he was "pressured" to change the classification of an email to render it unclassified. This pressure came from someone within the FBI, who said he had been contacted by Undersecretary of State Patrick Kennedy, who "had asked his assistance in altering the email's classification in exchange for a 'quid pro quo.'" The quid pro quo was that, if the FBI would say the email was unclassified, the State Department would allow the FBI to "place more Agents in countries where they are presently forbidden."

So, to add to the corrupt revenue agency and the corrupt justice department, we now have a corrupt national law enforcement agency and a corrupt foreign ministry – willing, indeed, to subordinate national security and its own diplomatic policy to the personal needs of Hillary Clinton. Needless to say, if you get your news from ABC, CBS, NBC, CNN, The Washington Post, The New York Times, etc, etc, you will be entirely unaware of all this. Which is the way they plan on operating for the next eight years.

A small but telling point: Wikileaks' Julian Assange has lived in the Ecuadorian Embassy in London for over four years. But not until he leaked against Hillary was his Internet cut off. Hillary, out of office, has a swifter and more ruthless global reach than Hillary in office on the night of Benghazi. And, should she win, her view of her subjects is that we should have the same information access as Ecuadorian Embassy refugees.

And, should she win, I will delete all of my previous posts and become a registered Democrat. It would be futile to do anything else.

Contract with the American voter
October 23, 2016

Will this be the largest missed opportunity in American history: 'Trump's Contract with the American Voter'.[390] Anyone who supports Clinton will be forever stained with the stupidity of supporting the imposition of a slave state in place of freedom. The contract can be found in the Appendix.

You can also find it all outlined here in detail, naturally not in an American press but in *The Daily Mail:* 'Trump's 'Gettysburg address''[391] where the heading continues, "makes closing argument for choosing him and unveils first-100-days agenda as he promises 'the kind of change that only arrives once in a lifetime'."

~

What do we have in common anymore?
October 24, 2016

I stopped reading Jonah Goldberg's pseudo-conservative nonsense ages ago – it's been literally a decade – and have thought of him as irrelevant to anything that matters for a long long time. He has nothing to teach me about anything I think of as important. But here is something that begins with an attack on JG, but which has a much more important message. It's titled, 'Seven Degrees of Jonah Goldberg',[392] but is dealing with an entire disease, not the particular carrier who's named in the article title. It is by the highly insightful Publius Decius Mus who has been cited here twice before. You can find his other articles referenced at the link. Here is the problem that the official conservative battalions have failed to achieve.

> *We failed to preserve a true understanding the principles of the Declaration of Independence. We failed to preserve the proper working order of the Constitution. We failed to protect and nurture that virtue in the people necessary to sustain the Constitution. We failed to defend the family from*

---

[390] assets.donaldjtrump.com/CONTRACT_FOR_THE_VOTER.pdf.
[391] *Daily Mail Australia,* 22 October 2016.
[392] amgreatness.com, 22 October 2016.

relentless assault. We failed to maintain any semblance of a shared public morality. We allowed—through a combination of active cheering and ineffective opposition—demographic and cultural replacement. We lent a great deal of our talent to serve rapacious interests in the name of "economic freedom." All the things we were supposed to conserve—the nation, its people, its way of life, its governing structure—we have not conserved.

This all seems irrefutably clear to me [and me]. Yet official conservatism says I am insane for saying so. So I ask: what do we have in common anymore?

PDM then repeats the exact words he previously wrote, which is again a complete mirror of what I think myself:

If Hillary wins, there will still be a country, in the sense of a geographic territory with a people, a government, and various institutions. Things will mostly look the same, just as—outwardly—Rome changed little on the ascension of Augustus. It will not be tyranny or Caesarism—not yet. But it will represent, in my view, an irreversible triumph for the administrative state. Consider that no president has been denied reelection since 1992. If we can't beat the Democrats now, what makes anyone think we could in 2020, when they will have all the advantages of incumbency plus four more years of demographic change in their favor? And if we can't win in 2016 or 2020, what reason is there to hope for 2024? Will the electorate be more Republican? More conservative? Will constitutional norms be stronger?

And to the #NeverTrumpers, he says this, which I agree with more than with all the rest:

To be a conservative or a Republican and to sit it out, or to criticize Trump, is in this circumstance to favor Hillary. That's just a fact. Trump is the underdog and needs all the help he can get. Every defection or abandonment hurts him and makes it more likely that she will win. If she wins, she will be a disaster for the right and for the country—on precisely the terms that Goldberg and so many others have always said she would. I therefore find it mind boggling that they could do anything, however slight, that might help her win.

It is self-defeating to stress the negatives that Trump brings with him, whatever they may be. So far, there is nothing that has come to my notice for which Hillary is actually superior, not a thing. If your aim is not to see Hillary lose if that means that Trump wins, then you are just as much the enemy as Obama himself.

~

Is there nothing these people don't corrupt?
October 24, 2016

In this case, we are talking about polling. The aim is to get people voting for Republicans not to bother since it's all over. This is from Zero Hedge: 'New Podesta Email Exposes Dem Playbook For Rigging Polls Through "Oversamples".'[393]

> Now, for all of you out there who still aren't convinced that the polls are "adjusted", we present to you the following Podesta email, leaked earlier today, that conveniently spells out, in detail, exactly how to "manufacture" the desired data. The email starts out with a request for recommendations on "oversamples for polling" in order to "maximize what we get out of our media polling."
>
> I also want to get your Atlas folks to recommend oversamples for our polling before we start in February. By market, regions, etc. I want to get this all compiled into one set of recommendations so we can maximize what we get out of our media polling.
>
> The email even includes a handy, 37-page guide with the following poll-rigging recommendations. In Arizona, over sampling of Hispanics and Native Americans is highly recommended:
>
> Research, microtargeting & polling projects
>
> — Over-sample Hispanics
>
> — Use Spanish language interviewing. (Monolingual Spanish-speaking voters are among the lowest turnout Democratic targets)
>
> — Over-sample the Native American population
>
> For Florida, the report recommends "consistently monitoring" samples to make sure they're "not too old" and "has enough African American and

---
[393] zerohedge.com, 23 October 2016.

Hispanic voters." Meanwhile, "independent" voters in Tampa and Orlando are apparently more dem friendly so the report suggests filling up independent quotas in those cities first.

– Consistently monitor the sample to ensure it is not too old, and that it has enough African American and Hispanic voters to reflect the state.

– On Independents: Tampa and Orlando are better persuasion targets than north or south Florida (check your polls before concluding this). If there are budget questions or oversamples, make sure that Tampa and Orlando are included first.

Meanwhile, it's suggested that national polls over sample "key districts / regions" and "ethnic" groups "as needed."

– General election benchmark, 800 sample, with potential over samples in key districts/regions

– Benchmark polling in targeted races, with ethnic over samples as needed

– Targeting tracking polls in key races, with ethnic over samples as needed

The aim is to have the poll record as closely as possible the outcome they are intending to rig on the day. And what may be the most astonishing part is that were it not for the leaked emails, no one would have heard a thing about any of this even though hundreds of people must be in on the scam.

~

Political idiots
October 25, 2016

This is by 'Publius Decius Mus'[394] and 'the people he describes'[395] are everywhere to be seen:

> *To be a conservative or a Republican and to sit it out, or to criticize Trump, is in this circumstance to favor Hillary. That's just a fact. Trump is the underdog and needs all the help he can get. Every defection or abandonment hurts him and makes it more likely that she will win. If she wins, she will be a disaster for the right and for the country—on precisely the terms that many*

---

[394] en.wikipedia.org/wiki/Publius_Decius_Mus_(consul_340_BC)
[395] amgreatness.com, 22 October 2016.

others have always said she would. I therefore find it mind boggling that they could do anything, however slight, that might help her win.

These people are idiots, disgusting low-life political morons. It really is impossible to describe the imbecilic pomposity of anyone who takes an even-handed weighing up of both sides in the election this year, never mind those sunshine conservatives who are all-in for Hillary. Are they really that stupid, that out of it? If Hillary wins, there is no coming back.

~

"There is no third option, there is no compromise, there is no sitting out the election"
October 27, 2016

Speaking of political idiots,[396] this has just come my way which might help some see things more clearly: 'Conservative leaders step up for Trump, warn of a "Clinton Progressive Police State".'[397] If the title doesn't make you see the point, perhaps the introduction to the publication will:

> *Longtime conservative maven Richard Viguerie has produced an instant publication for these final, frantic days before the election, consisting of essays penned by a group of 18 conservative leaders who include Brent Bozell, Gary Bauer, Jerry Falwell Jr., Craig Shirley, Joseph Farah, David Keene and James Dobson.*
>
> *Mr. Viguerie says the compilation is meant to "attack the idea that not voting for Donald Trump somehow advances conservative principles." The 25-page booklet is titled "Hail Hillary: Is a Clinton-Progressive Police State in America's Future?"*
>
> *Interesting. Some in GOP circles seem to suggest there's virtue in shunning Mr. Trump.*
>
> *"Hail Hillary is a cannonball through the doors of the ivory towers of those conservative who continue to obdurately claim that a Hillary Clinton presidency might not be that bad, that the country can recover after four or eight years, and that her policies won't be aimed at marginalizing, if not*

---

[396] catallaxyfiles.com, 27 October 2016.
[397] *The Washington Times,* 26 October 2016.

outlawing, the conservative worldview," says Mr. Viguerie.

"This is now a binary choice: Donald Trump and Mike Pence vs. Hillary Clinton and Tim Kaine. In this battle there is only the victory or defeat of constitutional liberty and the rule of law. In this battle there is no third option, there is no compromise, there is no sitting out the election. I'm all in for Trump and Pence."

Anyone who cannot see the difference a Trump administration would make in comparison with an administration led by Hillary is so out of it politically that there is never any further reason to pay attention to a thing they say about the great issues of our time.

~

If you were a Trump voter would you tell your friends?
October 28, 2016

Since we know the media never say what's true but only what will help Hillary, the question I have been pondering is why they keep repeating the election is over and Hillary has won. This can only cause some Hillary voters not to bother. But more importantly, it will also cause some Trump voters not to bother. The conclusion they have reached is that it is better to keep Trump supporters home (possibly since for Democrats, you don't even need to show up to vote – or even still be among the living).

But this is too strange an election to know anything about the final result (see Brexit). A blow-out in either direction is still possible. Certainly, if the election were in Australia, Hillary would win in a landslide, just as Obama would have done in both 2008 and 2012. Now, I don't know whether this is whistling past the graveyard but I do find it interesting: 'Hidden' Trump vote becomes formidable force.[398]

Despite media hysteria and a daily influx of polls, a persistent conversation has emerged about the huge, hidden population of Americans who could suddenly step forward and vote for Donald Trump. It is a powerful, unknown

---
[398] *The Washington Times*, 27 October 2016.

factor with much potential — and one which makes Democratic strategists plenty nervous.

There are no standard ways of measuring this demographic. They could be evangelicals, dispossessed working-class folk, or disenchanted fans of Sen. Bernard Sanders and third party candidates. They could be small business owners, doubting Democrats, active-duty military, veterans, bikers, patriots, law enforcement personnel, seniors who remember another America, or impoverished millennials. Second Amendment fans and pro-lifers are certainly part of the hidden vote. No one knows the precise demographics, though there will be insight in future exit polls.

All of them, however, found something to like in Mr. Trump, and their motivation is paramount. National polls have consistently revealed that Trump voters are more passionate and engaged than those who favor Hillary Clinton.

"I still think Trump may win the election. The polls are very weird. We've seen how off they were with Brexit and the last UK general election. A hidden Trump vote is not unimaginable at all," writes Powerline analyst Steven Hayward.

He points to a recent rousing speech made by Michael Moore before a live audience. The renegade filmmaker appears appreciative of Mr. Trump's outsider status and plainspoken pitch, and that he is hated by the press and corporate America. A grinning and f-bombing Mr. Moore relished making this prediction about election day:

"Joe Blow, Steve Blow, Bob Blow, Billy Blow, Billy Bob Blow — all the Blows will get to blow up the whole [expletive] system because it's their right. Trump's election is going to be the biggest [f — k] you in human history and it will feel good," Mr. Moore told his audience.

The structure of polls are works of history, and where we now are is unprecedented. A couple of bits from Drudge on how unusual things are:

More Jewish Voters Going Against Tide...
Trump fans rally in Jerusalem's Old City...

BLACK ACTIVIST BLASTS CLINTONS...
Anger Over 'Using' Father's Death...
'These people will co-opt anything to push agenda'...

Merkel says FACEBOOK, GOOGLE 'distort perception,' demands they 'reveal algorithms'...

Zuckerberg's 'Free Basics' A Dictator's Dream...

Merkel's problem is hilarious in that she has "launched a broadside at internet media giants, accusing them of 'narrowing perspective,' and demanding they disclose their privately-developed algorithms. Merkel previously blamed social media for anti-immigrant sentiment and the rise of the far right." But if they did, it was never their intention, if you listen to what Sheryl Sandberg and Mark Zuckerberg have been saying. But Merkel's larger point applies to the polls as well.

> *"These algorithms, when they are not transparent, can lead to a distortion of our perception, they narrow our breadth of information."*

It ain't over, and it may not be over even after the weight-challenged person has sung.

~

But what about her policies?
October 29, 2016

There is certainly some kind of demented distorted thought process that allows Democrats to vote for Hillary in spite of everything. The latest everything at Drudge:

> *Computer seized in Weiner probe prompts FBI to take new steps in Clinton email inquiry*
> *CAMPAIGN ROCKED*[399]

And from the last of these:

> *Approximately 10 percent of Abedin's emails released through Judicial Watch Freedom of Information Act requests were addressed to one of Mills' various personal email addresses.*
>
> *Several were found to contain such highly sensitive material that the State Department redacted 100 percent of the content pages, marking many pages with a bold stamp reading "PAGE DENIED."*

The real question is whether any of it matters to the 51%.

---

[399] wnd.com, 6 September 2016.

All we like sheep
October 30, 2016

All of the stories from Drudge are crucial but for me one stands out:

HILLARY AT WAR WITH FBI
DEMS RAGE AS SURVIVAL IN DOUBT
LYNCH MOVED TO SPIKE COMEY
HUMA GOES INTO HIDING
TENS OF THOUSANDS OF EMAILS
Homeless woman attacked by mob for defending Trump's Hollywood star...
HILLARY HELL WEEK: 10-POINT VANISH IN WASHPOSTABCNEWS...
Poll Tampering?[400]

How Clinton campaign allowed hacking of Podesta's e-mail account...

It may take all of the information that has come from two entirely different directions – from Wikileaks on one side and the Weiner investigation on the other – but the role of the media in distorting and suppressing what the public needs to know to make an informed decision remains to me the greatest scandal of them all. You cannot trust the press. The sudden ten-point fall in the Washington Post-ABC News poll, all before the latest revelations, is a reminder that what you read in the papers is almost entirely what those on the left want you to read. This is the question posed by the report:

> *Just yesterday we wrote about the very curious ABC / Wapo poll which seemed to show Hillary's blow-out 12-point lead from last Sunday get cut in half in a matter of just two days. But the ABC/Wapo enigma continues to grow today as their latest poll shows the presidential race has now tightened to just 2 points, which is within the margin of error. Ironically, these new results do not reflect the latest FBI bombshell as polling was concluded on October 27th and it still includes an 8-point sampling advantage for democrats...*
>
> *Now, while ABC / Wapo claim that the 10-point swing (in less than a week) was driven by changes in "who's intending to vote," we find it quite curious that their own data shows just a 2-point swing in people who said they were "certain to vote" on 10/23, when the poll reflected a 12-point*

---
[400] zerohedge.com, 29 October 2016.

Hillary lead, and 10/27 when the lead had collapsed to just 2 points. So, are we really expected to believe that a 2-point swing in voter intentions somehow translated to a 10-point swing in the poll results? Not likely...something tells us it had a little more to do with including "ethnic 'oversamples' as required."

We are fed lies from the very top through to every official and unofficial organ of government to keep us in line. It has required a politically-driven independently-wealthy billionaire with a flair for publicity to perhaps bring us to the point of some kind of change in the way the United States – and pretty well all of the democracies – are governed. But it's not over yet. At least there is more hope for change than there was a week ago, which even the Washington Post and ABC are being forced by circumstance to reveal.

~

The right question is whether the media is off track
October 31, 2016

The great genius of the Clinton campaign is to make it seem that Hillary and Trump are just two of a kind, with no signifcant difference between them in what each would bring to the presidency. So when you read on Instapundit[401], remember Peggy Noonan supported Obama not just in 2008 but also in 2012. She is another Democrat shill pretending to be a Republican. This is what she wrote:

> *What I'm thinking about this week is a focus group led by Peter Hart, the veteran Democratic pollster, Tuesday night, in Charlotte, N.C., still a toss-up state. Present were a dozen late-decider voters, three Democrats, six Republicans and three independents.*
>
> *What struck me about the group wasn't its new insights, which were few. What was powerful was its averageness, its confirmation of what you've already observed. The members weren't sad, precisely, but they were unillusioned. They were seeing things with clean eyes and they were disappointed. They wanted a candidate they could trust and believe in.*
>
> *Which when you think about it shouldn't be too much to ask.*

---

[401] pjmedia.com/instapundit, 30 October 2016.

Raise your hand, said Mr. Hart, if you like both candidates. No one did. Raise your hand if you like one candidate. No one did. Raise if you don't like either. All 12 did. . . .

Mr. Hart asked: Will the next generation be better off? No one raised a hand. This is not news; it's been a cliché since the crash of 2008. You get used to the data: Americans no longer assume their children will have it better than they did. But it was striking to see these dozen thoughtful people keep their hands down.

Asked what has been lost in America, one respondent said security for kids: "They can't just go out and play." "Innocence for kids," said another. Parents no longer feel the world, even the immediate one, is a safe place.

What is missing in America? "A freshness," said a middle aged man. He went on to speak of the 1950s, "Ozzie and Harriet," when things seemed newer somehow and assumptive of progress.

Is America off track? They all nodded.

The people she describes are so deluded that it is breathtaking.

~

The top ten of the (so far) top 100 wikileaks
October 31, 2016

The Top 100 Most Damaging Wikileaks (so far).[402] There is nothing new in any of it for anyone who has been paying attention. What makes Wikileaks and now the Weiner additions so devastating is that the media cannot avoid covering them and therefore slowly – very slowly – the tide may be turning against the most morally corrupt individual ever to run for President from a major party. Here are the top ten of the (so far) top 100, but I've added in Number 100 to show what a deep bench there is. You should also go to the link to see the detail which really is overwhelming.

> 1. *Obama lied: he knew about Hillary's secret server and wrote to her using a pseudonym, cover-up happened (intent to destroy evidence)*
> 2. *Hillary Clinton dreams of completely "open trade and open borders"*

---

[402] themillenniumreport.com, 29 October 2016.

3. *Hillary Clinton took money from and supported nations that she KNEW funded ISIS and terrorists*

4. *Hillary has public positions on policy and her private ones*

5. *Paying people to incite violence and unrest at Trump rallies*

6. *Hillary's campaign wants "unaware" and "compliant" citizens*

7. *Top Hillary aides mock Catholics for their faith*

8. *Hillary deleted her incriminating emails. State covered it up. Asked about using White House executive privilege to hide from Congress*

9. *Bribery: King of Morocco gives Clinton Foundation $12 million to have meeting with Hillary, 6 months later Morocco gets weapons*

10. *State Department tried to bribe FBI to un-classify Clinton emails (FBI docs)*

100. *Obama picked people in his administration from the suggestion list of CiTi bank advisor/Wall Street shill*

The proof that the media have the astonishing power to hide and distort is shown by the polls that say Obama still has a plus-50% approval rate. After Syria, Obamacare, the open southern border and the state of the economy, and that's just to begin with, you have to wonder what he could have done to make things worse. But elect Hillary and we may yet find out.

~

A week is a long time in politics
November 1, 2016

It's Melbourne Cup day in an American election year but the election is not today. The constitution determined that presidential elections should be held on the first Tuesday **after the first Monday** in November. I don't know the official reason why but my guess is that back in 1787 they decided not to have the election the day after Hallowe'en so that everyone could spend the day righting their outhouses and cleaning the soap off the windows. But whatever the reason, it has meant that this year there is another week to go.

In my view, had the election been held today, Hillary would have won.

The extra week has the potential to reverse this outcome, as the media are forced to report on the corruption and incompetence of Hillary Clinton, as revealed in the emails released. A week from now, it is possible that enough independents, and even some traditional Democrats, will have become sickened at the thought of a Clinton presidency to allow Trump enough of a margin to win in spite of the certain illegality of Democrat election practice.

And the stories provide nothing new, but with the FBI now saying that the investigation into Hillary is now open again, attention is being paid. And this is what even the New York Times, Washington Post and ABCBSNBC are being compelled to cover.

> *LA TIMES TUESDAY: FBI Investigators had planned to conduct new email review over several weeks. It now hopes to complete 'preliminary assessment' in coming days, but agency officials have not decided how, or whether, they will disclose results publicly... Developing...*
>
> *CARVILLE CRACKS: Asserts FBI, GOP and KGB in Cahoots... Podesta's BFF At DOJ Will Be In Charge Of New Probe...*
>
> *45% say scandal worse than Watergate...*
>
> *BUCHANAN: Pres. Hillary would go way of Nixon...*
>
> *Clinton unfavorable rating hits new high...*
>
> *Pollster: 'Dam About to Break'...*
>
> *22 million ballots already in...*
>
> *CITI: Black swan could throw vote off course...*
>
> *STUDY: Networks Attack Comey Over Clinton 3 to 1...*
>
> *TRUMP TARGETS DEMOCRATIC STATES IN FINAL ASSAULT...*

And the straightforward fact is that even if elected, Hillary could not govern. These are not placid times, and it is not too much to say that the fate of the West is being decided for us right now. More from Drudge:

> *BORDER BLOWN OPEN...*
> *ILLEGALS FLOOD IN...*
> *FEDS HIDE NUMBERS...*
> *'WORST WE'VE EVER SEEN'...*
> *SESSIONS: 817,740 CROSSED LAST YEAR!*

Leaked Images Show Illegals Strolling Across Open Border...
Merkel's Germany descends into lawlessness...
'Losing control of streets'...
Putin preps army of robots...
Nuke Sub Off Brit Coast...
NATO, Russia to hold parallel drills...

I know enough Democrat voters to appreciate how obnoxiously determined they are to vote for Hillary. We met a woman in a cafe yesterday who decided to join into a conversation I was having with my wife. Her issue. Trump treats women badly. The infuriating reality was that she knew no facts about anything. No facts at all about any of the policy matters that will determine the future of the Western world. We are staring at the fall of the American Republic and she is worried only about the sexual practices of alpha males. No analogy with Bill would even be entertained. My wife even brought up Bob Hawke and his womanising, but she was determined not to be dissuaded by anything anyone might say.

Yet it really is the policy differences that matter. For a rundown of what those differences are you can go to 'WHERE CLINTON AND TRUMP STAND – ON EVERY MAJOR ISSUE'.[403] Just looking at the list of issues ought to terrify anyone, and then there are Hillary's policy positions which are inferior in every case.

~

Raisin' Kaine to the highest office in the land
November 1, 2016

Is all of this a charade to make Tim Kaine president? The evidence of how much that goes on is make-believe to fool the rubes is now massive. This is B-grade movie plot, but does fit the facts.

From the start, the selection of Tim Kaine was a curiosity since he is 100% from the Obama side of the Democratic Party and Hillary would never under ordinary circumstances have picked one of Obama's closest

---

[403] frontpagemag.com, 25 October 2016.

associates. As in:[404]

> Kaine held the key fundraising position of Democratic National Committee chairman during the entire run-up to Obamacare's passage, as the Democrats passed that unpopular 2,400 page legislation without a single Republican vote. But Kaine's ties to Obama go back further. In November of 2005, during Obama's first year in the Senate, Obama campaigned for Kaine in the Virginia gubernatorial race. Just over a year later, in February of 2007—as the Los Angeles Times reports—Kaine became the first statewide elected Democrat outside of Illinois to support Obama's presidential bid against the Democratic heir apparent, Hillary Clinton.
>
> The Clintons are not exactly known for their short memories. So how is it that someone who was among the first to break ranks with Hillary in 2007 was rewarded with the top prize that she could grant in 2016? Could it be that Clinton decided that the largely unknown Kaine was such a big political asset that she should let bygones by bygones? Or could it be that Clinton, who has tied herself to Obama and is highly dependent on his help in turning out the Democratic base, was told whom to pick?

Or could it be that Obama had the ability to short circuit any presidential ambitions Hillary might have had by getting the Department of Justice and Loretta Lynch to prosecute for unambiguous violations of national security laws that forbid government officials to use private email servers, which still comes down to whether she was told whom to pick.

Comey the first time round did nothing, against all of the evidence and the clear views of the rest of the FBI. So she owed Obama to no end, if for nothing else, for keeping her out of jail, since if Lynch (ie Obama) had said indict, indicted she most surely would have been. This time round, however, Comey has raised the possibility of prosecution. But more importantly, 'Obama has not condemned Comey'[405] for raising these issues now.

> Earnest [Obama's press secretary] did reiterate that President Barack Obama thinks Comey is a man of "integrity" who didn't do anything to "intentionally" influence the impending election when he offered Congress sketchy details about a new line of inquiry into the scandal over Clinton's

---

[404] weeklystandard.com, 28 September 2016.
[405] politico.com, 30 October 2016.

use of a private email server at the State Department.

Do you really think that is designed to help Hillary or to set things up to have her in jail once she wins the election.

Third, let me note how incredible it is that 650,000 emails have ended up in Weiner's laptop, some of them highly classified and none of which he would have been sent by anyone, especially not his estranged wife, Huma Abedin. So let's add this in to the rest:[406]

> *Abedin claims to be at a loss as to how her emails got onto Anthony's laptop. That surprise could well be genuine....*
>
> *Weiner's laptop contains 650,000 emails? If he sent or received 200 emails a day, 365 days a year–a considerable number!–it would take 3,250 days, or just about nine years, to accumulate 650,000 on the laptop's hard drive. It is not clear–to me, anyway–what would cause such a large number of emails to reside on the laptop, absent some sort of bulk downloads.*

Bulk downloads, you say. Who would do it? Who could do it? Huma is out of sight and probably has no idea what took place, while Weiner is facing many years in jail for sexting an underage teenager. Whatever she may know or wish, he is likely to be highly cooperative.

Where does it come down to? That Clinton wins the election and then is forced to resign making Kaine president. My hope is that this all ends as conjecture when Trump wins the election. But if she wins, then we will see whether all of this is out there waiting to happen.

~

A sense of Huma
November 2, 2016

There is this video on the life history of Huma Abedin, with the title, "Hillary's #1 aide Huma Abedin: Undeniable ties to terrorists & 9/11 funders (Watch before voting!)", does raise some questions that everyone seems determined to ignore.

---

[406] powerlineblog.com, 30 October 2016.

Which reminds me of the worldwide absence of "lone wolf" Islamist attacks anywhere in the world. May be just a coincidence, but it is eerie.

On the other hand, there is this: 'Islamic State-Linked Magazine Urges 'Lone-Wolf' Attacks in West to Avenge Mosul.'[407]

> *An Islamic State (ISIS)-linked propaganda magazine, published in English, Arabic, and French by the Nashir Media Foundation, is urging jihadists in Europe and the United States to carry out deadly "lone-wolf" attacks to avenge the terrorist group's losses in Mosul.*
>
> *In the second issue of the magazine, titled Nashir – Now Fight Has Come, the writers remind Muslims across the globe of the "privilege" they have residing "among our enemies who live peacefully in their countries," notes the Foreign Desk (FD).*
>
> *"Every soldier fights on the Caliphate land [in Iraq and Syria] wishes to be in your place. We can cut the tail of the snake but it will sooner grow again. But you have its head," adds the magazine.*
>
> *"Brave Mosul is bleeding. You should stop its bleeding by carrying out exhaustion operations of the Enemy's power and blood ... cut their heads by your knives, let us hear your guns blasting their heads," it also states, according to FD.*

But please, not until November 9th

~

My presentation on the American election
November 3, 2016

I spoke to one of the branches of the Liberal Party last night about the American election. They obviously chose me since they wanted someone who might speak positively about Donald, which is what they most certainly received from me. Here were my opening points:

> *1) If you are not for Trump and are even tempted to vote for Hillary, you ought to consider shifting to the Greens.*
>
> *2) I do not prefer Trump in the sense of the lesser of two evils. I prefer*

---
[407] breitbart.com. 1 November 2016.

Trump as the best imaginable choice to "Make America Great Again", or more realistically, as the last possible chance to save Western civilisation from disintegration.

3) If you do not see this then you are blind to everything that is going on, almost all of which is hidden from view by a media that is almost as corrupt as Hillary.

I then discussed all of the policies that are in parallel with the Coalition's. You know:

- *border protection*
- *dealing with terrorism and Islamic jihad*
- *market-based policies to encourage recovery*
- *lower taxes and certainly no "death taxes"*
- *reduced public spending*
- *removal of Obamacare and an open national market for health insurance*
- *Supreme Court appointments who are constitutional scholars*
- *suppressing voter fraud*
- *understanding climate change is a fraud*
- *encouraging fracking and coal-based sources of power*

You know, sanity for a change. The Q&A made it quite an evening, but I am happy to report, the sentiment of the room was definitely with me. A very unusual experience, I can tell you.

~

How did Hillary get so rich?
November 3, 2016

Trump's new ad via Instapundit:[408]

> CULTURE OF CORRUPTION: Trump's Closer: How Did Hillary Get So Rich? "The Clintons made several millions off of book deals, but made a lot more off of their connections to power and monied interests, including $57.5 million during the four years Hillary Clinton served as

---

[408] pjmedia.com/instapundit, 2 November 2016.

> *Secretary of State. Donald Trump has occasionally made reference to this, but he's making it an explicit argument in the final week with his new ad, "Corruption." Washington Post analyst Chris Cillizza is impressed. . . . Don't forget that the Clintons had been in federal office continuously from January 1992 to February 2013, a period of twenty-one years, while they amassed a nine-figure net worth. Only a small portion of that came from book advances, while their speeches and especially Bill's consultancy income derived almost entirely from Hillary's status as a Senator and later as Secretary of State. (See Laureate Education for an $18 million example, where Bill was paid eight figures to be an honorary chancellor.)"*

How she gets a single vote remains beyond me. Have the last eight years really been that great that we should want four more like it, if not actually worse?

And also via Instapundit, which for the first time puts me in complete agreement with Obama:

.@POTUS says if @realDonaldTrump elected, he'll reverse "every single thing I've done" on jobs, health insurance, climate change, et al.

One can only hope.

~

Hillary pro and con
November 3, 2016

I have come across two articles today, each providing their last set of public advice before the election. For Hillary, we have that NYT political writer Thomas Friedman with his vapid and inane 'Donald Trump Voters, Just Hear Me Out'.[409] I did hear him out, and it comes down to concern that Trump has been known to eat with his elbows on the table. I only bring it to your attention as evidence that there is no case for Hillary of any

---
[409] *The New York Times*, 2 November 2016.

substance. You do have to laugh at this, when immigration to the US is almost entirely third-world peasants with no first-world skills who will be living on welfare for generations. Meanwhile, all you folks looking for jobs and decent incomes, well you will just have to depend on the welfare state.

> *The smartest thing we can do now is to keep our economy as open and flexible as possible — to get the change signals first and be able to quickly adapt; create the opportunity for every American to engage in lifelong learning, because whatever jobs emerge will require more knowledge; make sure that learning stresses as much of the humanities and human interactive skills as hard sciences; make sure we have an immigration policy that continues to attract the world's most imaginative risk-takers; and strengthen our safety nets, because this era will leave more people behind.*

And on the other side, we have Ann Coulter 'My Final Argument for Trump.'[410] It's almost as if she had read Friedman's arguments since she manages to plough through them all, one by one. Her article comes with a language warning. This is her basic premise.

> *For every argument the media make against Trump, Hillary's worse.*

And from there she goes through thirteen different issues giving both sides. I will start you off with the first, but go read all thirteen.

> *(1) Eleven years ago, Trump said on a secretly recorded tape that celebrities can do anything — even grab a woman's p*ssy.*
>
> *Hillary, born-again Victorian virgin, campaigns with Beyonce, who performs a duet with the words "curvalicious, p*ssy served delicious."*
>
> *Hillary is thrilled to have the support of Madonna — who has publicly offered to give blow jobs to anyone who votes for Hillary. (She'll even remove her teeth!)*
>
> *Hillary's campaign has deployed Miley Cyrus to canvas for her — when Cyrus is not busy inviting men in the audience to reach up and grab her p*ssy. (Here's a video of delicate flower Miley Cyrus in action.)*
>
> *When Vernon Jordan was asked by CBS' Mike Wallace what he talked about while golfing with Bill Clinton — aka Hillary's husband — he answered: "P*ssy."*
>
> *Oh, and 11 years before Teddy Kennedy ran for president as the Conscience of*

---

[410] breitbart.com, 2 November 2016.

the Democratic Party — *he killed a girl. After grabbing her p*ssy.*

If this p*ssy business is the clincher for you, then you really are too stupid to vote.

~

Election map the weekend before
November 5, 2016

Here it is from Real Clear Politics.[411] Three days before the election, it is Clinton/Kaine 298 v Trump/Pence 240. Florida going (R) makes the vote 269-269. But it only went (R) in 2000 because of Elio Gonzales, remember him? Otherwise Gore would have won just like this.

~

The argument for Western civilisation
November 5, 2016

You can see Trump's two-minute final ad: "The Argument for America" at the link.[412]

Meanwhile I am looking at what passes for financial sense at the AFR where its coverage of the American election is from #Never Trump's master moron, Bill Kristol, with the heading "Not My Kind of Conservative". Presumably, Hillary is more his kind of conservative, although what exactly will be conserved by four years of Hillary is an unknown.

It is now down to the wire. The drift is towards Trump but Democrat larceny never ends. What makes this exceptional is that even now, with all of the media only one way, it is still possible that Trump may win.

---

[411] realclearpolitics.com, 4 November 2016.
[412] hotair.com, 4 November 2016.

The revolt of the dispossessed
November 6, 2016

I have been re-reading Christopher Lasch's brilliant *The Revolt of the Elites and the Betrayal of Democracy*[413] which was published more than a decade ago. It's about the we-know-what's-best-for-you types who have risen to the top of power structures across the world. A brief but inadequate summary but you'll get the point:

> *Controversy has raged around Lasch's targeted attack on the elites, their loss of moral values, and their abandonment of the middle class and poor, for he sets up the media and educational institutions as a large source of the problem. In this spirited work, Lasch calls out for a return to community, schools that teach history not self-esteem, and a return to morality and even the teachings of religion. He does this in a nonpartisan manner, looking to the lessons of American history, and castigating those in power for the ever-widening gap between the economic classes, which has created a crisis in American society. The* Revolt of the Elites and the Betrayal of Democracy *is riveting social commentary.*

If you want to understand the attractions of Donald Trump, there is no better place I can think to look. And if you want an even better idea what it's all about, you should read 'The economic losers are in revolt against the elites by Martin Wolf' [perfect name][414] in *The Financial Times*.

> *Losers have votes, too. That is what democracy means — and rightly so. If they feel sufficiently cheated and humiliated, they will vote for Donald Trump, a candidate for the Republican party's presidential nomination in the US, Marine Le Pen of the National Front in France or Nigel Farage of the UK Independence party. . . .*
>
> *It is not hard to see why ordinary people, notably native-born men, are alienated. They are losers, at least relatively; they do not share equally in the gains. They feel used and abused. After the financial crisis and slow recovery in standards of living, they see elites as incompetent and predatory. The surprise is not that many are angry but that so many are not.*
>
> *Branko Milanovic, formerly of the World Bank, has shown that only two*

---

[413] goodreads.com/book
[414] *The Financial Times,* 27 January 2016.

parts of the global income distribution enjoyed virtually no gains in real incomes between 1988 and 2008: the poorest five percentiles and those between the 75th and the 90th percentile. The latter includes the bulk of the population of high-income countries.

The Clinton Foundation is the perfect example of how our elites operate. They shaft you and steal your money, and most importantly, they use government as their major tool to syphon the wealth of the hard-working majority to themselves and their friends.

~

Where's the outrage?
November 7, 2016

It is now fully understood that the Democrats will do everything they can to steal this election, and this is the official view of the left from the President on down [Criminal President Obama Encourages Illegal Aliens to Vote – Promises No Repercussions (VIDEO)[415]]. The question is whether Trump can win beyond the range of deceit. So, as we head into the home stretch.

> *CONFUSED COMEY CLEARS HER AGAIN!*
> *TRUMP: 'SHE'S PROTECTED BY RIGGED SYSTEM'*
> *POLL: THISCLOSE*
> *TRUMP MARATHON SUNDAY*
> *CLINTON WARNS 'FAKE' WIKIS COMING*

Astonishing reversal by Comey, somehow managing to sift through 650,000 emails in a few days. It still seems to me that the aim is to make Tim Kaine president. She wins and is then indicted seems simple enough, but of course she first has to win. Comey re-opening the investigation suddenly brought Trump back to life so here they close it again. That they did shift back does make it seem that there now is a genuine possibility that Trump could win.

But what most of this has done is sidetrack the election from Trump's main issue, which is open borders. The United States will be about as wealthy as Argentina when all this is over, with the same sort of

---
[415] thegatewaypundit.com, 6 November 2016.

distribution of income. Fascinating to have watched all of this even if extremely depressing.

~

Some call it treason
November 8, 2016

These are the kinds of things you will know only if you put yourself in the way of knowing them. The number of people we associate with who do not even know the existence of Wikileaks never mind their contents is quite astounding. You would not even know it's possible, never mind that these are the issues they choose to ignore:[416]

> *John Podesta, Hillary's campaign chair, who was also a counselor to President Obama at the time, was the recipient of the 2014 email which was released today.*
>
> *Assange promised his latest batch of leaks would lead to the indictment of Hillary, and it looks like he was not kidding. The email proves Hillary knew and was complicit in the funding and arming of ISIS by our 'allies' Saudi Arabia and Qatar!*
>
> *"the governments of Qatar and Saudi Arabia, which are providing clandestine financial and logistic support to ISIL…" Clinton wrote*
>
> *The media is yet to report on this, even though Wikileaks has a 10-year history of being 100% accurate in their leaks, never once releasing info that proved to be false.*
>
> *…Can you guess why?*
>
> *Maybe it has something to do with the fact that The Saudi's brag about funding 20% of Hillary's Presidential campaign, and along with Qatar, are among the largest donors to the CLINTON FOUNDATION.*
>
> *Is it any mystery now why ISIS has flourished under the Obama/Clinton administration? The United States has created armed and funded the terrorists overthrowing Syria via our Terrorist State allies. When you know this it makes you look at the situation in Syria differently. Perhaps*

---

[416] freedomsfinalstand.com, 7 Nobember 2016.

Russia and Iran are the ones fighting ISIS, it stands to reason once you know we are fighting Russia, and at the same time arming ISIS.

Clinton's campaign and her Clinton Foundation are literally funded by the SAME PEOPLE who are funding ISIS and killing hundreds of thousands of innocents in the Middle East, and now, even here at home.

This is nothing short of TREASON. Hillary must be sent to trial and held accountable for crimes against humanity and Treason against the United States of America.

We know the media will do all in their power to bury this story so it is up to us to use social media to make sure every voter in America knows this before they cast their vote for president on Nov 8th. You know what to do ...

There are already more than enough reasons not to vote for Hillary and then to convict. All by way of making Tim Kaine president

~

A day in the death of the American Republic
November 8, 2016

Plucked from Drudge on election eve.

UPDATE: MS-13 Terrorize Suburb...
Spike in Illegals...
ISIS continues its 'Get Out the Vote' jihadi campaign...
Communities struggle with Muslims' arrival...

Leaked Documents Reveal Expansive Soros Funding to Manipulate Elections...
Hacking a Voting Machine...
Used in 13 States!
Undercover journalist in full burka offered Huma Abedin ballot in NYC...

WIKI: DNC and CNN colluded on questions for Trump...
Dirty Donna Sent EVEN MORE Debate Questions From CNN To Clinton...
CNN EXEC'S HUSBAND TIPPED PODESTA ABOUT

POLLING…
WASH POST Writer Asked DNC For Anti-Trump Research…
COLUMN: Media Sees Itself As Part of Govt. whose actual title is *"How the Political Media's Corruption Destroyed America's Most Crucial Institutions"*

Govt Workers Outnumber Manufacturing by 9,977,000…
Leaked Bill Clinton Speech: Obama Years Left No Hope For White Working Class…

COMEY THE CLOWN…
Top Clinton Donors Gave Big Bucks to FBI Investigator's Wife…
DOJ Proposal Slow Walks Her Email Release Past 2020!
WIRED: Yes, They Can Vet 650,000 Emails In 691,200 Seconds…

And this is what we know about that's going on. There is a lot more we will never know but all of it along the same lines as what we see above.

And if you want to see the kind of Sunshine Conservatives I despise, there is a button that is doing the round which says:

I begrudgingly voted

Fuck this shit 2016

The difference between Trump and Hillary is so immense you have to be a voting-for-a-living type at the bottom of the income pile, or else a complete idiot. With Trump you are getting everything a conservative ought to want. If you are so dumb and ignorant about what is at stake this time round, then you are as big a fool as anyone who has ever lived. Such dummies on the right, who take their opinions from the *New York Times* and *Washington Post!*

Political ecstasy
November 9, 2016

There is a providence that protects idiots, drunkards, small children and the United States of America.
-- Otto von Bismarck

And He may also be keeping an eye out for the rest of us as well.

There are not many moments like this that come along in a lifetime. We went out tonight to see that brave Canadian climate sceptic, Tim Ball, discussing his costly adventures in climate change. His legal bills are now over a million. It does not come cheap to wrangle with these people, but he seemed pretty content with life as it has unfolded. But he was certainly as thrilled as I am about what a Trump presidency will mean. It also means that the political fights have only just begun.

And this was as improbable a victory as I have ever seen. And the big losers are not just Hillary, the Clintons and the Clinton Foundation. We can also add to the cart the #NeverTrumps, the #OccasionallyTrumps and the Sunshine Conservatives who have revealed themselves. And of course, there is the media. Watching the ABC when I came home was one of those precious experiences that for someone such as myself who almost never watches TV, gave such immense pleasure, as much on the plus side for me as the negatives must have been for them as revealed by the misery on their faces. The same kind of pleasure watching Megyn Kelly as I replayed the afternoon on Fox that I had missed going out.

I might also throw in that perhaps the biggest loser of them all is Obama. He has been a global disaster, but his eight years will be swept, as those of his kind like to say, into the dustbin of history. There will be an ample amount of damage to clean up, some which will never be fixed, but at least come January he will be history and have no successor. I wish I could say we can then all start again, but we can at least start a fairly decent salvaging operation.

So to go back to the quote, either Bismarck was absolutely right or the planets were lined up just exactly right, but who could have predicted any of it. You could see Trump learning on the job and getting the polish together just a bit more each day. He turned his vague aims into a series of specific policy proposals that make profound sense for those of us who pay attention to such things. There were the Wikileaks, Comey's decision not to prosecute, then the Weiner revelations followed by Comey's decision to re-open the case, and then finally his reversal. Not to mention Hillary's disastrous record in politics where her only success was to become possibly the most brazen political liar in history. As for everything else, there was not a single actual success of any kind she could point to that might give anyone the slightest notion that she could handle the office of the Presidency, even if she were healthy, which she clearly is not.

On the negative side, of course, there was some locker-room talk from back in 2005. That was the only issue ever brought up in Hillary's favour. I never heard another reason to vote for her or against Trump by those who sided with the Democrats, and I did try to find out. How history hinges on such things, in the way that Romney travelling with a dog on the roof of his car might have cost him the presidency in 2012. But that was then; this is now. Hurray for our side, but there now really is a lot to do.

APPENDIX

DONALD J. TRUMP CONTRACT WITH THE AMERICAN VOTER

What follows is my 100-day action plan to Make America Great Again. It is a contract between myself and the American voter — and begins with restoring honesty, accountability and change to Washington

Therefore, on the first day of my term of office, my administration will immediately pursue the following six measures to clean up the corruption and special interest collusion in Washington, DC:

- *FIRST, propose a Constitutional Amendment to impose term limits on all members of Congress;*
- *SECOND, a hiring freeze on all federal employees to reduce federal workforce through attrition (exempting military, public safety, and public health);*
- *THIRD, a requirement that for every new federal regulation, two existing regulations must be eliminated;*
- *FOURTH, a 5 year-ban on White House and Congressional officials becoming lobbyists after they leave government service;*
- *FIFTH, a lifetime ban on White House officials lobbying on behalf of a foreign government;*
- *SIXTH, a complete ban on foreign lobbyists raising money for American elections.*

On the same day, I will begin taking the following 7 actions to protect American workers:

- *FIRST, I will announce my intention to renegotiate NAFTA or withdraw from the deal under Article 2205*
- *SECOND, I will announce our withdrawal from the Trans-Pacific Partnership*
- *THIRD, I will direct my Secretary of the Treasury to label China a currency manipulator*
- *FOURTH, I will direct the Secretary of Commerce and U.S. Trade Representative to identify all foreign trading abuses that unfairly impact American workers and direct them to use every tool under American and international law to end those abuses immediately*

- FIFTH, *I will lift the restrictions on the production of $50 trillion dollars' worth of job-producing American energy reserves, including shale, oil, natural gas and clean coal.*
- SIXTH, *lift the Obama-Clinton roadblocks and allow vital energy infrastructure projects, like the Keystone Pipeline, to move forward*
- SEVENTH, *cancel billions in payments to U.N. climate change programs and use the money to fix America's water and environmental infrastructure*

Additionally, on the first day, I will take the following five actions to restore security and the constitutional rule of law:

- FIRST, *cancel every unconstitutional executive action, memorandum and order issued by President Obama*
- SECOND, *begin the process of selecting a replacement for Justice Scalia from one of the 20 judges on my list, who will uphold and defend the Constitution of the United States*
- THIRD, *cancel all federal funding to Sanctuary Cities*
- FOURTH, *begin removing the more than 2 million criminal illegal immigrants from the country and cancel visas to foreign countries that won't take them back*
- FIFTH, *suspend immigration from terror-prone regions where vetting cannot safely occur. All vetting of people coming into our country will be considered extreme vetting.*

Next, I will work with Congress to introduce the following broader legislative measures and fight for their passage within the first 100 days of my Administration:

1. Middle Class Tax Relief And Simplification Act. An economic plan designed to grow the economy 4% per year and create at least 25 million new jobs through massive tax reduction and simplification, in combination with trade reform, regulatory relief, and lifting the restrictions on American energy. The largest tax reductions are for the middle class. A middle-class family with 2 children will get a 35% tax cut. The current number of brackets will be reduced from 7 to 3, and tax forms will likewise be greatly simplified.

The business rate will be lowered from 35 to 15 percent, and the trillions of dollars of American corporate money overseas can now be brought back at a 10 percent rate.

2. End The Offshoring Act Establishes tariffs to discourage companies from laying off their workers in order to relocate in other countries and ship their products back to the U.S. tax-free.

3. American Energy & Infrastructure Act. Leverages public-private partnerships, and private investments through tax incentives, to spur $1 trillion in infrastructure investment over 10 years. It is revenue neutral.

4. School Choice And Education Opportunity Act. Redirects education dollars to gives parents the right to send their kid to the public, private, charter, magnet, religious or home school of their choice. Ends common core, brings education supervision to local communities. It expands vocational and technical education, and make 2 and 4-year college more affordable.

5. Repeal and Replace Obamacare Act. Fully repeals Obamacare and replaces it with Health Savings Accounts, the ability to purchase health insurance across state lines, and lets states manage Medicaid funds. Reforms will also include cutting the red tape at the FDA: there are over 4,000 drugs awaiting approval, and we especially want to speed the approval of life-saving medications.

6. Affordable Childcare and Eldercare Act. Allows Americans to deduct childcare and elder care from their taxes, incentivizes employers to provide on-side childcare services, and creates tax-free Dependent Care Savings Accounts for both young and elderly dependents, with matching contributions for low-income families.

7. End Illegal Immigration Act Fully-funds the construction of a wall on our southern border with the full understanding that the country Mexico will be reimbursing the United States for the full cost of such wall; establishes a 2-year mandatory minimum federal prison sentence for illegally re-entering the U.S. after a previous deportation, and a 5-year mandatory minimum for illegally re-entering for those with felony convictions, multiple misdemeanor convictions or two or more prior deportations; also reforms visa rules to enhance penalties for overstaying and to ensure open jobs are offered to American workers first.

8. Restoring Community Safety Act. Reduces surging crime, drugs and violence by creating a Task Force On Violent Crime and increasing funding for programs that train and assist local police; increases resources for federal law enforcement agencies and federal prosecutors to dismantle criminal gangs and put violent offenders behind bars.

9. Restoring National Security Act. Rebuilds our military by eliminating the defense sequester and expanding military investment; provides Veterans with the ability to receive public VA treatment or attend the private doctor of their choice; protects our vital infrastructure from cyber-attack; establishes new screening procedures for immigration to ensure those who are admitted to our country support our people and our values.

10. Clean up Corruption in Washington Act. Enacts new ethics reforms to Drain the Swamp and reduce the corrupting influence of special interests on our politics.

On November 8th, Americans will be voting for this 100-day plan to restore prosperity to our economy, security to our communities, and honesty to our government.

This is my pledge to you.

And if we follow these steps, we will once more have a government of, by and for the people.

www.ingramcontent.com/pod-product-compliance
Lightning Source LLC
Chambersburg PA
CBHW060938230426
43665CB00015B/1984